The Woman
Who Laughed
at God

The Woman Who Laughed at God

THE UNTOLD HISTORY
OF THE JEWISH PEOPLE

Jonathan Kirsch

VIKING

VIKING COMPASS
Published by the Penguin Group
Penguin Putnam Inc., 375 Hudson Street,
New York, New York 10014, U.S.A.
Penguin Books Ltd, 27 Wrights Lane
London W8 5T2, England
Penguin Books Australia Ltd, Ringwood,
Victoria, Australia
Penguin Books Canada Ltd, 10 Alcorn Avenue,
Toronto, Ontario, Canada M4V 3B2
Penguin Books (N.Z.) Ltd, 182-190 Wairau Road,
Auckland 10, New Zealand

Penguin Books Ltd, Registered Office:
Harmondsworth, Middlesex, England

First published in 2001 by Viking Compass,
a member of Penguin Putnam Inc.

10 9 8 7 6 5 4 3 2 1

LIBRARY OF CONGRESS CATALOGING-IN-PUBLICATION DATA
Kirsch, Jonathan, 1949–
    The woman who laughed at God: the untold history of the Jewish people / Jonathan Kirsch.
        p. cm.
    Includes bibliographical references and index.
    ISBN 0-670-03009-0
    1. Judaism—History. 2. Judaism—Essence, genius, nature. 3. Jews—Identity. I. Title.
    BM157.K55 2001
    296'.09—dc21   2001026880

This book is printed on acid-free paper. ∞

Printed in the United States of America
Set in Goudy
Designed by Helene Berinsky

For Ann Benjamin Kirsch,
my beloved wife and lifelong friend,
wise counselor and woman of valor.

For Jennifer Rachel Kirsch and Adam Benjamin Kirsch,
my accomplished, beautiful, and cherished children.

And for
Judy Woo and Eui Sook (Angie) Yoon,
my dear friends and colleagues,
whose support and encouragement
were essential to the writing of this book.

Remember us in life,
and health, and strength,
O Lord who delights in life,
and inscribe us in the Book of Life . . .

Yes, God is a writer, and we are both the heroes
and the readers. We know that the angels have nothing
but praise. Three times a day they sing: Sublime! Perfect!
Great! Excellent! But there must be some angry critics, too.
They complain: Your novel, God, is too long, too cruel.
Too little love. Too much sex. They advise cutting. . . .
But about one quality we all agree: God's novel has suspense.

—ISAAC BASHEVIS SINGER

CONTENTS

ACKNOWLEDGMENTS

As always, I have relied on the constancy and companionship of my beloved wife, Ann Benjamin Kirsch, and our children, Jennifer Rachel Kirsch and Adam Benjamin Kirsch, in all of the work that I do, including this book.

Andrew M. Solomon was my principal research assistant, working in the libraries at Columbia University and UCLA, and his accuracy, enterprise, diligence and good cheer were indispensable in making sense of 3,000 years of Jewish history!

Leonard Braman, too, shared his research skills, and I was able to draw on research materials that were gathered for my previous books by my son, Adam, and Vera Tobin.

Clare Ferraro at Viking Penguin has long encouraged and supported my work, starting with *The Harlot by the Side of the Road* and continuing over the years through the publication of this book.

I have also been privileged to work with Janet Goldstein and Beena Kamlani at Viking Penguin, each of whom brought their wisdom, insight, taste, and discernment to bear upon the manuscript of this book, as well as Miriam Hurewitz, Yelena Gitlin, and Ann Mah.

Laurie Fox is not only my agent but also my muse, and it was over a cup of coffee with Laurie at a cliffside restaurant in La Jolla that *The Woman Who Laughed at God* was first conjured up.

Linda Chester has always been welcoming and encouraging to me and my family, both in work and in life, and I am grateful to Linda and all of her colleagues at the Linda Chester Literary Agency for making so many opportunities for me over these many years.

At the offices of Kirsch & Mitchell in Los Angeles, where the early morning hours have been devoted to this book, I have been blessed with the companionship and colleagueship of my friend and law partner, Dennis Mitchell, and our co-workers, Judy Woo and Angie Yoon, to whom this book is affectionately co-dedicated.

I will always owe a debt of gratitude to my colleagues in publishing who are also my dear friends, including Marie Coolman, Heather Smith, Robin Benway, and Liz Williams.

Among the radio and television hosts who do the important work of calling attention to books, my own among them, I am especially grateful to Connie Martinson, Larry Mantle, Joe Skelly, Warren Olney, and Michael Cart.

Among the booksellers across the country who have welcomed me and my books into their stores, I am especially grateful to Doug Dutton, Diane Leslie, Lise Friedman, and Ed Conklin at Dutton's in Brentwood, Stan Hynds and Linda Urban at Vroman's in Pasadena, Stan Madson and Jeanne D'Arcy at the Bodhi Tree in West Hollywood, Peggy Jackson at Borders in Montclair, Michael Graziano at Borders in Pasadena, and Katie O'Laughlin at Village Books in Pacific Palisades.

Rabbi Michael Gotlieb at Kehillat Maarav in Los Angeles has always been generous in sharing his wisdom, insight, and encouragement with me and my whole family.

Finally, and with a full heart, I acknowledge the following generous people, each of whom has supported me and my work in many different but crucial ways:

At the *Los Angeles Times*, Bret Israel, Elena Nelson Howe, and Susan Freudenheim in the Southern California Living section, and Steve Wasserman, Tom Curwen, Nick Owchar, Cara Mia di Massa, Susan Salter Reynolds, and Ethel Alexander in the Book Review.

At the Publishers Marketing Association, Jan Nathan and Terry Nathan.

Tony Cohan at Acrobat Books, a stalwart of the Freedom to Write program of PEN Center USA West and the publisher of my books on publishing law.

At the *Jewish Journal*, Robert Eshman.

My mother and stepfather, Dvora and Elmer Heller.

My beloved aunt, Lillian Heller Conrad.

My daughter-in-law, Remy Holzer, and her family, Harold, Edith, and Meg Holzer.

Among my fellow writers, I am especially and deeply grateful to K. C. Cole, Carolyn See, Diane Leslie, Jack Miles, Bernadette Shih, Eric Lax, Dolores Sloan, and April Smith.

Donald Harman Akenson, Karen Armstrong, David Noel Freedman, and Richard Elliott Friedman, each of whom is an accomplished scholar from whose work I have benefitted beyond measure.

Rabbi Allen Freehling, the Rev. Peter Gomes, Rabbi David Wolpe, Rabbi Will Kramer, Rabbi Harold Schulweis, Rabbi Isaiah Zeldin, Rector J. Edwin Bacon, Jr., and Pastor Mitch Henson.

Sheldon Kadish and Mary Ann Rosenfeld, Raye Birk and Candace Barrett Birk, Len and Pat Solomon, Scott Baker, Jacob Gabay, Inge-Lise DeWolfe, Fred Huffman, Jill Johnson Keeney, and Rae Lewis.

The Woman Who Laughed at God

ONE

And Sarah Laughed

We are a people—one people.

—THEODOR HERZL, *The Jewish State*

• • •

There are six million Jews in America, and six million Judaisms.

—JACOB RADER MARCUS

Who is a Jew? Or, to put the question more bluntly, who is entitled to regard himself or herself as an authentic Jew, a faithful Jew, a "good" Jew?

The question was first asked several thousand years ago by the original authors of the Hebrew Bible, and it is still being asked today by both religious and secular Jews in Israel and throughout the Diaspora. After three millennia, we are no closer to a definitive answer—indeed, the only honest and accurate answer is that Judaism is not now, and never has been, a monolithic faith or a homogenous people. In fact, the history of the Jewish people is such a rich and colorful tapestry with so many threads of belief and practice that scholars prefer to speak of it in the plural: not Judaism but "Judaisms."

Of course, some Jews have always insisted on defining Judaism as a set of commandments literally written in stone, a moment of revealed truth that is fixed in time and place. At any point in the last three thousand years of Jewish history, we will find a few zealous Jews who have drawn a circle around a set of rituals and beliefs that they regard as essentially and authentically Jewish, and they have condemned as an apostate any Jew who dares to step outside the circle of orthodoxy as they define it. Ironically, even the most assimilated and secular Jews in the modern world seem to concede the point when they say of themselves: "I'm not very Jewish.": the unspoken premise is that Jewishness is a fixed point, and all but the most traditional Jews have strayed from authentic Judaism to one degree or another.

But there is quite another way to look at the history and destiny of the Jewish people. No single moment can be fixed as the time and place where Judaism reached its highest or purest expression. No single tradition in Judaism can be regarded as authentic and authoritative to the exclusion of all others. Starting in antiquity, and continuing without interruption to the present day, Judaism has been defined by generation upon generation of courageous men and women who felt both inspired and empowered to reimagine and reinvent what it means to be a Jew. After three thousand years of rich and daring innovation, an argument can be made that diversity rather than orthodoxy is the real core value of Judaism—and the only quality that all of the many "Judaisms" share in common.

Priestesses and Goddess Worshippers, Guerillas and Generals

That is exactly why it is so treacherous to focus on what is sometimes called classical or normative Judaism in seeking to understand what it really means to be a Jew. Hidden away behind the facade of classical Judaism is a rich and strange array of Judaisms, and for every tradition, there is a countertradition. As we shall come to see, Judaism has encompassed piety and prayerfulness but also mysticism and ecstasy, not only the ghetto but also the barricade, the gun and the plow as well as the Torah and the Talmud. Along with the more familiar figures of Jewish tradition—patriarchs and prophets, rabbis and sages, and martyrs in heartbreaking abundance—Jewish history is also populated with priestesses and goddess worshippers, astrologers and magicians, generals and guerillas, freethinkers and revolutionaries.

Many of these Judaisms have been hotly condemned when they have not been written out of Jewish history altogether. The practice of idol worship and goddess worship among the ancient Israelites was so distressing to the original authors of the Bible that they condemned it as "the abomination of desolation" (Dan. 11:31).[1] The mystical and ecstatic practices of Kabbalism and Hasidism were once dismissed as "malignant growths in the body of Judaism" by one influential Jewish historian.[2] Even a figure as pious and learned as the medieval Talmudist called Maimonides was condemned as an apostate in his own lifetime, and his writings were put to the flames at the behest of the more militant rabbis. The seventeenth-century philosopher Spinoza, nowadays regarded as the archetype of the modern Jew precisely because he insisted on reading the Torah with an open mind, was excommunicated by the Jewish community of Amsterdam for "abominable heresies."[3]

Even the most recent and dramatic experiences in Jewish history have been the source of bitter contention. The single greatest catastrophe in Jewish history—the murder of six million Jewish men, women, and children by Germany and its collaborators during the Second World War—is regarded as a political as well as a theological mystery. Did so many Jews die because they had forgotten the ancient and authentic Jewish tradition of "the fighting Jew," a tradition that begins with the biblical King David in the Book of Samuel? Or did they die because they had forgotten the elaborate and demanding code of religious law that begins with the biblical Moses, thus suffering the fate that God threatens to inflict on the Chosen People in the Book of Deuteronomy?

No less controversial is the single greatest achievement of the Jewish people in the last two thousand years—the founding of a Jewish homeland in Palestine in the aftermath of the Holocaust. Modern political Zionism can be seen as the latest of the many Judaisms, a fulfillment of the oldest and most pious aspiration of the Jewish people by a generation of Jews who were willing to pick up a gun and fight. Yet Zionism is condemned by some ultraobservant Jews who believe "with perfect faith," as Maimonides puts it, that Jewish sovereignty in the Holy Land must await the coming of the Messiah.[4] For some Jews, Zionism is the ultimate betrayal of Judaism, and for other Jews, Zionism *is* Judaism. That is why many secular Jews in Israel regard citizenship in a Jewish state as the single most authentic expression of their Jewishness, and a few ultraobservant Jews affirm their allegiance to the Palestine Liberation Organization in preference to the State of Israel.

The War Among "Judaisms"

Diversity of belief and practice is so characteristic of Judaism, in fact, that it is the stuff of both somber Talmudic commentary and countless Jewish jokes. A story is told, for example, about a Jewish castaway who is plucked from a tropical island after being stranded for thirty years. He insists on conducting his rescuers on a tour of the island, proudly showing them all the comforts and conveniences that he built for himself during his long years of solitude—a cabin, a vegetable garden, a well, and not one but two synagogues.

"Why two synagogues?" asks the captain of the ship.

"To *that* one," answers the castaway, pointing to one of the synagogues, "I *never* go!"

Now, it's perfectly true that the sheer number of factions within the Jewish community—and the bitter frictions between them—are sometimes laughable. Among the ultraobservant Jews who live in self-contained neighborhoods around New York, all of whom pride themselves on the strict observance of the dietary laws of *kashrut*, the followers of one rabbi will sometimes reject another rabbi's *heksher*—the seal of approval indicating that a food product has been deemed kosher by a particular rabbi. When a prominent Conservative rabbi in Los Angeles invited a leading Orthodox rabbi to join him at a Friday evening service in a gesture of Jewish ecumenicalism, the Orthodox rabbi accepted the invitation—but when the service started, he pointedly retreated to a corner and prayed with his back to the congregation. And some of the ultraobservant Jews of the Mea Shearim district in Jerusalem, who believe that the founding of the Jewish state was an act of apostasy, have used crudely printed scrip to avoid sullying their hands with the currency of the State of Israel.

Still, the war among Judaisms is not always a laughing matter. When a Conservative synagogue in Brooklyn was defaced with a swastika and set afire, for example, the culprits turned out to be not neo-Nazi skinheads but a gang of radical Jews who called themselves "T.O.R.A.H."— "Tough Orthodox Rabbis and Hasids." Jewish men and women who dare to pray together at the Western Wall in Jerusalem are likely to be pelted with rocks and dirty diapers by ultraobservant Jews: "Go back to Germany," they taunt, "and let them finish the job!" Tragically, an obscure point of Talmudic law was invoked by a few Jewish zealots to justify the assassination of Yitzhak Rabin, the Israeli war hero and political leader who shared a Nobel Peace Prize for his efforts at peacemaking. Significantly, the term that is sometimes used in Israel to identify ultraobservant Jews—*haredim*—derives from the Hebrew word for "fearful," which is used in the sense of "God-fearing" but also suggests how fiercely they condemn their less observant fellow Jews.*

The bitter conflict in the Jewish world may be an open wound but it is hardly a fresh one. Precisely the same clash—the clash between a strict and sometimes punishing Judaism and a kinder, gentler Judaism—can be traced all the way back to distant biblical antiquity. The Torah preserves the contending arguments of various authors who simply cannot agree on who God is or what God wants—sometimes Yahweh is a grizzled desert vagrant trying to cadge a free meal and sometimes a celestial king on a heavenly throne, sometimes a fatherly and forgiving deity and sometimes a bloodthirsty "God of Armies." The first patriarch, Abraham, feels at liberty to argue with God himself, and so does Moses.

The Talmud, a vast anthology of rabbinical commentary that is the font of classical Judaism, can be described as one long and noisy debate

---

*I use the capitalized term "Orthodox" to identify Jews who belong to the highly observant congregations and communities that center on "Modern Orthodoxy," and I use "ultraobservant" to identify the various religious movements (such as, for example, Hasidic Jews as well as the so-called Mitnagdim) that are even more traditional and more strictly observant than Modern Orthodoxy. See Chapter 6 ("In the Ruined Citadel").

about the meaning of Judaism that began fifteen hundred years ago and is still going on. Another Jewish joke sums it up: "Two Jews, three opinions." That is why there is no Jewish counterpart to the pope, no Jewish catechism, no Jewish version of the Inquisition. Significantly, the Talmud records one especially heated debate on a point of religious law in which God himself is moved to speak out from on high—and God is outvoted! So diversity of belief and practice is nothing new in Judaism. Indeed, it is an ancient and authentic tradition—perhaps the most authentic Jewish tradition of all.

The Red Heifer

Of course, some examples of diversity in Judaism are affirmed and celebrated throughout the Jewish world. The so-called Ashkenazic Jews trace their ancestry back to the Jewish communities of Central and Eastern Europe, Sephardic Jews to Spain, and "Oriental" Jews to Babylon, Persia, and elsewhere in the ancient Near East. Each community practices a slightly different form of Judaism—Ashkenazic Jews regard rice as a forbidden food during Passover, for example, but the Sephardic Jews do not; Ashkenazic tradition prohibits the naming of a newborn after a living relative, but Sephardic tradition requires it. Yet all of these communities are regarded as thoroughly and authentically Jewish despite their profound differences in matters of ritual, cuisine, language, and folkways.

Other expressions of diversity are more controversial. To be an authentic Jew, or so goes the argument of Orthodoxy and other highly observant movements in Judaism, one must bear the full weight of the Jewish religious law as set forth in the Torah and the Talmud. But each of the progressive movements in Judaism—Conservative, Reform, and Reconstructionist—has come up with its own understanding of what points of Jewish religious law ought to be preserved and what points ought to be simplified, modernized, or abandoned. And the vast majority of Jews, both in Israel and in the Diaspora, have purged their lives of all but a few symbolic gestures—they may circumcise their sons, engage a rabbi to perform a wedding ceremony, or show up in synagogue for a few hours on Yom Kippur, but their Jewishness is not defined by religious observance.

That is why Jews cannot agree on something so fundamental as what constitutes the practice of Judaism.

So it is that Jews express their Jewishness in every imaginable way. An ultraobservant Hasidic *rebbe* is so meticulous about keeping kosher that he will not even drink a glass of wine if it comes from a vintner that employs non-Jews—the functional definition of "kosher wine" under Jewish religious law—while an ultrahip Jewish yuppie yields to the nostalgic longing for a pastrami sandwich even though he is concerned about his cholesterol count. Jewish men in some congregations still thank God in their morning prayers "for not having made me a woman," while in other congregations, the liturgy and the Torah itself have been rewritten in gender-neutral language by women rabbis. Ultraobservant Jews, preparing for the day when the Temple will be rebuilt and animal offerings will be resumed in Jerusalem, resort to genetic engineering to breed the "red heifer" whose sacrifice is mandated in the Torah. At the same time, secular Jews in New York and Los Angeles consult the ancient mystical teachings of the Kabbalah to improve their sex lives. Each one defines his or her Jewishness in a wholly different way, and yet all of them insist on regarding themselves as Jews.

The Laughing Matriarch

If we ask the toughest question of all—what do all these varieties of Judaism really have in common?—we will find no easy answers. That's exactly what historian Jacob Rader Marcus means when he looks at six million Jews in America and sees "six million Judaisms."[5] But we will find some intriguing and provocative clues in what I have called "The Untold History of the Jewish People," the surprising and even shocking moments over the last three thousand years when Jewish men and women dared to break out of the circle of orthodoxy and express their Jewishness in new and inventive ways.

As an emblematic example of one such moment, I have chosen the biblical account of the remarkable encounter between God and the woman called Sarah. The scene in the Book of Genesis opens with Abraham, then nearly one hundred years old, as he idles at the opening of his

tent near a grove of oak trees in the Judean wilderness. The old man, perhaps dozing in the shimmering heat of the late afternoon, suddenly real-
izes that three men are standing outside his tent—two of them, the Bible
reveals, are angels of death on their way to destroy the cities of Sodom
and Gomorrah for their sinfulness, and the third man is God himself.
Suddenly, Abraham rises to his feet, hastens to greet the strangers, and
begs them to tarry at his encampment.

Abraham orders his elderly wife, Sarah, to prepare a meal of curds
and milk, veal chops and fresh bread. "And he set it before them," the
Bible tells us, "and he stood by them under the tree, and they did eat"
(Gen. 18:8).[6] Sarah is not permitted to join the menfolk at their meal,
but she lingers by the tent-flap and listens to their conversation.

"I will return to you next year," God vows to Abraham, "and your
wife Sarah shall have a son!" (Gen. 18:10) (New JPS).

The words strike Sarah as not merely surprising but ridiculous. After
all, she has been barren all her life, and now, at the age of ninety, she is
beyond all hope of childbearing. So startling is God's promise, in fact,
that Sarah cannot contain herself.

"And Sarah laughed within herself," the Bible reports, "saying:
'Withered as I am, am I still to know enjoyment—and my husband so
old!' "

God apparently overhears Sarah's laughter because he now addresses
a question to *both* Sarah and Abraham.

"Why did Sarah laugh, saying 'Shall I in truth bear a child, old as I
am?' " God wants to know. "Is anything too hard for the Lord?"

"I laughed not," lies Sarah.

"No," insists God, "but you did laugh" (18:12–15).[7]

Elsewhere in the Torah, God is shown to be wrathful and punishing,
and human beings are shown to cringe and cower in fear of him. And for
good reason, too—God is perfectly capable of scourging and even killing
men and women who are not sufficiently compliant and deferential. But,
at the moment of his tête-à-tête with Sarah, all of our expectations about
who God is and what God wants of us are tweaked. Sarah is so unafraid
of the Almighty that she laughs at his words and then lies to his face.
The all-knowing and all-seeing God of Israel is so taken aback that he is

forced to ask why she is laughing at his solemn promise. For all of her audacity and boldness, God responds only with petulance rather than punishing wrath. And, as if to symbolize how little Sarah fears God, the
child she bears in fulfillment of God's promise is named *Yitzhak* ("I
laughed"), a pun on the Hebrew word for laughter (*tsa-hak*).

Classical Judaism is troubled by the laughing matriarch. Much is said
about Sarah in the rabbinical tales that we find in the Talmud and the
Midrash—she is so beautiful, even in her old age, that all other women
are "like monkeys by comparison," goes one such tale, and she is regarded
as the greatest among the seven women who are honored as prophetesses
in pious Jewish tradition.[8] But the high spirits that prompted her to
laugh at God are mostly passed over in a kind of embarrassed silence by
the rabbinical storytellers, and some of the ancient translators of the
Bible into Aramaic went so far as to rewrite the biblical text to remove
any reference to Sarah's audacious laughter.[9] Nowadays, Sarah is invoked
along with the other matriarchs in the "egalitarian" liturgy of the more
progressive movements in Judaism, but her remarkable encounter with
God is rarely, if ever, mentioned at all.

Yet the woman who laughed at God embodies one of the essential
values of Judaism—the audacity, boldness, and daring that are summed
up in the Yiddish word "chutzpah." Like so many other moments in the
"untold history" of the Jewish people, as we shall see, the encounter between God and Sarah reminds us that Judaism is not a fossil-religion, not
a fly caught in amber and preserved over the millennia, but something
fully and vigorously alive, something that acknowledges and affirms what
human beings really are and what they really do, something that lives
and endures precisely as it grows and changes.

TWO

The People of the Book

Aboriginal Creation myths tell of the legendary totemic beings who had wandered over the continent in the Dreamtime, singing out the name of everything that crossed their path—birds, animals, plants, rocks, waterholes—and so singing the world into existence.

—BRUCE CHATWIN, *The Songlines*

Let us begin where the Bible begins: "*B'reh-sheet*" ("In the beginning") is the very first word of the Hebrew Bible, a work that presents itself as the official history of the people who will one day come to be called the Jews. Starting with the very moment of creation, and spanning several thousand years of human experience, the biblical history of the Jewish people is sometimes exalted, sometimes sordid, and sometimes baffling. As profoundly misunderstood and misused as it may be, the fact remains that the Bible is, and has always been, the document by which Judaism has defined itself.

Jews like to call themselves "the People of the Book," a phrase that honors the intimate connection between the Bible and the people who were its original writers and readers. By one of the many rich ironies that decorate Jewish history, the phrase itself originated with Muhammad, founder of Islam, and it is used in the Koran to describe both Christians *and* Jews. Still, the Jewish people have embraced it precisely because "the Book"—that is, the Bible—is the touchstone of Jewish law, ritual, and tradition. Although, as we shall soon see, Judaism has grown into something drastically different from the faith that is actually described in the Bible, the Jewish people have always understood themselves and explained themselves to the rest of the world by reference to the Bible.* "God, Torah and Israel are one" goes a credo that is preserved in the work of Jewish mysticism known as the Zohar.[1]

The Bible presents itself as a work of history, but it can be deceptive and even dangerous to regard the biblical text as history in the modern sense. After centuries of scratching in the rock and sand and soil of the Holy Land, the enterprise once known as "biblical archaeology"—that is, the search for archaeological evidence to prove that the Bible is historically true—has produced only meager results. Not a single item of archaeological evidence unambiguously confirms what we read in the Bible about people or events before King David, who supposedly lived and reigned starting around 1000 B.C.E. But the evidence for the glorious King David is oblique at best—a fragmentary inscription on a stone monument dating as far back as the ninth century B.C.E. appears to refer to the dynasty (or "house") of David, but the stela postdates the supposed life of David by at least a century or so.

Sometimes, the archaeological record squarely contradicts what is recorded in the Bible. The very earliest mention of Israel outside the Bible, for example, is an Egyptian stela of the thirteenth century B.C.E., a period in which a couple million Israelites were supposedly marching out of Egypt, across the Sinai Peninsula, and into the land of Canaan. But, contrary to the saga of liberation and conquest that is reported in the

---

*What we call the Bible is identified in Hebrew as the *Tanakh*, an acronym that refers to its three principal components: the Torah ("Law" or "Instruction"), the *Neviim* ("Prophets"), and the *Ketuvim* ("Writings"). The Torah consists of the first five books of the Bible, also known as the Five Books of Moses, the Pentateuch ("Five Scrolls"), or the *Chumash* ("Five"). The *Neviim* consist of early historical books (Joshua, Judges, Samuel, and Kings) and the writings of the Prophets (Isaiah, Jeremiah, Ezekiel, and the twelve others who are described as the "Minor" Prophets). The *Ketuvim* are a miscellaneous collection of writings, including Psalms and Proverbs, Job and Ruth, Ezra and Nehemiah.

Book of Exodus, the Egyptian stela preserves a boast by a pharaoh called Merneptah that the nation and people of Israel had been utterly destroyed: "Israel is laid waste, his seed is not."[2]

According to pious tradition in Judaism, Christianity, and Islam, of course, the Scriptures are regarded as literally true. The first five books of the Bible were given on Sinai "from the mouth of God to the hand of Moses," as we recite in the liturgy of the Torah-reading service. But modern biblical scholarship suggests that the Bible can and should be understood in much the same way that we approach the myths and legends of other ancient and primitive peoples as embodied in *their* sacred writings. Thus, for example, the myth of origin that appears in the opening passages of the Bible—"And God said: 'Let there be light,' and there was light" (Gen. 1:3) (JPS)—can be understood as an ancient Near Eastern counterpart to the Dreamtime of the aboriginal people of Australia, who believe that the world was sung rather than spoken into existence at some magical moment in the far distant past.

The God of History

Deeply embedded in the Bible is the simple but revolutionary idea that the God of Israel is a god of history, and that is why the Bible presents itself as a work of history. Stripped of its rich mythical and theological decoration, the Bible can be read as a factual account of the twelve tribes that descended from Abraham, Isaac, and Jacob—how they wandered across the ancient world, sought refuge in Egypt under Joseph, passed into slavery, and then marched out again under Moses, conquered the land of Canaan under Joshua, united into a single kingdom under David and Solomon, fell into bitter tribal rivalry again when the "United Monarchy" cleaved into a northern kingdom and a southern kingdom, and finally suffered a series of military and political defeats that ultimately deprived them of national sovereignty and sent them into a long diaspora.

Significantly, all of these crucial events are credited by the biblical authors to God himself: "The Lord will bring a nation against thee from far away, as the vulture swoopeth down," Moses is shown to prophesy in the Book of Deuteronomy. "And the Lord shall scatter thee among all peoples, from the one end of the earth even to the other end of the earth" (Deut. 28:49, 64).³ Only when they are liberated by the Persians in 538 B.C.E. does a remnant return to Jerusalem and rebuild the Temple, and it is the emperor Cyrus II who is hailed in the Book of Isaiah as the Messiah—God's anointed one—precisely because the god of history chooses a pagan from far-off Persia to work his will in the Holy Land.

Indeed, the distinction between a god of history and a god of nature is crucial to understanding the Bible and its role in Judaism. Across the ages and around the world, the gods and goddesses who were worshipped in various pagan faiths were imagined to manifest themselves in natural objects—mountains and rivers and oceans, caves and rocks and trees—and to work their will through natural phenomena such as thunder and lightning, floods and earthquakes, and, above all, the fertility of animal and vegetable life. The Jewish understanding of God, as it was first articulated in the Bible, was something wholly new and different: the God of Israel is a cosmic deity who cannot be contained on a single sacred mountain or in a single grove of trees, and whose powers are not confined to flood and fire. Rather, the God of Israel prefers to express himself through the words that ordinary human beings are inspired to speak and write, and he works his will through the deeds that they are inspired to do.

"The lofty conception . . . that the God of nature is also the God of history," wrote Heinrich Graetz, an influential Jewish historian of the nineteenth century, "is a product of a people that possessed a keen eye for the unusual and the wonderful."⁴

To be sure, the Bible presents itself as an historical narrative. One of the enduring credos of Judaism, which originated in ancient Israel as a formula for sacrificial offerings and is now recited during the observance of Passover, is actually a thumbnail sketch of a thousand years or so of biblical history:

My father was a fugitive Aramean. He went down to Egypt with meager numbers and sojourned there; but there he became a great and very populous nation. The Egyptians dealt harshly with us and oppressed us; they imposed heavy labor upon us. We cried to the Lord, the God of our fathers, and the Lord heard our plea and saw our plight, our misery, and our oppression. The Lord freed us from Egypt by a mighty hand, by an outstretched arm and awesome power, and by signs and portents. He brought us to this place and gave us this land, a land flowing with milk and honey (Deut. 26:5–9) (JPS).

But when we read the Bible with open eyes and an open mind, we will come to see that it is *not* a work of history in the conventional sense. The various sources who authored and edited the biblical text do not always agree with each other on the details of biblical history, great or small. When Noah sought to find dry land after the Flood, for example, did he send out a raven (Gen. 8:7) or a dove (Gen. 8:10) or both? Was the father-in-law of Moses named Jethro (Exod. 3:1) or Reuel (Exod. 2:18) or Hobab (Judg. 4:11)? Did David slay Goliath (1 Sam. 17:49–50) or was it a man called Elhanan (2 Sam. 21:19)? Even something so fundamental as the name and nature of God himself is the subject of debate among the biblical sources, and it turns out that the God of Israel—like Judaism itself—can be understood in many contrasting and sometimes conflicting ways.

So the diversity that has always characterized Judaism begins in the Torah itself. The biblical sources confirm that the Israelites embraced a rich and strange assortment of beliefs and practices, and even the orthodoxy of ancient Israel was something very different from what we recognize as Judaism today. That is why the Bible is the best place—the *only* place—to start in a quest for the many Judaisms of antiquity.

Who Really Wrote the Bible?

The Bible, according to the common wisdom of modern biblical scholarship, is a work of human authorship, composed and compiled by many different authors, men and women alike, working at different times and places over a period of a thousand years or so and embracing a variety of beliefs about who God is and what God wants. Though Jewish fundamentalists in the modern world may regard the idea as heretical, it was apparent a thousand years ago even to those who regarded the Bible as Holy Writ.

For example, a Jewish physician called Isaac ibn Yashush, who lived in Spain during the eleventh century, noticed that the Edomite kings who are listed in Chapter 36 of the Book of Genesis actually lived and reigned long after the death of Moses, the supposed author of Genesis and the rest of the Five Books of Moses. Surely, he suggested, the king list must have been inserted into the text by someone other than Moses. Isaac was condemned as "Isaac the Blunderer" by Abraham ibn Ezra, a Spanish rabbi of the twelfth century, but the rabbi seemed to concede that the good doctor's only real blunder was his lack of discretion rather than his sharp-eyed reading of the Torah. "[I]f you understand, then you will recognize the truth," wrote Rabbi ibn Ezra, "and he who understands will keep silent."[5]

Here begins the old and honorable but sometimes dangerous tradition of reading what is actually written in the Bible. "It is clearer than the sun at noon that the Pentateuch was not written by Moses but by someone who lived long after Moses," insisted Baruch Spinoza, the seventeenth-century philosopher who was excommunicated by the Jewish community of Amsterdam for holding such opinions and speaking them aloud.[6] By the late nineteenth century, the pioneers of modern Bible scholarship had begun to identify and describe the various human authors and editors who created the biblical texts and whose ideas are preserved in the Bible as we know it today. Nowadays, only the most fundamentalist Jews still insist on regarding the Bible as the word of God in a literal sense; the rest of the Jewish world is willing to entertain the idea that it is actually the work of men and women who may have been God-inspired but were also thoroughly human in both their methods and their motives.

The Woman Who Laughed at God

The very first clue to the multiple human authorship of the Bible is also the single best example of the startling diversity of belief that is accommodated and even encouraged by the biblical authors. Although the closest thing to a catechism and a credo in Jewish tradition is a line of text from the Book of Deuteronomy that declares the oneness of God—"Hear O Israel, the Lord thy God, the Lord is One" (Deut. 6:4)—God has always meant different things to different people. And nowhere are the many faces of God displayed with greater variety than in the Bible itself.

At one moment, for example, the Bible depicts God as a desert wanderer who shows up at the tent of Abraham and Sarah to cadge a meal of veal and curds—God has not yet handed down the law that will one day be interpreted to prohibit the mixing of milk and meat (Deut. 14:21), and so he is perfectly willing to eat *trayf* (Gen. 18:1–8). At another moment, God resembles one of the pagan storm gods and mountain gods whom the Bible finds so abominable: "Now Mount Sinai was altogether on smoke, because the Lord descended upon it in fire," goes a passage in the Book of Exodus, "and the whole mount quaked greatly" (Exod. 19:18) (JPS). At yet another moment, God is the Ancient of Days, a white-haired king seated on a throne of fire and attended by "ten thousand times ten thousand" angels (Dan. 7:9–10). And God agrees to reveal himself to the prophet Elijah in the most sublime passage of all:

> And, behold, the Lord passed by, and a great and strong wind rent the mountains, and broke in pieces the rocks before the Lord; but the Lord was not in the wind; and after the wind an earthquake; but the Lord was not in the earthquake; and after the earthquake a fire; but the Lord was not in the fire; and after the fire a still small voice (1 Kings 19:11–12) (JPS).

The classic proof for the multiple human authorship of the Bible— and the starting point for identifying and describing the various biblical sources—begins with the most basic question of all: What is God's name? One biblical source, who is known in Bible scholarship as the Yahwist or J, calls God by his personal name, Yahweh.* Another biblical source,

---

*The Yahwist is called "J" because the name of God is spelled "Jahweh" in German, the language of the pioneering Bible scholars of the eighteenth and nineteenth centuries, and is sometimes rendered in English as "Jehovah." By long tradition in Judaism, however, the name of God is not

known as the Elohist or E, generally calls God by a descriptive noun rather than a personal name—"*Elohim,*" a plural noun that can be literally translated as "gods." Not only does each source call God by a different name, but each one presents God in a very different way.

J gives us a deity who is approachable and companionable, if sometimes also cranky and impulsive. After sitting down to dinner with Abraham and Sarah, according to J, God promises the aged couple that Sarah will bear a son. The old woman finds the idea so preposterous that she is moved to impulsive laughter, and God reacts to the sound of Sarah's laughter in a way that reveals not his mighty wrath but his hurt feelings. "Why did Sarah laugh?" asks God, protesting just a bit too much for a God who is supposed to be omnipotent and saying of himself: "Is anything too hard for Yahweh?" (Gen. 18:13–14).[7]

E, by contrast, gives us an all-seeing and all-knowing deity who flatly refuses to manifest in human form and inspires only blood-shaking terror in his Chosen People. According to E, for example, God calls to Moses from a burning bush atop the sacred mountain called Horeb—and Moses hides his face like a child because, as E tells us, "he was afraid to look upon Elohim" (Exod. 3:6).[8] Thus, J shows us that an old woman might giggle at God and suffer no consequence at all, but E suggests that a man is worthy only if he lives in abject fear of God.

The points of conflict among the biblical sources are not merely objects of curiosity. Rather, they go to the heart of what the Bible teaches about who God is and what God wants. When God reveals to Abraham that he intends to kill every man, woman, and child in the sin-soaked cities of Sodom and Gomorrah, for example, J gives us a scene in which Abraham reprimands God—"Wilt thou indeed sweep away the righteous with the wicked?" (Gen. 18:23) (JPS)—and then haggles with him like a bazaar merchant. Would God spare Sodom if there were fifty righteous men and women in the city? What if there were only forty? How about thirty? Finally, Abraham extracts a promise from God that he will not

spoken aloud, and we do not know exactly how the Hebrew word is actually pronounced. Based on this tradition, the Hebrew word for God's personal name, consisting of consonants that correspond with "YHVH," is usually rendered as "the Lord" in pious translations of the Bible.

destroy Sodom if he finds only ten righteous men and women. And yet, when God demands that Abraham offer up Isaac as a human sacrifice, E gives us a very different scene in which Abraham is willing to comply without a word of protest—"And Abraham stretched forth his hand, and took the knife to slay his son" (Gen. 22:10) (JPS)—and spares Isaac only when God abruptly calls the whole thing off (Gen. 22:12).[9]

The same tension can be seen when we compare the writings of the Priestly Author, a biblical source who is wholly concerned with the meticulous observance of ritual law in every detail, and the Prophets, who insist on looking into the hearts and minds of the Israelites. "And the anointed priest shall take of the blood of the bullock and bring it to the tent of meeting," goes a typical passage in the Book of Leviticus on the rites of sacrifice that are nothing less than a priestly obsession. "And the priest shall dip his finger in the blood, and sprinkle of the blood seven times before the Lord, in front of the veil of the sanctuary" (Lev. 4:5–6). But the prophet Isaiah voices the disgust of God at the hypocrisy of those who piously observe the fast days while forcing their laborers to stay at work. "Do you call that a fast?" asks an angry God, and he goes on to describe "the fast I desire":

> *To unlock the fetters of wickedness*
> *And untie the cords of the yoke,*
> *To let the oppressed go free.* . . .
>
>   .   .   .   .
>
> *It is to share your bread with the hungry,*
> *And to take the wretched poor into your home;*
> *When you see the naked, to clothe him,*
> *And not to ignore your own kin.*
>   (Isa. 58:5–7) (New JPS)

Most significant of all is the simple fact that *all* of these conflicting ideas about God—and much else that is contrary to what is taught in traditional Judaism—have always coexisted within the pages of the Torah.

The Angel in the Flame

The Yahwist and the Elohist are not the only authors whose differing takes on history and theology have been teased out of the Torah by modern Bible scholarship. A third source, who is obsessively concerned with ritual matters, religious law, and other aspects of priestcraft, is known as the Priestly Author or P. The Book of Deuteronomy, so distinct from the rest of the Torah in its theology and its rhetorical style, is attributed to a source called the Deuteronomist or D. All of the various strands of authorship were woven together by yet another source known as the Redactor or R. That is why the Bible must be read as an anthology rather than a seamless work of authorship by a single source, human or divine.

During the long process of biblical authorship, many of these various sources felt at liberty—or perhaps even obliged—to fix what they found wrong with both the history and the theology of ancient Israel as it was reflected in the biblical texts. Revision of the text was a tool of reinterpretation. Thus, for example, one nameless source, who was apparently uncomfortable with the notion that God and human beings are able to encounter each other without the assistance of a duly consecrated priest, may have rewritten key scenes to suggest that God is always accompanied by an intermediary when he deigns to reveal himself to ordinary men and women. That is why, some scholars believe, angels have been inserted into some of the most familiar passages of the Bible, often lamely and sometimes confusingly, as when God calls to Moses from a burning bush:

> And *the angel of the Lord appeared unto [Moses]* in a flame of fire out of the midst of a bush; and he looked, and, behold, the bush burned with fire, and the bush was not consumed. . . . And . . . *God called unto him out of the midst of the bush*, and said, "Moses, Moses." And he said, "Here am I" (Exod. 3:2, 4) (JPS) (Emphasis added).

Sometimes, the Bible preserves two entirely different accounts of the same life or the same event. Thus, for example, one early biblical author called the Court Historian is credited with the intimate and candid biography of King David that appears in the Book of Samuel, where we are allowed to see David not only as a courageous war hero, compassionate father, glorious king, and pious worshipper of Yahweh, but also as a bandit, mercenary, trickster, shakedown artist, seducer, adulterer, voyeur, exhibitionist, and even murderer. But another author, known as the Chronicler, came along several centuries later and composed the revisionist version of David's life story that is preserved in the Book of Chronicles, where all of the salacious details have been cut out and only a plaster saint remains.

"See what Chronicles has made out of David!" exclaimed Julius Wellhausen, one of the early and influential figures in modern Bible scholarship.[10]

The Things That Are Concealed

During and after the Babylonian Exile of the sixth century B.C.E., the priests and scribes who were the custodians of the sacred writings of Israel felt at liberty to act as censors. Some of the texts in their care were ancient and revered: the biblical life story of King David in the Book of Samuel may date back to the lifetime of David himself, for example, and a few passages of the Bible, such as the Song of Miriam (Exod. 15:21) and the Song of Deborah (Judg. 5), may be even older, perhaps the very oldest fragments in the entire Bible. But the texts that are collected in the Bible were worked and reworked over the centuries by a series of priestly authors and editors who were committed to theological law and order.

That is why, for example, some of the biblical sources—like their spiritual successors in strictly observant Judaism—insist that what God wants of the Chosen People is, above all, simple obedience to the 613 *mitzvot* (commandments) that were revealed to Moses on Mount Sinai, a body of law that concerns itself wholly with life as it is lived down here on earth. Certain passages in the Bible suggest that so long as a man does not sleep with his sister, for example, or plow his field with an ox and an ass yoked together, or shave the corners of his beard, he will be blessed by

God. If, however, he does any of those things, he will be cursed. This is what Moses really means when he is shown to say, so famously and so memorably, "I have set before thee life and death, the blessing and curse; therefore choose life" (Deut. 30:19).

The same biblical sources—again, like their heirs in the strictest traditions of Judaism—condemn mystical yearnings in general and magical practices in particular. "If there arise in the midst of thee a prophet, or a dreamer of dreams," warns Moses, "saying, 'Let us go after other gods,' thou shalt not hearken unto the words of that prophet, or unto that dreamer of dreams" (Deut. 13:2–4).[11] The ban on the practice of the black arts extends to "a soothsayer, or an enchanter, or a sorcerer, or a charmer, or one that consulteth a ghost or a familiar spirit, or a necromancer" (Deut. 18:10–11), and the penalty is death: "Thou shalt not suffer a witch to live," goes one bloodthirsty clause in the Book of Exodus (Exod. 22:17). Theological speculation ought to be left to the experts, the Bible seems to say, and ordinary men and women ought to content themselves with the here and now.

"The secret things belong unto the Lord our God," says Moses, "but the things that are revealed belong unto us and to our children for ever, that we may do all the words of this law" (Deut. 29:28) (JPS). But something deep in human nature prompts us to go in search of the "secret things"—that is why Adam and Eve earned a place in the theological hall of fame—and the biblical censors were unsuccessful in their efforts at concealment of forbidden truths. Through the cracks in the wall that was built up around the oldest texts in the Bible, we can see that the Israelites were no less curious and no less daring than anyone else in the ancient world, a time and place in which most people felt free to mix and match gods and goddesses, rites and rituals, according to their own whim and inspiration. Indeed, the effort to censor the Bible—an effort that begins within the pages of the Bible itself and continued long after the biblical canon was closed—has been a failure. Crucially, the works of both the Court Historian *and* the Chronicler are preserved, and we can see for ourselves much of what we are not supposed to see at all.

We do not know exactly why so many provocative and troubling passages were allowed to remain in the Bible by the very people who tried to clean up the text. Perhaps some of the most scandalous or self-contradictory stories were so familiar to the people of ancient Israel that the priests and scribes did not feel free to leave them out; perhaps they fretted that the original readers of the Bible would not accept it as authentic if, for example, the torrid but star-crossed love affair of David and Bathsheba were cleaned up or cut out entirely. Perhaps the inclusion of two versions of the same incident—what scholars called a "doublet"—is a wink and a nod from the biblical author that is meant to convey his own doubt about the historical accuracy of either one. And, for some of the biblical sources, the notion that David was both "a man of blood" and "a man after God's own heart" is itself an affirmation of faith: the will of God prevails even in the face of flagrant disobedience of his sacred law.

Whatever the reason, however, we are fortunate that the biblical censors were so halfhearted in their efforts. And if we dare to draw back the thin veil that they drew across the more provocative passages of the Bible, we can glimpse a landscape of startling richness and diversity, the very landscape in which the many expressions of Judaism first flowered in such profusion.

What Moses Believed

"We do not know what the faith of the Patriarchs was," insists Harold Bloom in *The Book of J*, "or what Moses believed."[12] But the Bible allows us to see that the faith of ancient Israel was something far different and far more diverse than what has been preserved in Jewish tradition. Indeed, the religion that is actually described in such blood-soaked detail in the pages of Exodus, Leviticus, Numbers, and Deuteronomy—a religion based on elaborate rituals of animal sacrifice by an hereditary priesthood at a single central sanctuary—is so unlike what we know today as Judaism that Jacob Neusner calls it "proto-Judaism,"[13] and Donald Harman Akenson uses the newly minted term "Judahism" to distinguish it from "Judaism."

"This is not a trick word," insists Akenson. "The religion of Judah, based on Temple sacrifice to Yahweh, up to the destruction of the Second Temple in 70 C.E., is distinct historically from its descendent, the post-Temple faith, usually known as 'Rabbinic Judaism.' "[14]

First of all, the ancient Israelites were not originally or always strict monotheists. An intriguing clue to what Moses actually believed can be found in a prayer that is uttered in synagogues all over the world to this very day: *"Mee khah-moh-kha b'elim Adonai."* According to the Book of Exodus, these words were first uttered by Moses in praise of God after the miracle at the Red Sea, when the waters were parted to permit the Israelites to cross on dry land and then closed again to destroy the pursuing army of Pharaoh. "Who is like You among the heavenly powers, Hashem!" goes the English translation of the prayer in one modern prayerbook.[15]

But the pious translation is inaccurate, and intentionally so. "Hashem," for example, is a Hebrew word that literally means "the Name" and is traditionally used in place of the word that actually appears in the biblical text: *Yahweh*, the personal name of God. According to the practices of ancient Israel, the name of God was uttered only on the holiest day of the year, Yom Kippur, only by the High Priest, and only in the Holy of Holies in the Temple at Jerusalem. By the second century B.C.E., even the High Priest was forbidden to speak "this glorious and awful Name" (Deut. 28:58). By long and devout tradition in Judaism, the word that appears in prayers and biblical passages as Yahweh is read aloud as "Hashem" or "Adonai."

But even more deceptive is the rendering of the Hebrew word *elim* as "heavenly powers." Other Jewish translations are equally evasive: the word *elim* is translated as "the mighty" or "the celestials" in various Bibles.[16] In fact, *elim* is a Hebrew noun that literally means "gods," and the words of Moses as reported in Exodus can be rendered in a way that suggests he was not quite the strict monotheist he is reputed to have been in Jewish tradition: "Who is like you, O Yahweh, among the *gods*?" is the real meaning of what Moses is reported to have said in the Bible (Exod. 15:11).[17]

So Moses—or, perhaps more accurately, the biblical author who composed the so-called Song of Moses in Chapter 15 of the Book of Exodus—may not have believed that Yahweh is the one and only god. Rather, his words can be understood to suggest only that Yahweh is better than all the other gods and goddesses—or, perhaps, that Yahweh is the best of all gods only as far as the Israelites are concerned. Although the Book of Deuteronomy presents us with the pristine declaration of monotheism that is the closest thing to a catechism in Judaism—"Hear O Israel, the Lord thy God, the Lord is One" (Deut. 6:4)—the Bible seems to preserve, almost inadvertently, a more open-minded and affirming attitude toward polytheism than the later biblical authors were willing to allow.

"The Brazen Serpent That Moses Had Made"

Another fundamental idea in Jewish tradition is that God detests not only the worship of rival gods and goddesses but also the making of idols that are imagined to depict or embody them. "Thou shalt not make unto thee a graven image," goes the Second Commandment, "nor any manner of likeness, of any thing that is in heaven above, or that is in the earth beneath, or that is in the water" (Exod. 20:4). So sacred is the Second Commandment that, when the Israelites make and worship the notorious Golden Calf, God vows to exterminate the Chosen People—man, woman, and child—and start over again with Moses and his two sons. Only when Moses stands up to God and challenges *him* to keep the faith—"Turn from thy fierce wrath," Moses boldly implores, "and repent of this evil against thy people" (Exod. 32:12) (JPS)—does God spare the Israelites from divine genocide. Even so, God insists on death for anyone who has committed the sin of idolatry, and Moses carries out a bloody purge of the men and women who had joined in the worship of the Golden Calf:

> Thus saith the Lord, the God of Israel: Put ye every man his sword upon his thigh, and go to and fro from gate to gate throughout the camp, and slay every man his brother, and every man his companion, and every man his neighbour (Exod. 32:27) (JPS).

Yet, even in the life story of Moses, the Bible allows us to see that the law against the making of graven images was not always enforced with perfect zeal. Moses himself is shown to fashion a serpent out of brass and use the graven image as a magical cure for snakebite, all at the specific bidding of God himself: "Every one that is bitten, when he seeth it, shall live" (Num. 21:8–9). In fact, one of the biblical authors confirms that the brass snake was preserved for centuries in the Temple at Jerusalem, where it was cherished along with other relics of the Exodus. Not until the reign of Hezekiah, a reformer-king of the eighth century B.C.E., did some of the more devout and literal-minded Israelites wake up to the fact that the graven image of a snake—and, especially, the uses to which the so-called Nehushtan was put—were a plain violation of the Ten Commandments.

"And he broke in pieces the brazen serpent that Moses had made," the Book of Kings reports of Hezekiah, "for unto those days the children of Israel did offer to it" (2 Kings 18:4).

Moses is not the only revered figure who is shown in the Bible to traffic in graven images. Rachel, the favorite wife of the patriarch Jacob, filched her father's collection of household idols, known in the Bible as *teraphim,* or so J reports in the Book of Genesis without a hint of disapproval. Michal, daughter of Saul and wife of David—each one of them anointed by God as a king of Israel—apparently kept a collection of *teraphim* in her own home, and she used one to trick the death squad sent by her father into thinking that her husband was asleep in bed when he was already on the run (1 Sam. 19:13–16). The Court Historian, who tells the tale in the Book of Samuel, also allows the incident to pass without comment.

Only when we reach the Book of Kings and the writings of the Prophets do the biblical authors enforce the laws against idolatry wholeheartedly and embrace monotheism as the official theology of ancient Israel in plain language. It is the prophet Jeremiah (c. 640–587 B.C.E.), for example, who rules out any notion that Yahweh is merely the best of all possible deities: the gods and goddesses worshiped by the pagans (and not a few Israelites) are "no-gods," as he puts it (Jer. 2:11, 5:7) (JPS). And it is Josiah, a king who reigned in the late seventh century, who seeks to purge the faith of ancient Israel of the last traces of polytheism and paganism.

The good king Josiah, according to his admirers among the biblical authors, purifies the Temple of Yahweh at Jerusalem by dragging out and destroying the idols and other paraphernalia used for the worship of the Canaanite god Baal and his consort Asherah. He carries out mass executions of the priests who make sacrificial offerings "to the sun, and to the moon, and to the constellations, and to all the hosts of heaven" at hill shrines around Jerusalem and the tribal homeland of Judah, and he burns their bones down to ash. And he tears down the houses where men are offering themselves as temple prostitutes and women are put to work at weaving the vestments used for the worship of Asherah.

"No king before him had turned to the Lord as he did, with all his heart, and with all his soul, and with all his might, following the whole law of Moses," goes the account in the Book of Kings, echoing the distinctive rhetorical flourishes of the Deuteronomist, "nor did any king like him appear again" (2 Kings 23:4–7, 25).[18]

Almost inadvertently, the biblical author concedes that the pious Josiah was a rarity among the people of Israel. Before and after Josiah, the Israelites and their kings are lured into all of the practices that the Bible condemns as "abominations"—idol worship and ritual intercourse and even human sacrifice. Even King Solomon, who is said in the Bible to have been blessed by God with "wisdom and understanding and largeness of heart" and who is mandated by God to build the Temple at Jerusalem, is also plainly depicted as an apostate who is seduced into idolatry by his several hundred foreign wives and concubines (1 Kings 11:5–13) (JPS). "Upon every high hill, and under every leafy tree, thou didst recline, playing the harlot," complains Jeremiah of his fellow Israelites (Jer. 2:20) (JPS), conjuring up the orgies of sexual excess that both the authors of the Bible and the makers of Hollywood epics associate with the worship of pagan gods and goddesses.

So the schism between belief and practice was a fact of life in ancient Israel. The Bible itself attests that the Israelites, their kings, and even their priests were as susceptible as anyone else in the ancient world to the charms and seductions of paganism and polytheism. The invisible

God of Israel—so austere, so aloof, so demanding—was always in competition with the more alluring gods and goddesses and the beguiling artifacts and rituals by which they were worshipped. Even when the biblical author seeks to shock his readers with a description of the pagan excesses that King Josiah stamped out—the groves and high places where the idol worshippers gathered, the altars and standing stones and living trees that were the object of worship, the "houses of sodomites" where the ritual paraphernalia was prepared, the incense that was burned in celebration of "the sun, the moon, the planets, and all the host of heaven"—he betrays himself by allowing us to see how seductive it all must have seemed to the Israelites themselves (2 Kings 23:4–7).

If the Bible is a work of history at all, then, it is the history of how the fundamentalists of ancient Israel tried—and failed—to enforce a strict orthodoxy on the rest of the Israelites. The Josianic reform, as it is known in biblical scholarship, was spotty and short-lived, and the faith of ancient Israel was never wholly purged of paganism and polytheism. Indeed, the Bible can be read as one long song of despair over the failure of the Chosen People to live up to the lofty standards of faith and conduct set for them by their priests and prophets. When Moses is shown in the Book of Deuteronomy to scold the Israelites yet again—"Behold, while I am yet alive with you this day, ye have been rebellious against the Lord; and how much more after my death?" (Deut. 31:27)—surely we are hearing the voices of the disappointed and frustrated biblical authors who lived long after his supposed lifetime.

Real History

In the Bible, as elsewhere, history is written by the victors—or, at least, the survivors. Tellingly, the strictest of the biblical sources—the Deuteronomist, the Priestly Author, and perhaps even the Elohist—have all been linked to the priestly caste of ancient Israel, and they put their own political and theological imprint on everything that we read in the Bible. Not only the long and sometimes tedious codes of biblical law and ritual but even the most thrilling tales of military and sexual adventure are shaped—and sometimes distorted—by their real goal of winning the hearts and minds of the original readers of the Bible. And, for that reason, it is treacherous to read the Bible as history even when it invites us to do so.

The story of creation in the Book of Genesis, for example, is self-evidently a work of myth, not science, and it is intended as a statement of theology rather than a factual account of how the world came into existence. Its rich poetic imagery recalls (and may have been inspired by) the creation myths of the pagans among whom the Israelites lived. For example, the Epic of Gilgamesh, an early work from Mesopotamia that long predates the Bible, includes a flood story not unlike the one told about Noah, and the motif of a creator-god imposing order on the watery forces of chaos can be found in mythological works all over the ancient Near East. Even the Orthodox movement in modern Judaism is willing to concede that "those seven 'days' of creation may in fact have been periods of extremely long duration," as Rabbi Hayim Donin puts it, "that correspond to 'stages' rather than days similar to our own twenty-four-hour day."[19] And biblical scholars insist that the original readers of the Bible did not regard it as literally true.

"[T]he audience of the biblical writers had its own literary idiom," explains Bible scholar Nahum M. Sarna. "[W]e must not confuse the idiom with the idea, the metaphor with the reality behind it."[20]

Indeed, the Bible itself suggests that the biblical authors regarded the story of creation as not much more than a curtain-raiser. The history of the world from the day of creation to the calling of Abraham is covered in eleven short chapters, which take up only eleven *pages* in the Bible that was handed to me on the day I was called to the Torah as a *bar mitzvah*. The rest of the Book of Genesis, along with the other thirty-eight books of the Hebrew Bible in their entirety, is devoted to an account of the ancient Israelites and their descendants, the Jewish people. And the whole of the Bible can be read as a pair of parallel histories, a sacred account of the dealings between God and humankind that appears side by side—or sometimes layer upon layer—with a secular account of how human beings deal with each other. In fact, much of the Bible—Judges, Samuel, Kings, and many of the later books—is entirely devoid of divine miracles of any kind. By the time we reach the Book of Esther, God is not mentioned at all.

"It is real history," enthused Sigmund Freud, an amateur Bible critic, about the biblical life story of King David, "five hundred years before Herodotus, the 'Father of History.' "[21]

Or is it?

"One Who Struggles with God"

The history of Israel, as we find it in the Bible, starts with Abraham, a restless nomad who is called by God from the city of Ur in Mesopotamia and promised a homeland in a distant place called Canaan. Abraham begat Isaac, as the King James Version puts it, and Isaac begat Jacob, and Jacob begat twelve sons, each of whom is regarded as the founder of a tribe. After Jacob wrestles by night with a deeply mysterious figure who might be an angel or God himself, his name is changed to Israel (*Yisrael*), a Hebrew word that is understood to mean "one who struggles with God." And that is why the Israelites are known in the Bible quite literally as "the Children of Israel" (*B'nai Yisrael*).

Significantly, it is the fourth-born son of Jacob, a man called Judah, on whom the richest blessings are bestowed. Indeed, the whole of the Bible can be read as a saga in which younger sons—Jacob, Joseph, Judah, Moses, David, and Solomon, among others—prevail over their older siblings. And it is the tribe of Judah that will survive and prevail over the other tribes of Israel—the tribe that will produce David, the king who unites the twelve tribes into a single nation and conquers the city of Jerusalem as its royal capital; and Solomon, the king who builds the all-important Temple to Yahweh in Jerusalem; and, one day, the Messiah, the "anointed one" whom God will send to redeem the people of Israel. And it is the Jews—called *Yehudim* in Hebrew—who are the modern survivors of the tribe of Judah (*Yehudah*) and the inheritors of the tradition that is described so convincingly in the pages of the Bible.

Until very recently, in fact, the biblical saga of early Israel was regarded as essentially if not entirely historical by scholars. Abraham, for example, is shown in the Bible to purchase the Cave of Machpelah in Hebron as a burial place for his wife, Sarah (Gen. 23:9). The transaction is commemorated even today at the so-called Tomb of the Patriarchs in the modern Arab town of Hebron. And the incident is so convincing that a contemporary historian, Paul Johnson, describes it as "perhaps the first passage in the Bible which records an actual event, witnessed and described through a long chain of oral recitation and so preserving authentic details."[22]

Johnson can be credited with a gracious concern for the sensibilities of his Jewish readers in describing what actually happened at Hebron in distant biblical antiquity—"This is where the 4,000-year history of the Jews, in so far as it can be anchored in time and place, began," he writes[23]—but the fact is that modern scholarship makes no such claim. Jews and Muslims have long fought with each other over what they both regard as a sacred site; some sixty-seven Jews were killed during Arab rioting in Hebron in 1929, and some twenty-nine Muslims were killed when an Israeli physician opened fire on an Arab prayer service at the Cave of the Patriarchs in 1994. But, as it turns out, they are fighting over a myth: "The only indisputable fact in all this is the cave at Hebron cannot possibly be the biblical Cave of Machpelah," writes Magnus Magnusson. "[I]t is in fact a manmade water cistern, once carefully plastered to prevent the water seeping into the rock."[24]

No archaeological evidence of any kind confirms the existence of Abraham, Isaac, or Jacob, or any of the exploits attributed to them in the Bible. "Most Bible scholars and archaeologists have abandoned the question of the Patriarchs altogether," says Bible scholar Ronald Hendel. "They don't regard Abraham as having anything historical to say."[25] And nothing in the vast archaeological record of ancient Egypt preserves even a memory of Moses or the liberation of the Israelites from slavery under Pharaoh or any of the other events of the Exodus, most of which are nowadays regarded as purely legendary. "Do we possess any historical testimony about Moses?" muses Bible scholar Elias Auerbach in his own study of Moses. "We have none."[26]

Israelite Shleppers and Canaanite Shleppers

One of the core values of the Bible is what Auerbach calls "the desert-ideal," the notion that the Israelites are nomadic wanderers who are untainted by the comforts and corruptions of city life.[27] The Tenth Commandment—"Thou shalt not covet thy neighbor's house (Exod. 20:14)—may have originated as a rejection of *all* houses by a people who aspired to the freedom of movement that only a tent dweller enjoys. And though the Bible occasionally refers to the Israelites as "Hebrews" (*ibrim*), the biblical authors may intend to describe them as *habiru*, a term that is commonly used in extra-biblical writings to describe anyone who lived outside the settled communities of the ancient world. The notion of the Israelites as outsiders is summed up, as we have already seen, in a simple credo: "A wandering Aramean was my father" (Deut. 26:5) (JPS).

The idea that the Israelites were outsiders who were chosen by God as "mine own treasure from among all the peoples" (Exod. 19:5) (JPS) is soaked with meaning in biblical theology, which teaches that God bestowed the Torah and the Promised Land upon the Israelites as a sign of his special favor: "Because he loved thy fathers," explains Moses to the Israelites, "and chose their seed after them, and brought thee out [of Egypt] with his great power, to drive out nations from before thee greater and mightier than thou, and to bring thee in, to give thee their land for an inheritance" (Deut. 4:37–38) (JPS). Indeed, the separateness and the "chosenness" of the Israelites are essential and inseparable elements of Jewish religious tradition: the most enduring rites and rituals in Judaism, including circumcision, the sanctity of the Sabbath, and the laws of *kashrut*, are meant to remind the Chosen People of their unique calling and, not incidentally, to keep them separate and apart from everyone else.

But the very idea of the Israelites as outsiders who arrived in the land of Canaan as conquerors has been called into question by modern science and scholarship. The search for archaeological evidence that Israelites were outsiders who wandered through the ancient world before invading Canaan has been fruitless. The biblical account of the Battle of Jericho, for example, has been shown to be "a romantic mirage," according to Israeli archaeologist Israel Finkelstein, director of the department of archaeology at Tel Aviv University; the archaeological record reveals that no settlement existed at the site of Jericho at the time when Joshua was supposedly blowing those famous trumpets and those walls were a-tumbling down.[28] Even the fundamental notion that the Israelites and the Canaanites were two wholly different peoples has been challenged by some modern scholars, who argue that the people who came to identify themselves as Israelites actually emerged from within the native-dwelling peoples of Canaan at a date far earlier than the supposed period of the Exodus. "The early Israelites were—irony of ironies!—themselves originally Canaanites," explains Finkelstein.[29]

And so the biblical claim to the separateness and chosenness of the Israelites turns out to be a matter of theology rather than history. But the whole controversy is still capable of political repercussions in the modern Middle East. Just as so-called biblical archaeologists try to validate the Bible with what they find in the ground, the Zionist movement and the modern Jewish State of Israel have always taken a certain comfort in evidence of the "material culture" of ancient Israel; a distinctive style of calligraphy or architecture or pottery that can be characterized as "Israelite" strengthens the thread that links modern Israel with the ancient state of the same name.

Yigal Yadin, for example, who was both an accomplished archaeologist and a celebrated war hero during the early years of the modern Jewish state, served as chief of staff of the Israel Defense Forces and the excavator of Masada, an ancient desert fortress that has come to be regarded as a symbol of Jewish survival. And nowadays Palestinian Arabs are following the example of their Jewish counterparts in Israel by putting archaeology in service to nation-building. "Did you know the Canaanites were actually Arabs?" Abu Khalaf, director of the archaeology department at Al-Quds University, enthused to American journalist Amy Dockser Marcus. "Our habits and traditions go back to the Canaanites. They came from the Arabian peninsula looking for water. Abraham didn't arrive until two thousand years later."[30]

But the ambiguities in the archaeological record cut both ways, and neither the Jews nor the Arabs can really distinguish their distant ancestors from one another simply by digging facts out of the ground. Indeed, like so many other points of conflict in the modern Middle East, the facts are almost beside the point; Arabs and Jews insist on regarding themselves as separate and distinct from one another, and the most militant among them refuse to acknowledge that the two rival claimants to the Holy Land share *anything* in common. The Bible itself plainly asserts that both Isaac, the second patriarch of the Jewish people, and Ishmael, the traditional forefather of the Arab people, were sons of Abraham. But some Arab archaeologists, acting on the same patriotic impulses that motivate some Israeli archaeologists, insist on claiming kinship with the Canaanites precisely because the Bible insists that they were original owners of the Holy Land.

Ironically, the most recent archaeological findings suggest that all of the biblical distinctions between Israelites and Canaanites, so crucial to ancient Jewish theology and modern Palestinian nationalism, may be mostly a matter of myth. And, if so, the Arab claim to kinship with the Canaanites turns out to be a claim of kinship with the Jews. All of the people who lived in the land of Canaan during the early biblical era seem to have spoken the same language, worshipped the same gods and goddesses, lived in the same kind of houses, and stored their wine and grain in the same kind of jars. "The Israelite shleppers," as Finkelstein puts it, "weren't that much different than the Canaanite shleppers."[31]

A Paper Empire

Even more unsettling, however, is what the archaeologists have *not* found. Most of the crucial events described in the Bible, and most of the men and women depicted in its pages, are wholly absent from the archives and inscriptions that have survived from distant antiquity. And so, if we were forced to reconstruct the history of ancient Israel on the archaeological record alone, it would be a very different account from the one we are accustomed to reading in the pages of the Bible.

David, for example, is celebrated in the Bible as the king who forges the warring tribes of Israel into a single nation, conquers the Jebusite city of Jerusalem and makes it the seat of government, triumphs over the enemies of Israel on every border, and ultimately reigns over an empire that stretches "from the River of Egypt unto the River Euphrates" (Gen. 15:18).[32] Solomon, his son and successor, crowns his father's efforts by building a glorious temple in Jerusalem for the worship of Yahweh, the centerpiece of the faith of ancient Israel and the only place in all of Israel where sacrifice to God was officially sanctioned. And, according to one theory of Bible authorship, the biblical life story of David and Solomon as told by the Court Historian may have been composed by an eyewitness who actually lived and worked in the royal court of the Davidic kings.

All of this supposedly took place around 1000 B.C.E. and shortly thereafter, an era when history was literally being written in stone (as well as on clay tablets and sheets of papyrus) by the peoples and countries that surrounded Israel. And yet, other than the biblical authors, not a single observer in the ancient world took note of David or Solomon or any of their supposed exploits. Aside from the stela that was discovered at Tel Dan, which postdates the supposed life of David and mentions only the "House of David" rather than David himself, no mention of David or Solomon has been detected in any written source outside the Bible itself. Nor has the soil of Jerusalem yielded a single artifact that can be linked to the kingdom that David supposedly created or the Temple that Solomon supposedly built.

"Without the biblical accounts, history would be totally unaware of the very existence of the twin founders of the tenth-century expansion of Israel/Judah into a major power, and archaeology would have been able to do little to indicate that it had ever taken place," observes Magnus Magnusson. "As far as archaeology is concerned, it was a paper (or papyrus) empire only."[33]

A startlingly different impression of ancient Israel is given by the men and women who work at the cutting edge of archaeology and Bible scholarship. If David and Solomon existed at all, the revisionists suggest, they were rude tribal chieftains rather than the glorious kings and emperors who are depicted in the Bible. Jerusalem in the tenth century B.C.E. was only a village, and all of Israel was a rural backwater whose meager population survived by tending flocks and herds, raising grapes and olives, and selling their produce into the international trade that served

Egypt and Assyria. The faith of ancient Israel was a colorful miscellany of rites and rituals, some of which focused on the deity known as Yahweh and a great many others of which did not. Not until the late seventh century B.C.E., they insist, did the biblical saga emerge from the mists of myth and legend into the full light of history, and only then did the kingdom of Judah, the Temple at Jerusalem, and the religion of Israel even begin to resemble what is described in the Bible.

The scholars who make these arguments are authentic revolutionaries, and proud of it. Unlike the so-called biblical archaeologists of the nineteenth and early twentieth centuries, who were said to work with "a shovel in one hand and a Bible in the other," they claim to leave their Bibles at home and let the archaeological evidence speak for itself. And their reading of that evidence calls into question some of our most cherished assumptions about the origins of the Bible and the history of the Jewish people.

The Man Who Invented Biblical Israel

Among the revisionists at work today are non-Jewish scholars whose rhetoric strikes many Jewish readers as shrill and inflammatory. "We can now say with considerable confidence that the Bible is not a history of anyone's past," insists Thomas L. Thompson, perhaps the most radical of all revisionists in contemporary biblical scholarship, who argues that the Bible is no more reliable than similar collections of legend and lore that originated in Egypt, Mesopotamia, and Phoenicia. "Today, we no longer have a history of Israel."[34]

By his lights, such obscure kings as Omri and Ahab, who reigned in the northern kingdom of Israel in the ninth century B.C.E., are more likely to have been flesh-and-blood human beings than David and Solomon, and a now-forgotten town called Lachish was larger, richer, and more significant than Jerusalem during the period when the latter supposedly served as the royal capital of the United Monarchy. The biblical writings were composed *after* the Babylonian Exile, he insists, and the Bible as we have it dates back only to the second century B.C.E., when the Dead Sea Scrolls were being cached away in the caves near Qumran.

"There never was a 'United Monarchy' in history and it is meaningless to speak of pre-exilic prophets and their writings," insists Thompson. "The history of Iron Age Palestine today knows of Israel only as a small highland patronate lying north of Jerusalem and south of the Jezreel valley. Any history we write of this people will hardly resemble the Israel we thought we knew so much about only a few years ago"[35]

But some Jewish scholars, too, have reached many of the same disturbing conclusions. Thus, for example, Israeli archaeologist Israel Finkelstein is willing to affirm that Jerusalem, nowadays claimed by some Jews as the "eternal capital" of Israel, "only belatedly—and suddenly— rose to the center of Israelite consciousness" during the reign of King Josiah in the late seventh century B.C.E. And, according to Finkelstein, the version of history that we read in the Bible can be understood as a work of propaganda composed by Josiah and the priesthood that supported him to validate their own fierce ambitions toward a puritanism in religion and a "pan-Israelite" reach in politics. From the royal court and the Temple of Yahweh at Jerusalem—"hardly more than a small Middle Eastern market town," as Finkelstein describes it, "huddling behind its walls and gates"—Josiah aspired to expand the House of David and the cult of Yahweh into an imperial government and a state religion that would encompass all of ancient Israel.[36]

"Such is the power of the Bible's own story that it has persuaded the world that Jerusalem was always central to the experience of all Israel, and that the descendants of David were always blessed with special holiness," write Finkelstein and his collaborator, Neil Asher Silberman, "rather than being just another aristocratic clan fighting to remain in power despite internal strife and unprecedented threats from the outside."[37]

Such ideas may be shocking, but they are not new. The Book of Deuteronomy was characterized by one nineteenth-century Bible scholar as a "pious fraud" because it came to light under highly suspicious circumstances during the reign of Josiah and all too conveniently endorsed the reforms that he was undertaking. Thus, for example, the earlier books of the Bible suggest that the Patriarchs, Moses and David, among others, were perfectly free to offer sacrifices to Yahweh at various sites around Israel and even beyond its borders, whereas the Book of Deuteronomy introduces the wholly new idea that Yahweh accepts sacrifices only from "the place which the Lord your God shall choose out of all your tribes to put his name there" (Deut. 12:5) (JPS), a phrase that was understood to mean the Temple at Jerusalem and nowhere else in all of Israel.

So it turns out that Josiah, an obscure figure who is never invoked in Jewish prayer or folklore, may be the single most crucial figure in all of Jewish history, the man who literally invented biblical Israel. According to the Bible, he was a pious king who sought to bring the faith of ancient Israel into compliance with God's will as it was revealed in the long-lost scroll that was discovered in the Temple at Jerusalem. A more cynical reading of the biblical text suggests that Josiah was an ambitious, willful, and clever king who sought to unify the Israelites under his leadership by making sure that they regarded Jerusalem not only as the royal capital but also as the single holiest place in all of Israel. Whatever his actual motives, however, Josiah worked a revolution in the beliefs and practices of ancient Israel. During his thirty-one-year reign as king of Judah, a shiny new theology was minted, a bloody purge of old believers was carried out in its service, and the core texts of the Bible were reworked, quite literally, in his image.

"It is not just that King Josiah is seen in the Bible as the notable successor to Moses, Joshua, and David," argues Finkelstein. "[T]he very outlines of those great characters—as they appear in the biblical narrative—seem to be drawn with Josiah in mind." Above all, it is Josiah who "dramatically changed what it meant to be an Israelite, and laid the foundations for future Judaism," by redefining the faith of Israel and thus the destiny of the Jewish people.[38]

The Prisoner's Rations

Josiah is hardly a unique figure in Jewish history, and we will meet his kindred spirits again and again in the pages that follow. He imagines God to be a strict and demanding deity, he insists that God must be worshipped according to narrow and rigorous laws, and he condemns anyone and anything that fall outside his own orthodoxy. Still, the crucial point to bear in mind is that Josiah was *not* successful in enforcing his harsh new regime on the people of Israel, and the clash between orthodoxy and diversity remains the single most consistent and enduring theme of the Bible and Jewish history alike.

Josiah, the Bible reports, does not live to complete his crusade. He finds himself caught between the two warring empires of Assyria and Egypt, and he is killed in battle against the pharaoh Neco II at a place called Megiddo in 609 B.C.E. Josiah's body is brought back to Jerusalem in his war chariot. First one and then another of his sons is crowned as king in his place. But each of Josiah's sons lapses into the same apostasies and heresies that the puritanical Josiah tried but failed to stamp out, and, as the biblical mantra goes, "did that which was evil in the sight of the Lord" (2 Kings 23:32, 37) (JPS). And, the biblical author insists, the long-suffering Yahweh loses patience with the faithless men and women of Judah as he already did with the Lost Ten Tribes of Israel.

> I will remove Judah also out of my sight, as I have removed Israel, and I will cast off this city which I have chosen, even Jerusalem, and the house of which I said: "My name shall be there" (2 Kings 23:27) (JPS).

Soon a catastrophic new threat appears on the borders of Israel: "Nebuchadnezzar, king of Babylon, came up," the Bible reports (2 Kings 24:1). The Babylonian Conquest of 586 B.C.E. leaves Jerusalem in ruins and the Temple razed to the ground. The aristocracy, the intelligentsia, and the priesthood are carried off in chains to far-off Babylon, leaving behind only "the poorest sort"—the so-called *Am Ha'aretz* ("people of the land")—to scratch out a living by tending the flocks and dressing the vines (2 Kings 24:14, 25:12). Jehoiachin, grandson of Josiah, reigns as king of Judah for only three months before he is exiled to Babylon as well, and his successor, Zedekiah, is later taken from the throne, forced to witness the execution of his own sons, then blinded and sent to prison (2 Kings 25:7, Jer. 52:11). And thus ends the reign of the very last king in whose veins ran the blood of David and the earthly dynasty that had provided Israel and Judah with monarchs for more than four hundred years.

Here, at perhaps the single most bitter moment in biblical history, we find a passage for which archaeology has retrieved hard evidence out of the soil of Babylon. Archaeologists working at the site of ancient Babylon in the late 1930s uncovered a cache of clay tablets inscribed in the distinctive cuneiform (wedge-shaped) lettering of the ancient world. Remarkably, the tablets recorded the oil rations that were issued to various Judeans living in the court of Nebuchadnezzar (ca. 630–562 B.C.E.). One man in particular is described on a clay tablet as "*Ya'u-kinu*, the king of the land of *Yahudu*"—that is, Jehoiachin, King of Judah— and his ration of oil is given as precisely five liters each month.[39]

The Holy Seed and the "Am Ha-aretz"

The biblical authors go on to describe how Cyrus, emperor of Persia, conquers the Babylonians, brings the Exile to an end in 538 B.C.E., and sends the former captives back to Judah to rebuild the Temple. "All the kingdoms of the earth hath the Lord, the God of heaven, given me," says Cyrus, a pagan who is made to piously credit the God of Israel for his victories in battle, "and he hath charged me to build him a house in Jerusalem" (Ezra 1:2). The Second Temple is far smaller and far less ornate than the one that Solomon built and the Babylonians destroyed, and the land of Israel is now only a province of the Persian Empire; but the Law of Moses is restored and the offerings to Yahweh are resumed. And, significantly, the people whom earlier biblical authors knew as the Israelites are now called the Jews (*Yehudim*).

Still, the biblical account does not conceal the tensions that afflicted the Jewish community in the province that the Persians called Yehud. The first efforts at rebuilding the Temple are a failure, it is revealed, and for a reason that is all too familiar to modern Jews—a bitter conflict arose within the Jewish community. The poor folk who had remained in Judah during the Babylonian Exile, the *Am Ha'aretz*, fall into conflict with the returnees over the question of who is and who is not entitled to regard himself as a Jew, a question that is raised here for the first time but will echo down through centuries of Jewish history to our own day.

At first, the *Am Ha'aretz* seek to join in the task of rebuilding the Temple: "Let us build with you, since we too worship your God" (Ezra 4:2) (New JPS). But their offer is spurned: "It is not for you and us to build a House to our God," says Zerubbabel, a scion of the House of David who is appointed by the Persian emperor to lead the first wave of returnees back to Judah, "but we alone will build it" (Ezra 4:3) (New JPS). Thus spurned, the *Am Ha'aretz* try to prevent the reconstruction of the Temple with threats of violence and by denouncing the returnees to the Persian emperor as "wicked and rebellious" (Ezra 4:12) (NEB). Eventually, the emperor Darius sides with the returnees and allows the Temple to be completed, but only "the Israelites who had come back from exile" and those who had "separated themselves from the people of the land" are permitted to join in the joyous ritual of rededication or taste the flesh of the first lamb to be sacrificed to Yahweh at the so-called Second Temple (Ezra 6:21–22) (NEB).

The origins of the *Am Ha'aretz* are mysterious, and the term itself has taken on harsh meanings in Jewish usage. The Book of Ezra seems to suggest that they are descendants of the foreigners who are settled in the land of Israel by the Assyrians after the conquest of the northern kingdom. But the *Am Ha'aretz* apparently regard themselves as Jews, and they may have been the peasantry of Judah who were left behind during the Babylonian Exile or a remnant of the Lost Ten Tribes of Israel who sought refuge in the southern kingdom. Eventually, the term came to be used in some Jewish circles to describe any Jew who is untutored in the Torah or who is insufficiently observant of law and tradition—a "boor" or an "ignoramus."[40] But the Bible is clear on one cruel but crucial point: the Jewish community is to be purged and purified, and not every man or woman with Jewish blood is to be regarded as an authentic Jew.

"So now make confession to the Lord, God of your fathers, and do His will," says Ezra, "and separate yourselves from the *Am Ha'aretz* and from the foreign women" (Ezra 10:11).[41]

Not only are the *Am Ha'aretz* to be wholly excluded from the Jewish community by the returned exiles, but a distinction is to be made between those Jews who have kept themselves separate and apart from the "abominable practices" of the non-Jews, and those Jews who have tainted "the holy seed" of Israel by marrying non-Jews and bearing children with them (Ezra 9:1–2).[42] Under Ezra—"a ready scribe in the Law of Moses" and a leader of the returned exiles (Ezra 7:6)—an inquisition is conducted, the Jews who dared to intermarry are searched out, and the Jewish community is purged of all non-Jewish wives and children. "And the seed of Israel separated themselves from all foreigners, and stood and confessed their sins," reports Nehemiah, the governor appointed to rule the province of Yehud by the Persian emperor. " 'We will not give our daughters in marriage to the foreign population or take their daughters for our sons' " (Neh. 9:2, 10:31).[43]

Spirits and Demons, Witches and Magicians

Here the saga of ancient Israel as it is recorded in the Bible comes to an end, and here the biblical author strikes a note of hope and redemption: the once glorious kingdom of Israel may have been reduced to a province of the Persian Empire, but at least Jerusalem is restored to the Jewish people, the Temple is rebuilt and rededicated, and the Law of Moses is reestablished. Among the causes for celebration, as far as Ezra and Nehemiah are concerned, is the triumph of a puritanical elite with a clear, strict, and narrow sense of Jewish identity and Jewish destiny. "And they offered great sacrifices that day, and rejoiced, for God had made them rejoice with great joy; and the women also and the children rejoiced; so that the joy of Jerusalem was heard even afar off," reports Nehemiah. "Thus I cleansed them from everything foreign. Remember me, O my God, for good" (Neh. 12:43, 13:30–31).[44]

But, as it turns out, neither the Jewish people nor their sacred writings were "cleansed" of the foreign influences that men like Ezra and Nehemiah found so repugnant. The Jewish homeland remained a place that we would today describe as ethnically, culturally, and religiously diverse. The Am Ha'aretz remained in the majority, and the population of Judah included the divorced wives and disinherited children who had been forcibly separated from their Jewish husbands and fathers. Even the returned exiles, who regarded themselves as the purified and sanctified aristocracy of Judaism, were deeply imprinted with the culture of the place where they had spent the years of captivity, the land of Babylon.

"By the rivers of Babylon, there we sat down, yea, we wept, when we remembered Zion," the exiles once sang, according to a heartfelt line of verse that is preserved in the Book of Psalms (Ps. 137:1). But when they returned to the Jewish homeland, they had been so thoroughly "Babylonianized" that the two men who led the first wave of returnees, Sheshbazzar and Zerubbabel, are reported in the Bible to bear names that are purely pagan and specifically Babylonian in origin (Ezra 1:11, 2:2).

Babylon is used in the Bible as a kind of code word for apostasy. And yet Babylon was the probable source of many traditions that were woven deeply and intricately into the fabric of Judaism over a period of several centuries. From the Babylonians, some scholars suggest, the Jews may have borrowed the tales of the Flood and the Tower of Babel, the lunar calendar and the seven-day week, the principle of jurisprudence that calls for "an eye for an eye and a tooth for a tooth." Even the solemn observance of the Sabbath, perhaps the single most crucial ritual in traditional Judaism, owes something to the pagan culture of Babylon: the word *Shabbat* may derive from *shapattu*, a Babylonian word that means "day of the quieting of the heart (of the god)" and refers to the day of the full moon in the Mesopotamian lunar calendar.[45]

So the Jewish people—or, more accurately, the priests and scribes who acted as guardians of the sacred writings of Judaism—may have aspired toward purity and uniformity in belief and practice, but the "People of the Book" never lived up to the lofty expectations that are set forth in some of the most familiar (and demanding) passages of the Bible. Ironically, the Torah itself bears the fingerprints of men and women whom "a ready scribe" like Ezra must have regarded with real horror—the practitioners of various "Judaisms" that were deeply influenced by the pagan cultures of the ancient world and thus fell far outside the bounds of biblical law and theology. Hidden in plain sight in the pages of the Torah, as we shall see, are idols and idol worshippers, spirits and demons, witches and magicians, all of the "abominations" that biblical orthodoxy tried but failed to eradicate.

THREE

A Goddess of Israel

Why should I lie beneath you, when I am your equal?
—LILITH, "the First Eve," to Adam,
Alphabet of Ben Sira

Not a stone remains of the Temple that Solomon built in Jerusalem. None of the sacred relics that were locked away in the inner sanctum known as the Holy of Holies—a jar of manna, the Ark of the Covenant, and the two stone tablets on which Moses inscribed the Ten Commandments—survived the destruction of the Temple in 586 B.C.E. All that we know of the First Temple, the single holiest site in biblical history, is what we read in the pages of the Bible.

But the soil of the Holy Land has yielded up literally hundreds of figurines of ivory and clay that depict naked women, some touching their breasts or genitals or both. They are examples of what the biblical authors know as *teraphim*—idols of various fertility goddesses whose adoration is condemned in the Bible with such fear and loathing. These beautiful and beguiling figurines have been found in every major archaeological site across Israel, and they allow us to glimpse a pantheon of gods and goddesses, demons and demigods, and the complex rites and rituals by which they were worshipped. And, even though biblical law excludes women from the priesthood in particular and the affairs of men in general, and prefers them to live out their lives as daughters, wives, and mothers, it is clear that the women of ancient Israel served as priestesses and prophetesses, judges and generals, shamans and soothsayers.

The *teraphim* tell us of a people who were bold, curious, and daring, and they reflect a spirit of invention and innovation that turns out to be one of the core values of Judaism. In fact, as we shall come to see, the same spirit can be traced without interruption through three thousand years of Jewish history, and it is fully alive in the Judaisms of the new millennium.

"Their Gods Shall Be a Trap unto You"

Even the strictest of the biblical sources are forced to admit that the Israelites engaged in all kinds of forbidden beliefs and practices—the worship of pagan gods and goddesses, the making and use of idols, the practice of sacred harlotry and ritual intercourse, the black arts of divination and magic-working—and they feel obliged to explain why. In fact, the question and the answer lay at the very heart of biblical theology and remain one of the defining principles of orthodoxy in Judaism.

To put it simply, the Bible calls on the Chosen People to obey the Law, promising them the richest of blessings if they do and the most harrowing of curses if they don't. Indeed, God has decided to put the Chosen People to a test of faith by tempting them with the pleasures of paganism and seeing for himself whether they yield or resist. The priests and the prophets are forced to admit that only a few of the Chosen People actually live up to God's high expectations, but they hold out the hope that the "stiff-necked" Israelites will overcome their flaws and failings and turn out to be better than they are shown to be in the Bible.

All of biblical history is soaked with the same theological assumptions. At first, God promises the land of Canaan, "a land flowing with milk and honey," to the Israelites even though it is already occupied by "nations greater and mightier than thou" who regard it as *their* homeland. "I will send an angel before thee," God says, "and I will drive out the Canaanite, the Amorite, and the Hittite, and the Perizzite, the Hivite, and the Jebusite" (Deut. 4:38, Exod. 33:1, 2). And, promptly upon their arrival in the Promised Land, the Israelites are instructed by God to purge the land of all traces of paganism and polytheism:

Ye shall surely destroy all the places, wherein the nations that ye are to dispossess served their gods, upon the high mountains, and upon the hills, and under every leafy tree. And ye shall break down their altars, and dash in pieces their pillars, and burn their Asherim* with fire; and ye shall hew down the graven images of their gods; and ye shall destroy their name out of that place (Deut. 12:2–3).

Later, it turns out that God actually expects the Israelites to fight their way into Canaan on their own resources and conquer the Canaanites by force of arms. But the Israelites achieve only a partial victory, and they find themselves forced to share the land of Canaan with its native tribes; the Jebusites, for example, drive off the invaders and succeed in preserving their sovereignty over their mountain stronghold at Jerusalem. Defeat in battle, according to the Bible, is the will of Yahweh, the god of history who is angered yet again by the apparent preference of his Chosen People for the worship of gods and goddesses. And so the God of Israel, acting on a punishing if rather perverse impulse, protects the people of Canaan and preserves their tantalizing idols and shrines as a temptation and a test of faith.

"I will *not* drive them out from before you," God now says, "but they shall be unto you as snares, and their gods shall be a trap unto you" (Judg. 2:1–3).

Common Folk and Kings

All of the Israelites—not only the common folk but even the kings and princes—fall into the trap that God has set for them, according to the Bible. Starting with Solomon himself, all but a few of the kings of Israel and Judah show themselves to be idol worshippers, easily seduced by their pagan wives and concubines into building altars and offering sacrifices to Asherah and Baal and "all the host of heaven" and practicing the black arts of divination and soothsaying and other "enchantments." One

---

*An *asherah* (*asherim* in the plural) was an upright pole or a living tree by which the Canaanite goddess Asherah was worshipped.

king of Judah called Manasseh goes so far as to cast his own son on the altar fire as a human sacrifice. Again and again, God threatens to punish his faithless people—"Behold, I will bring such evil upon Jerusalem and Judah, that whosoever heareth of it, both his ears shall tingle" (2 Kings 21:12)—and, again and again, the people of Israel call God's bluff by doing exactly "that which was evil in the sight of the Lord" (Judg. 2:11).

What makes it all so bewildering to the biblical authors is the simple fact that the Israelites *choose* to sin. Humankind, after all, enjoys the divine gift of free will, the Bible concedes, and it is up to us to make our choices and take our chances. That is exactly what Moses really means by the oft-quoted phrases of Deuteronomy: "I have set before thee life and death, the blessing and the curse; therefore choose life, that thou mayest live, thou and thy seed" (Deut. 30:19).

Defeat and dispersion, drought and famine, pestilence and plague, madness and blindness, slavery and sexual humiliation, are among the curses that God will inflict upon the people of Israel if they fail to obey the Law, according to the Book of Deuteronomy. But the Deuteronomist is not content with generalizations. Rather, he wants his readers to *feel* the sting of his words—to experience what he calls "astonishment of heart" (Deut. 28:28)—and so he goes into the kind of detail that is intended to turn the reader's stomach and break the reader's heart. "Tumors and scabs and itches" will afflict you, he warns his reader, and you will suffer from malignant boils that will not heal. You will take a wife, "and another man shall lie with her" (Deut. 28:27–30).[1] Besieged by your enemies and literally starving to death, you will be reduced to cannibalism of the most debased kind:

> Then you will eat your own children, the flesh of your sons and daughters whom the Lord your God has given you. The pampered, delicate man will not share with his brother, or his wife, or his own remaining children, any of the meat which he is eating, the flesh of his own children. And the pampered, delicate woman will not share with her own husband the afterbirth which she expels, or any boy or girl that she may bear. She will herself eat them secretly in her extreme want (Deut. 28:53–57).[2]

All of these threats are uttered by the Deuteronomist in the name of God and in the hope that they will deter the men and women of Israel from yielding to the temptation of pagan ways. And, notably, the practices that he warns against are depicted as something wholly alien to the pious tradition of Israel. But the same text can be read from an entirely different point of view: the practices and beliefs that are denounced as "abominations" in the official theology of the Bible can be seen as an organic and authentic countertradition in the history of ancient Israel.

Gynarchy

According to the Book of Jeremiah, a community of Jews in Egypt worshipped a goddess that he calls the "Queen of Heaven," a deity that scholars identify with Anath or Astarte, both of them goddesses in the pantheon of the ancient Near East. Like other goddess worshippers, the Jewish women in the Egyptian diaspora light altar fires to the Queen of Heaven, bake and eat "crescent-cakes marked with her image" (Jer. 44:19) (NEB), pour out libations as drink offerings to the goddess, and burn incense or perhaps even sacrificial animals in her honor. They are joined in these rituals by their menfolk—"And is it we that offer to the Queen of Heaven without our husbands?" they taunt the old prophet (Jer. 44:19)—but it is clearly the women who serve as priestesses. And when Jeremiah calls on them to return to orthodoxy at the risk of their lives—"High and low alike will die by sword or by famine," he quotes God as saying, "and will be an object of execration and horror, of ridicule and reproach" (Jer. 44:12) (NEB)—they boldly and flatly refuse.

The defiant speech of the Jewish women in reply to Jeremiah is unique in the biblical record. They claim the right to freedom of religion and full participation in the rituals of worship. They assert that the Queen of Heaven is worthy of worship precisely because she is more effective than Yahweh, the King of the Universe, in protecting and providing for them. And, above all, they insist that goddess worship is an old and honored tradition among the Jews. "We will not listen to what you tell us in the name of the Lord," the women boldly declare. "We intend to fulfill all the promises by which we have bound ourselves" (Jer. 44:15–16) (NEB).

We will burn sacrifices to the Queen of Heaven and pour drink-offerings to her as we used to do, we and our fathers, our kings and our princes, in the cities of Judah and in the streets of Jerusalem. We then had food in plenty and were content; no calamity touched us. But from the time we left off burning sacrifices to the Queen of Heaven and pouring drink-offerings to her, we have been in great want, and in the end we have fallen victims to sword and famine (Jer. 44:16–18) (NEB).

Jeremiah retorts with bitter sarcasm. "Well, then, fulfill your vows by all means," he says. "But listen to the word of the Lord—'I am on the watch to bring you evil and not good' " (Jer. 44:25–27).[3] For Jeremiah, as for the other priests and prophets who shaped the official theology of the Bible, the worship of the Goddess of Heaven is not merely a quaint and colorful variant of Jewish tradition—it is what God specifically condemns as "this abominable thing that I hate" (Jer. 44:4). Indeed, the whole point of the tale as it is recorded in the Book of Jeremiah is to explain why the history of the Jewish people is so weighted with suffering. " 'Thus said the Lord of hosts, the God of Israel,' " Jeremiah quotes God as saying, " 'Ye have seen all the evil that I have brought upon Jerusalem, and upon all the cities of Judah' " (Jer. 44:2).

So the angry old prophet allows us to glimpse a faith that may be far older than the orthodox theology that he seeks to enforce with such fury. Here we are able to see a Jewish community in which women regard themselves—and, significantly, are regarded by their menfolk—as fully empowered to play a role that is otherwise denied to them in biblical law and tradition. Here is a Jewish community in which women serve as priestesses and perhaps even as political leaders. For exactly this reason, historian Salo Baron describes the place that Jeremiah visits as "a gynarchy"—a community ruled by women.[4]

At this point in the biblical narrative, tradition crosses with counter-tradition, and the result is a spark and a flash that illuminates the landscape of ancient Israel and reveals what the biblical authors tried so hard to conceal. At the deepest layers of the biblical text lies the tantalizing suggestion that God, like the men and women he is shown to create, was not always seen as a bachelor and a loner. God, too, may have enjoyed the company of a female companion who was his queen and consort.

"Raped by the Pen"

Significantly, the Jewish women who stand up to Jeremiah in Egypt are much more engaged in the spiritual life of their community than their sisters back in the land of Judah—or so the biblical authors would have us believe. According to the Bible, the women of Israel were afforded no opportunity at all to participate in the rituals of worship that were conducted at the Temple in Jerusalem—menstruation renders women ritually impure under biblical law, and so the priesthood of ancient Israel was exclusively male. If women approach the Temple at all, they are permitted to come no closer than the so-called Women's Court, an outer enclosure that also accommodated storage rooms and the Chamber of Lepers!

The quarantine of menstruating women is only the starting point of the disabilities imposed upon women by biblical law. A woman does not inherit the property of her father under the Law of Moses unless he dies with no surviving sons, and she is always at risk of divorce at her husband's whim. "A woman shall not wear that which pertaineth to a man," the Torah decrees (Deut. 22:5), and the law was understood to prohibit not only cross-dressing but any conduct by a woman that is properly reserved to a man, ranging from the offering of ritual sacrifice to the use of weapons of war. Indeed, the only approved roles for a woman are defined in terms of a subservience to a man: she is first a dutiful daughter to her father, then a faithful wife to her husband, and finally a caring mother to her son. A married woman who is widowed before bearing a child falls between the cracks of biblical law, and she is regarded as a pariah with no lawful role to play in the community.

"Patriarchy," Kate Millett writes in *Sexual Politics*, summing up the feminist case against of the Bible and Judeo-Christian tradition, "has God on its side."[5]

The first feminist critique of the Bible was articulated in the late nineteenth century by the pioneering suffragist Elizabeth Cady Stanton, who dismissed Sarah, Rebekah, Leah, and Rachel, four women who are cherished above all others in Jewish tradition, as unworthy of our esteem: "All untruthful," she wrote of the Matriarchs in *The Woman's Bible* (1898), "and one a kleptomaniac." And she condemns the Bible as a tool for the oppression of women in general: "Whatever the Bible may be made to do in Hebrew or Greek," she writes, "in plain English it does not exalt and dignify woman."[6]

> The Bible teaches that woman brought sin and death into the world, that she precipitated the fall of the race, that she was arraigned before the judgment seat of Heaven, tried, condemned and sentenced. Marriage for her was to be a condition of bondage, maternity a period of suffering and anguish, and in silence and subjection she was to play the role of a dependent on man's bounty for all her material wants, and for all the information she might desire on the vital questions of the hour, she was commanded to ask her husband at home.[7]

The critique has only grown harsher over the last century or so. Aghast at such biblical horror stories as the account of the nameless concubine who runs away from her husband and is literally gang-raped to death (Judg. 19) or the four hundred young virgins who are consigned to rape en masse by an equal number of soldiers (Judg. 21), feminist Bible critic Anne Michele Tapp has condemned the Book of Judges and other biblical writings as a collection of "gynosadistic" texts in which "women lived only as objects to be bartered, abused and sacrificed."[8] At the core of the Bible, argues Tapp, is a rancor toward women so sharp and so brutal that it is literally life-threatening. "The ideologies expressed through these [stories]," she argues, "are both degrading and deadly for women."[9]

Even the beautiful and beguiling Bathsheba, whose star-crossed love affair with King David is regarded as one of the great love stories of the Bible, is reduced to victimhood by J. Cheryl Exum, who insists that Bathsheba is "raped by the pen" in the hands of the biblical author. "This is no love story," Exum writes of the deeply erotic encounter between David and Bathsheba. "The scene is the biblical equivalent of 'wham, bam, thank you, ma'am.'" And she indicts both the writer and the reader on charges of voyeurism when it comes to the moment when

David first spies Bathsheba at her bath: "Art, film, and pornography provide constant reminders that men are aroused by watching a woman touch herself," she insists. "And if Bathsheba is purifying herself after her menstrual period, we can guess where she is touching."[10]

Still, if we listen carefully to the tales told in the Bible, we may hear the voices of women raised in both story and song—"countervoices within a patriarchal document," as one feminist Bible critic, Phyllis Trible, puts it.[11] The effort to find and work these veins of gold in the patriarchal bedrock of the biblical text began in distant antiquity, continued over the centuries and millennia of Jewish history, and still goes on today.

The Women Who Wrote the Bible

In fact, certain portions of the Bible—including some of its most crucial and exalted passages—may have been written by women. Two of the texts that are regarded as among the oldest in all of the Bible, for example, are believed by some scholars to have been composed by the very women who are identified as their authors—Miriam and Deborah, each one described in the Bible as a prophetess. The Book of Judges, which preserves some of the most appalling tales of violence against women in all of the Bible, has been described as "the literature of a feminist intelligentsia."[12] And the source we know as J, who is credited with the thread of storytelling that runs through the Five Books of Moses, may have been a woman, too.

The Song of Miriam (Exod. 15:21), which celebrates the miraculous victory over the army of Pharaoh at the Red Sea, is attributed to the woman who is identified in the Bible not only as the sister of Moses but as a prophet in her own right. Once thought to be only a fragment of text, the two-line song is now understood to be a call-and-response song preserved in its entirety. Miriam sings out the first verse—"Sing ye to Yahweh, for he is highly exalted—and the women of Israel, dancing around her with tambourines in hand, sing back: "The horse and his rider hath he thrown into the sea." Notably, Moses is not mentioned at all, and some scholars argue that Miriam may have been the heroine of a separate storytelling tradition that came to be attached to the story of Moses only later, and the description of Miriam and Moses as siblings may have been wholly fabricated.

The Song of Deborah is attributed to an Israelite woman who serves as a chieftain (or, as the Bible puts it, "judge") as well as a prophetess and even a battlefield commander. Deborah orders a man called Barak to lead the army of Israel into battle against Sisera, a Canaanite general, but Barak refuses to go to war unless Deborah goes with him. "I will surely go with you," she taunts, "but the journey that you take will not be for your honor, for Yahweh will give Sisera over into the hand of woman" (Judg. 4:9).[13] Significantly, the Hebrew word that was once thought to identify Deborah by reference to her husband—traditionally rendered in English as "the wife of Lappidoth" (Judg. 4:4)—may be an obscure Hebrew word that describes her own qualities of courage and daring: "A woman of flames."[14]

Even more startling is the assertion that the Book of Judges—a book in which women are shown to be raped not by the pen but by men—may have been composed by "a deeply religious woman who is satirizing men who play God," according to one feminist Bible critic,[15] or perhaps even "a woman secretly harboring sympathies for the goddess," according to another scholar.[16] Indeed, Judges has been characterized as a book of readings originally compiled by members of the "feminist intelligentsia" of ancient Israel and used by them to muster the "courage to live marginally, in a fashion resembling witches in New England."[17]

Most important of all, the argument has been made that the Yahwist, an author of genius whose work is the real glory of the Torah, was a woman. Richard Elliot Friedman, author of *Who Wrote the Bible?*, is among the first Bible scholars to raise the intriguing notion that J was a woman, while Harold Bloom elaborates upon the same idea in *The Book of J* by suggesting that she was "a *Gevurah* ('great lady') of post-Solomonic court circles, herself of Davidic blood, who began writing her great work in the later years of Solomon, in close rapport and exchanging influences with her good friend the Court Historian, who wrote most of what we now call 2 Samuel."[18]

One clue that suggests J may have been a woman—and an example of the countertraditions that can be teased out of the Bible—is a tale that J tells about Rachel, the favorite wife of the patriarch Jacob and one of the four Matriarchs who are so beloved in Jewish tradition. Jacob and his two wives, Rachel and Leah, are fleeing from his father-in-law, Laban, who follows in hot pursuit. Laban, however, is less concerned about his two daughters than about his purloined collection of *teraphim*. Rachel, as it turns out, is the one who filched the household idols, and she has hidden them in a camel saddle. When her father catches up with the runaways and starts ransacking their tents in search of the missing idols, Rachel seats herself atop the saddle. And when he approaches Rachel to look beneath the saddle, she warns him away.

"Let not my lord be angry that I cannot rise up before thee," Rachel tells her father, "for the manner of women is upon me" (Gen. 31:35).

The joke, of course, is on Laban. Like the Priestly Author, whose code of law regards a menstruating woman and a leper with roughly the same degree of revulsion, Laban sees his daughter as unclean and untouchable during her period. Rachel knows it, counts on it, and subtly ridicules her father for it. Laban backs away from Rachel, searches the rest of her tent in vain, and leaves without his cherished *teraphim*. And thus does J make light of the sternest traditions of ancient Israel: she invites us to join her in laughing out loud at how men chase after idols but run away from menstruating women.

The Harlot by the Side of the Road

One of the enduring themes of the Bible—and a *cause de guerre* among some feminist Bible critics—is the primal notion of the woman as temptress and seductress. Eve, the very first woman, is also first in a long line of famous seducers that includes Bathsheba, Jezebel, and not a few of the one thousand wives and concubines of King Solomon. And, significantly, women are often shown in the Bible to lure men not only into forbidden sexual practices but, more crucially, into forbidden religious practices, too.

After all, when Eve tempts Adam to taste the forbidden fruit in the Garden of Eden, it is not only because the fruit is "good for food and a delight to the eyes" but, more crucially, because it bestows forbidden knowledge and power on anyone who dares to eat it: "In the day ye eat thereof, then your eyes shall be opened," the serpent tells Eve, "and ye shall be as God" (Gen. 3:5, 6). Ever since Eve, sexual temptation and religious apostasy have been regarded as two sides of the same coin in biblical tradition.

But here, too, a countertradition is hidden in plain sight in the pages of the Bible—a woman can be a seducer *and* a heroine at the same time. And, once again, it is J who dares to ridicule the piety and pomposity of men, celebrate the courage and vision of a woman, and illustrate the surprising diversity in the traditions of ancient Israel, all in the story of a seductive young Canaanite woman named Tamar and her famous father-in-law, Judah.[19]

According to the charming and beguiling tale as it is told in Genesis 38, Tamar is a childless widow who disguises herself as a harlot and lays an elaborate sexual ambush for her father-in-law. She tricks Judah into thinking she is a common whore, excites his sexual appetite, and engages in an act of roadside prostitution that results in the birth of twin sons. At the climax of the story—a surprise ending worthy of O. Henry—Judah discovers that Tamar is guilty of prostitution, incest, and bastardy, and yet he says of her, "She is more righteous than I" (Gen. 38:26).

In what sense is Tamar righteous? To decode the hidden meaning in Judah's words, we need to recall the predicament of a childless widow in ancient Israel: since she has neither a husband nor a son to protect her, she falls outside the roles permitted to a woman under biblical law. And we need to know that biblical law provides a right and a remedy for a woman like Tamar. The so-called Levirate tradition obliges a male relative of a deceased man—usually the brother-in-law of the widow, known in Latin as a *levir*—to engage in sexual intercourse with the widow and, hopefully, to impregnate her with a male child. The infant is regarded as the offspring of the dead man rather than of his biological father, and he inherits the dead man's estate. Marriage between the widow and the brother-in-law is not required; the whole point is to make the childless widow into a mother and thus preserve her role in the community.

For Tamar, a Canaanite woman who marries into an Israelite family, the situation is even more dire: she is the ultimate outsider. But Tamar, according to the tale as told by J in the Book of Genesis, is twice denied her rights as a childless widow. Judah's second-born son, Onan, refuses to do his duty, famously "spilling his seed on the ground" in an ancient form of birth control known as coitus interruptus and thus preventing Tamar from impregnation (Gen. 38:9).[20] So solemn is the obligation to impregnate a childless widow, the biblical author tells us, that God strikes Onan dead for shirking it.

Judah has a third son, Shelah, who is now obliged to do what his older brother refused to do, but Judah is reluctant to send him to Tamar—after all, two of his sons have shared her bed, and both of them are now dead. So he makes the excuse that Shelah is yet too young, and he sends Tamar back to her father's house to await the day when Judah will call on Shelah to go to her—a day that Tamar fears will never come. So she resorts to seduction in order to trick Judah into performing the role of the *levir* in place of his sons. And that is exactly why Judah judges the seducer to be more righteous than the man she seduces: "Because I did not give her to my son Shelah" (Gen. 38:26) (NEB). Tamar may have played the harlot with her own father-in-law, but she is still a righteous woman because she has only claimed the right to which she is entitled by the laws and customs of ancient Israel.

So righteous is Tamar, in fact, that J bestows upon her the very highest praise that one can earn in the Bible—one of the twin sons that is born of her coupling with Judah turns out to be the direct ancestor of King David, and David himself is the direct ancestor of the Messiah. But for the daring act of seduction by a Canaanite woman, the story suggests, there would be no tribe of Judah and thus no Jews, no David and thus no Messiah.

Mixed Marriages

The Law of Moses condemns intermarriage with non-Israelites in general and Canaanites in particular: "Thou shalt make no covenant with them, neither shalt thou make marriages with them," God says. "Thy daughters thou shalt not give unto his son, nor his daughter shalt thou take unto thy son." And the ban on intermarriage touches one of the hot buttons of both biblical theology and Jewish tradition, then and now: "For he will turn away thy son from following me, that they may serve other gods," God explains. "So will the anger of the Lord be kindled against you, and he will destroy thee quickly" (Deut. 7:2–4).

But, according to yet another direct contradiction between Bible law and Bible history, the biblical saga is decorated with more than one successful intermarriage. Judah is not the only son of the patriarch Jacob who marries out; Joseph, who rises to the rulership of Egypt and shelters Jacob and his other sons during a famine, takes the daughter of an Egyptian high priest as his wife (Gen. 46:20). Ruth, a Moabite woman who seduces and then weds an Israelite man called Boaz, is another non-Israelite whose blood runs in the veins of King David himself, and her tender words to her mother-in-law remind us that the Israelites are shown in the Bible to be a multiethnic people: "Thy people shall be my people," says Ruth, "and thy God, my God" (Ruth 1:16). And David is married to Bathsheba, whose first husband is a Hittite and who may have been a non-Israelite herself.[21] If so, then King Solomon is the child of a mixed marriage, and the Temple that he builds in honor of the God of Israel is the handiwork of a *mishling.*

Perhaps the greatest irony of all is the fact that the man who promulgates the law against intermarriage is himself wed to a non-Israelite woman. And the marriage of Moses to Zipporah, daughter of the pagan high priest of Midian, is just as crucial as the coupling of Judah and Tamar in biblical history. Indeed, the tale of how Zipporah saves the life of Moses is perhaps the single strangest passage in all of the Bible, a fly in amber that may preserve some of the oldest and oddest traditions of the Israelites. "We are peering into the deep recesses of a primordial, absolutely mythological religion," argues Bible scholar Elias Auerbach, "which is far older than the time of Moses."[22] Some scholars, in fact, believe that the tale is a remnant of the strands of paganism that are so deeply woven into the biblical fabric that they have almost—but not quite—disappeared from sight.[23]

God, Moses, and Zipporah

Moses, a fugitive from Pharaoh, is working as a shepherd for his father-in-law, Jethro, when he is called by God to return to Egypt, liberate the Israelites from slavery, and lead them to the Promised Land. On the first night of the trek back to Egypt, however, God suddenly turns on Moses: "Yahweh met him," the Bible bluntly reveals, "and tried to kill him" (Exod. 4:24).[24] Only because of the courage, insight, and ingenuity of Zipporah is Moses spared; she may be a pagan, but she seems to intuit that the God of Israel requires a blood ritual of some kind to appease his anger, and she circumcises her son then and there. "Then Zipporah took a flint, and cut off the foreskin of her son, and cast it at his feet," the Bible reports. "So [Yahweh] let him alone" (Exod. 4:25–26).[25]

The classic rabbinical explanation for God's attempt on the life of Moses is pious enough—Yahweh seeks to kill Moses because he has neglected to circumcise his son, a duty imposed on Israelites ever since Abraham (Gen. 17:12), and Zipporah succeeds in changing God's mind by performing an emergency circumcision. More daring commentators, however, suggest that the Bible actually preserves a myth borrowed by Israelites from one of the many pagan cultures that they encountered. Perhaps, as one feminist Bible scholar proposes, the story is a "Hebraized" version of the Egyptian myth of Isis.[26] Or, even more likely, the tale may have originated among the Midianites: Moses, a newcomer to Midian and a self-proclaimed "stranger in a strange land" (Exod. 2:22), has angered one of the gods of Midian by trespassing on his sacred precincts, and Zipporah makes a blood offering to appease the Midianite deity. When we witness God's attack on Moses, Sigmund Freud suggests, we are seeing not Yahweh, the God of Abraham, Isaac, and Jacob, but Jahve, a tribal god of Midian who has been transplanted into the Torah, "an uncanny, bloodthirsty demon who walks by night and shuns the light of day."[27]

Indeed, according to a theory of biblical scholarship called the Midianite Hypothesis, more than one element of the biblical saga may have been borrowed from the culture of Midian. Moses, for example, encounters God for the first time—and is told God's secret name, Yahweh—on a sacred mountain in Midian. He is tutored in the art of governance by his father-in-law, Jethro, the high priest of Midian. And it is Jethro, rather than Moses himself—or his brother, Aaron, the first high priest of the Israelites—who makes the very first sacrificial offering to Yahweh in the wilderness. "If Jethro was a priest who offered sacrifices to Yahweh, presumably he was a priest of Yahweh," writes Bible scholar Murray Lee Newman, Jr., summing up the Midianite Hypothesis. "And if Moses first learned the name of Yahweh in this period, he probably learned it from Jethro."[28]

To some Jewish scholars, the Midianite Hypothesis is not merely unconvincing but also downright offensive because it suggests that some of the most cherished elements of the Torah may be secondhand goods. "The hypothesis has not been unjustly described," writes philosopher and Bible scholar Martin Buber, "as 'an explanation of *ignotum ab ignoto*,'"—a theory that relies on the unknown to explain the unknown.[29] To historians of religion, however, Jewish and non-Jewish alike, it is an unremarkable example of what is called syncretism, the mixing and matching of religious beliefs and practices that was a commonplace of the ancient world, at least until the strictest of the biblical authors tried to eradicate it once and for all.

The Mosaic Distinction

No one in the ancient world would have been surprised or shocked to find a congregation in which both the God of Israel and the Queen of Heaven were worshipped by the same people at the same time. No one would have been puzzled or put off by the phantasmagorical quality of a deity who appeared as Yahweh at one moment, Jahve at the next moment, and sometimes both of them at once. And, above all, no one would have thought to punish a man or a woman merely because he or she offered sacrifices to one god rather than another god or, for that matter, many gods and goddesses all at once.

No one, that is, except a prophet like Jeremiah or a king like Josiah, each of whom set himself the task of purifying the faith of ancient Israel. Syncretism is an appealing idea to many of us; indeed, the free market in religious beliefs and practices that has come to be called the New Age is really something very old, and the modern Jewish syncretist who keeps the Sabbath, practices Zen meditation, and calls himself a "BuJew" is honoring the most ancient tradition of all. But the single most revolutionary idea in the Bible, and the one with the most blood-chilling consequences, is the simple notion that Yahweh is not merely the best of all gods, but the one and only god. For men like Phinehas, Jeremiah, and Josiah—and the biblical sources who recorded their words and deeds in the Bible—syncretism is the ultimate sin because it fails to distinguish between the single shining truth that is revealed in the Torah and the other beliefs and practices of humankind, all of which are dismissed as an "abomination."

"Let us call the distinction between true and false in religion the 'Mosaic distinction,'" proposes Egyptologist Jan Assmann, "because tradition ascribes it to Moses."[30] Yet the "Mosaic distinction" is not always apparent in the Bible. As we have seen, some of the biblical authors have allowed the fingerprints of paganism and polytheism to remain in the margins of the Torah. The wife of Moses and the mother of his two sons is plainly depicted as a pagan woman from Midian, and one particularly baffling passage in the Book of Numbers suggests that Moses has a second wife who is a woman of color—a "Cushite," the biblical term for an Ethiopian (Num. 12:1). And Moses himself is often shown to be a deeply humane and compassionate man, a "true Empath," as one contemporary Bible commentator puts it, rather than a Grand Inquisitor.[31]

Indeed, one of the great and enduring traditions of Judaism is the stirring sense of social justice that Moses is shown to embrace: "Justice, justice, shalt thou pursue," he enjoins the Israelites (Deut. 16:20). And many of the laws that he hands down are fired with the powerful idea that doing God's will and caring for one's fellow human beings are one and the same thing: "He doth execute justice for the fatherless and the widow, and loveth the stranger, in giving him food and raiment" (Deut. 10:18). And God is not content with high ideals and bland generalities: Moses pauses to specify that a laborer must be paid his wages on the same day that he earns them. A landowner must leave the corners of his fields unharvested so that the poor may find something to eat. A Hebrew man or woman who is sold into slavery must be set free in the seventh year of servitude. At perhaps the most sublime moment in all of the Torah, Moses promulgates a series of laws that call on the Israelites to not only respect and protect the stranger who lives among them but to *love* the stranger, and to do so out of solidarity with a fellow human being rather than out of blind obedience to divine law. "The stranger that sojourneth with you shall be unto you as the home-born among you, and thou shalt love him as thyself; for ye were strangers in the land of Egypt: I am the Lord your God" (Lev. 19:34).

The irony of these words and phrases is deep and bitter. At one moment, the Bible calls on the Israelites to love the stranger, and, at another moment, to fear and loathe and even kill him. "Thou shalt smite them, then thou shalt utterly destroy them," God says of the seven native-dwelling nations of Canaan; "thou shalt make no covenant with them, nor show mercy unto them" (Deut. 7:2). Whereas one of the biblical authors shows us Moses as a man of the deepest compassion, another biblical author shows us Moses as a generalissimo and a Grand Inquisitor. When the Israelites make and worship the Golden Calf, Moses argues with Yahweh, "face to face" and even "mouth to mouth" (Deut. 34:10, Num. 12:8), in an effort to keep him from exterminating the Chosen People—and then he carries out a bloody purge of his fellow Israelites.

"Have Ye Saved All the Women Alive?"

Even if the Bible shows Moses in a highly successful mixed marriage, the sternest of the biblical sources refuse to leave the impression that Israelites might safely do the same. To make the point, the Torah includes a cautionary tale about what happens when ordinary Israelites follow the example of Moses by consorting with Midianite women.

The setting of the story is the frontier between Canaan and Moab, where the Israelites are preparing for the long-awaited and long-delayed invasion of the Promised Land. After forty years of wandering in the wilderness, the slave generation has died out and the twelve tribes of Israel have been forged into a free people and an army of conquest. And, like any other army in times of idleness, the soldiers of Israel begin to fraternize with the local women, both Moabites and Midianites. The pagan women lure the men of Israel into both sexual adventure and religious apostasy, and so the Israelite men join the Midianite women both in their beds and in their shrines, where they participate in rituals of sacrifice and sacred intercourse that celebrate the pagan god Baal. And God makes it clear that fraternization under these circumstances is a capital crime.

"Make the Midianites suffer as they made you suffer with their crafty tricks," God tells Moses, "and strike them down" (Num. 25:16–18) (NEB). The first act of vengeance is carried out by a man called Phinehas, grandson of the very first high priest of Israel, against a man called Zimri, a prince of the tribe of Simeon. Zimri strolls through the encampment of the Israelites in the company of his lover, a highborn Midianite woman called Cozbi, and they boldly enter one of the tents for a quick tryst. Phinehas catches them in the act, so to speak, and so he is able to kill both of them with a single thrust of his spear.

But the carnage is not over yet. Moses sends out Phinehas and an army of twelve thousand men on a punitive expedition against the Midianites, and they march back to the camp in total victory—not a single Israelite soldier has fallen in battle, but every man among the Midianites has been slain. The scene is described by the biblical author in appalling if authentic detail: Phinehas and his soldiers are followed by thousands of captive women and children, herds and flocks, and carts piled with gold and silver, all taken from the slaughtered Midianites as prizes of war. But Moses is not pleased at the sight, and he addresses a single query to the triumphant general of his army: "Have ye saved all the women alive?" (Num. 31:15).

Then Moses calls on the commander to correct the oversight—all the women and all the male children of Midian are put to the sword. Only the virgin girls are spared, and they are handed over to the men-at-arms as slaves. Elsewhere in the Bible, Moses may appear as a liberator and a lawgiver—"Thou shalt love the stranger as thyself" is one of his pronouncements (Lev. 19:34)[32]—but, here and now, Moses is what we would call a war criminal.

The rabbis whose writings are collected in the Talmud and the

Midrash spend much ink and breath in explaining and elaborating upon the Torah. No line of text is too obscure to draw their attention, and they display an impressive measure of enterprise and imagination in trying to make sense of even the most baffling passages. But the murder of the Midianite women and children at the command of Moses seems to baffle them, and a rabbinical tale about Zimri and his Midianite lover offers no explanation or justification for the incident.

Zimri brings Cozbi before Moses, or so the Talmudic tale goes, and he demands to know whether the Midianite woman is permitted or forbidden to him as a sexual partner.

"Forbidden," answers Moses.

"How then canst thou assert that she is forbidden to me?" demands an indignant Zimri. "For then thy wife would be forbidden to thee, for she is a Midianite like this woman."[33]

Moses has no answer to Zimri's pointed question, and neither do the rabbis who tell the tale. But the ending of the Talmudic tale and the biblical text are exactly the same. According to the Talmud, Phinehas overhears the argument between Zimri and Moses, sees that Moses is "doomed to impotence" by his own hypocrisy, and so takes it upon himself to punish the lovers by slaying them. Thus does Phinehas show exactly how the "Mosaic distinction" is applied to any Israelite who dares to love a Midianite—any Israelite, that is, except Moses himself.

Prophetesses and Assassins

The clash between tradition and countertradition in the Bible is always fiercest when it comes to women, whether they are depicted as mortal or divine. And we can see for ourselves that women were much more active in the spiritual life of ancient Israel—and much more powerful in matters of war and politics—than the Priestly Author or the Prophets are willing to admit.

How, for example, are we supposed to regard Miriam? She is presented in some passages of the Bible as a wholly positive figure—the older sister of Moses, the liberator and lawgiver, and Aaron, the first high priest, and a prophetess in her own right. She is one of many women in the Bible whose heroism serves to preserve the life of Moses against every threat; when Pharaoh orders the slaughter of the male babies of the enslaved Israelites, it is the mother of Moses who sets him afloat on the Nile in a little boat of reeds, Miriam who follows the boat to make sure that her baby brother is carried to safety, and the daughter of Pharaoh who rescues him from the river and raises him to manhood. Miriam leads the women of Israel in song and dance after the victory over the Egyptians at the Red Sea. In fact, the word that is used to describe Miriam in the Bible (*nebhiah'ah*), which is usually translated as "prophetess," can also be rendered as "the ecstatic" or "the enthused," thus suggesting that Miriam is a compelling and charismatic woman who is uniquely capable of inspiring the Israelites and moving them to dervishlike expressions of spirituality.[34]

And yet, lest the biblical reader become *too* enthusiastic about a woman, Miriam is depicted with a certain unmistakable contempt in other biblical passages. She is shown to challenge Moses over the very question of spiritual leadership: "Hath Yahweh spoken only with Moses?" she boldly declares along with her brother Aaron. "Hath he not spoken also with us?" (Num. 12:2). And, as we have seen, she is made to utter a baffling but unmistakably racist slur on her brother: "And Miriam and Aaron spoke against Moses because of the Cushite [Ethiopian] woman whom he had married" (Num. 12:1). Crucially, God is shown to punish Miriam—but not her male co-conspirator, Aaron—for her *chutzpah* in claiming to be the equal of Moses: "Behold, Miriam was leprous, as white as snow" (Num. 12:10). Only when Moses pleads with God to spare Miriam—"Let her not, I pray, be like something stillborn, whose flesh is half eaten away when it comes from the womb" (Num. 12:12)[35]—is she restored to health. But Miriam is still punished with seven days of exclusion from the camp: "If her father had but spit in her face," says God, "should she not hide in shame seven days?" (Num. 12:14).

The same double bind can be found at odd moments throughout the Bible. The single most revolutionary idea in the religious reforms of King Josiah, as we have seen, is the notion that Yahweh accepts sacrificial

offerings from only a single site in all of Israel—the Temple in Jerusalem. And we have seen that women are wholly excluded from the
rituals of worship that are conducted in the Temple and from the priesthood that conducts them. Yet, when King Josiah discovers the lost scroll
that seems to bestow the divine seal of approval on his newfangled ideological agenda—the scroll that is believed to have been the Book of
Deuteronomy—the high priest of the Temple feels compelled to bring
the document to a prophetess called Huldah and ask *her* to judge
whether or not it is authentic (2 Kings 22:14). Only when Huldah gives
her blessings to the scroll are its laws regarded as authoritative.

In fact, the Bible is littered with clues that women were *not* always
relegated to the roles of daughter, wife, and mother, and women did *not*
always rely on sexual seduction as their only effective weapon. More
than once, for example, a king or a general is approached by a "wise
woman" who feels perfectly free to confront the powerful man with his
own hypocrisy. The "wise woman of Tekoa," for example, tricks King
David into conceding that he has erred by refusing to recall his son from
exile. "Out of your own mouth, your majesty," the old woman boldly tells
the king, "you condemn yourself" (2 Sam. 14:13).[36] A "wise woman," according to some scholars, may have been a formal role assumed by a few
gifted women, the Bible-era equivalent of an advocate or a bard whose
powers of speech were highly valued in ancient Israel.

A few women even raise a hand in an act of violence against a man, a
rare reversal of the customary order of things in the biblical world. The
prophetess Deborah, as we have already seen, leads the army of Israel
into battle against a Canaanite general called Sisera. And Deborah tells
the remarkable tale of Jael, a Kenite woman who encounters Sisera after
he has fled from the battlefield in defeat. When Sisera appears at her tent
in search of shelter and sustenance, she gives him a bowl of milk, makes
a bed on the floor of her tent, waits until he is asleep—and then strikes
him dead. Out of deference to the biblical law that forbids a woman to
use anything that "pertaineth to a man," she is shown to assassinate Sisera with a hammer and a tent peg rather than a sword or a dagger, but
Deborah praises her valor in a song that is still capable of thrilling us
with its lyricism and chilling us with its graphic violence:

Above women in the tent shall she be blessed.
Water he asked, milk she gave him;
In a lordly bowl she brought him curd.
Her hand she put to the tent-pin,
And her right hand to the workmen's hammer;
And with the hammer she smote Sisera, she smote through his head,
Yea, she pierced and struck through his temples.
At her feet he sunk, he fell, he lay;
At her feet he sunk, he fell;
Where he sunk, there he fell down dead.

(Judg. 5:24–27)

Of course, Miriam and Huldah and the "wise woman" of Tekoa may be assertive but they are surely not apostates, which must have been some small comfort to the fussier biblical authors. And even a woman as bold and decisive as Jael, yet another non-Israelite woman with a crucial role in biblical history, fits comfortably within the official theology of the Bible. After all, none of these powerful women traffic in *teraphim* or pour out drink offerings to the Queen of Heaven! But the Bible also preserves the memory of a few extraordinary women who fall wholly outside the bounds of orthodoxy as it is preached by the priests and prophets. And it is exactly here that we glimpse the most forbidden countertraditions of all.

Ghostwife

One such woman is identified in the Book of Samuel only as "the witch of En-dor." She is plainly described by the Court Historian as a practitioner of the black magic—"a woman that divineth by a ghost" (1 Sam. 28:7)—but an even more provocative way of rendering the biblical Hebrew is suggested by one Bible scholar. She is not merely a witch, according to P. Kyle McCarter Jr.'s lively translation, but a "ghostwife."[37] And some highly subversive notions are buried just beneath the surface of the biblical tale in which the ghostwife encounters Saul, "God's anointed" and king of Israel.

Saul ruthlessly enforces the biblical laws that condemn the black arts: "There shall not be found among you one that useth divination, a soothsayer, or an enchanter, or a sorcerer, or a charmer, or one that consulteth a ghost or a familiar spirit, or a necromancer" (Deut. 18:10–11). So, the king dutifully "banished from the land all who trafficked with ghosts and spirits," or so the Bible says (1 Sam. 28:3). And yet, when the prophet Samuel dies and Saul finds himself cut off from all communication with Yahweh, Saul is so lonely and so desperate that he seeks out someone to put him in touch with the dead man. Donning a disguise and traveling in the darkness of night, Saul shows up at the house of the witch of En-dor, who apparently escaped his purge, and begs her to conjure up the ghost of Samuel.

"Why then layest thou a snare for my life, to cause me to die?" she asks Saul, who conceals his identity by hiding his face behind a cloak.

"As Yahweh lives," Saul vows, "no punishment will fall upon you for this thing" (1 Sam. 28:9–10).

A double irony is at work in the biblical tale. Saul may be God's anointed, but he is perfectly willing to break the divine law against witchcraft when God falls silent and stops answering his queries. Even more shocking, however, is the suggestion that although black magic may be an "abomination," it is wholly effective—the witch of En-dor effortlessly conjures up the ghost of Samuel from the underworld.

"What seest thou?" asks Saul.

"I see a god," the woman whispers, "coming up out of the earth" (1 Sam. 28:13).[38]

Saul is shown to converse at length with the ghost of Samuel, who predicts the death of Saul and his sons in battle—"Tomorrow shalt thou and thy sons be with me" (1 Sam. 28:19)—and then returns to the spirit world, leaving Saul alone with the "ghostwife." But, as it turns out, she is a good witch, and now she strikes a tender and even maternal note. "I listened to what you said and I risked my life to obey you," says the witch of En-dor to the king of Israel. "Now listen to me: let me set before you a little food to give you strength for your journey" (1 Sam. 28:21–22) (NEB).

Now it is possible that the encounter between God's anointed and a "ghostwife" is merely an exercise of poetic license by the Court Historian, a storyteller of real genius. Saul, after all, is depicted as a hapless and impulsive man who forfeits the favor of God—indeed, he seeks out a witch precisely because God has abandoned him. Even so, the scene sizzles with a forbidden subtext. The biblical condemnation of black magic can be traced back to the old bugaboos of idolatry and polytheism, and the same commandment that condemns soothsayers and sorcerers also condemns "any one that maketh his son or his daughter pass through the fire" (Deut. 18:10)—a reference to human sacrifice. And the commandment itself ends with a pious equation: magic equals apostasy. "For whosoever doeth these things is an abomination unto the Lord, and because of these abominations, the Lord thy God is driving them out from before thee," the Deuteronomist insists. "Thou shalt be whole-hearted with the Lord thy God" (Deut. 18:12–13).

"That is the religion of Moses," Martin Buber sums it up, "the man who experienced the futility of magic."[39]

But magic is *not* always shown to be futile in the Bible, and never is it more effective than in this tale. The woman whom Saul seeks out is, in fact, a highly competent practitioner of witchcraft and conjurer of ghosts. She is undeterred by the law of God or the decree of his anointed king, and she even manages to overcome the will of the ghost himself, who complains bitterly when he is summoned by the witch of En-dor: "Why hast thou disquieted me, to bring me up?" (1 Sam. 28:15). Nor is the "ghostwife" presented in the Bible as malevolent in the slightest degree; in fact, she comes across as a stereotypical Jewish mother who prevails on Saul, spent and distraught by his encounter with a ghost, to restore himself with a *nosh*. "Eat, eat," we might imagine her saying to the king, and the Bible confirms that Saul complies with the gentle but firm demand of a woman who comes across as both a good witch and a good mother.

Women Who Bewail Their Virginity

Perhaps the most provocative passage of all is a tale in the Book of Judges that focuses on a young woman known only as "daughter of Jephthah." She is the only child of a soldier of fortune who makes a rash vow to Yah-

weh on the eve of battle: if Yahweh grants him victory against his enemies, he will make a burnt offering of "whatsoever cometh forth out of
the doors of my house to meet me" (Judg. 11:31). Not unpredictably, it is
Jephthah's daughter who greets him after his God-given victory, whirling
in dance and playing a tambourine like the women who once circled
Miriam at the Red Sea. Jephthah regretfully but dutifully prepares to fulfill his vow; God may have stopped Abraham before he offered up his
son, Isaac, as a human sacrifice, but he remains silent when Jephthah is
ready to cast his virgin daughter on the altar fire. But, intriguingly, the
Bible preserves a curious last request from Jephthah's daughter and a
haunting coda to the whole tragic tale:

> And she said unto her father: "Let this thing be done for me: let me
> alone two months, that I may depart and go down upon the moun-
> tains, and bewail my virginity, I and my companions." And it came
> to pass at the end of two months, that she returned unto her father,
> who did with her according to his vow. And it was a custom in Israel,
> that the daughters of Israel went yearly to lament the daughter of
> Jephthah four days in a year (Judg. 11:37, 39–40).[40]

Nowhere else in the Bible is Jephthah's daughter mentioned, and we
know nothing about the annual retreat that is described in the Book of
Judges. But even these few intriguing words are enough to excite the
imagination of some biblical scholars. Perhaps, they suggest, Jephthah's
daughter and her companions were acolytes in what they breathlessly describe as a "sex cult." Perhaps the scene described in Judges actually recalls the memory of a ceremony in which the sacrifice is symbolized by
sexual intercourse: "Israelite women were dedicated to the deity (presumably Baal) by an act of ritual defloration."[41] Or perhaps the dimly remembered ritual—"the ancient and primitive custom of annually
bewailing the dead or ousted spirit of fertility during the dry or winter
season"—is quite literally a human sacrifice.[42]

Significantly, the god or goddess whom Jephthah's daughter may have
worshipped—and to whom young virgins may have been sacrificed—is
always described in conventional biblical scholarship as a *foreign* deity

who has been borrowed from an alien culture. If the "sex cult" was not devoted to one of the deities from the Canaanite pantheon, then perhaps the women offered devotions to one of the figures from the Greek myths that faintly resemble the tale of Jephthah's daughter: Persephone, who is taken captive by the king of the underworld but is periodically released to visit her mother, the goddess Demeter; or Artemis, a virgin goddess who watches over women in childbirth; or Iphigenia, a virgin who is selected for sacrifice to Diana but is spared in order to serve the goddess.

So even the secular Bible scholars of the modern era buy into the assumptions of the ancient biblical authors: if a deity other than Yahweh was worshipped in ancient Israel, then it must have been one of those abominable gods and goddesses that Yahweh set before the people of Israel as a snare. But there is another way of looking at goddess worship among the Israelites—as a countertradition of the greatest antiquity, and one that honors the universal need of humankind to see themselves in the deities they worship. If men and women come in pairs, so do their gods and goddesses. And, as we shall see, the archaeological record suggests that the Israelites, too, believed that Yahweh, the God of Israel, wanted and needed the companionship of a female consort, a goddess of Israel.

Lady Asherah of the Sea

Not long ago, at an archaeological site in the Sinai called Kuntillat 'Ajrud, a large ceramic storage jar, more than three feet high, was dug out of the sandy soil. The jar has been dated to as far back as the late ninth century B.C.E., a period when the Law of Moses and its strict credo of monotheism ("The Lord is One") had been in effect for four hundred years or so, at least according to the Torah. But the jar is inscribed with a sentiment that is starkly at odds with the official theology of the Bible: "May you be blessed by Yahweh *and by his Asherah*."[43]

Asherah, as we have seen, is identified in the Bible as a Canaanite goddess—and an especially dangerous and detested one. According to the biblical authors, Asherah is depicted in the rituals of idolatry in the form of a carved wooden pole set upright in the ground or, perhaps, a liv-

ing tree. These so-called *asherim* are found all over the land of Israel—
"upon the high mountains, and upon the hills, and under every leafy
tree" (Deut. 12:2–3)—and a graven image of Asherah is even placed in
the Temple at Jerusalem by various Israelite kings, ranging from Re-
hoboam, son of Solomon, to Manasseh, who is said to have offered his
own son as a sacrifice (2 Kings 21:6–7). At every mention of Asherah in
the Bible, she is condemned as something alien, vile, and forbidden:
"that which was evil in the sight of the Lord, after the abominations of
the nations, whom the Lord cast out before the children of Israel" (2
Kings 21:2).

Asherah is cast in a much warmer light in a collection of inscribed
tablets from the fourteenth century B.C.E. that were recovered from the
site of ancient Ugarit, now called Ras Shamra, in what is now Syria. The
tablets confirm that Asherah was regarded by the Canaanites as the
wife and consort of their supreme god, El, and the mother of all other
gods and goddesses in the Canaanite pantheon, some seventy in all, including Baal and Anath. Her formal title is "Lady Asherah of the Sea,"
and she rules over the oceans even as her husband, El, rules over the
heavens. Asherah is depicted in Canaanite mythology as a caring and
nurturing mother figure and a wetnurse who suckles both gods and
kings.[44]

What is revolutionary about the inscription at Kuntillat 'Ajrud and
others like it is the suggestion that both the Israelites *and* the Canaanites
embraced Asherah with equal fervor and with an equal sense of inti-
macy. Until the so-called Josianic reformation, when a new orthodoxy
was imposed on the faith of ancient Israel, the Israelites apparently regarded "Yahweh and his Asherah" as husband and wife, king and queen.
Each one was equally worthy of worship, and some Israelites—like the
women described in the Book of Jeremiah—preferred the goddess over
the god. What is more, they apparently felt free to worship the divine
couple with the aid of ritual objects that may be fairly called "idols" but
probably served a function closer to icons—that is, works of art that are
intended to inspire reverential prayers rather than objects that are imagined to be the physical manifestation of a god or goddess. Perhaps, then,

Asherah or some deity very much like her is not merely a goddess borrowed from the Canaanite pantheon but an authentic goddess of Israel.

"As a Male Embraces a Female"

If we reread the Bible in this strange new light, many other traces of forbidden beliefs and practices come into sharper focus. Perhaps the rituals
and paraphernalia of paganism that are described in the Bible as the
"snares" of the seductive stranger were, in fact, authentic expressions of
what the ancient Israelites really believed and really did in the service of
their beliefs. Indeed, the very passages that seem to describe the most
cherished ideals of monotheism may have originated as expressions of a
much older tradition of polytheism and idolatry.

According to the Torah, for example, the Ark of the Covenant is a
chest fashioned out of acacia wood and decorated with a pair of cherubim of beaten gold—not those fat little angels of Renaissance art but
fierce creatures with the torso of a beast and the face of a human being.
So sacred is the Ark that anyone who dares to look inside is struck dead
(1 Sam. 6:19), and so revered is it that the Israelites carry it through the
wilderness of Sinai for forty years. The Ark is ultimately placed in the
Holy of Holies of the Temple that Solomon builds in Jerusalem, where it
remains in safekeeping for four hundred years or so until it disappears
from the biblical record during the Babylonian Conquest in 586 B.C.E.

Exactly what was locked away inside the Ark? The Bible insists that
it was the repository of the most sacred relic in the history and religion of
ancient Israel, the two stone tablets on which Moses inscribed the Ten
Commandments. Some daring scholars, however, wonder out loud
whether the Ark actually represents a far older tradition, one that begins
with "Yahweh and his Asherah" and the *teraphim* that are found in such
abundance. Perhaps, as Julius Morgenstern argues, the two sacred stones
that came to be described in the Bible as the tablets of the Law originally
"represented Yahweh and, in all likelihood, His female companion."[45]

And what are we supposed to make of the two golden cherubim that
adorn the Ark? When an Israelite king called Jeroboam uses golden

calves to decorate the sanctuaries that he establishes at Bethel and Dan in open competition with the Temple at Jerusalem, the author of the Book of Kings condemns him as an apostate. But the cherubim, too, appear to be in violation of the Second Commandment, which sternly prohibits the making of "any manner of likeness of any thing that is in heaven above or that is in the earth beneath" (Exod. 20:4). And perhaps the cherubim that adorn the Ark represent something even more sternly forbidden—a figurative representation of both the God and Goddess of Israel.[46] "The Cherubim were joined together," goes an ancient tradition preserved by the revered medieval Talmudist called Rashi, "and were . . . embracing each other as a male embraces a female."[47]

Such heretical ideas, of course, are precisely what the priests and the prophets of ancient Israel—and, for that matter, pious Talmudic sages like Rashi—sought to stamp out. And the suggestion that the Chosen People worshipped both a god and a goddess of Israel in distant antiquity can be trumped with a simple theological shrug—yes, of course, some of them did, and they were godless sinners who fell into the trap that Yahweh had set for them.

A Goddess of Israel

But the biblical authors, who were eyewitnesses to the faith of ancient Israel as it was actually practiced, may protest too much when they insist so stubbornly that every expression of faith in ancient Israel other than the worship of Yahweh according to biblical orthodoxy is something alien and abominable. Perhaps the Israelites, like every other people in every age and every corner of the world, yearned for a mother-goddess as well as a father-god.

"There can be no doubt that the goddess to whom the Hebrews clung with such tenacity down to the days of [Josiah], to whom they returned with such remorse following the destruction of the Jerusalem Temple, was, whatever the prophets had to say about her, no foreign seductress," insists Bible scholar and cultural anthropologist Raphael Patai, "but a Hebrew goddess, the best divine mother the people had had to that time."[48]

In fact, the yearning for a mothering deity runs so deep in both the biblical text and Jewish tradition that it could never be wholly stamped out. If a biblical author succeeds in suppressing the Hebrew goddess in one place, she always seems to spring up again in another place. Thus, for example, a provocative line of text in the Book of Judges reveals that Deborah—prophetess, judge, general, and "a woman of flames"—always seats herself beneath a certain palm tree in the hill country, and that is where the Israelites go to hear her oracles, commands, and judgments (Judg. 4:4). A living tree, as we have seen, is one of the symbols of the goddess Asherah, who is described in the Bible as a Canaanite deity but in the Kuntillat 'Ajrud inscriptions as the consort of the God of Israel. Does the pointed reference to "the palm-tree of Deborah" preserve the forbidden memory of a priestess of the Hebrew goddess, we might wonder, or perhaps even the goddess herself?

Similar speculation is focused on the figure of Miriam. One of the biblical authors may report that God punishes Miriam with leprosy when she claims to hear the divine voice as clearly as Moses does, but she is elsewhere described as the protector of her brother, a prophetess in her own right, and a leader of prayerful song and dance among the women of Israel. Does the biblical figure of Miriam, too, recall a woman who was a priestess as well as a prophet? Or is she a stand-in for one of the goddesses who populate the myth and legend of the ancient world?

Significantly, Miriam is made over in the folk traditions that are recorded in various rabbinical writings, where she is recalled with striking warmth as a mother figure who watches over the Israelites throughout their wanderings. The ugly incident in the Torah that ends with a divine curse of leprosy seems to be entirely forgotten, and the rabbis insist she dies wholly free of sin. Indeed, according to one cherished tale, God is prompted by Miriam's special merit to provide the Israelites with a source of fresh water that follows them throughout their forty years in the wilderness. "God wrought this great miracle for the merits of the prophetess Miriam, wherefore it also was called 'Miriam's Well.' "[49] And the water that flows from Miriam's Well is described as nothing less than magical: "[E]very conceivable kind of plant and tree" sprouted in abundance, "and these trees, owing to the miraculous water, daily bore fresh fruits."[50]

So the female figure in Jewish tradition is a shape-shifting spiritual entity who asserts herself against every attempt of priests and prophets, rabbis and sages, to snuff her out. She appears in various guises, some of them dark and demonic, some benign and even divine. At one moment she is Lilith, a she-devil who seduces men and slays mothers and babies; at another moment she is the Shekinah, the queen and consort of God himself. But she is always a woman who refuses to be ignored.

"Why Should I Lie Beneath You?"

Lilith is mentioned only once in all of the Bible, a single line of text in the Book of Isaiah that describes all the terrible things that will happen when Yahweh finally wreaks vengeance on a sinful world. The voice belongs to the prophet Isaiah, and the point of view belongs to the strictest traditions of orthodoxy:

> *Wildcats shall meet hyenas,*
> *Goat-demons shall greet each other;*
> *There too the lilith shall repose,*
> *And find herself a resting place.*
> (Isa. 34:14) (New JPS)

As used by the prophet Isaiah, "lilith" apparently refers to a seductive she-demon who first appears in Sumerian mythology, a harlot-vampire who seduces men but gives them neither sexual satisfaction nor children, and the term is rendered in some English translations of the Bible as "night monster." Here is yet another example of how the Bible freely borrows from foreign cultures and then "Hebraizes" what has been borrowed. Lilith is turned into an authentic element of Jewish folk tradition, where she is regarded as "the first Eve." And she illustrates, too, the process of invention and reinvention that is the beating heart of Judaism: she starts out as a creature of flesh and blood, turns into a vile and dangerous demon, then comes full circle in our own era as an icon of autonomy and self-expression among modern Jewish women.

Lilith is mentioned only rarely and briefly in the Talmud and other rabbinical writings, but she is fleshed out in *The Alphabet of Ben Sira*, a satirical and more than slightly heretical collection of tales that may date back to the tenth century C.E.[51] Indeed, the scandalous nature of *The Alphabet* is proof that the Jewish tradition of midrash was broad and accommodating enough to include some highly impious writings. The purported author, Ben Sira, is depicted as both the son and grandson of the prophet Jeremiah, conceived when the holy man is forced to engage in an act of masturbation in a bathtub later used by his own daughter. And, although we know nothing about the flesh-and-blood author, he is plainly "a writer with an anarchistic tendency," as one scholar puts it, "who used satire to ridicule all the institutions of established religion in his day."[52] Indeed, his retelling of the tale of Lilith allows us to see how Lilith came to embody, at the same time, the aspirations of Jewish women to be powerful and the fear that Jewish men felt toward powerful women.

Lilith is the first woman to be created by God, according to the folk tradition that is summed up in *The Alphabet of Ben Sira*, and the first wife of Adam. Since God fashions her out of the same clay that he uses to make Adam, Lilith regards herself as his equal. And so, when Adam demands that Lilith submit to sexual intercourse, Lilith refuses to assume the missionary position.

"I will not lie below you," Lilith insists, "but above you."

Adam insists on what he regards as his male prerogative, and Lilith resorts to a strictly forbidden form of "name magic" to resolve the marital spat: she utters the name of God, an act that bestows magical powers on anyone who knows the secret name and dares to say it aloud. Thus empowered, she rises into the air and flies off. Adam, earthbound and flummoxed, appeals to God to do something about his runaway wife.

"The woman you gave me," he complains, "has fled from me."

God vows to send three angels to find Lilith and bring her back. And here the tale reveals, yet again, that the God of Israel is not quite as all-seeing, all-powerful, or all-knowing as he is sometimes shown to be in the Bible. As when God goes in search of Adam and Eve in the Garden of Eden, it appears that he does not know where Lilith is, cannot compel her to return, and is unable to predict whether she will do so willingly.

"If she wants to return, all the better," God allows. "If not, she will have to accept that one hundred of her children will die every day."

The angels catch up with Lilith at the Red Sea—the same body of water where, countless years later, the army of Pharaoh is destined to die by the hand of God—and demand that she return to Adam. Lilith laughs off God's dire threat and refuses to rejoin her husband. Faced with her stubborn refusal, God replaces Lilith with a second and more dutiful wife for Adam—the biblical Eve. But God carries out his threat against Lilith, and she is cursed to bear children and watch them die through all of eternity as a punishment for defying the King of the Universe.[53]

Jewish folk tradition embellishes upon the original tale of Lilith in curious ways, some of them beguiling and some horrific. To replace her doomed babies, whom God condemns to death by the hundreds, she resorts to seduction of men in equally great numbers. When a man awakens from a "wet dream," the rabbis explained, it is because Lilith has descended upon the sleeping man and engaged in an act of sexual intercourse with him in order to satisfy her lust—or, to look at the same encounter from Lilith's point of view, to impregnate herself with new babies to replace the ones who have died. Other versions depict Lilith as unable to bear children at all: her womb is barren, her breasts give no milk, and she couples with men without giving them the pleasure of orgasm. In both versions, however, she is a dangerous seducer. "It is forbidden for a man to sleep alone in a house," warns one rabbi of the first century c.e., "lest Lilith get hold of him."[54]

Lilith is depicted as even more threatening to women and babies. Because she is jealous of women who bear healthy babies, she stalks the virgin bride on her wedding night, the fecund wife, the laboring mother, and the newborn child; only an amulet inscribed with the names of the three angels who confronted Lilith at the Red Sea is effective to stop her from killing mothers and babies. Lilith is blamed for infertility, miscarriages, and deaths of mother or baby in childbirth; that is why she has been called "a [product] of the morbid imagination," as James A. Montgomery puts it, "of the barren or neurotic woman, the mother in time of maternity, the sleepless child."[55] And Jewish women as recently as the last century still resorted to hanging amulets on cribs and muttering magical incantations to keep her at bay.

Still, no matter how vile she is made out to be in rabbinical writings, Lilith is not a wholly unsympathetic figure. After all, her only real offense is her claim to a position of equality in the marriage bed, an act of self-assertion that God is shown to punish far beyond the biblical proportions of "an eye for an eye, a tooth for a tooth." And, even if she is turned from an aggrieved woman into a demonic baby-killer in the Bible and the Talmud, she has been rescued and rehabilitated in the countertraditions of Judaism, both ancient and modern. Nothing better illustrates the vitality and inventiveness of Judaism than the many ways in which Lilith is depicted in Jewish storytelling.

Wife, Lover, and Daughter

If Lilith is the demonic manifestation of the female spirit in Judaism, then her benign counterpart is the figure known variously as the Matronit ("Matron"), the Bride, the Sabbath Queen, or sometimes just "the Lady." Most often, however, she is called the Shekinah, and she is understood to represent "the loving, rejoicing, motherly, suffering, mourning, and, in general, emotion-charged aspect of deity."[56] Like Lilith, the Shekinah surfaces in startling ways and surprising places over the long history of Judaism.

"Shekinah" is derived from the Hebrew word used in the Torah to describe the tent (*Mishkon*) where God is said to dwell among the Israelites as they wander through the wilderness during the Exodus. The Shekinah is presented in the Talmud as a manifestation of God that human beings can see and hear—"the pillar of cloud by day, and the pillar of fire by night," according to a passage in the Book of Exodus (Exod. 13:22). When the same idea was taken up by the practitioners of Kabbalah in the medieval work of Jewish mysticism known as the Zohar, the Shekinah came to be understood as something separate and apart from Yahweh. And, since *shekinah* is a feminine noun in Hebrew, the term that came to be used in the mystical traditions of Judaism suggests a spiritual entity that is human in form and female in gender. "[T]he very mythologies so suppressed in the Bible erupted in the heart of Jewish mysticism," explains Rabbi Lynn Gottlieb, "and Shekinah became YHVH's wife, lover, and daughter."[57]

The Shekinah is conjured up in the mystical writings of Kabbalism in language that is richly metaphorical and sometimes even phantasmagorical. She is likened to the waxing moon and the waning moon, the morning star and the evening star, a primordial body of water, a queen, a well, a tree, and a serpent, all of which "hark back to images that once belonged to the ancient goddesses of the Near East," as Rabbi Gottlieb points out.[58] Here the Kabbalists seem to understand the allure of such ideas, and they dare to insinuate them into their own mystical musings about God. If the Jewish people, like everyone else in the world, yearn for a caring and comforting mother figure to counterbalance the stern and punishing father figure whom we encounter in the Torah—and if they are cautioned by their rabbis against the "abomination" of goddess worship—then the Shekinah is an outwardly safe alternative to the she-deities who were once openly worshipped as Asherah or the Queen of Heaven.

But something deeply subversive is at work here. The practitioners of Kabbalah did not content themselves with vague if lyrical phrasemaking; rather, they imagined exactly what it would be like when God and the Shekinah encountered one another in the celestial bedroom—and they decided that they would behave like any mortal couple in the same circumstances. "Some say that as long as the Temple stood the King would come down from his heavenly abode every midnight, seek out his wife, the Matronit, and enjoy her in their Temple bedchamber," goes one interpretation of the mystical writings of the Zohar, referring to God as "the King" and the Shekinah as "the Matronit." "Others say that the King and the Matronit coupled only once a week, on the night between Friday and Saturday." Thus impregnated, the Matronit would give birth both to "human souls and to angels"—and thus inspired, the pious but passionate Kabbalists imagined that it was their duty, too, to engage in sexual intercourse with their wives on the Sabbath.[59]

Lilith, too, surfaces in sometimes shocking ways in the musings of Kabbalism. When the Temple is destroyed and the Jewish people are driven from the Holy Land into the Diaspora, the Kabbalists suggest, God insists on remaining behind on the sacred mount in Jerusalem where the Temple once stood. The Shekinah, however, is a devoted mother who refuses to abandon the Children of Israel; she rises from Mount Zion and trudges with them into exile. Deprived of both his queen and his bedchamber, God recruits a "slave goddess" to replace the Shekinah, "one of the handmaidens of the Matronit who used to 'sit behind the handmill.' " She is none other than Lilith, who is now raised from slavery, given a place in the divine marriage bed, and allowed to reign over the Holy Land in place of the exiled Shekinah.[60]

All of these steamy imaginings were condemned at first by the Talmudic rabbis and sages who have always served as the guardians of orthodoxy in Judaism. They were scandalized by the suggestion that God is *not* One, but they were powerless against the allure of the Shekinah: "The fact that . . . no other element of Kabbalism won such a degree of popular approval," writes Gershom Scholem, the leading historian of mystical traditions in Judaism, "is proof that it responded to a deep-seated religious need."[61] Eventually, the Shekinah succeeded in insinuating herself into traditional Judaism, where even otherwise pious Jews seem to respond to her compassionate and companionable ways. And the Shekinah, like Lilith, has been recruited by the latest generation of Jewish seekers who see in her the same promise of a renewed and reinvigorated Judaism that once inspired the Kabbalists of a thousand years ago.

"The More Wives, the More Witchcraft"

Still, the yearnings and strivings of Jewish women are deeply alarming to the strictest practitioners of Judaism. The same misgivings that prompted the priestly and prophetic authors of the Bible to regard women as seducers, harlots, and witches also infected the rabbis and sages who took their place after the destruction of the Second Temple in 70 c.e. Just as women are excluded from the priesthood and the rites of sacrifice at the Temple in Jerusalem under biblical law, they are excluded from the rabbinate and the rituals of worship in the synagogue under the Talmudic law that still prevails among the strictly observant movements of Judaism.

"A woman's thought is only for her beauty," the Talmud teaches, and her sexual nature is so insistent and so treacherous that "[a] man should walk behind a lion rather than behind a woman."[62] A man who kisses or embraces a woman other than his mother, wife, or daughter, according to the *Shulhan Arukh*,* is at risk of "stimulat[ing] lewd thoughts within himself, causing erection and the vain discharge of semen, God forbid."[63] And, as in the Bible, the Talmudists always seem to equal sexuality with apostasy: "The more wives," the Talmud warns, "the more witchcraft."[64]

Now and then, the rabbis and sages will praise a woman for her piety, wisdom, or generosity. But, more often, a woman is singled out in the Talmud or the Midrash only because she has supported her husband in *his* prayer, study, and good works. Thus, for example, a rabbi's wife is celebrated in one tale only because she waits until the Sabbath is over before telling her pious husband that his two sons have died on the Lord's day of rest—"Because God is owed a Sabbath unmarred by mourning, she restrains her own grief as a mother."[65] Tellingly, a woman's life is regarded as explicitly less valuable than a man's in the Talmud, where it is written that if a choice must be made between saving a man or a woman in an emergency, it is the man who must be saved first.[66] And what is the heavenly reward that a dutiful and faithful wife may expect when her life comes to an end? According to the Talmud, she will serve as her husband's footstool throughout eternity in the World to Come!

Indeed, if a woman is praised at all in rabbinical tradition, it is only because she has managed to overcome what the rabbis regard as the flawed nature of women in general. "Four qualities are ascribed to women," goes one passage in the Midrash. "They are gluttonous, eaves-

---

*The *Shulhan Arukh* ("Set Table"), composed by Joseph Caro (1488–1575), is a highly influential summary of the religious law (*Halakhah*) that is set forth at length in the Talmud and other rabbinical writings.

droppers, lazy, and jealous." Women are "querulous and garrulous," according to another passage. "Ten measures of speech descended to the world; women took nine and men one." Above all, the Talmud insists, women are deeply seductive by nature, and men are their helpless victims: the touch of a woman's hand, the sound of a woman's voice, even the sight of a woman's hair are regarded as so powerfully tempting that ordinary men cannot resist their own impulses toward carnality.

The point is made in one of the rabbinical tales told about a woman called Beruriah, the daughter of one revered rabbi, the wife of another, and one of the few woman reputed to be a scholar in her own right. She is a kind of stock figure in the Talmud, where she serves as a rare example of piety, modesty, and fidelity among women. Even Beruriah, however, is shown to be a victim of her own womanly nature in one particularly distasteful Talmudic tale, where she makes light of the notion that women are easily seduced, and her husband resolves to put her to the test. The good rabbi prevails on one of his own students to test his wife's virtue by attempting to seduce her, and the student proves himself to be remarkably diligent in trying to do so. At last, Beruriah yields to the young man's wooing and her own sexual yearnings; the rabbi's wife and the rabbi's student become lovers. When the affair is revealed, Beruriah literally hangs herself in shame, and her husband runs away in disgrace.

"This is the story," observes commentator Rachel Adler, "through which our teachers truly break our hearts."[67]

"Is the Hebrew Goddess Dead?"

"Is the Hebrew goddess dead," asks anthropologist and historian Raphael Patai provocatively, "or does she merely slumber, soon to awaken rejuvenated by her rest and reclaim the hearts of her sons and lovers?"[68]

In a sense, the question has been answered by contemporary Jewish women, religious and secular alike, who feel fully empowered to reclaim Jewish history as their own and remake Jewish traditions in their own image. That is why, as we have seen, much of the most daring biblical scholarship is the work of women, some of whom see the Bible as nothing less than "a feminist manifesto"[69] while others declare themselves appalled and alienated by what they find in the Torah and the Talmud. And that is why some men and women, who are both militant and observant, dared give both Judaism in general and God in particular a human face.

The first and most dramatic ritual innovation was the *bat mitzvah*, first introduced in 1922 when Judith Kaplan, daughter of the founder of the Reconstructionist movement, Mordecai M. Kaplan, was called to the Torah to celebrate her religious coming-of-age, a ritual previously afforded only to sons. An even more dramatic innovation was the ordination of women as rabbis: Sally Priesand was the first rabbi to be fully ordained in the Reform movement in 1972, Sandy Eisenberg Sasso was ordained in the Reconstructionist movement in 1974, and the Conservative movement soon followed their example.

Other obstacles have fallen, too. women are seated with men in the synagogue, counted in the prayer quorum (*minyan*), and afforded the opportunity to put on a *tallis* (prayer shawl), a *kipah* (skullcap), and *t'fillin* (phylacteries) and to read from the Torah—all of which are frowned upon or outrightly forbidden to women in Orthodoxy and other ultraobservant branches of Judaism. Still more recently, the traditional prayer books used in Reform, Reconstructionist, and Conservative synagogues have been revised to conform with the so-called egalitarian movement in Judaism. God is rendered in strictly gender-neutral terms—"Sovereign" rather than "King"—and both the Patriarchs *and* the Matriarchs are honored in the liturgy. "God of Our Fathers," goes the newest version of an old prayer, "and Our Mothers."

Wholly new traditions have been minted to broaden and celebrate the role of women in Judaism. Until recently, for example, only the birth of a baby boy was marked with such ancient rituals as the *B'rit Milah* ("Covenant of Circumcision") or the *Pidyon Ha'Ben* ("Redemption of the Firstborn"), a ceremony in which a firstborn male child is symbolically redeemed from the biblical obligation to devote himself to the service of God by payment of silver coins to a *kohen*, a Jewish man who traces his ancestry back to the priesthood of ancient Israel. Nowadays, however, the birth of a baby girl, too, will be celebrated in many congregations with a baby-naming ceremony or an even more elaborate ritual called a *B'rit Bat* ("Covenant of the Daughter") or a *Shalom Bat* ("Welcome to the Daughter"). And some of the most innovative rituals are wholly invented: one Jewish mother adapted the traditional observance of the new moon, *Rosh Hodesh,* to celebrate her daughter's first menstruation, and she fashioned a silver ornament to commemorate the event, a thoroughly syncretistic charm that depicts a tree, a moon, a Star of David, and a bit of red coral to symbolize a drop of blood!

Sometimes the newest traditions are a matter of impulse and improvisation. My mother, Dvora, was raised in a secular home in Brooklyn where Jewish values were expressed through Labor Zionism rather than Orthodoxy. When my grandmother took my mother and her twin sisters to Palestine in 1926, she dressed up the three girls in Arab garb to symbolize the notion of a binational state for Jews and Arabs; and my mother was taught to sing the "Internationale" as well as "Hatikvah" at a socialist youth camp in upstate New York. And, years later, when I married my wife, Ann, she improvised on the sacred tradition of conducting a bride to the *mikveh* for a ritual bath before her wedding—Dvora and Ann visited a health club for a soak in the Jacuzzi. The invented ceremony was strictly secular, of course, but the *kavannah*—their spiritual intent in taking a dip together—was something ancient and earnest.

But, as we have seen, the spirit of invention is wholly authentic to Jewish tradition—or, more precisely, it is an expression of the many threads of tradition and countertradition that make up the rich tapestry of Judaism. Just as Sarah felt at liberty to laugh at God's words and suffered not at all for her audacity, just as the Kabbalists felt at liberty to redefine God as both male and female, some modern Jews have dared to embrace a new set of "Judaisms." Thus, for example, Lilith has been reimagined as a woman of valor rather than a demonic baby-killer—"She radiates strength [and] assertiveness," insist the editors of *Lilith,* a feminist journal that invokes the figure of Lilith as a rallying point for Jewish women[70]—and the Shekinah has been placed on an equal footing with God himself.

"Lo and behold!" writes Rabbi Lynn Gottlieb, who dared to replace *"Adonai"* ("Lord") with *"Shekinah"* in a prayer service, thus allowing both the rabbi and her female congregants to "finally picture ourselves created in God's image." "The 'Goddess' was alive and well in the midst of my own tradition."[71]

FOUR

The Fighting Jew

*Out of blood and fire and tears and ashes, a new
specimen of human being was born, a specimen
completely unknown for over eighteen hundred years,
"the Fighting Jew."*

— MENACHEM BEGIN, *The Revolt*

When President George W. Bush assembled a small crowd of religious leaders for a "photo op" at the White House, his staff recruited one man who embodied the near iconic attributes of the Jew—a gray-haired rabbi with a yarmulke and a long pointed beard, a figure who could have stepped out Marc Chagall's equally iconic *The Praying Jew*. And that was the whole point—the presidential handlers wanted to make sure that the scene included at least one figure who would "read" as Jew. For a couple of thousand years, and even today, the eternal Jew is the pious and prayerful Jew, an old man bent over his holy books, a man wholly devoted to God, Torah, and Israel.

Long before the praying Jew, however, the world knew only the fighting Jew. The starting point, as with everything in Jewish tradition, is the Bible: David is depicted in the Book of Samuel as a bandit, a guerilla, and a mercenary before he is elevated to the loftier but no less violent roles of king and conqueror. "Thou hast shed blood abundantly, and hast made great wars," God scolds his beloved David in the Book of Chronicles (1 Chron. 22:8) (JPS); and Bible critic Robert Alter likens the deathbed hit list that David gives to his son, Solomon, as "a last will and testament worthy of a dying Mafia capo."[1]

After David, as we shall soon see, came Judah Maccabee, founder of a guerilla army that defeated the successors of Alexander the Great in one of the first successful wars of national liberation in recorded history. Then came the so-called Sicarii ("dagger men"), who literally invented the art of political terrorism, and the other Jewish revolutionaries who dared to wage war against Rome, the greatest superpower of the ancient world. And, finally, came Simon Bar Kokhba, a freedom fighter with messianic aspirations whose insurrection against the Roman occupation of Judea in the second century C.E. was the last assertion of Jewish sovereignty for nearly two millennia.

So the fighting Jew represents yet another countertradition in Jewish history. Only after the defeat of Bar Kokhba did the Jewish people finally put down the sword and pick up the Torah, addressing their prayers to God while, at the same time, petitioning the pagan emperors and Christian princes and Muslim sultans under whom they lived for protection and favor. Once their will to resist was finally crushed, the Jews turned inward; the ghetto was not only a place of confinement for Jews in the Diaspora but also a hothouse where they were able to preserve their oldest and most cherished traditions. Ironically, the People of the Book seemed to forget that the Bible is, among so many other things, a treatise on the art of war and a saga of war and conquest by their distant ancestors, and they cut themselves off from their own authentic martial traditions. Thus, the rabbis and sages of the Talmud recall David not as "a man of war" and "a man of blood," which is exactly how the Bible describes him, but as someone very much like themselves. "Whatever leisure time his royal duties afforded him," the studious and prayerful rabbis insisted, "he spent in study and prayer."[2]

Even today, long after the world witnessed the resurrection of the fighting Jew during two world wars, the Holocaust, and the struggle to create the first Jewish state since the Maccabees, the whole subject is only sparingly mentioned in a conventional Jewish education outside Israel. Until I met an Israeli whose first name is Giora, for example, I had never heard the name and I simply did not know that Simon Bar Giora was a revolutionary leader of the first century B.C.E., the Jewish equivalent of Spartacus, and a warrior who struck his Roman adversaries as so fierce and so fearful that they demonized him by calling him a cannibal. The fighting Jew, not unlike the goddess of Israel, is a countertradition that fundamentally redefines what it means to be a Jew.

That is why, for example, a writer who chose to celebrate Jewish gangsters in a book he titled *Tough Jews* seeks to justify his fascination with them by, remarkably enough, invoking the memory of the Holocaust. Rich Cohen praises Arnold Rothstein, the man who was reputed to have fixed the 1919 World Series, as "the Moses of the underworld,"[3] and he pauses to point out that Rothstein met one of his protégés, Meyer Lansky, at a bar mitzvah. Apparently never having heard of Bar Giora or Bar Kokhba or any of *their* modern protégés, he embraces the "tough Jew" as a more inspiring role model than the six million Jewish men, women, and children whom he recalls only as helpless and pathetic victims.

"[R]emembering Jewish gangsters is a good way to deal with being born after 1945, with being someone who has always had the Holocaust at his back, the distant tom-tom: *six million, six million, six million*," writes Cohen in *Tough Jews*. "[H]ere was another image, closer to home—Jews with guns, tough, fearless Jews. Don't let the yarmulke fool ya. These Jews will kill you before you get around to killing them."[4]

Among the "tough Jews" whom Cohen overlooks is Menachem Begin, who was condemned by British authorities as "Terrorist Number One" when he was a leader of the Zionist underground in Palestine before Jewish statehood and who later earned the Nobel Peace Prize as prime minister of Israel. Begin, too, invokes the memory of the Holocaust and what he regards as the passivity of its victims when he praises "the Fighting Jew" in his memoir, *The Revolt*: "That Jew, whom the world considered dead and buried, never to rise again, has arisen," writes Begin. "[A]nd he will never again go down to the sides of the pit and vanish from off the earth."[5] And when Begin remarks that the fighting Jew has been "completely unknown to the world for over eighteen hundred years," he is pointing all the way back to the *original* tough Jews—Judah Maccabee and Simon Bar Kokhba and Simon Bar Giora.

Alexander's Dream

No single event in Jewish history is quite so thoroughly misunderstood and misrepresented as the war of liberation that was fought by Judah and the Maccabees, a struggle that is commemorated and celebrated in the Jewish festival of Chanukah. Their revolt is generally described as "a battle of religious liberty," as Herman Wouk sums it up in *This Is My God*, and yet freedom of religion meant something very different to the Maccabees of the second century B.C.E. than it does to us. Judah and his cohorts, not unlike Ezra and Nehemiah, sought to purify the practice of Judaism, to cleanse it of foreign taint, and to impose a strict fundamentalism on their fellow Jews by any means necessary. The very same struggle that was first undertaken by the priest Phinehas and the prophet Jeremiah and the reformer-king Josiah—the struggle between orthodoxy and diversity—was carried on by Judah and the Maccabees with even greater passion and ferocity.

As with so much else in Jewish experience, the saga of Judah and the Maccabees begins in the cracks of world history. The land of the Jews remained a provincial backwater of the mighty Persian Empire for a couple of centuries after the end of the Babylonian Exile in 538 B.C.E. The Temple had been rebuilt, although on a much more modest scale than the glorious one the Babylonians had pulled down, and the daily rituals of animal sacrifice had been resumed. Isolated and undisturbed, the Jewish people enjoyed an interval of relative peace and harmony under the benign neglect of an emperor who reigned in far-off Persia and did not much concern himself with the affairs of his Jewish subjects.

And then came the Macedonian who would change the course of Jewish history forever, the man known to history as Alexander the Great.

Alexander was a willful young man who marched out of Macedonia at the head of an army with the goal of making himself master of the Greeks, then subjugating the Persian Empire, and finally conquering the rest of the known world. He only skirted the coastal fringes of Palestine on his way to Egypt, but he is assigned a much more commanding role in rabbinical tradition, if only because the Hellenistic culture that Alexander carried with him around the ancient world figures so crucially and so corrosively in Jewish history.

According to a tale in the Talmud, for example, Alexander marches on Jerusalem with the intent of conquering the city and destroying the Temple. The High Priest, dressed in white vestments, and a delegation of elders, all of them carrying torches, walk out to greet Alexander and beg for mercy. As soon as Alexander sees the high priest, however, he climbs down from his war chariot and prostrates himself on the ground. Alexander has seen the high priest in a dream, and the mysterious old man has revealed that Alexander is destined to defeat the Persian king who reigns over the Jews. Suddenly face to face with the man he had seen in his dream, Alexander resolves to spare Jerusalem and to bestow his imperial favor on the Jewish people.

"Should a great king like you," his officers protest, "prostrate yourself before this Jew?"

"The image of this man," Alexander explains, "wins my battles for me."[6]

The tale is purely fanciful. Alexander never bothered to visit Jerusalem, a provincial hill town of no strategic importance. But it is true that Alexander won his battles against the Persian king who was the overlord of Yehud, and sovereignty over the Jewish province passed to the empire that Alexander founded and over which he very briefly reigned. At his death in 323 B.C.E., Alexander's generals divided up the empire among themselves, and the land of the Jews eventually passed to the dynasty that was founded by a commander called Seleucus. By 198 B.C.E., Judah was under the rule of the so-called Seleucid kings of Syria, and it was against them that the Maccabees eventually went to war.[7]

The revolt of the Maccabees, as we shall see, was provoked by the insulting and oppressive reign of a particularly vile and hateful king called Antiochus IV. So brutal was the Syrian king, who called himself Antiochus Epiphanes ("Antiochus the Manifestation of God"), that he was dubbed Antiochus Epimanes ("Antiochus the Madman") by a courageous punster who witnessed his excesses. But, ironically, the outrages of Antiochus the Madman ultimately mattered less in Jewish history than the culture that he embraced and symbolized, a culture that is still celebrated as the highest expression of Western civilization. Indeed, the Maccabees regarded as abominable the very thing that many of their fellow Jews found irresistible—a vigorous, worldly, sophisticated, and pleasure-seeking way of life that originated in Greece and spread all over the ancient world, a way of life that scholars call Hellenism.

Coca-Cola Colonialism

What the Maccabees regarded as most repugnant about Hellenism is exactly what fundamentalists in the modern world find so objectionable about American culture—its energetic cosmopolitanism, its encouragement of both intellectual speculation and physical pleasure, and its corrosive effect on the oldest and most cherished traditions. Above all, they detested Hellenism precisely because it was so easygoing about matters of faith. Alexander himself, like any civilized man or woman in the ancient world, was a practicing syncretist who paid homage to the gods of Egypt when in Egypt and to the Chaldean deities when in Babylon. According to a legend preserved by one ancient historian, Alexander is even shown to visit the Temple in Jerusalem and offer sacrifices to the God of Israel!

Among the Jews who found themselves under the rule of Alexander's successors were men and women who were beguiled and bedazzled by Hellenism. Not unlike modern Saudi princes with MBAs and Brooks Brothers suits—and not unlike a modern American Jew who goes to law school instead of yeshiva and favors a discreet body-piercing and a tasteful rose tattoo over *payess* (earlocks) and *tsit-tsits* (ritual fringes)—some of the Jews in ancient Israel distanced themselves from the traditional expressions of Judaism and embraced the newfangled ways of Hellenism. So the snares of assimilation and apostasy had been set yet again—and, yet again, the Jews hastened toward them. The Maccabees, as the theological heirs of Josiah and Jeremiah, Ezra and Nehemiah, resolved to do something about it.

Talibanism

So it was that the aristocracy and intelligentsia of Judea began to imitate the manners of their overlords. Rich, influential, and powerful Jews began to speak and write in the Greek language—significantly, the earliest translation of the Bible into a language other than Hebrew is the so-called Septuagint, a Greek translation produced in Alexandria as early as the third century B.C.E. "They frequented the theatres and sports meetings, held drinking bouts, and generally adopted the Greek manner of gay living," according to historian Simon Dubnow.[8] They sent their sons to gymnasia, a Greek system of schooling that included military and physical exercises that were unknown in traditional Jewish schools, and the young men participated in the athletic games that were the glory of Greek culture.

Pious Jews were especially outraged when young men adopted the Greek practice of competing in Olympic-style athletic contests in the nude and consorting with female dancers and singers—"the attractive vice," as the pioneering nineteenth-century historian Heinrich Graetz puts it, "which the Judaeans learned from the Greeks."[9] To credit the version of history that has been preserved in devout Jewish tradition, the Hellenizers were so craven that they even sought to conceal the fact that they had been circumcised by resorting to a primitive form of cosmetic surgery, "submit[ting] to painful operations in order to remove the sign of the covenant which distinguished them visibly from other people," according to Graetz, "and thus to avoid the ridicule of the Greeks on the occasion of the Olympic games."[10]

Tellingly, the most militant Jews—a faction known as the Hasidim ("Pious Ones")*—were alarmed most of all by the open-minded and easygoing ways of the Letzim ("Scoffers"), as the Hellenized Jews were known. The militants feared that the contemplation of philosophy and the celebration of physical beauty would distract their fellow Jews from

---

*Not to be confused with Hasidism, an ecstatic religious movement within Judaism that first emerged in Eastern Europe in the eighteenth century and is still an influential and highly visible faction within ultraobservant Judaism in the modern world. (See Chapter 8.)

the strict religious practice demanded by the Laws of Moses, and they condemned those who embraced Hellenism as "violators of the law" and "evildoers against the Covenant."[11]

"Where the Hebrew asked: 'What must I do?' the Greek asked: 'Why must I do it?'" quipped the nineteenth-century English critic Matthew Arnold, and the twentieth-century Jewish historian Abram Leon Sachar offers an epigram of his own: "The Hebrew believed in the beauty of holiness, and the Greek believed in the holiness of beauty."[12]

The man who picked up the banner of fundamentalism was Judah Maccabee, and the Hasidim rallied to his leadership. Judah can be seen as a brilliant military tactician and an earnest patriot who aspired to restore political sovereignty to his people. But he can also be seen as a religious zealot who inspired in the soldiers under his command the willingness to kill and to die in service to the invisible God of Israel. And he declared war not only on the Syrian occupiers of the Jewish homeland, but also on those of his fellow Jews who chose not to fight but to switch.

For that reason, biblical historian Thomas Thompson, ever the controversialist, characterizes the white-hot political and religious idealism of the Maccabees as the ancient equivalent of "Talibanism."[13] The comparison is intentionally provocative, but it is not wholly wrong. Just as the Taliban guerillas of modern Afghanistan are motivated by a potent blend of nationalism and fundamentalism, the Maccabees and their allies among the Hasidim of ancient Judea were fired by a righteous wrath against both their foreign overlords and their fellow Jews. Just as the Taliban see themselves as soldiers in a *jihad*, the Maccabees were warriors in a holy war. And, in both instances, the enemy includes not only the foreigner but friends and relations, too.

"The Abomination of Desolation"

Even before Judah and the Maccabees rose up in revolt against the Syrian army of occupation, the land of the Jews was already approaching a state of civil war. Rival factions within the Jewish community conspired against each other to put one of their own in the office of High Priest at the Temple in Jerusalem and to put themselves under the protection of one or another powerful foreign king. The fundamentalists curried favor with the Ptolemaic king in Egypt, and the assimilationists courted the Seleucid king in Syria. By the time Antiochus IV marched into Judea in 168 B.C.E. with the goal of keeping it within *his* sphere of influence, he found a country in chaos.

Antiochus did not bother himself with the finer points of Jewish politics, and he resolved to impose law and order on his unruly subjects by carrying out a general massacre that lasted three days. Jewish men, women, and children were put to the sword without inquiry as to whether they were Hasidim or Hellenists. To add insult to injury, the Syrian king defiled the sanctity of the Holy of Holies—the innermost chamber of the Temple, a place regarded by the Jews as so sacred that only the High Priest himself was permitted to enter—and he carried off the altar and the menorah, the cups and bowls and censers, even the crowns that adorned the Torah scrolls, all of them fashioned out of silver and gold, as spoils of war.

Unlike Alexander the Great, and contrary to the customary practice of the pagan world, Antiochus sought to root out the practice of Judaism once and for all, or so we are told by the chroniclers who composed the First and Second Book of Maccabees. Worship of the God of Israel was forbidden, and the three fundamental rites of Judaism—circumcision, the observance of the Sabbath, and the dietary laws of *kashrut*—were specifically criminalized. The Jews were commanded to offer sacrifices to the Greek pantheon of gods and goddesses, and they were to use only those animals that Jewish law regarded as ritually impure. Ironically, the open-mindedness that was the most appealing quality of Hellenism was suddenly replaced with a bestiality that seems to anticipate the worst excesses of the Crusades, the Inquisition, and the Holocaust.

In the hope of destroying the will to resist, Antiochus ordered the Temple in Jerusalem to be rededicated to the worship of pagan deities in a ceremony that was designed to insult and humiliate the Jewish people. A pig was to be slaughtered and offered in sacrifice on the holy altar of Yahweh. Its flesh was to be cooked and eaten in public by the High Priest. Its offal was to be poured over the scrolls of the Torah. As if to make Hellenism as repulsive as possible, an image of Zeus, principal deity of the Greek pantheon, was installed in the Temple where the God of Israel was believed to dwell: "The abomination of desolation" is how the distraught author of the First Book of Maccabees describes it (1 Macc. 1:54) (NEB).

The same outrages were carried out throughout Judea by squads of Syrian soldiers. Synagogues and schools were torn down, and pagan altars were erected in every village and town. Torah scrolls were burned, and anyone who was caught with one was tortured to death: "They were whipped with rods and their bodies were torn to pieces," one ancient historian reports, "and they were crucified while they were still alive and breathed." Mothers who dared to circumcise their newborn sons in defiance of the king's decree were put to death with special cruelty—mother and child were strangled, and the child was hung from the neck of his mother, "as they were upon the crosses."[14]

A remnant of pious Jews sought to save themselves from these horrors by fleeing from the towns and villages and taking refuge in the wilderness. A thousand Jewish men, women, and children sheltered in caves, but they were searched out and rousted by an expeditionary force of Syrian soldiers from the garrison in Jerusalem. The death squad showed up on the Sabbath—and so it was on the Sabbath that the killing began.

The Sabbath Massacre

Something crucial happened in those caves on the morning of the Sabbath massacre—an old and cherished ideal of Jewish piety was murdered along with the men, women, and children who embraced it and were willing to die for it, and a wholly new ideal would soon take its place. And, to understand Jewish history and tradition, to understand what it really means to be a Jew, we must understand what happened there.

The pious Jews in those caves were observing the Sabbath when they first spotted the approaching Syrian soldiers. Precisely because it was the Lord's day of rest, and precisely because they were so pious, the Hasidim refused to raise a sword against the enemy or even to pile one stone on another to create a barricade at the mouth of the cave. Filled with true belief, and unwilling to desecrate the Sabbath by defending themselves, they died in smoke and flames as the Syrians tossed firebrands into the caves and burned the unresisting Jews alive in their refuge.

The Hasidim were what we would recognize today as "Bible literalists." Since the Torah plainly and sternly forbids "any manner of work" on the Sabbath (Exod. 20:10), they regarded themselves as duty bound to do nothing in their own defense. And they took Moses at his word when they read his caution against interpretation of the sacred text: "All this word which I command you, ye shall observe to do," insists Moses. "Thou shalt not add thereto, nor diminish from it" (Deut. 13:1).[15]

The very same idea is still alive today among Jewish fundamentalists in the modern world who insist that the Ten Commandments and the rest of the Law are, both literally and figuratively, written in stone. But the plight of the Hasidim, who died as martyrs because they refused to lift a hand in self-defense on the Sabbath, was not lost on their fellow Jews in antiquity. Fatefully, the Maccabees decided for themselves that the Torah does not require blind and suicidal obedience, and they interpreted the Law to permit the bearing of arms even on a holy day or the Sabbath—whenever the enemy chose to fight, the Maccabees would fight, too.

The Maccabees are credited with three crucial innovations, two of which are firsts in world history: "They . . . invented martyrdom," observes Rabbi Emil Fackenheim, and "theirs was the first war in history fought in defense of a faith." And the third innovation of the Maccabees is no less historic, but quite specific to Judaism: they empowered themselves to bend the Mosaic law to their own will. "Violation of the Torah in defense of it is not a violation" is how they reasoned it out; "it is an interpretation."[16]

The single most enduring legacy of the Maccabees, then, is the simple but crucial decision to treat the Torah not as something written in stone but as something alive and life-affirming. Ironically, if the Maccabees can be accused of Talibanism, they can also be credited with both courage and creativity in freeing themselves from at least one of the bonds of true belief. In contrast to the notion that authentic Judaism is not only a monotheistic but also a monolithic faith, and contrary to those who insist on treating Judaism as a fossil religion, it is the example of the Maccabees at their moment of greatest innovation that has sustained Judaism and the Jewish people for the last two thousand years.

A Dagger Under the Old Man's Cloak

Modin is a village located some thirteen miles north of Jerusalem, and it is here that an old man called Mattathias seeks refuge when Antiochus marches into Jerusalem and defiles the Temple where he had served as a priest. According to the Book of Maccabees, he brings along with him to Modin his family, including five sturdy sons—Johanan, Simon, Eleazar, Jonathan, and Judah. The family name is rendered as Hasmon in Hebrew and Hasmoneus in Greek, but they are best remembered in Jewish tradition by a term that is derived from Judah's nickname—Maccabee, or "the Hammer."*

One day, a Syrian officer and a squad of soldiers arrive in Modin to enforce the royal decree against the practice of Judaism, and the Hasmoneus family shows up in strength. Mattathias, as a priest and an elder, is singled out to set an example for the rest of the village by offering the first sacrifice to the pagan gods. He refuses with a stirring cry of resistance: "Heaven forbid we should ever abandon the Law," he proclaims. "We will not obey the command of the king" (1 Macc. 2:21–22) (NEB). And when another Jewish man steps forward and offers to do what Mattathias has refused to do, the old man draws a dagger from his cloak and strikes down the apostate Jew and then the Syrian officer.

" 'Follow me, every one of you who is zealous for the Law and the Covenant!' " Mattathias is shown to say in the Book of Maccabees. "Thus Mattathias showed his fervent zeal for the law, just as Phinehas had done by killing Zimri" (1 Macc. 2:26, 27) (NEB).

At this moment, the Book of Maccabees likens Mattathias to the

---

*Some scholars argue that Maccabee is actually an acronym for a praise song first sung by Moses after the miraculous victory of the Israelites over the Egyptians at the Sea of Reeds: "*Mi k'mocha b'elim adonai* ("Who is like unto thee, O Yahweh, among the gods?") (Exod. 15:11) (NEB). (See Chapter 2.)

holy warrior whom we encountered in Chapter Two, the man who assassinated a prince of Israel called Zimri and his Midianite lover and then carried out a punitive expedition that ended with the murder of the men, women, and male children of Midian. More than two thousand years later, Phinehas is still being invoked as a symbol of violence in the service of religious zeal: one ultraobservant rabbi in Israel recently declared that any Jew who dared to "marry out" ought to suffer "the fate of Zimri." From Phinehas to Mattathias to the extremists in modern Israel, zeal in defense of the Law has always inspired some Jews to shed the blood of fellow Jews.

That's why it is an oversimplification, if not an outright distortion, to characterize the revolt of the Maccabees as "a battle for religious liberty." To be sure, the Maccabees went to war against Antiochus to win back the right to worship the God of Israel. And they empowered themselves—and generation upon generation of Jews after them—to interpret the ancient laws of the Torah in new and creative ways. But the Maccabees also made war on their fellow Jews whom they deemed to be insufficiently zealous for the Law and the Covenant. They skirmished with the Syrians, but they also raided Jewish towns and villages, destroying pagan altars and "chastising" the Hellenizers who were too friendly with the Syrian overlords. The only religious liberty that mattered to the Maccabees was their own.

So fierce were the Maccabees that their weapons of war included not only the sword and the spear but also the knife wielded by a *mohel* in the ritual of circumcision. If they found a Jewish boy whose parents had failed to circumcise the child, whether out of fear of the Syrians or out of defiance of the Law of Moses, the Maccabees piously (and sometimes forcibly) completed the ritual. Indeed, some sources suggest that the Maccabees and their successors did not confine the practice of forcible circumcision to infants—the genitals of uncircumcised adolescents and adults, too, were put to the knife. As the Maccabees saw it, forcible circumcision was "not an act of tyranny," explains historian Steven Weitzman, "but an act of zeal required to restore the social boundaries between Jews and Gentiles in the Holy Land."[17]

Circumcision, like the dietary laws of *kashrut* and the strict observance of the Sabbath, are all outward signs of membership in a people that is taught to regard itself as chosen by God, "a kingdom of priests and a holy nation" (Exod. 19:6). Not incidentally, they serve the function of encouraging the physical separation of the Chosen People from everyone else; a Jew who strictly observes the laws of *kashrut*, for example, cannot sit down to a meal in comfort and confidence with anyone but another Jew who is equally scrupulous. And circumcision is perhaps the single most dramatic and effective marker of Jewish identity, a "sign of the Covenant" that is literally carved into the flesh.

A Great Miracle Happened There

Another innovation of the Maccabees was the artful use of guerilla warfare against the Syrian army, a strategy that may have been inspired by the saga of young David in the Book of Samuel. Mattathias led his sons and their followers into the countryside, where they sought refuge in caves and crags, sallying forth to carry out ambushes and skirmishes against small units of the Syrian army. But if the Syrians marched out of their strongholds in force, the Maccabees scattered and disappeared.

On the death of Mattathias, the post of commander-in-chief fell to one of his younger sons, Judah. By now, the ranks of the Maccabees had swelled with new fighters—"those whom the prevailing cruelty and wretchedness had cured from their infatuation for things Greek," as Graetz puts it[18]—and so Judah was finally able to lead his army into open battle against a Syrian army in 166 B.C.E. So confident of victory were the Syrians that a gaggle of slave merchants followed the army to shackle any Jewish survivors. But Judah whipped his soldiers into a righteous frenzy with a stirring battle speech, then led them in a daring maneuver that allowed the Maccabees to fall upon the enemy from an unexpected direction. The Syrian general was slain, the Syrian army fled the battlefield in open rout, and Judah picked up the sword of the fallen commander and carried it in battle against the enemy for the rest of the campaign.

The Maccabees, no longer confined to guerilla operations, defeated the Syrians in a series of set-piece battles. At last, Judah and his army entered Jerusalem, cleansed the city of its pagan paraphernalia, and reconsecrated the Temple in 164 B.C.E. with prayers and offerings. The priests returned to the altar of Yahweh, and the daily sacrifice of rams and goats was resumed. And, even if the thought never occurs to most of us, it is the resumption of animal sacrifice to Yahweh in the cleansed and purified Temple that we celebrate during the candle-lighting ceremonies over the eight days of Chanukah, a Hebrew word that is variously rendered as "inauguration," "dedication," and "purification."

Although it appears nowhere in the Book of Maccabees or other ancient histories, a cherished tale is told in the Talmud about the rededication of the Temple. A small cruse of holy oil was found in the ruined precincts of the Temple, only enough to light the lamps of the sanctuary for a single day, but the meager supply of oil then burned for eight whole days. "A great miracle happened there" (*Nes Gadol Haya Sham*) is the aphorism that recalls the miraculous event, and the first letter of each word in the Hebrew phrase is inscribed on the sides of the *dreydl*, the spinning top that is used to play a lighthearted game of chance in Chanukah celebrations today.

But the saga of the Maccabees is something far more solemn—and something with far graver consequences—than is suggested by the modern observance of Chanukah. The Maccabees were ruthless soldiers who fought a war of national liberation to restore Jewish sovereignty in the old tribal homeland of Judah for the first time since the Babylonian Conquest in 586 B.C.E. And, at least according to pious Jewish tradition, they fought a holy war to cleanse and purify not only the Temple but the whole of the Jewish people. The most dangerous and enduring threat to Judaism was found not in the cruel decrees of Antiochus the Madman but in the comforts and pleasures of assimilation. "[A] 'Kulturkampf' between Judaism and Hellenism" is how one historian sums up the real meaning of the Maccabean revolt.[19]

"A Peaceful Battle Against Assimilation"

None of these meanings has survived in the contemporary celebration of Chanukah. What began as "the last and least of the minor holidays," as Herman Wouk points out, is now the emblematic expression of Judaism for many Jews and most non-Jews.[20] The zealotry of the Maccabees—the assassinations, the forced circumcisions, the battles fought and won—is eclipsed by candle lighting and gift giving and the singing of the single most insipid song in the otherwise stirring repertoire of Jewish music: "I have a little dreidl, I made it out of clay. . . ."

A stinging irony has attached itself to the celebration of Chanukah. The motive of the Maccabees, and especially their allies among the Hasidim, was to compel their fellow Jews to shun the easygoing ways of Hellenism and embrace the Law of Moses in all of its rigor—or so goes the traditional reading of Jewish history. And that is why, for example, they forced the more neglectful of their fellow Jews to carve into their own flesh "the sign of the Covenant," a symbol of their chosenness and separateness. But Chanukah, the holiday that commemorates the Maccabees, has become, as Wouk puts it, "an official symbol of mutual courtesy and tolerance," an exact and complete analog to Christmas and an opportunity for Jewish children to ape the ways of their Christian neighbors.[21]

Now and then, a few modern zealots will try to remind their fellow Jews of the original meaning of Chanukah. "Not in twenty centuries has Hanukah been so important a festival as it has become in our own day," wrote one Jewish author in *Jewish Holidays and Festivals*, a book first published during World War II and intended for the instruction of children and families in basic Jewish observances. "We understand a little better, perhaps, what it means to enjoy liberty and to have heroes and heroines." But the author does not pour out his wrath on the Nazis and their collaborators, latter-day reincarnations of Antiochus the Madman who were, even then, murdering Jewish men, women, and children all over Europe. Rather, he rants and rails against a much more intimate enemy:

> We also realize what it means to have Hellenists. Today we call them assimilationists—Jews who do not care whether the holidays and customs are observed, whether the Hebrew language, the Bible, and Jewish history are studied, whether Palestine is rebuilt, whether the Jewish community is well organized, whether, in fact, the Jewish people and the Jewish religion survive or not. Hanukah, each year,

reminds us of the conflict between the Hasidim and Hellenists of old and inspires us to wage a peaceful battle against assimilation.[22]

But the ultimate irony is that the worldview of Jewish zealots, then and now, is based on a false premise; indeed, a fresh reading of the historical evidence suggests that some of our most cherished ideas about the Maccabees may be wrong. The Maccabean revolt need *not* be seen as a death match between the Hasidim and the Hellenists, the pietists and the assimilationists. Even in the lifetime of Judah Maccabee himself, it was possible to be a Judean patriot, an observant Jew, and a civilized human being, all at the same time.

Ready to Die

Of course, the oldest ideas about the Maccabees are very old indeed. The First and Second Book of Maccabees, where the saga of the Maccabees is first recorded, were probably composed around the turn of the first century B.C.E., not long after the events they purport to describe. But both books are clearly the work of special pleaders who want their readers to regard "the traditional Jewish way of life" as something pure and exacting and who admonish them "not to abandon the Law." Indeed, the battle speeches attributed to Judah Maccabee in the Book of Maccabees are meant to inspire martyrdom in later generations just as they are shown to do in his own lifetime. "His words put them in good heart," writes the author of the Second Book of Maccabees, "and made them ready to die for their laws and for their country" (2 Macc. 2:3; 8:18, 21) (NEB).[23]

If we read the old traditions in the full light of history, however, it appears that Judah and the Maccabees were never quite as zealous in their war on Hellenism as the Book of Maccabees *or* Jewish tradition makes them out to have been. Judah himself apparently engaged in negotiations with the Syrians, seeking to make an honorable peace with the enemy rather than fight unto victory or death. After the death of Antiochus (163 B.C.E.) and Judah (160 B.C.E.), the Syrians and the Maccabees worked out an armistice that conceded the de facto independence of the

Jewish state and yet, at the same time, allowed a Syrian garrison to remain in the fortress of Acra in Jerusalem, a place where both Syrian soldiers and Hellenized Jews sheltered for more than two decades after the Temple had been reclaimed and rededicated.

The Hasmonean kings who ruled after the Maccabees went even further in making peace with Hellenism. Indeed, they were as thoroughly Hellenized as any Jews in the ancient world, adopting Greek names, titles, dress, and manners, engaging in commerce and diplomacy with the Hellenistic kingdoms that were their allies, and conducting wars against their enemies with Greek weapons and tactics. Once again, the distinction between traditional Judaism and its many countertraditions turns out to be a matter of theory rather than practice, and the "purity" of belief and practice sought by the fundamentalists in Judaism to be purely a myth. "We can no longer contrast 'Palestinian Judaism' as an unadulterated form of the ancestral faith with 'Hellenistic Judaism' as the Diaspora variety that diluted antique practices with alien imports," insists historian Erich Gruen. "Jews did not face a choice of either assimilation or resistance to Greek culture."[24]

Jews, in other words, could be—and were—both pious and worldly at the same time, a notion that is as hotly debated in the Jewish world today as it was two millennia ago.

Conversion or Death

Under Judah Maccabee and his brothers, the land of the Jews achieved sovereignty for the first time in four hundred years, and the Hasmonean kings who ruled after them carved out an empire very nearly as large as the one ruled by King David. They supplied themselves with mercenary armies in the Greek style, and they renewed old alliances with the Greek city-state of Sparta and the Roman republic. At the same time the Jewish kings were making their own peace with Hellenism, however, they were still resorting to terror in the name of true belief. On the death of Simon, the last of the original Maccabee brothers, the office of high priest, military commander, and political ruler of the Jewish state passed

to Simon's son, John Hyrcanus (175–104 B.C.E.). And it was John Hyrcanus who resolved to do to the Samaritans and the Idumeans exactly
what Antiochus had tried to do to the Jews.

The Samaritans lived in what had once been the northern kingdom
of Israel until the Assyrian conquest of the eighth century B.C.E., and
they saw themselves as coreligionists of the people of Judah—they, too,
regarded the Five Books of Moses as holy writ and worshipped the God
of Israel. Whether or not the Samaritans were descendants of the Ten
Lost Tribes of northern Israel—and thus blood-related to the Jews—is
still a matter of debate, but it is plain that the Samaritans differed with
the rest of the Jewish people on other articles of faith. The Samaritans
did not embrace the other biblical writings that make up the Hebrew
Bible, for example, and they insisted on the right to offer sacrifices to
Yahweh at a temple of their own on Mount Gerizim. So Hyrcanus
marched into Samaria, laid waste to its capital city, and pulled down
the temple on Mount Gerizim; like Josiah, he sought to preserve the
monopoly of the Temple and the priesthood of Jerusalem in the worship
of Yahweh.

The Idumeans, who lived in the hill country and the desert to the
south of the Hasmonean state, have been linked to the biblical Edomites,
and were described as an Arabic people even in antiquity. Hyrcanus, not
unlike the most militant Jews in modern Israel, aspired to sovereignty
over the whole of *Eretz Yisrael* as it is described in the Bible. But he was
not content with defeating the Idumeans in battle and bringing them
under his rule. For the first and last time in all of history, a Jewish army of
conquest offered a cruel choice to a defeated enemy, a choice that would
be given to countless Jewish men and women over the centuries to
come—they were compelled to choose between conversion and death.

The Jewish kings who descended from the Maccabees eventually
turned against their own people, too. One of the sons of John Hyrcanus,
a man whose Hebrew name was Jonathan but who adopted the Greek
name Alexander Jannaeus (103–76 B.C.E.), was such a convinced Hellenist that he refused to perform some of the ancient Jewish rituals that
were regarded as "barbarous" by the Greeks.[25] During a ceremony in observance of the biblical holiday of Sukkot, a festival that features the

etrog (citron) among its symbolic foodstuffs, pious Jews whose fathers and grandfathers had once rallied to Judah Maccabee now expressed their disgust and outrage by pelting his nephew with *etrogim*.

The king responded by setting his mercenary army on his own people, killing six thousand of them and sparking a civil war that lasted six years and left fifty thousand dead, at least according to the ancient sources. At the moment of his worst excess, Alexander Jannaeus is said to have hosted a victory banquet at which his guests were entertained with the mass crucifixion of eight hundred of his fellow Jews in the gardens of the palace.

The Empty Room

Such chaos could not be confined to the little Jewish kingdom. Indeed, the pious Jews who opposed Alexander Jannaeus appealed to the Syrian king to intervene on their behalf—"the successors of the Hasidim," as historian Solomon Grayzel exclaims, "asking the Syrians to help them against a descendant of the Maccabees!"[26] And, when the death of Alexander Jannaeus sparked a new civil war, the various pretenders to the Jewish throne courted the favor of Rome, the newest and greatest superpower in the ancient world. Each of the contenders would have happily accepted the patronage of pagan Rome, but the Roman Empire responded in a way that pleased none of them even as it fundamentally and catastrophically changed the course of Jewish history.

At first, the rival factions assumed that their bribes and blandishments would put one or another Jewish king on the throne. The Roman general Pompey, for example, was presented with a rich gift from the Temple of Yahweh in Jerusalem—an exquisite vine of worked gold that eventually ended up in the Temple of Jupiter in Rome—but, as it turned out, the Romans were unwilling to prop up an expansionist Jewish state within their own sphere of influence in the Near East. Pompey put an abrupt end to the intrigue among the various Jewish factions with a directness and decisiveness that was characteristic of the Romans: he marched into Jerusalem at the head of an army in 63 B.C.E., declared the land of Judah to be a province of the Roman Empire, and installed a series of puppet rulers who were denied the title of "king" and answered only to their Roman masters.

According to the ancient chronicles, Pompey and his legionnaires fought their way into the Temple even as the priests were conducting the daily sacrificial offerings to the God of Israel. So intent were the priests on doing their sacred duty, however, that as soon as one of them was struck down by a Roman sword or spear, another would take his place at the altar. So fierce were the pious Jews who threw themselves into combat against the invincible Roman army that twelve thousand of them were cut down before Jewish resistance was finally crushed. And when the fighting was over, Pompey resolved to see for himself exactly what was secreted away in the Holy of Holies of the Temple in Jerusalem, a chamber that no one except the High Priest was permitted to enter.

What happened next is an oft-told tale in Jewish tradition, and one that shimmers with sublime meaning in Jewish theology. The Roman general expected to find something strange and remarkable in the inner sanctum that the Jews held to be so sacred and so sternly forbidden to human eyes—an idol or an icon that would reveal, at last, what the supposedly invisible God of Israel really looked like. But when Pompey ripped aside the curtain with the point of his bloodied sword and strode into the Holy of Holies, all he found was an empty room.

A moment of even sharper irony followed. At first, the Romans permitted one of the Hasmonean royals to serve as high priest and "ethnarch" in the new Roman province of Judea, but they recruited his counselor, Antipater, to serve as a surrogate of Rome in the Jewish seat of government. And when Antipater died in 42 B.C.E., a victim of poisoning by someone even more adept at intrigue than himself, the Romans eventually settled on one of Antipater's sons to rule Judea as their liege. Now Antipater and his sons were Idumeans—a people of Arabic origins—but Antipater's family had been forcibly converted to the Jewish faith during the reign of the Hasmoneans. And so, when the Roman overlords of Judea put a crown on the head of Antipater's son in 40 B.C.E., it was an Arab who was dubbed "King of the Jews." His name was Herod, and he was the last man in recorded history to bear that exalted and resonant title.

Bandits and Brigands

Herod may have been crowned as King of Judea in Rome, but he was unable to seat himself on his new throne until three years later. The last of the Hasmonean pretenders to the throne of Judah took up arms against Herod and his Roman patrons, and the King of the Jews was forced to follow a Roman army into a ruined Jerusalem. Even after he finally claimed the throne in 37 B.C.E., his long reign was constantly disrupted by acts of armed resistance carried out by courageous young men who were characterized by the Romans as "bandits" and "brigands," although we might be more inclined to call them patriots and partisans. The fighting Jews of Herod's reign were never willing to defer to superior strength when it came to their faith in the God of Israel or their insistence on regaining the political sovereignty that the Jews had known so briefly.

Herod's first experience with the fighting Jew dated back to the days before kingship, when he served as governor of Galilee and struggled to maintain law and order in the Roman province. From the Roman point of view, the armed bands who carried out acts of highway robbery and home invasion were common criminals, but the more patriotic Jews must have seen them as righteous and heroic, a new generation of Maccabees. Indeed, the poorest and the most pious Jews must have taken some pleasure in seeing how the so-called bandits and brigands plundered the estates of the richest Jews, whose wealth was gained or preserved by reason of their collaboration with the Roman authorities and their Idumean puppet king. Although the accounts of the Jewish outlaws of the first century B.C.E. in conventional Jewish histories are cursory and slightly embarrassed in tone, as if the historians are reluctant to claim kinship with the "tough Jews" of antiquity, they can be seen as the ancient Jewish equivalent of Robin Hood and Pancho Villa and Che Guevara— "patriot-highwaymen," as historian Solomon Grayzel puts it.[27]

The chronicles of the Romans and their collaborators are full of sputtering rage toward these unruly Jews, but they also allow us to see an equal measure of Jewish rage that simmered just beneath the surface among the common folk of ancient Judea. And, now and then, an act of banditry was the spark that ignited the flame of open revolt among the

Am Ha'aretz. When an imperial courier was robbed on the road near a village called Beth-Horon, for example, the Roman procurator was outraged by the fact that the villagers did nothing to arrest or pursue the robbers. To punish them for their dereliction of duty, he ordered the village elders to be arrested and marched to Jerusalem in chains, but the operation spun wildly out of control when a Roman soldier ripped up a Torah and tossed it on a fire. Suddenly, the single act of highway robbery was eclipsed by a general uprising—"The Jews, as if their whole country was in flames, assembled in frantic haste . . . in their thousands," goes one ancient account[28]—and they dispersed only after the soldier was turned over to the mob, forced to run a gauntlet of angry Jews, and then put to death.

An early warning of the rancor between the King of the Jews and his Jewish subjects can be detected in an incident that took place during Herod's early days as governor of Galilee. Herod had captured and hanged a man called Hezekiah, who is called an "archbrigand" in the ancient sources[29] but was regarded as a victim of injustice by the Sanhedrin, the council of seventy elders that served as a religious supreme court. The Sanhedrin charged Herod with the crime of imposing a death sentence on Hezekiah and his men without a trial under Jewish law. But when he appeared to answer the charge, Herod refused to wear the customary black garb of the penitent and, instead, marched into court in full regalia, accompanied by a detachment of soldiers bearing swords and spears. Cowed by this show of force, the Sanhedrin hastily adjourned and scattered from the hall.

"If you will not judge this man now," warned an elder called Shemayah, the only member of the Sanhedrin willing to speak out against Herod, "the time will come when he will judge you and show you no mercy."[30]

Shemayah may have been a lone voice among the elders of the Sanhedrin on the day of Herod's abortive trial, but there would soon be other Jews who followed his example in challenging the authority of Rome and its puppet king. They would not rely on the niceties of Jewish law; rather, they would resort to the dagger, the sword, and the spear. And when they finally rose up in open rebellion against Rome, the distinction between outlawry and revolution, always hazy and indistinct, disappeared altogether. Significantly, it was the son of the "archbrigand" Hezekiah, a man called Judah of Gamalah, who later organized the freedom fighters who wrote themselves into the history of the Jewish people as the Zealots, one of several bands of fighting Jews that rose up in a war of national liberation against the greatest superpower in the ancient world.

Herod the Great

The Western Wall in the Old City of Jerusalem is revered in Jewish tradition as the last surviving relic of the Temple that was the single holiest site in the faith of ancient Israel. Long after the Temple was destroyed in 70 C.E. and the rituals of animal sacrifice to Yahweh came to an end, the Western Wall remained an enduring symbol of Jewish faith and Jewish nationhood. Even today, Jews will push folded pieces of paper on which earnest prayers are written into the cracks between the stonework in the pious hope that their words will catch the attention of the God of Israel. Here, we are told in the Book of Deuteronomy, is the very place where the God of Israel "causes his name to dwell."

And yet it is here, too, that we bump into yet another painful irony. The Western Wall is not a remnant of the First Temple, the one that Solomon is shown to build in the Book of Kings. Nor is it a remnant of the Second Temple, the one that Zerubbabel is shown to build in the Books of Ezra and Nehemiah. Indeed, it is not a remnant of *any* version of the Temple. Rather, the Western Wall is a short section of the retaining wall that King Herod erected in order to expand the construction site where he built what really ought to be regarded as the *Third* Temple, an opulent work of monumental public architecture that was one of the wonders of the Roman Empire and helped to earn him the sobriquet "Herod the Great."

Such were the unintended and unforeseen consequences of the Hasmonean policy of forcible conversion. Herod's grandfather, as we have seen, was an Indumean, a man of Arab descent, who had embraced Judaism only at the point of the sword; but now it was Herod who ruled

over the land of the Jews as a convert to Judaism and a Roman puppet king. And Herod was so thoroughly soaked in Greco-Roman culture
that he aspired to turn the Temple of Yahweh into a showpiece of classical architecture. He did not merely refurbish the Second Temple—he
built a glorious new temple around the old one, a rich confection of
Hellenistic architectural and ornamental flourishes that was meant to
(and did) rival anything that might be found elsewhere in the Roman
Empire. As if to acknowledge the *realpolitik* of the kingdom he ruled,
Herod affixed the emblem of Rome—a golden eagle—to the gateway to
the Temple.

"Whoever has not beheld Herod's building," goes a Talmudic saying
that refrains from actually describing what Herod built as the Temple,
"has not seen anything beautiful in his life."[31]

Herod is among the strangest figures in the rogue's gallery of Jewish
history. Cruel, cunning, and coldhearted, he was always willing to
scourge and slay his enemies, real and imagined. He would disguise himself and mingle with the crowds in order to eavesdrop on what they were
saying about their king. At the slightest provocation and on the merest
suspicion, Herod slaughtered not only his Jewish subjects by the thousands but his own blood relations, and all for the same reason—he suffered from a near-paranoid fear of political intrigue and personal
betrayal.

Thus, for example, Herod adored and cherished his wife, Mariamne—an authentic Jewish princess of the Hasmonean royal house—
but Herod's sister, Salome, whispered false accusations of adultery against
her sister-in-law. Mariamne, Salome insisted, had slept with the very
man whom Herod had charged with the task of guarding his wife's
chastity while he was away from the palace! At last, Herod was persuaded to order the execution of his beloved Mariamne and the man he
suspected of being her lover. Later, the grief-stricken Herod was seen
wandering the halls of his palace, forlornly calling out the name of his
dead wife and commanding his servants to summon her to his side. But
his remorse over the murder of Mariamne did not stop him from putting
to death the two sons she had given him, each one charged with treason
on trumped-up evidence and then strangled to death in his prison cell.

"I had sooner be Herod's swine," cracked the Roman emperor Augustus, "than his son."[32]

As Shemayah had predicted when Herod confronted the Sanhedrin over the hanging of Hezekiah, the king was no less ruthless in dealing with the traditions and institutions of the Jewish state. The Sanhedrin was stripped of any real authority in affairs of state, and its elders were permitted to decide only matters of religious law. The High Priest served at Herod's pleasure, and even the vestments he wore while officiating at the Temple were placed in the king's safekeeping. A special role was assigned to the non-Jewish soldiers in Herod's army, including four hundred men from Gaul who had previously served as Cleopatra's bodyguard—a gift from Augustus—and the elite unit of Germans and Thracians who guarded the Jewish king from his Jewish subjects. Anyone who sought to serve the king was required to take a loyalty oath to Herod, and anyone suspected of being insufficiently loyal was put to torture.

Herod may have been half-mad, but he was wholly effective in keeping himself alive and his kingdom intact. "For sheer ability," enthuses historian Cecil Roth, "he ranks perhaps second to none in all Jewish history."[33] And the Temple in Jerusalem was hardly the only symbol of his kingship: Herod built seaports, stadiums, and sanctuaries, and he decorated the cities and towns with amphitheaters, baths, colonnades, fountains, and gymnasiums. His terror of an uprising by his unruly Jewish subjects prompted him to build a series of fortified palaces across the length and breadth of the land of Judea. On his death, Herod the Great left behind a rich architectural legacy that has lasted much longer than the Temple itself.

Among the most enduring of Herod's monuments to himself is one of the strangest—a palace in the middle of a wasteland, a miragelike fortress perched atop a rugged peak that rises abruptly from the floor of the Judean desert near the Dead Sea. The site was first fortified in a crude way by the Maccabees, but the royal citadel that Herod built for himself included three separate palaces and, significantly, an impregnable complex of walls and watchtowers, a series of storehouses for arms and provisions, and a cistern that held 200,000 gallons of water, all of it designed to withstand a long siege. The place is called Masada, and it was in the defense of Herod's fortress that, ironically, the most zealous of the Jews later offered one of the most memorable demonstrations of their patriotism and their faith.

But Herod himself, as it turned out, did not have need of the desert fortress at Masada. Despite a lifelong terror of death by treachery and violence, the king died in bed. His final illness may have been a gruesome ordeal—the symptoms, as catalogued by one ancient historian, included fever, itching, pain in the bowels, swelling of the feet, difficulty in breathing, and "mortification of the genitals, producing worms"—but he died with his kingdom intact and his crown on his head. Still, even as he lay dying, Herod recognized how deeply he was loathed by his own subjects. "I know," he confided to his sister Salome, "the Jews will greet my death with wild rejoicing."[34]

In fact, the merest word that Herod was mortally ill prompted a couple of rabbis to send their students to the Temple with instructions to pull down the golden eagle that Herod had placed there in defiance of the Law of Moses. As the crowd cheered, the most daring of the young men lowered themselves by ropes from the roof and started cutting away the despised symbol of Rome. But they were stopped and arrested by the royal constabulary, along with some forty of their fellow students, and all of the exuberant young men were marched under guard to the palace for judgment and punishment. The premature uprising so outraged the dying Herod that he summoned up enough strength to rise from his deathbed for one last official act—the King of the Jews ordered the rabbis to be burned alive and the others to be turned over to the royal executioner.

Once the worms claimed Herod once and for all, however, the passions that he had managed to suppress during his lifetime could no longer be contained. At first, only a few bold men and women joined the Jewish underground, striking here and there at targets of opportunity that symbolized Roman authority or Jewish collaboration. Not unlike the IRA or the PLO, the Jewish resistance fighters of the first century B.C.E. were willing to carry on a low-grade war of national liberation that lasted decades and linked generation to generation. Ultimately, the rebellion spread throughout the land of Judea, and what had begun as a series of isolated brushfires turned into the general conflagration that has come to be called the Jewish War.

"Perverse Fanatics"

Here we come upon one of the countertraditions in Jewish history that have been rigorously and successfully repressed. "Tough Jews" like the ones that Herod tried but failed to exterminate during his long reign have been dismissed by both ancient and modern historians as "perverse fanatics," "wild men," and, at best, "pious robber chieftains surrounded by a false halo of sanctity."[35] Devout Jewish tradition is not much kinder, and the Jews who rose up in open rebellion after Herod's death—the Zealots and the Sicarii, among others—are recalled in rabbinical writings as "murderers" when they are mentioned at all.

"It is amazing, and not wholly creditable, that among Jews he is barely remembered," writes historian Cecil Roth about the "patriot-highwayman" called Simon Bar Giora, "and when he is, in terms almost of caricature."[36]

Rabbinical Judaism, as we have seen, shunned the tradition of violence that is written so prominently into ancient Jewish history. For the same reason that David is turned from a warrior king into a pious scholar in the tales of the Talmud—and just as the sages of the second century condemned Simon Bar Kokhba as the "Son of a Lie"—the rabbis of classical Jewish tradition preferred to distance themselves from the Zealots and the Sicarii. After all, *all* of the Jews who resorted to violence against Rome ended up in defeat, and the ones who were not killed in battle or tortured to death by the enemy took their own lives. And so, as the Jewish people struggled to survive in the Diaspora, where they sought only to go along and get along with the powers that be, they rejected the example of the fighting Jew, whether he was a "patriot-highwayman" or a soldier in the army of a sovereign Jewish state.

And yet the "bandits" and "brigands" who so vexed the Roman Empire were regarded in their own lifetimes as heroes by the *Am Ha'aretz*, the poor and the powerless of ancient Judea, if not by the Jewish aristocracy or the rabbinical elite. And they represent a crucial countertradition in Jewish history whose neglect, as Menachem Begin suggests, brought catastrophic consequences to countless generations of Jewish men, women, and children. By the time the Jewish people encountered Nazi Germany and its allies, they were out of touch with their own martial traditions. And so, when Begin speaks of the fighting Jew who emerges after a slumber of eighteen hundred years, he is harking all the way back to Judah of Gamala and Simon Bar Giora, the Zealots and the Sicarii, and the other "tough Jews" who raised a sword in defense of the Jewish people.

Like the Maccabees before them, the Jews who skirmished with Herod and then rose up in open rebellion against the Roman Empire can be seen as authentic revolutionaries, full of patriotic and religious zeal, rather than common criminals. Judah of Gamala, for example, condemned the taking of a census in Judea as a sacrilege; he regarded it as a symbol of submission to a worldly king and thus an insult to Yahweh, the King of the Universe. The same notion can be found in the Bible, where Satan is blamed for giving King David the idea of taking a census (1 Chron. 21:1)! But Judah also condemned the census for purely political reasons: the gathering of census data is an essential preliminary to conscription and taxation. And, significantly, when Judah and the Zealots succeeded in driving the Romans out of Jerusalem, they burned the public archives where the records of indebtedness and servitude were maintained for the convenience of the propertied classes of ancient Judea.

Many of the property owners, of course, were Jewish—not the *Am Ha'aretz* who suffered under the burden of debt and slavery, but the highborn and Hellenized families who were not averse to the rule of the Romans and, in fact, may have enriched themselves by active collaboration with them. Thus, for example, Simon Bar Giora and his followers, men and women alike, raided the estates of rich and privileged Jews whom they regarded as collaborators and traitors. And Simon Bar Giora played the Moses-like role of liberator, setting free the slaves of the wealthy families whom he and his cohorts attacked and ransacked. For that reason, one modern historian compares him to Spartacus, and another calls Bar Giora and his comrades in arms "the communists of the time."[37]

The Jewish collaborationists were singled out for a new and dramatic form of political terrorism by an urban guerilla faction known as the Sicarii. A member of the Sicarii, dressed as an ordinary citizen and mingling in the crowds of Jerusalem, would single out a Jew whom he knew to be friendly with the Romans. The disguised assassin would place himself next to the chosen victim, draw a dagger out of his cloak, surreptitiously stab the man to death, raise a cry of alarm as if he were merely a witness to the murder, and then slip away in the resulting commotion, leaving behind a bloody corpse as a caution to any other Jews who might be collaboratively inclined. *Sica* is the Latin word for the curve-bladed dagger that the terrorists favored, and the term "Sicarii" became a badge of honor among the Jewish resistance fighters. Significantly, their very first victim was the High Priest of the Temple in Jerusalem, a Jew whose friendly relations with the Romans were open and notorious.

What moved the Jews to fight, however, was never a matter of politics alone; the same religious zeal that had inspired the Maccabees in their long war against the Syrians burned in the hearts of the Jews who resisted the rule of Rome. During the war that Herod fought to claim his crown, for example, he pursued some "bandits" to a cliffside cave where they sheltered against their pursuers. Herod contrived to lower a few of his men from the cliff top in baskets so they could haul out the fugitives and drop them to their deaths. But one of the fugitives was seen to cut the throats of his wife and children before taking his own life, apparently preferring to die by his own hand rather than allowing himself or his family to fall into Roman hands. Perhaps nothing expresses more eloquently the tradition of zeal that runs in an unbroken thread from Phinehas to Josiah to Judah Maccabee to the Zealots and the Sicarii— and nothing else is needed to prove that such Jews were not "bandits" at all but freedom fighters who preferred death over dishonor.

Twenty-four Judaisms

*As for that house, God had for certain long ago doomed
it to the fire; and now that fatal day was come, according
to the revolution of ages.*

—JOSEPHUS, *The Jewish War*

On the ninth day of the Hebrew month of Av in 586 B.C.E., the
imperial army of Babylon looted and burned the Temple of
Solomon in Jerusalem. And, on the very same day in 70 C.E., the imperial army of Rome under Titus did exactly the same to the so-called Second Temple, the one that Herod had built to win the admiration of the
Roman world. That these two events took place on the same date may be
explained as a coincidence, or an act of divine will, or perhaps just a
pious fiction. Both events, however, are a matter of recorded history. To
this day, in fact, the ritual objects that were plundered from the ruined
Temple and carried off as spoils of war can be seen depicted on the Arch
of Titus in Rome—including a menorah so grand in scale that eight soldiers were needed to lift it—and we can hold in our hands the very coins
that were struck in honor of the victory, with *"Judaea Capta"* ("Judea
Captured") inscribed over a palm tree that shelters an upright Roman
soldier and a weeping Jewish woman.

The Ninth of Av (*Tisha B'Av*) is a day of fasting and mourning in the
Jewish calendar. Even today, pious Jews signify their grief over the de-

struction of the Temple by going unshaven, abstaining from both sexual relations and study of the Torah, and sitting on a low stool in the manner of a mourner who "sits *shiva.*" Yet if the destruction of the Temple in 70 C.E. marks the end of something sacred in Jewish tradition, it also marks the beginning of rabbinical Judaism, a new and vital faith that would prove to be far more crucial to the survival of the Jewish people than a temple built of cedar and stone.

Of the many Judaisms that flowered at that moment in history, rabbinical Judaism was clearly the most successful. After 70 C.E., priests were wholly replaced by rabbis—the word "rabbi" literally means "my master" and honors the role of the rabbi as a teacher. The Temple in Jerusalem was replaced by the synagogue, a house of prayer and study—and not a single synagogue but a countless number of them. The altar of sacrifice, where sheep and goats were butchered and burnt whole as sacrificial offerings to the God of Israel, was replaced by the *shulhan*, the table on which—then as now—the scroll of the Torah is unrolled and read aloud to the prayerful and studious congregants. Although the elaborate rules and procedures for ritual offerings are preserved in both the Torah and the Talmud—and the morning and afternoon prayer services in the synagogue are a faint echo of the morning and afternoon sacrifices in the Temple—the fact is that the old orthodoxy was wholly superseded by a new one.

The birth of classical Judaism, which rose from the flames of the ruined Temple in 70 C.E. and endures to this day, is an undeniably stirring drama. And the emblematic figure in that story is a revered rabbi called Yohanan Ben Zakkai,[1] one of the thousands of Jewish men, women, and children who were caught inside the walls of Jerusalem during the long Roman siege that preceded the destruction of the Temple. Buried away in the back story of Yohanan Ben Zakkai are clues to the old traditions that were obliterated along with the Temple, and the new ones that flowered in their place.

The Rabbi in the Coffin

Yohanan Ben Zakkai, according to rabbinical tradition, is a peace-loving sage and scholar who opposes the making of war against Rome. He foresees the failure of Jewish resistance, the ruin of Jerusalem, and the destruction of the Temple. He even prophesies that Vespasian, the general who commanded the expeditionary force in Judea, will rise to the rank of Roman emperor—a prophecy that ultimately earns him the favor of Vespasian and the opportunity to escape from Jerusalem in 68 C.E. and find refuge in the coastal town of Yavneh. There he is able to establish a yeshiva where the vast body of Jewish law and learning will be preserved even as the Temple is razed and the Jewish people are sent into their long exile.

His flight from Jerusalem, as one version of the story goes, is accomplished by a clever if undignified ruse. His followers place him in a coffin, add a chunk of rotting meat to simulate the odor of a putrefying corpse, and seek permission from the Jewish soldiers on the barricades to pass the coffin out of the besieged city for burial. Fooled by the sickening stench, the guards hasten the coffin on its way. Once beyond the fortifications, the coffin is unsealed, the rabbi rises to his feet, and he is escorted to Vespasian. The old Jewish rabbi greets the Roman general with a polished Latin phrase that amounts to a prophecy of his future high office: *"Ave domine imperator!"* ("Hail Lord and Emperor!") And, thus flattered by the use of a title that he has not yet won, Vespasian grants the rabbi permission to join the other sages at Yavneh—and thus is Judaism saved from extinction.

The tale is mostly fanciful, and what is left out of the rabbinical saga is details that cast Yohanan Ben Zakkai in a rather more ambiguous light. The Jewish resistance against Rome can be seen as a heroic war of national liberation fought by a determined guerilla army against a pagan army of occupation. But Yohanan Ben Zakkai belonged to a faction that sought to make peace with Rome, and one reason that he contrived to leave the embattled city of Jerusalem was to escape the reign of terror that the Zealots and their allies inflicted upon Jews who were regarded as too friendly to Rome. That is why it was necessary to smuggle the rabbi out in a coffin; the soldiers who guarded the gates were as concerned with keeping fainthearted Jewish defenders *in* Jerusalem as they were with keeping the Roman attackers out.

Significantly, no such implication of disloyalty to the Jewish cause is found in the rabbinical sources, where Yohanan Ben Zakkai is celebrated as one of the leading sages of his generation and, indeed, one of the saviors of Judaism. From our perspective, we can identify him as one of the inventors of what we recognize today as rabbinical Judaism, a faith that replaced blood sacrifice and temple ritual with study, prayer, and good works. At Yavneh, Yohanan Ben Zakkai and other sages like him undertook the creative and crucial enterprise that would eventually result in the canonization of the Hebrew Bible in 90 c.e. and the completion of the Talmud in 500 c.e.—the very roots of the "Tree of Life" that is Judaism today. "[H]e deliberately diverted Judaism," insists historian Cecil Roth, "from the heroic but dangerous path on which it had begun to tread."[2]

Even while the Temple still stood, however, Yohanan Ben Zakkai was already making over the faith of ancient Israel by abrogating some of the weirder rites and practices that are described in the Torah. If a woman is suspected of adultery, for example, the Torah prescribes a ritual of sympathetic magic to determine her guilt or innocence: the priest is to write the curses for adultery on a parchment, wash the ink into a vessel, mix it with holy water and dust from the floor of the Tabernacle, and then force the woman to drink the potion. If she is innocent of the charge, nothing will happen, but if she is guilty, then she will be betrayed by her own body with telltale signs of guilt: "Her belly shall swell, and her thigh shall rot" (Num. 5:27). Or, as another example, if the corpse of a murdered man is found but his murderer is not, the Torah instructs the priests to break the neck of a heifer as a symbolic punishment (Deut. 21:4). But Yohanan Ben Zakkai argued for the abandonment of these rites, so primitive and atavistic, even though they were plainly written into the code of laws that devout Jews believe to have passed "from the mouth of God to the hand of Moses."[3]

In place of superstition and sympathetic magic, Yohanan Ben Zakkai preached a faith in which prayer and piety were tempered with compassion and good works. Thus, when the Temple was destroyed—and with it the whole apparatus of animal sacrifice—he was ready to supply an entirely new approach to the worship of God. One of the most meaningful of the many stories told about him depicts an encounter between

Yohanan Ben Zakkai and a rabbi called Joshua who insists that the Jews are now doomed because the altar of sacrifice where they atoned for their sins is gone and there is no place else where they are permitted to make guilt offerings as specifically commanded in the Torah. Not unlike the Maccabees two centuries before, Yohanan Ben Zakkai feels empowered to interpret the Torah according to the changing demands of the world in which he lived. And thus his affirming response to the despairing Joshua is one of the defining moments of Jewish history, a moment of daring innovation and invention.

"My son, be not grieved," says Yohanan Ben Zakkai, who goes on to quote the words of the prophet Hosea. "We have another atonement as effective as this, and what is it? It is acts of loving-kindness, as it is said, 'For I desire mercy and not sacrifice.' "[4]

Twenty-four Judaisms

The Talmud preserves a suggestion that the rabbis and sages of antiquity blamed the Jewish people for their own misfortune. God allowed the Temple to be destroyed, they propose, precisely because the Jews had splintered into so many sects and schisms, each one at war with the others, and none of them worthy of the place where the God of Israel "caused his name to dwell." In fact, one ancient rabbi counted no less than twenty-four various sects and schisms—two dozen "Judaisms"—within the shattered Jewish world of the first century. "Israel did not go into exile," the Talmud insists, "until it had turned into twenty-four parties of heretics."[5]

Yohanan Ben Zakkai, however, embraced one of the many different "Judaisms" that competed for the hearts and minds of the Jewish people. He was a leading member of the Pharisees, perhaps the most familiar and ultimately the most successful of the competing factions. The Pharisees, unlike various other movements in Judaism, believed in resurrection, life after death, and divine rewards and punishments in "the World to Come," all of which are borrowed from or influenced by Greek and other pagan creeds. Above all, the Pharisees embraced the simple but crucial idea that a pious Jew is fully empowered to interpret and innovate upon the Torah. It's an idea that can be traced back to the Maccabees and all the way forward through the next two thousand years of rabbinical Judaism. And it's an idea that continues to keep Judaism and the Jewish people fully alive today.

The idea is best expressed in the fact that the Pharisees recognized the authority of two bodies of law: the 613 commandments of the Torah as preserved in written form in the Pentateuch ("Five Scrolls"), and the so-called Oral Torah, an ever-growing collection of laws and customs that were preserved through oral transmission from generation to generation over the centuries. According to a tale in the Talmud, the Oral Torah, too, was given to Moses on Sinai, invisibly written between the lines of the Torah. But the rabbinical tale misses the whole point of the oral tradition in Judaism: the Oral Torah is an accumulation of law that reflects the pragmatic and highly creative efforts of the Jewish community to answer questions and solve problems that are not squarely addressed in the Torah itself.

By contrast, the Sadducees, principal rivals of the Pharisees, recognized the authority of the Torah alone and rejected not only the oral law but the whole process of discussion and debate, invention and innovation, that created the Oral Torah in the first place and sustained it as a vital and growing organism. The Sadducees represented the wealthy and aristocratic elements of the Jewish people, and they guarded the primacy of the Temple and the privileges of the priesthood in the spiritual and political life of the Jewish state. Indeed, the very term "Sadducee" probably derives from the name of Zadok, the High Priest who served the two greatest kings in Jewish tradition, David and Solomon. Among the many points of conflict between the Sadducees and Pharisees was the insistence of the Sadducees on a strict and literal reading of the Torah, a fact that helps to explain why the Pharisees survived and the Sadducees did not. Rabbinical Judaism in all of its richness is the legacy of the Pharisees, but the Sadducees are remembered only as the die-hard advocates of an idea that failed—the idea of Bible literalism. And so enduring is the bad odor of the Sadducees that the term is sometimes used in the Talmud as a code word for "heretics" and "Gentiles."

Yet a third faction was the Essenes, a sect that rejected not only the

Pharisees and the Sadducees but the status quo of the Jewish state in its entirety. Afire with utopian dreams and apocalyptic nightmares, they fled to the desolate wilderness of the Judean desert and set up little enclaves where they studied their own fearful texts, practiced their own harshly ascetic disciplines, and awaited the terrible but glorious day when God would finally judge the Jewish people once and for all. They scorned the rest of the Jewish community in much the same way that Ezra once disdained the *Am Ha'aretz*, and they regarded themselves in much the same way that Ezra looked on the "Holy Seed," the cleansed and purified elite. So strict was their vow of celibacy that cold baths were a ritual obligation, for example, and so devout was their observance of the Sabbath that they were expected to refrain from bowel movements from sundown to sundown. The Essenes probably included the men and women whose desert encampments were discovered at a place called Qumran and whose library consisted of what we today call the Dead Sea Scrolls.

But the "Judaisms" of the first century C.E. were hardly limited to the Pharisees, Sadducees, and Essenes. The countertraditions of Judaism— the two dozen sects and schisms that so troubled the Talmudic sages—included a great many other expressions of the spiritual and political longings of the Jewish people. A few of them are deeply familiar to us because of what happened after they branched off from Judaism: John the Baptist was a Jewish sectarian, for example, and so was a charismatic preacher from Galilee known in Aramaic as Yehoshua (Joshua) and in Latin as Jesus. Many more of them are so unfamiliar that the ancient writings preserve only their names and little or nothing about their teachings: the "Knockers" and the "Awakeners," for example, the "Water Drinkers" and the "Morning Ablutionists" and the "Sun Worshippers," and the nameless followers of various self-proclaimed prophets and royal pretenders and would-be messiahs, one called Athronges the Shepherd and another called Simon the Royal Slave and yet another who is recalled only as "the Egyptian."

The Zealots, too, were among the many rival "Judaisms" that existed at this decisive moment in history. These rival Judaisms made their appeal to not only the educated and propertied elite that regarded itself as the "Holy Seed" but the poor and disempowered Jews who composed the

Am Ha'aretz. The Zealots were not content with the theological debate that raged among the city dwellers of Jerusalem or the self-mortification of the desert monastics at the Dead Sea; they were "Fighting Jews" for whom physical courage and military prowess were as crucial as piety and true belief.

"The Sights You See Will Drive You Mad"

The Zealots, as we have noted, were founded by Judah of Gamalah, the son of an "archbrigand" who had been hanged by Herod as a common criminal. But the lengthy Roman occupation of Judea had long since hammered the "bandits" and "brigands" into partisans and guerillas, and the Jewish War was the crucible that fully transformed them into patriots and revolutionaries who fought a war of national liberation. Their ranks included not only the old stalwarts but also the slaves whom they had freed from servitude and the poor folk whose debt records they had burned. At the same time, the Zealots and their allies in the Jewish resistance embraced the same blend of patriotism and fundamentalism that had once characterized the Maccabees, and the acts of terror carried out by the Sicarii were pointedly directed at Jewish collaborators rather than at Roman procurators or legionnaires.

By the time Yohanan Ben Zakkai was preparing his flight to Yavneh, however, the Romans had already managed to corner the Jewish fighters behind the walls of Jerusalem. And the defenders of the besieged city fought each other with as much resolve and ruthlessness as they fought the Romans. The Zealots controlled the Temple, Simon Bar Giora and the Sicarii dominated the upper city, and various other factions took and held strongholds around Jerusalem. Still, the rival forces in what amounted to a civil war in miniature agreed on one thing: "ruthless action against all who favored compromise," according to historian Cecil Roth, "or even breathed the word 'surrender.' "[6] And so Jerusalem endured not only a siege but also a reign of terror not unlike the one that would later be visited on Paris during the French revolution.

Famine, plague, and the random impact of stones and arrows fired into the city by the surrounding Roman army took thousands of lives during the prolonged siege of Jerusalem that finally ended with the destruction of the Temple in 70 C.E. Indeed, the holy city was a scene of horror and desperation that is predicted in the Book of Deuteronomy, which was composed several hundred years earlier but applies with uncanny accuracy to the events of the Jewish War. "The sights you see will drive you mad," Moses is shown to warn the Israelites in Deuteronomy, describing how the menfolk will one day fight their own wives for the flesh of their children and how the womenfolk will be reduced to eating the afterbirth of their newborns at an unspecified moment in history when Israel will be conquered by a foreign army (Deut. 28:34) (NEB).

Now the old prophecy came to pass. One Jewish woman within the walls of Jerusalem, literally driven mad with starvation during the Roman siege, roasted and ate the flesh of the baby who had suckled at her breast. When a few of her fellow Jews caught the aroma and searched her out, they demanded to know where she had hidden the roasted meat. "This is mine own son!" cries the desperate Jewish mother. "Come, eat of this food, for I have eaten of it myself!"[7]

Only when the rebels heard the ominous sound of Roman battering rams at work on the outer defenses of Jerusalem did they put an end to the reign of terror and the civil war and turn to the defense of the city. By then, however, it was too late. The Romans set fire to the gates of Jerusalem, fought their way into the city, and trapped the last of the Zealots and the Sicarii and the other Jewish soldiers on the Temple Mount. At last, the defenders were defeated, the Temple itself was destroyed, and the Roman victory in the Jewish War was complete. Simon Bar Giora was taken to Rome, where he was dragged in chains behind the triumphant Roman general who had captured him and then thrown to his death from a high rock.

A few of the Zealots managed to escape from Jerusalem after it fell to the Roman army, and they sought refuge in the fortress that Herod had built on the rugged peak called Masada. As they sheltered within its impregnable walls, a Roman army encamped at the base of the mountain, and a labor battalion of Jewish prisoners of war were set to work on a ramp that would allow the Romans to reach the fortifications for a final assault. Eleazar Ben Yair, the rebel leader, exhorted the men and women who had followed him to Masada to take their own lives rather than surrender. The defenders cast lots to determine who would be charged with the task of cutting the throats of the nearly one thousand men, women, and children before taking their own lives. When the Romans finally breached the walls in 72 c.e., they found only Jewish corpses.

Peacemakers and Swordbearers

Simon Bar Giora and Yohanan Ben Zakkai represent two sets of conflicting values and strategies that are deeply woven into the fabric of Jewish history. The rebel commander, of course, is moved to violence by a distrust and even hatred of secular authority that is first and often expressed in the Torah and the Prophets. The old rabbi, by contrast, is convinced that the authority of secular government is the best defense against the violent impulses of his fellow human beings, a notion that is first recorded in the Oral Torah. What's at stake in the contest between these two opposing traditions, as we shall come to see, is the very survival of the Jewish people.

Simon Bar Giora was honoring the older of the two traditions when he raised a sword against the armies of the Roman emperor and their Jewish collaborators. Moses himself is shown to caution the Israelites against the excesses of rule by a king, and the prophet Samuel delivers a tirade against monarchy when the Israelites clamor for a king of their own. "This," warns Samuel, "will be the manner of the king that shall reign over you."

> He will take your sons to be his horsemen and to plow his ground and to reap his harvest and to make his instruments of war, and they shall run before his chariots. And he will take your daughters to be perfumers and to be cooks, and to be bakers. And he will take your fields, and your vineyards, and your oliveyards, even the best of them. And ye shall cry out in that day because of your king whom ye shall have chosen, and the Lord will not answer you in that day (1 Sam. 8:11–18).[8]

Yohanan Ben Zakkai considered the hard facts of Jewish history and reached an entirely different conclusion about kings in particular and secular authority in general. His point of view, too, can be found among the traditions and countertraditions that are recorded in the Bible, where the atrocities and excesses of ordinary men and women—murder and dismemberment, gang rape and mass abduction, riot and civil war— are explained as the inevitable result of ungoverned humankind: "In those days there was no king in Israel," goes the mantra of the Book of Judges, "[and] every man did that which was right in his own eyes" (Judg. 21:25). The same notion was spoken aloud by one of Yohanan Ben Zakkai's contemporaries, Rabbi Hanina. "Pray for the peace of the ruling power," goes his aphorism as preserved in the Oral Torah, "since but for fear of it men would have swallowed each other alive."[9]

The Torah itself shows us a moment when the Israelites are confronted with a choice between making peace with a powerful ruler and making war against him over a matter of honor. Dinah, the only daughter of the patriarch Jacob, has been sexually disgraced by a Canaanite prince called Shechem, although it is not entirely clear whether the incident was a rape, a seduction, or a Romeo-and-Juliet love affair between young people from different tribes. In any event, Shechem falls in love with Dinah, and his father, a chieftain of the Canaanites, asks Jacob to consent to the marriage of the young man and woman—and he suggests that the marriage will bring an era of prosperity and peaceful coexistence to the Israelites and Canaanites.

"Let us ally ourselves in marriage; you shall give us your daughters, and you shall take ours in exchange," proposes Hamor, the Canaanite chieftain. "The country is open to you; make your home in it, move about freely, and acquire land of your own" (Gen. 34:9–10).[10]

Jacob is perfectly willing to accept the offer, but two of his twelve sons, Simeon and Levi, are secretly shocked at the notion, and they carry out a guileful and ruthless conspiracy to frustrate their father's efforts at peacemaking. Invoking the divine law and pious tradition of the Israelites, they insist that the bridegroom and his father and the entire male population of Canaanites submit to circumcision as a preliminary to the marriage of Shechem and Dinah. And, once the Canaanites have been rendered helpless and confined to their beds by the painful surgical procedure, the two brothers strap on their swords, slip into the unsuspecting town, and slaughter them all.

"You have made my name stink among the people of the country," complains Jacob when he learns of the massacre that his sons have carried out. "My numbers are few; if they muster against me and attack me, I shall be destroyed."

"Is our sister to be treated as a common whore?" retort Simeon and Levi, a pair of vengeful young men for whom honor matters far more than *realpolitik* or military exigencies (Gen. 34:30–31).[11]

The bitter confrontation between a statesmanlike father and his militant sons will be repeated again and again over the long history of the Jewish people. Peacemakers like Rabbi Yohanan Ben Zakkai followed Jacob's way, and swordbearers like Simon Bar Giora followed the way of Simeon and Levi. Before the Jewish War finally came to an end, the rival factions among the Jewish people would literally swallow each other alive.

The Turncoat General

So the Zealots picked up the sword, the Pharisees retreated into piety and study, and the Essenes waited out the end of the world in self-imposed isolation. But another strategy for survival that figures crucially in the preservation of the Jewish people throughout history—making peace with the ruling powers rather than fighting or fleeing—was also at work during the Jewish War. The man whose life and work best symbolizes that strategy is the same man to whom we are indebted for most of what we know about the Jewish world in the first century C.E., a man called Josephus.

Flavius Josephus, as his name is recorded in his own considerable writings, was born in Jerusalem in 37 C.E. as Yoseph Ben Mattitiyahu, a wealthy and aristocratic Jew of priestly descent. Yoseph studied under the Pharisees, the Sadducees, and the Essenes, as well as a hermit known as Bannus the Anchorite, or so he says of himself, and he acquired a familiarity with Greco-Roman culture on a journey to Rome in the year 64. And, thanks to his high standing in the Jewish community, Yoseph was recruited at the age of thirty to serve as governor general of Galilee. But his sympathies—or, perhaps more accurately, his self-interest—lay with the Romans, and he counseled his fellow Jews against the folly of making war on Rome until it became too dangerous to say such things out loud. And so, when he was called upon to lead a Jewish army in the war against the Romans, he turned out to be a halfhearted general, and he surrendered to Vespasian at the first opportunity. Unlike the Maccabees or the Zealots, Josephus preferred dishonor over death, and he managed to avoid the mass suicide carried out by his fellow Jewish fighters at the moment of surrender.

To hear Josephus tell the tale, he promptly offered Vespasian the very same prophecy that is credited to Yohanan Ben Zakkai in rabbinical tradition: Josephus revealed to Vespasian that he was destined to be emperor of Rome. Thus did he succeed in ingratiating himself with the Roman conqueror of Judea, who not only spared the life of the defeated Jewish general but brought him to Rome as a guest rather than a captive, afforded him shelter and sustenance, and made it possible for him to spend the rest of his life as a Roman citizen and a man of letters. And thus did Yoseph Ben Mattitayhu, the turncoat general of the Jewish War, reinvent himself as Flavius Josephus, author of histories and memoirs that survive to this day as a remarkable eyewitness account by a man who was a participant in some of the most decisive events in the history of the Jewish people.

Josephus freely admits that he put himself in service to the Romans during the Jewish War. At the siege of Jerusalem, he was repeatedly sent by Titus, son of Vespasian, to harangue his fellow Jews in the hope of persuading at least a few of the fainthearted to open the gates and allow the Romans to enter. He was rewarded for his efforts with taunts and jests and, eventually, a well-aimed stone that struck his head and knocked him out cold, and he was very nearly carried off by a few vengeful Jews intent on rough justice. He expresses only contempt and loathing for the very men whom we might prefer to see as Jewish patriots and freedom fighters: Josephus is our principal source for the accounts that characterize the Zealots, the Sicarii and their comrades-in-arms as "bandits" and "brigands." He blames the Jewish rebel leaders for blundering into the catastrophe of the Jewish War out of misdirected ambition—and he blames the Jewish people for blindly and stupidly following their leaders into war.

"God takes care of mankind," Josephus muses, "but men perish by those miseries which they madly and voluntarily bring upon them-selves."[12]

But one crucial point must not be overlooked: Josephus never re-nounced his faith or his identity as a Jew, and he never regarded himself as a betrayer of Judaism or the Jewish people. Quite to the contrary, he earnestly believed that the war against Rome was a tragic mistake that brought only catastrophe to the Jews, and he was convinced that he had acted in the best interests of the Jewish people by turning his coat and joining the Roman cause.

Of course, the turncoat general has been regarded as so odious that he has been mostly written out of pious Jewish tradition. Yet Josephus cannot be so readily written off. He may have been arrogant and opportunistic and self-serving, but he always regarded himself as, above all, an advocate for his fellow Jews. *Against Apion*, for example, is an earnest and even heroic effort by Josephus to defend the Jewish people against the slanders of anti-Semitic agitation and propaganda, in which he used his own celebrity and his considerable rhetorical skills to refute the "impudent lies" of Apion and other Jew-haters of the ancient world.[13] Indeed, *all* of the writings of Josephus, just like those of another highly assimilated Jew-ish author of the first century, Philo of Alexandria, represent an effort to retell and reinterpret Jewish history and religion in terms that were de-signed to ingratiate the Jewish people with the Greco-Roman world. And so, again like Philo, Josephus can be seen as someone who tried to be both be a good Jew and a good Hellenist at the same time.

That is why, as painful as it may be for some of us to admit, the ma-jority of modern Jews tend to resemble Josephus more than, say, the pious Yohanan Ben Zakkai or the zealous Simon Bar Giora. More often than not, the strategy for survival that Josephus embraced in antiquity served the Jewish people well over the next two thousand years of their history. Only in the twentieth century—and only against the barbarism of Nazi Germany and its allies—did the strategy of accommodation and assimilation turn out to be an utter failure. As historian Mireille Hadas-Lebel puts it, Josephus can be seen as "a man aspiring to become a citizen of the world."[14] For any modern Jew who shares the same aspiration, Josephus is both an example and a caution.

The Coming of the Messiah-King

Among the most innovative and longest-enduring traditions in Jewish history is a notion that is mentioned only briefly and obliquely in the Bible itself—the God of Israel will one day send a savior to redeem the Jewish people from their earthly sufferings. The title by which we know the savior and redeemer is, of course, "Messiah," a term that derives from the Hebrew word *mashiach* and literally means "anointed one." As used in the Bible, the word identifies anyone who has been singled out by God for a special role in history: Saul and David, for example, are "anointed ones" in the sense that the prophet Samuel pours oil over their heads during the ritual of coronation. Starting with the destruction of the Temple, however, and continuing over the next two millennia, the yearning for a Messiah will be transformed first into something mystical and even magical, and, much later, into a wholly secular and political movement that created the modern State of Israel.

The doctrine of the Messiah first emerged as the solution to a theological problem that confronted the Jews of antiquity when the Davidic dynasty finally came to an end in 586 B.C.E. After all, God is shown to promise eternal and unconditional kingship to the house of David in the Book of Samuel: "Thy throne shall be established forever," God tells David (2 Sam. 7:16). When, despite God's plain and unequivocal promise, no mortal king sat on the throne of David in Jerusalem after the Babylonian Conquest, his words were reinterpreted in a wholly new way. God did not mean that a mortal king would always reign in the here and now. Rather, God would send a spiritual king—a Messiah—to redeem the Jewish people at some unknown and unknowable point in the distant future. According to a deeply mystical tradition, the Messiah would be "a shoot out of the stock of Jesse" (Isa. 11:1)—that is, a descendant of David.

"If the Messiah-King comes from among the living, David will be his name," goes the rabbinical spin that was put on the divine promise. "If he comes from among the dead, it will be David himself."[15]

By the time of the Jewish War, the sufferings of the Jewish people were so acute that the idea of the Messiah was transformed yet again; the soulful yearnings for the coming of a savior changed from a theological to a political matter. Simon Bar Giora, for example, and some of the other charismatic leaders of the Zealots did not discourage their followers from regarding *them* as likely candidates for messiahship. Some of the magicians and miracle workers who worked the crowds in the cities and towns of Judea sometimes struck the same provocative stance. And the political implications of posing as the Messiah were hardly lost on the Romans—the army of occupation in Judea was under standing orders from four successive emperors throughout the first century "to hunt out and execute any Jew who claimed to be a descendant of King David," a claim that was equivalent to an act of insurrection.[16]

Thus, for example, the guerilla commander who led a second war of liberation against Rome in 132 c.e., a man called Simon Ben Kosiba, was hailed as the "King Messiah" by the leading rabbi of his era, Rabbi Akiva ben Yosef. To symbolize his messiahship, Akiva changed Simon's name from Ben Kosiba to Bar Kokhba, an Aramaic phrase that means "Son of the Star."[17] Thus did Akiva invoke one of those ornate but oblique passages of the Torah in which generations of yearning Jewish readers detected the divine promise of a Messiah:

> *There shall step forth a star out of Jacob,*
> *And a scepter shall rise out of Israel.*
> (Num. 24:17) (JPS)

Akiva, however, was proven wrong. Bar Kokhba may have briefly succeeded in taking back Jerusalem from the Romans, and he certainly reigned long enough as the self-proclaimed *nasi* ("prince") of a sovereign Jewish state to mint his own coins—"Year One of the Redemption of Israel" is how his coinage is dated—but the Romans defeated him by force of arms in 135 c.e. Both the guerilla commander and the good-hearted rabbi were made to suffer a protracted and painful death by torture. According to an old and dolorous tradition, the so-called Bar Kokhba Revolt was finally crushed on the Ninth of Av, the same day on which the First and Second Temples were destroyed.

Significantly, the clearer-headed rabbis of Roman-occupied Judea had refused to join the revered Rabbi Akiva in embracing the "Son of the Star" as the Messiah, and they bestowed upon Bar Kokhba yet a third variation of his name—Bar Koziba, the "Son of a Lie." They saw how dangerous it could be to incite the patriotic fervor of the Jewish people, and they exhibited a certain healthy skepticism when it came to weighing the messianic claims of a man like Bar Kokhba: "Grass will grow in your jawbones, Akiva ben Yosef," said one pragmatic rabbi called Yohanan ben Tortha, "and the Messiah will not have appeared."[18] The defeat of Bar Kokhba imprinted on rabbinical Judaism something that would endure for the next eighteen hundred years—a fear of the fighting Jew and a loathing for the False Messiah.

Once rid of the latest generation of Jewish freedom fighters, the Romans resolved to put an end to the spirit of resistance among the Jews once and for all. As if to erase even the memory of Jewish sovereignty, the Roman province of Judea was renamed Palestina, a reference to the Philistines in place of the Jews. Jerusalem was renamed Aelia Capitolina in honor of the family name of the Roman emperor—a project that was announced even before the Bar Kokhba Revolt and may have been one of its causes. The Temple Mount was cleared of the last traces of the Second Temple, and a temple to Jupiter was raised in its place. Jews were evicted from Jerusalem and forbidden to come within sight of the Temple Mount except on a single day of the year set aside for a ritual of mourning that was characterized as an opportunity to "buy their tears."[19] Not until 1967, when the army of the modern State of Israel fought and won the Six-Day War, were Jerusalem and the Temple Mount restored to Jewish sovereignty.

"The Four Cubits of the Torah"

The Jewish people had known displacement and dispersion even in distant biblical antiquity, of course, but now their long exile began in earnest. The traditional homeland of the tribe of Judah was in ruin and desolation, and Judaism was sheltered and sustained in the far-flung communities of the Diaspora. And, according to the conventional wisdom of Jewish history, Judaism turned in on itself. War weary and heartbroken by a century of unremitting chaos and destruction, we are asked to believe, Judaism was defined by the peaceful and scholarly musings of the rabbis and sages as they are recorded in the Talmud and other rabbinical writings of antiquity. "From now on, Judaism contracted itself within the limits of the four cubits of the Torah," writes Ya'akov Meshorer, "and the earthly Jerusalem gave place to the heavenly Jerusalem."[20]

The truth is far more intriguing, if also less elegant and exalted. "Classical" Judaism may have become the focus of Jewish piety and scholarship, but it was never the only expression of Jewish aspirations. Some Jews, as we shall see, were alchemists and magicians and wonder workers. Some were mystics who spent their lives in the search for hidden and forbidden meanings within the Torah. To the distress and disgust of the rabbis and sages, the *Am Ha'aretz* were afforded the opportunity to worship God through the ecstasies of song and dance. Now and then, a Jew convinced himself that he was the long-awaited and long-delayed Messiah—and, on occasion, he managed to convince not a few of his fellow Jews, sometimes by feats of magic, sometimes by masterful rhetoric, and sometimes by force of a charismatic personality, thereby acting on the same impulse toward innovation and invention that has produced so many "Judaisms" over so many centuries.

Conventional wisdom, however, proposes that at least one strand of Judaism was entirely played out by the defeat of Bar Kokhba. The fighting Jew slumbered over the next two millennia and reawakened only in the twentieth century, when a fusion of messianism and nationalism prompted the explosion of Zionism that created the modern state of Israel and fundamentally redefined what it means to be a Jew. Only then did Jews begin to name their children Giora, and only then did Jewish men and women in uniform take an oath to the survival of the Jewish state amid the ruins of Masada, the very place where a thousand Jewish men, women, and children took their own lives rather than surrender to the enemy. Significantly, the stirring phrase "Never again" was used in modern Jewish tradition in reference to Masada long before it was applied to the Holocaust.

But the fact is that a faint memory of the fighting Jew—and, specifically, a memory of Bar Kokhba—is embedded deep within the traditions of rabbinical Judaism, a strand of Judaism that owes much more to the rabbi who was smuggled out of Jerusalem in a coffin than to the Jews who died on their feet on the ramparts through which he passed. Once a year, on the occasion of a Jewish festival called Lag Ba'omer, the children of the ghettos and the *shtetls* of Eastern Europe were permitted to leave the stuffy schoolrooms where they pored over the pages of the Talmud, and they were taken to the fields or the woods for a day of picnicking and a night of bonfires. And, by long tradition, the Jewish children were encouraged to fashion and play with bows and arrows.

The origins and meanings of Lag Ba'omer are buried under centuries of theological overgrowth. The name of the festival refers to the harvest days that are counted out on the Jewish ritual calendar—an *omer* is a sheaf of barley. Some Talmudic sources suggest that Lag Ba'omer marks the day when manna first fell from heaven to feed the wandering Israelites in the wilderness of Sinai, and others propose that it was the day when a plague that had afflicted the students of Rabbi Akiva finally abated. The tradition of the bow and arrow is given a lyrical and even a mystical interpretation in rabbinical writings: the bow is meant to symbolize the rainbow that God painted across the sky after the Flood as a symbol of his promise not to destroy humankind.

But the bow and arrow can be understood in a far more literal way. According to Yigal Yadin, the Israeli general and archaeologist who excavated both Masada and the desert refuge of Bar Kokhba, the traditional observance of Lag Ba'omer is meant to conjure up the Jewish rebels who made a last stand against the Roman army in the wilderness of Judea. Over the centuries and throughout the Diaspora, he explains, when Jewish children carried their bows and arrows into the countryside, they were playing "Bar Kokhba and the Romans" in the same way that American children play "cowboys and Indians."[21] And so it was that even the most bookish of Jewish children found out for themselves what it felt like to hold a weapon in their hands, thus honoring a tradition that had once preserved the Jewish people against their worst enemies and would do so again.

Six

In the Ruined Citadel

*I billeted a strong force overnight in a citadel laid waste
in former days by other generals.
And I said to my heart:
Where are the many people who once lived here?
Where are the builders and vandals, the rulers and
paupers, the slaves and masters?*

—Samuel Ha'Nagid, *"In the Ruined Citadel"*

Diaspora" is a word from the Greek that means "dispersion," but the Hebrew word used to describe the same phenomenon in Jewish history has a slightly different meaning—*galut* means "exile." And the word is meant to carry a sting of reproach: according to both the pious faith of Orthodoxy and the secular political agenda of Zionism, a Jew belongs in Israel. That is why, for example, a Jew who goes to Israel is called an *oleh*, "one who ascends," and a Jew who leaves Israel is called a *yored*, "one who descends." So sacred is the linkage between the Jewish people and their ancestral homeland in the land of Israel that the word *aliyah*—"ascent" or "going up," a word related to *oleh*—is used to describe both the honor of being called to the Torah and the act of emigration to Israel.

"Even a Gentile female slave, if living in Israel," insisted one ancient sage, trying to come up with a description of the single most degraded person he could imagine, "is assured a share in the world to come."[1]

Of course, as we have seen, a significant fraction of the Jewish people has *always* lived in the Diaspora. The first two dispersions date back to biblical antiquity: the northern tribes of Israel were scattered and lost after the Assyrian conquest of 722 B.C.E., and the tribe of Judah was carried off to exile in Babylon in 586 B.C.E. Even after the end of the Babylonian Captivity in 538 B.C.E., however, some Jews apparently preferred to remain in their new homes in Babylon, Egypt, and elsewhere in the ancient world. Nor did they regard themselves as second-class Jews; the Jews in the Egyptian cities of Elephantine and Leontopolis, for example, built temples of their own, thus defying the decree in the Book of Deuteronomy that awarded a monopoly on sacrifice to Yahweh to the Temple in Jerusalem.

After the Jewish War and the Bar Kokhba Revolt, however, the majority of the Jewish people came to live outside the land of Israel. They redefined themselves and reinvented their religion so they could remain Jews in far-flung communities all over the ancient world. Their Judaism—a Judaism stripped of priestly and Temple-based rituals and designed for export to the Diaspora—is what we recognize today as "classical" Judaism, a faith that can be practiced anywhere in the world where ten Jews gather together to pray. Indeed, the act of self-invention that created rabbinical Judaism in the first century C.E. is exactly what enabled the Jewish people to survive two thousand years in exile.

The Wailing Wall

The destruction of the Temple is still mourned in traditional Judaism. By pious tradition, musical instruments are excluded from the synagogue service precisely because they were once featured so prominently in the rituals of the long-lost Temple. The breaking of a glass at the climax of a Jewish wedding is intended as a reminder of the destruction of the Temple even at the moment of greatest joy. And, until very recently, the last remnant of the Temple in Jerusalem was called the Wailing Wall, a pilgrimage site where Jews gathered to keen and wail over the rubble that symbolized the fate of ancient Judaism.

"Deplorable sight," wrote Albert Einstein when he visited Jerusalem in 1922 and beheld "Jews swaying in anguished prayer" at the Wailing Wall. "[A] people with a Past without a Present."[2]

But it is also true that the new Judaism readily translated the Temple from a pile of rubble into a shimmering theological symbol. Yohanan Ben Zakkai, as we have seen, was quick to suggest that acts of *hesed*—loving-kindness—were as effective as the spilling of animal blood on the Temple altar as an expression of Jewish piety. Thus, for example, when the Roman emperor Julian offered to rebuild the Temple in Jerusalem in the fourth century C.E., the elders of the Jewish community in Rome regarded his offer with suspicion and distrust; they preferred the portable version of Judaism that had proved to be so well suited to survival in the Diaspora. A symbolic Temple was far more serviceable than a real one now that the Jews were forced to live at such distances from Jerusalem.

The long exile of the Jewish people would eventually come to an end in 1948 when Jewish statehood was restored in the land of Israel. After nearly two thousand years of dispersion, the so-called Law of the Return would assure citizenship in the new Jewish homeland to every Jew in the world. And then, at the moment of greatest victory during the Six-Day War in 1967, Jewish soldiers fought their way into the Old City of Jerusalem and established Jewish sovereignty over the Temple Mount for the first time since 70 C.E. As if to express the joy and triumph and redemption that the retaking of the Temple Mount represents in Jewish history, what was called the Wailing Wall for twenty centuries is now called the Western Wall.

Nowadays, it is considered distasteful and even slightly disgraceful in Jewish circles to use the mournful old phrase in reference to the Western Wall. And the disdain says something profound and crucial about how the Diaspora has come to be regarded in Israel: Jews need no longer wail over the Wall for the same reason they need no longer linger in the Diaspora; today, they can live in an independent Jewish state for the first time since the days of the Maccabees. The subtext of the new tradition, however, is something harsher and more judgmental: Jews who stubbornly remain in the Diaspora are shunning their duty to build and defend the Jewish homeland, and they are foolishly placing themselves at risk of fresh outbreaks of anti-Semitism, if not a new Holocaust. That is why, for example, the Museum of the Diaspora in Israel is described by historian Sander L. Gilman as "a counterweight to Yad Va-Shem," the memorial to the victims of the Holocaust—one acknowledges the achievements of the Diaspora and the other one admonishes us to remember the ultimate catastrophe of the Diaspora.[3] "[T]he overarching model for Jewish history has been that of the center . . . and the periphery," Gilman explains. " 'Israel,' the lost Garden of Eden, the City on the Hill, is its center; all the rest of Jewish experience is on the periphery of the Diaspora."[4]

Of course, the history of the Diaspora can be written as a series of assaults and insults that were intended not only to humiliate the Jewish people but to eradicate them. Indeed, we will encounter many of these outrages in the pages ahead. Some of the most notorious examples—the Crusades, the Inquisition, the Khmielnicki pogroms—are only the worst moments in a long ordeal of fear and pain, oppression and impoverishment, even mass murder. That is why, in a real sense, the Holocaust can be traced all the way back to the fifth century C.E., when the synagogue of Antioch was destroyed by a mob and the corpses in a local Jewish cemetery were dug up and put to the flames.

"Why did they not burn the living Jews," asked the Roman emperor Zeno when the incident was reported to him, "along with the dead?"[5]

But the history of the Diaspora is *not* a tale of unrelieved despair. Indeed, an argument can be made that classical Judaism in all of its richness is purely a phenomenon of the Diaspora, a faith and a culture that exists only because the Temple was destroyed and the Jewish people were scattered. Judaism continued to grow and change, to improvise and innovate, precisely because the Jewish people were continually confronted with both new perils and new opportunities in the Diaspora. And even if the cherished dream of a restored Jewish homeland took on life-or-death implications during the Holocaust, the Diaspora has never been more vital and vigorous than it is today, a fact that may not fit comfortably into the pieties of Orthodoxy or the theories of Zionism but remains self-evidently true.

Paper and Stone

To this day, some Jews still pore over the pages of the Talmud in conscious imitation of the very oldest traditions of rabbinical Judaism, committing long passages to memory and engaging in the classical form of dialectics known as *pilpul*. They strive to conform their lives to the vast assortment of rules and regulations for the practice of Judaism collectively known as *Halakhah*. Orthodoxy and other highly observant movements tether themselves to *Halakhah* with a short line; the Conservative movement is still linked to *Halakhah* but the line is much longer and looser; and Reform and Reconstructionist Jews have cut the cord—or, at least, that's how the Orthodox see it.

Inevitably, the point is made in a joke. A Jewish man buys a sleek new sports car and then seeks to find out whether the Talmud prescribes a suitable way to observe such a momentous event in one's life. He starts by visiting an Orthodox rabbi and asking if there is a *b'rukha* ("blessing") that one ought to recite over a Ferrari Testarossa. "What's a Ferrari Testarossa?" asks the Orthodox rabbi. So the man goes to a Reform rabbi and asks the very same question: "What's a *b'rukha?*" replies the Reform rabbi.

And yet, in fact, the Talmud itself is the result of a pious but daring act of self-invention that was occasioned by the destruction of the Temple in 70 C.E., a quantum leap in the history of the Jewish people. When the First Temple was destroyed and the Jews were marched off to Babylon, for example, they responded to the emergency with an act of literary invention—they gathered the various laws and legends of ancient tradition and created the core of a new work that we now know as the Torah. With the destruction of the Second Temple and the latest exile of the Jewish people, they responded with a new and even more daring work of authorship—they collected the so-called oral law that had accumulated over the centuries and created the core of a new work that we now know as the Talmud. And it is the Talmud, even more than the Torah itself, that is the beating heart of the revolutionary new faith that we call "classical" Judaism.

"[T]he Talmud is the most important book in Jewish culture," insists

Rabbi Adin Steinsaltz, the leading Talmudist of our own times, "the backbone of creativity and of national life."[6]

So it turns out that what we are taught to call classical Judaism can be seen as a kind of countertradition that replaced the old biblical faith. The Torah, with its 613 *mitzvot*, and the rest of the Hebrew Bible, with its fiery prophetic writings, remained the core of the new Judaism. But now the so-called Oral Torah, a body of religious law long preserved by the Pharisees as a purely oral tradition, was compiled and committed to writing in a work known as the Mishnah. Completed around 200 under the leadership of Judah Ha-Nasi ("Judah the Prince," c. 135–220), a sage who was regarded with such reverence that he is known in rabbinical tradition simply as "Rabbi," the Mishnah was the foundation stone of the latest and longest enduring of the many "Judaisms."

The Mishnah itself was the subject of elaboration and disputation by generation upon generation of rabbis and sages whose commentaries on the Mishnah are known collectively as Gemarah. Thus, the Talmud evolved into what can be described as the mating of Mishnah and Gemarah, the Oral Torah itself and the elaborations upon the Oral Torah by rabbis who felt fully empowered to debate among themselves and explain to the rest of us what God intended it all to mean. But the Talmud, like the Judaism that it spawned, is a living organism, and it cannot be contained within simple categories or definitions.

To the law and commentary was added a vast, rich, and almost phantasmagorical accumulation of what is loosely called *haggadah*—legend and lore, folktales and fairytales, aphorisms and witticisms, philosophical musings and mystical speculation. And the Talmudic enterprise continued to grow and change long after the original edition of the Talmud was completed around 500 C.E. Layer upon layer of commentary on the Talmud was added by new generations of rabbis and sages, and a whole literature of rabbinical elaboration upon the Torah, known generally as Midrash, sprouted and flowered in the fertile soil of Jewish selfinvention. "Free diversity" is how one scholar describes the astounding range of ideas that were discussed and debated in the rabbinical literature of classical Judaism. "In other words," writes G. F. Moore, "there is no such thing as 'orthodox' haggadah."[7] And the same idea is expressed in a charming Talmudic tale about a disputation among the rabbis over a particularly troubling point of Halakhah. So spirited is the debate that God himself is moved to offer his own opinion from on high—and God is outvoted!

"Even a voice from Heaven," goes one Talmudic aphorism, "must be ignored if it is not on the side of justice."[8]

Here we come upon a crucial fact about rabbinical Judaism, one that is not often conceded by ultraobservant Jews who claim to be the guardians of both Torah and Talmud. Unlike the Torah, the Talmud does not purport to record the sacred pronouncements of God. Rather, the Talmud is the minutes book in which the lively and sometimes bitter debates of rabbis and scholars are recorded. Indeed, the theme of argument and counterargument is expressed in the Talmud itself as an ongoing and thoroughgoing dispute between two rabbis of the first century B.C.E., Hillel and Shammai, a pair of sages who could not seem to agree on anything. The two rabbis and their disciples—*Bet Hillel* ("House of Hillel") and *Bet Shammai* ("House of Shammai"), as they are called in the Talmud—represent the classic division of Judaism between two contending approaches, one that is kind and gentle and one that is strict and stern. Hillel represents the first approach, Shammai the second, and there is an emblematic tale that demonstrates the difference between them.

One day, a Gentile approaches each of the two rabbis and demands to be taught the Torah "while standing on one foot," thus challenging each rabbi to sum up in a few words what Judaism is all about. Shammai responds with his customary harshness and impatience, refusing to waste any time on the taunting question and sending the man away. Hillel, by contrast, is willing to pause and answer the question: "Do not do unto your neighbor that which you would not have him do unto you," says Hillel, summing up all of Judaism in the sublime words of the Golden Rule. "The rest is commentary—now go and study."[9]

The tale of Hillel and Shammai illustrates the diversity of classical Judaism, the spirit of open debate that has shaped and sustained the Jewish people over the centuries. Indeed, the debate over the meaning and effect of Jewish religious law continues to this very day as new generations of rabbis issue their own commentaries and interpretations in the form of *responsa*, new answers to new questions posed to them by their fellow Jews. But the tale of Hillel and Shammai also points toward one of the core values of Judaism. Hillel, amiable and lenient, was famed and beloved for his "generosity, piousness, and love of mankind," as Rabbi Steinsaltz sums it up, and Shammai, irascible and exacting, was known for "his consistency to the point of extremity in everything he did."[10] The Talmud, which carefully ponders the contending points of view on virtually every aspect of Judaism, expresses a clear preference when judging between Hillel and Shammai. "Both are the words of the living God," goes a Talmudic saying, "and the decision is in accordance with the House of Hillel."[11]

The "free diversity" of rabbinical Judaism explains why there are actually *two* Talmuds. The so-called Jerusalem or Palestinian Talmud, actually completed in Tiberias around 400 C.E., is the work of sages who remained in the land of Israel. The Babylonian Talmud, longer and more comprehensive than the Jerusalem Talmud, was completed a century or so later by sages who lived and worked in the emblematic site of Jewish exile, Babylon. As if to remind us of the crucial role of the Diaspora in the making of classical Judaism, the Babylonian Talmud has long been regarded in rabbinical tradition as more authoritative than the Jerusalem Talmud.

The Thirteenth Tribe

Some offshoots of ancient and medieval Judaism are so far removed from their roots that they are no longer regarded as Jewish at all. The Samaritans, for example, split off from the people of Judah in biblical antiquity, when they insisted on the right to worship Yahweh at their own temple on Mount Gerizim in northern Israel. The schism deepened over the centuries as the Samaritans embraced the Five Books of Moses but rejected the Oral Torah and the whole edifice of Talmudic Judaism. The same rejection of the Talmud characterizes the Karaites, a Jewish sect that emerged in Persia and Babylonia in the eighth century C.E. and spread as far afield as the Baltic and the Crimea. Intriguingly, the

Karaites may have absorbed the remnants of several other ancient countertraditions in Judaism, including what was left of the Sadducees who
had once contended with the Pharisees when Judaism was still a Temple-
based faith. Today, a few Samaritans and Karaites can still be found in
Israel, the United States, and Europe, but they are ever-diminishing in
number.

Significantly, the Karaites are no longer regarded as a variety of Judaism because they succeeded in doing what pious Jews only claimed to
do—they "built a wall around the Torah" and thereby cut themselves
off from the growth and change that permitted rabbinical Judaism to survive and thrive all over the Diaspora. Ironically, the schism between the
Karaites and the Jewish people may have saved their lives during the
Holocaust, when a few Karaite communities in Europe fell under the
control of Nazi Germany. Baffled by the belief system of the Karaites, the
ever-meticulous German authorities actually sought out and consulted a
couple of eminent rabbinical scholars on the question of whether or not
the Karaites were, in fact, Jews. The rabbis assured the Germans that
Karaites were *not* Jewish—and thus spared them from the killing pits and
concentration camps.

Other Judaisms of the Diaspora may have been "home-grown," as
historian Nathan Schur puts it.[12] The Jews of Ethiopia believe that they
descend directly from King Solomon by way of his marriage to the Queen
of Sheba, a biblical event that long predates the Talmud and would explain why the Oral Torah is unknown in their tradition. Some scholars
dismiss such ancient lineage as purely legendary but are still willing to
entertain the notion that the Ethiopian Jews represent "a kind of fossilized ancient Judaism," preserving and practicing the long-lost traditions of the Essenes or the Therapeutae, an even more reclusive sect, or
perhaps the Jewish communities of ancient Egypt.[13]

But the latest scholarship suggests a much different—and much more
recent—origin for the practice of Judaism in Ethiopia. According to one
theory, which has been described as "controversial" and "challenging"
and even "painful," the Ethiopian Jews may have descended from Christians who broke away from the Ethiopian Church in the fourteenth and
fifteenth centuries and sought to distinguish themselves from their fellow

Christians by embracing some of the beliefs and practices of Judaism.[14] The Ethiopian Jews call themselves *Beta Esra'el* ("House of Israel"), but they came to be known among their fellow Ethiopians as Falashas—the word means "wanderers" and is regarded as an insult. More recently, they suffered a second insult from their fellow Jews when the Chief Rabbi of Israel ruled that they were "questionable Jews" who must submit to a ritual of formal conversion in order to qualify for Israeli citizenship under the Law of the Return.[15]

Still other "Judaisms" were, quite literally, washed up and stranded on far-flung shores. When a couple of thousand European Jews, seeking refuge from the Holocaust, managed to reach India in the 1930s and '40s, for example, they found three separate and distinct Jewish communities already there—the Baghdadis, the Cochin Jews, and the Bene Israel ("Children of Israel"). The so-called Baghdadis were wealthy traders who first emigrated to India from the old Jewish communities of Aleppo and Baghdad in the eighteenth century to set up an "Arabian Jewish Merchant Colony" at the encouragement of the British authorities in India. Many of the so-called Cochin Jews originated in the Middle East, too, but they also hailed from places as disparate as Spain and Persia, and they may have begun to arrive on the southwest coast of India near the city of Cochin as early as the first century C.E. Most exotic of all were the Bene Israel, a Jewish community that claims to descend from seven couples, all members of the Lost Ten Tribes of Israel, who were shipwrecked on the coast of India in 200 B.C.E.

The various Jewish communities of India offer some startling contrasts to the Jewish experience under Christianity and Islam. The Bene Israel, for example, remained "fighting Jews" long after most other Jews had retreated into the bookish world of the Talmud and the Torah, and they served proudly in the British army under the designation of "Native Jew Caste," fighting in the Indian Mutiny of 1857 and other military engagements that marked the long rule of the British in India. The Cochin Jews cherish a pair of ancient copper plates on which is inscribed a royal charter that raised a Jewish man named Joseph Rabban to kingship and granted him such kingly prerogatives as the power to levy taxes, the privilege to travel by elephant under the shade of a parasol, and the right to fire cannon salutes in celebration of Jewish weddings. In the fourteenth century, a Jewish poet traveled all the way from Spain to India in search of the legendary Jewish kingdom. "I longed to see an Israel king," wrote Rabbi Nissim. "Him I saw with my own eyes."[16]

What we learn from the Jewish experience in India, according to historian Matthew D. Slater, is that "Jews need not be persecuted in order to remain Jews."[17] But a closer examination reveals a more troubling subtext to the history of the Jews of India. Although they were never persecuted as Jews by British or Hindu authorities, they managed to find plenty of reasons to discriminate against each other as Jews. Thus, for example, the Bene Israel enforced a caste system of their own, favoring the lighter-skinned "white" Bene Israel, who were believed to be direct descendants of the original shipwrecked Israelites, over the darker-skinned "black" Bene Israel, who were regarded as the descendants of mixed marriages with local slaves. The Cochin Jews, too, discriminated within their own community: "Black Jews" were native-born Cochin Jews, "White Jews" were those who had fled from Europe to escape the Inquisition, and "Brown Jews" were the offspring of emancipated slaves who had arrived in India with Jews from Spain, Holland, and Arabia.

When the Baghdadi Jews showed up in the eighteenth century, the same ugly distinctions were made yet again. Not unlike the Jews who returned to Jerusalem from the Babylonian Exile and spurned the *Am Ha'aretz* whom they found there, the Baghdadis regarded the darker-skinned Bene Israel as second-class if not wholly inauthentic Jews. For that reason, the aristocratic Baghdadis excluded the Bene Israel from participation in their synagogue services, and even formally petitioned the British authorities to erect a wall in the Jewish cemetery of Bombay to separate the graves of the Baghdadis from those of the Bene Israel. Not until the twentieth century, when the Holocaust prompted them to work together to shelter Jewish refugees from Europe, did the Baghdadis and the Bene Israel begin to recognize, honor, and embrace one other as fellow Jews.

Each of these "Judaisms" remains in existence today—and many others, too, ranging from the "Mountain Jews" of Dagestan to the "cave-dwelling" Jews of North Africa—although some are sharply reduced in numbers and vastly changed in circumstances. Indeed, only a very few of the many Jewish communities of the Diaspora have disappeared entirely. For example, a few Jews managed to reach the far end of the Silk Road and establish themselves in the town of Kaifeng on the Yellow River in China perhaps as early as the first century c.e., but they were slowly obliterated by centuries of isolation and assimilation. By the time that rumors of a Jewish community in Kaifeng were investigated by Protestant missionaries in the mid-nineteenth century, all that remained were "fragments of Torah scrolls, prayer books, stone tablets and the faded memories of some members of the community."[18]

So, too, the storied kingdom of the Khazars survives in memory alone. The Khazars were a people of Turkish descent living in the Caucasus, and their khan famously converted to Judaism in the eighth century c.e. after allowing a Jew, a Christian, and a Muslim to each make the best case for his religion. The Jewish kingdom of the Khazars fell into decline and finally disappeared in the thirteenth century, although the author Arthur Koestler insists that their cuisine, haberdashery, and folkways are preserved in the Jewish *shtetl* culture of Russia and Eastern Europe. "[A] substantial part, and perhaps a majority of eastern Jews—and hence of world Jewry—might be of Khazar, and not of Semitic origin," proposes Koestler in *The Thirteenth Tribe*, a work that was clearly intended to tweak Jewish sensibilities and was entirely successful in doing so.[19]

Such oddities and curiosities aside, however, the fact remains that substantially all Jews in the world today, regardless of where they live or what language they speak, can be traced back to one of three major components of the Diaspora—Mizrahim, Sephardim, or Ashkenazim. Unlike breakaway sects like the Samaritans or the Karaites, or stranded Jews like the Bene Israel, or "home-grown" Jews like the "Falashas," all three of the major elements of the Diaspora were tied together by the Talmud and the ongoing rabbinical debate over its meaning and use. Perhaps the best evidence of diversity in Jewish history, then, is the fact that so many startlingly different strands of tradition were teased out of the very same fabric of rabbinical Judaism.

Three Judaisms

The first and oldest component of the Diaspora is identified by the Hebrew word *Mizrahim*—literally, "Easterners," or, according to the conventional if rather creaky English rendering, "Oriental Jews." Nowadays, the term is sometimes used to refer generally to *all* Jews who are *not* Ashkenazic; but, strictly speaking, the so-called *Yehude HaMizrah* ("Eastern Jews") are Jews who trace their origins to various places around the ancient Near East. Their distant ancestors may have settled in the lands adjoining Israel as far back as the Assyrian and Babylonian conquests, and the greatest concentrations of Mizrahim in antiquity were found in Babylon, Egypt, and Persia. Over the centuries, Jews spread across a vast expanse of the Mediterranean basin, ranging from North Africa through the Levant to Anatolia. Although these Jewish communities existed long before the rise of Islam in the seventh century c.e.—and, in fact, Muhammad himself was deeply influenced by the Jewish tribes who dwelled in his native Arabia—the culture of the Mizrahim was shaped by the experience of living in places where Arabic was spoken and Islam was practiced.

The second major component is the Sephardim, whose name derives from the medieval Hebrew word for Spain (*S'farad*) and describes a Jewish civilization that first established itself in Spain under Roman rule in the second century b.c.e., surviving and even thriving there for more than fifteen hundred years. Indeed, the Sephardic Jews reached their fullest flowering under the Moors, who ruled the Iberian Peninsula after the Arab conquest of the eighth century c.e., an era known rather wistfully as the Golden Age. Although it may strike the modern reader as bitterly ironic, the fact is that the Sephardic culture reached its highest expression under the rule of Islam, and some of the most accomplished, influential, and long-enduring works of science, medicine, poetry, philosophy, and theology by Jewish scholars and sages were composed in Arabic. So rich is the legacy of the Golden Age that, as late as the twentieth century, wealthy Jewish families in the United States who could trace their roots only to some muddy *shtetl* in Poland or Russia commissioned wishful genealogies in an effort to lay claim to a Sephardic pedigree.

The Golden Age came to ruin in the fifteenth century when a vengeful Spanish king and a militant Catholic church reasserted themselves and drove the Moors off the Iberian Peninsula. Ominously, the church turned its attention to the Jews who remained behind, and the Golden Age turned suddenly and tragically into a kind of proto-Holocaust. Jews were forced to convert to Catholicism under torture and threat of death. The so-called *conversos* who had submitted to the cross were put to torture again by the Inquisition to test the sincerity of their conversion, and the ones who were convicted of secretly practicing Judaism—they were called *marranos* ("pigs")—were turned over to royal authorities and burned alive in a ceremony of pious homicide known as an auto-da-fé ("act of faith"). At the same auspicious moment in history when King Ferdinand and Queen Isabella dispatched Christopher Columbus on the voyage that would result in the discovery of the New World, they decreed the total expulsion of Jews from Spain—and so, in 1492, the Sephardim began to seek out new places of refuge, the greatest number of them in North Africa and the far-flung empire of the Ottoman Turks, a smaller number in Italy, Holland, England, and, eventually, the Americas.

The Sephardim showed up in places around the Islamic world where the Mizrahim had long been settled, and the two Jewish communities encountered each other "like strangers from two different worlds," as anthropologist and historian Raphael Patai puts it.[20] Slowly, one community tended to dominate and absorb the other—the Sephardim, for example, largely disappeared into the older Jewish community of Morocco, but it was the other way around in Turkey. Nowadays, the old distinction between Mizrahim and Sephardim has been blurred, if not yet wholly erased.[21] Still, the oldest memories have not entirely disappeared—Jews of Iraq, who proudly trace their ancestry to ancient Babylon, and the Jews of Persia, where the biblical tale of Esther is set, still see themselves as distinct from the Jews whose ancestors left Spain a mere five hundred years ago.

The third and largest component is the Ashkenazim, whose name derives from the medieval Hebrew word for Germany (*Ashkenaz*) and nowadays describes Jews whose ancestors lived in the towns and cities, *shtetls* and ghettos, throughout Central and Eastern Europe, Russia, and the Ukraine. The earliest Jewish settlements in Europe may date back to Roman antiquity—an argument has been made that Jewish traders reached the northern shore of the Black Sea in the second century B.C.E., and captives taken during the Jewish War and the Bar Kokhba Revolt may have accompanied the Roman legions who penetrated what is now France, Germany, Hungary, and Romania. But, as with the Jews of Spain, the defining moment in the history of the Ashkenazim was an expulsion. Starting in the thirteenth and fourteenth centuries, the Jews of Germany were harried and driven into Poland, Russia, the Ukraine, and elsewhere in Eastern Europe.

And it is here that the distinctive language, cuisine, garb, music, and other folkways of the Ashkenazim flowered into the culture that *is* Judaism in the minds of many Jews and non-Jews alike. That is why, for example, a book of recipes titled *Simple Jewish Cookery* consists almost entirely of dishes borrowed from the Gentile populace of the places in Central and Eastern Europe where the Ashkenazim lived for centuries— sour pickles and pickled herring, kishka and kreplach and k'naydlach, bagels and lox and cream cheese. That is why a few of the ultraobservant Jews who can be seen even today in the Diamond District on 47th Street in Manhattan or the neighborhood of Mea Shearim in Jerusalem are dressed in the style of a well-attired Polish aristocrat of the eighteenth century—fur headdress, long black *kapote*, white stockings. And that is why *Fiddler on the Roof*, which is meant to conjure up and celebrate the Jewish experience, is based on the Yiddish stories of Sholem Aleichem, who was born in the Ukraine, and derives its iconic title and logo from the phantasmagorical paintings of Marc Chagall (1887–1985), who was born in Bielorussia.

Bride and Groom, Rice and Beans

Even the most traditional and observant Jews are generally comfortable in celebrating the richness and diversity of Judaism when it comes to the contrasts among Mizrahim, Sephardim, and Ashkenazim. So different are these "Judaisms" that a bride from a Polish-Jewish background and a groom from a Persian-Jewish background found it necessary to hand out a kind of instruction manual to the guests at their wedding so that each one's friends and relatives would understand the blend of rituals and observances that the couple had adopted for their marriage ceremony. And yet, even though both families are strictly observant, they were able to accept, if not quite embrace, the differences between the Jewish traditions that one family brought with them from Warsaw in the 1880s and the other family carried out of Teheran in the 1980s.

Some of these contrasts are quite colorful and dramatic, at least at first glance. A tradition among Ashkenazic Jews, as we have already noted, prohibits the naming of a baby after a living relative whereas a tradition among some Sephardic Jews actually requires it. Rice, peas, and beans are forbidden foods in traditional Ashkenazic homes during Passover, when only matzoh is to be eaten, but rice is generally permitted in Sephardic homes. Even here, however, the traditions vary from community to community: rice is forbidden by tradition among Moroccan Jews, and fresh peas and beans (but not dried ones) are permitted by tradition among Syrian Jews. Tellingly, *The Jewish Home Advisor* by Rabbi Alfred J. Kolatch—who carefully distinguishes among the folkways of Ashkenazic and Sephardic Jews as well as Orthodox, Conservative, Reform, and Hasidic Jews—offers two different recipes for *charoset*, a traditional Passover food that symbolizes the mortar used by the Israelites during their enslavement in Egypt, one called "Ashkenazic Charoset" and the other called "Sephardic Charoset."[22]

Even the pronunciation of the liturgy is different in Ashkenazic tradition, whose Hebrew is influenced by the Yiddish-tinged drawl of the *shtetl*, and Sephardic tradition, whose Hebrew is more accurate and more elegant. Thus, for example, the Ashkenazic custom is to replace the "t" sound in some words with an "s" sound: the blessing over the Torah in Ashkenazic tradition refers to *Toras Emes* ("Torah of Truth"), for example, rather than *Torat Emet*, which is the proper pronunciation of the Hebrew words. Nowadays, the Sephardic pronunciation has replaced the Ashkenazic pronunciation in Israel, where the ghettos and *shtetls* of Europe are not regarded with the same sense of nostalgia that we find in *Fiddler on the Roof*. And the old ways of pronouncing Hebrew and Aramaic are disappearing in the Diaspora, too; the last stand of the old

Ashkenazic dialect in many American synagogues is the Kaddish, the traditional mourner's prayer. Some prayer books in American synagogues still offer transliterations of the Kaddish that preserve the comforting sounds of sibilant consonants and drawling vowels at the moment of greatest bereavement: "*Yisgadal v'yiskadash sh'mei rabbaw*" rather than "*Yitgadal v'yitkadash sh'mei rabbah*" ("May His great Name grow exalted and sanctified").[23]

Even if the folkways of some Jews may strike other Jews as quaint and colorful, odd and exotic, they are not regarded as heretical precisely because all three groupings of Diaspora Judaism—Mizrahim, Sephardim, and Ashkenazim—recognize and submit to the authority of the Talmud. And the Talmud, as we have seen, embraces the principle of diversity in the custom and practice of Judaism, at least up to a point. For example, the Talmud preserves a passage in which six local customs that were unique to the Jews of ancient Jericho were reviewed by the sages, and three of these customs, including one that permitted the recitation of the *Shema* in a distinctive way, were granted rabbinical approval. Thus, the Jew whose tradition permits the eating of rice on Passover, or the naming of a child after a living grandfather, or the use of dates instead of honey to make *charoset*, is still entitled to regard himself or herself as a "Torah Jew."

"I Was Driven from One End of the Earth to the Other"

The emblematic figure of Judaism in the medieval world is a remarkable man whose name was Moses Ben Maimon (1135–1204). He is known in Jewish tradition as Rambam, an acronym based on his title and name (*Rabbi Moses Ben Maimon*), but he is also called Maimonides, a Hellenized version of his name that acknowledges his role in introducing Aristotelian philosophy into Jewish theology. Revered as he is, Maimonides was a figure of hot controversy in his own lifetime, an innovator whose writings were banned and even burned. And yet it is Rambam's life and work that illustrate exactly how Jews who lived in so many different places and so many different ways were bound together as a single people—*K'lal Yisrael*, the Community of Israel—throughout the centuries of dispersion and oppression.

Maimonides was born in the Spanish city of Cordoba, a place where the caliphs of the liberal and cosmopolitan Ummayid dynasty had once treated the Jewish community with generosity and toleration. Here the Golden Age of Spain reached its fullest flowering, attracting Jewish scholars, scientists, philosophers, and poets to Cordoba, where the caliph himself was attended by an influential Jewish court physician, and encouraging Jewish settlement in some fifty towns elsewhere in Spain. By the time Maimonides was born, however, the Ummayids had been driven out by their fellow Muslims and replaced by a series of ever more fundamentalist and ever more violent Islamic zealots. The latest Islamic rulers of Spain, the Almohads of North Africa, closed the synagogues where Jews prayed and the *yeshivot* where they studied Torah and Talmud, demanded conversion to Islam on the threat of death, and, even then, forced the converts to identify themselves with distinctive garb—a cap in the shape of a donkey saddle or a suit of clothing dyed bright yellow.

So Maimonides and his family did what Jews throughout the world and throughout history have done—they packed up their possessions, they left behind their home and they sought a place of refuge, first in Spain, then France, Morocco, Palestine, and finally Egypt. He was only thirteen when he began to run, but he managed to acquire a profound knowledge of Torah and Talmud and a mastery of medicine. By the time he settled in Fustat, the old city of Cairo, he was distinguished in both fields of expertise, serving as court physician to the Egyptian vizier and as head of the Jewish community of Egypt. Later, as the Crusades continued to rage in the Holy Land, he served as physician to the family of Saladin and turned down an invitation to do the same for a Crusader king, possibly Richard the Lionhearted, but he never stopped treating patients in the public hospitals and serving as judge in the Jewish communal court.

The life of Maimonides illustrates the precarious existence of Jews under both Christian and Islamic rule in the medieval Diaspora: "I was driven from one end of the world to the other," he writes of himself.[24] Significantly, Maimonides made his living as a physician and his brother made his as a trader in jewels and gemstones; both of these enterprises are highly portable and thus perfectly suited for a family of Jewish refugees who were harried from place to place. Wherever they went, they found a community of fellow Jews with whom they shared a common language, a common faith, and a common fate—the fact that the Jewish world of the Diaspora crossed political and religious boundaries enabled them to engage in the kind of international banking and commerce that was a fact of history before it became an anti-Semitic canard. And, like the rabbinical sage Yohanan Ben Zakkai as well as the turncoat general Josephus, they found it advantageous to place themselves in service to, and under the protection of, a powerful potentate, whether pagan or Christian or Islamic. Such were the strategies of survival in the Diaspora, and they worked as well for Maimonides as they did for countless thousands of other Jews.

Above all, however, Maimonides is celebrated in Jewish tradition because of something remarkable that he managed to accomplish even while living a life of stress and peril—he literally rewrote the vast body of Jewish law and restated the fundamental beliefs and practices of Judaism. Maimonides studied and mastered the voluminous Talmudic writings that had accumulated over the centuries as rabbis and sages elaborated upon the Torah and the Oral Torah, thus producing ever more detailed and complex expressions of *Halakhah*. He imposed order on the random accumulation of law and custom that took the form of commentaries upon commentaries upon commentaries. And he produced an authoritative, comprehensive, and practical legal code to instruct his fellow Jews in the practice of their faith, a fourteen-volume work known and revered in Jewish tradition as the *Mishneh Torah*.

On its completion in 1180 c.e., the *Mishneh Torah* sparked a theological civil war within Judaism. The orthodoxy of his own time and place condemned the work of Maimonides precisely because it was so creative and so daring—how could Maimonides, a wholly self-invented "second Moses," presume to break down the vast body of rabbinical law into its essential parts and then put them back together again in the form of an accessible and practical law code? But the *Mishneh Torah* is yet another countertradition that eventually insinuated itself into devout Jewish tradition. The very idea that once seemed so revolutionary—the idea of codifying the thousands of points of law in the *Halakhah*—is now embraced as a commonplace of Judaism. Indeed, it is orthodoxy and ultra-observant Judaism that cherishes and studies the *Mishneh Torah* and the other law codes that it inspired. And, above all, it was the availability of law codes like the *Mishneh Torah* that allowed the scattered Jewish communities of the Diaspora—from Amsterdam to Bialystok to Cordoba to Damascus—to remain a single Judaism.

A Guide for the Perplexed

The *Mishneh Torah* of Maimonides is a monumental achievement, but it is hardly his only one. Indeed, he is perhaps even more celebrated, especially outside Jewish circles, for a three-volume tour de force called *A Guide for the Perplexed*, a work of theology and philosophy that is regarded as one of the seminal works in the long intellectual tradition that ultimately produced the modern science of psychology. He authored tracts on health and self-improvement—mental, physical, and moral—and he issued stern warnings against adultery and homosexuality, overeating and excessive consumption of wine, wife-beating and witchcraft. And he produced the closest thing to a catechism that has ever existed in Jewish tradition, thirteen articles of faith that may seem to be utterly pious and yet carry a subtle subtext of sophistication and even fatalism.

"I believe with perfect faith that God is not physical," goes one of his thirteen principles, which cautions us against taking the Torah literally when God is described in anthropomorphic terms.[25] Another principle seems to echo the cautious words that were uttered to Rabbi Akiva about the coming of the Messiah: "I believe with perfect faith in the coming of the Messiah," declares a patient and practical Maimonides, "and though he may tarry, I will wait daily for his coming."[26]

The *Mishneh Torah* may not seem so very revolutionary to the modern reader. In fact, Maimonides can be seen as a practitioner of a very old tradition in Jewish history. Like Moses, like Ezra, like Yohanan Ben Zakkai, like Judah HaNasi, Maimonides is a man who felt fully empowered to teach Judaism to his fellow Jews. But Maimonides is a revolutionary figure precisely because he presumed to play the role of an Ezra or a Judah HaNasi. And, by doing so, he sought to break the old monopoly of the rabbinate and the Talmudic scholars over the religious life of the Jewish people. In fact, he called his work "Second Torah" because he regarded it as an essential counterpart to the Torah itself. "[A] man should read first the written law, i.e., the Pentateuch, and then he can read this book," Maimonides announces in the *Mishneh Torah*, "and he does not need any other book."[27]

Maimonides also rankled his fellow Jews because, not unlike Josephus, he strived to bring a sober and scholarly rationalism to Jewish ritual and belief—"to put the Torah and Greek wisdom together," in the words of one of his bitterest enemies, David Kimhi, who meant to bury Maimonides, not to praise him.[28] By cracking the hard shell of the Talmud and allowing the light of reason to fall on its pages, Maimonides hoped to improve the minds of his fellow Jews and, at the same time, to bring them into higher repute in the non-Jewish world in which they were forced to live. In that sense, Maimonides was, at once, following an old tradition and defining an entirely new one. "Maimonides was a great harbinger of the Jewish future," writes historian Paul Johnson, "indeed, of the human future."[29]

That is exactly why the *Mishneh Torah* was condemned so bitterly during the lifetime of Maimonides and long afterward by the most observant of his fellow Jews, a fact that is often overlooked in pious Jewish history. The whole undertaking was regarded as apostasy and blasphemy by the rabbinical authorities in France, where a *herem* ("ban") was issued against Maimonides' writings. The noisy debate within the Jewish world even attracted the attention of the Roman Catholic Church, whose Dominican inquisitors obliged the enemies of Maimonides by putting the *Mishneh Torah* to the flames in 1232.

Indeed, the so-called Maimonidean Controversy, which was still a point of contention in certain Jewish circles as recently as the early twentieth century, offers yet more evidence of the diversity that has always characterized Jewish tradition. The Talmud, as we have seen, frankly reports the spirited and sometimes bitter debate among rabbis and sages over the correct understanding and application of the Law, and, significantly, both sides of the debate are reported. That is why, for example, we know the position of Hillel *and* Shammai on any given point of disputation, even if "the decision is in accordance with the House of Hillel." But Maimonides chose to leave out the conflicting points of view and report only the specific point of law that he regarded as controlling. And that is precisely why his pious adversaries, recognizing and honoring the diversity of opinion that is written deeply into the Talmud, objected to the *Mishneh Torah*.

Over the centuries, several other codes came along to challenge the primacy of the *Mishneh Torah*, but the need for an accessible and practical compendium of Jewish customs, laws, rituals, and observances was no longer a matter of controversy. After all, how else could the Jewish people, scattered across the world in thousands of isolated communities, share a common understanding of what it meant to be a Jew? Ultimately, the most successful and the most enduring of the law codes, and the one that established itself as the definitive source of *Halakhah* throughout the Jewish world, was the *Shulhan Arukh* ("Set Table").

The author of the *Shulhan Arukh* was Joseph Caro (1488–1575). Born in Toledo, Spain, Caro based his work on the Sephardic tradition in which he was raised and tutored. Caro and family were among the Jews who were expelled from Spain in 1492, and he lived in Istanbul and elsewhere in the Turkish Empire before eventually settling in Palestine. But, crucially, the *Shulhan Arukh* was later amended by a Polish rabbinical scholar named Moses Isserles (c. 1525–1572) to include Ashkenazic sources and traditions. And so the *Shulhan Arukh* succeeded in the goal that Maimonides had set for himself and his *Mishneh Torah*— the treasure house of Jewish law and ritual was reduced to its essentials and made accessible to any Jew anywhere in the world who possessed the piety and the literacy to read it. Indeed, as early as 1574, the *Shulhan Arukh* was published in Venice in what we would call a pocket edition— "So that it could be carried in one's bosom," according to the publisher's blurb, "[and] referred to at any time and any place, while resting or traveling."[30]

Masters of the Good Name

Something essential is missing from the work of Maimonides, however, and from the whole edifice of stern and sober Judaism that was built upon its foundations: he is disapproving of the magic and mystery that are the root of all religion, including some of the most vivid and endur-ing expressions of Judaism. "[L]ies and falsehood, not fitting for Jews, who are intelligent and wise," writes Maimonides on the subject of the occult, and he dismisses all who believe in magic as "fools and ignora-muses, immature women and children."[31] In doing so, he is only affirm-ing one of the cherished values of classical Judaism, a faith that condemns every manner of witchcraft and wonder working, soothsaying and sorcery. "That is the religion of Moses," as Martin Buber puts it, "the man who experienced the futility of magic."[32]

And yet, as we have seen, the oldest traces of magic and mysticism in Jewish tradition are found in the Torah and the Talmud themselves. The Law of Moses may pronounce a death sentence on magic users of all kinds, but Moses himself is shown to perform feats of legerdemain with a kind of magic wand in the court of Pharaoh and to cure snakebite with a bronze serpent in the wilderness. The Talmud may warn that "magic [has] caused the destruction of all,"[33] but it also records the boast of one rabbi who insisted that he was able to turn cucumbers and melons into a living deer and the account of two other rabbis who used a mystical text called the *Book of Creation* every Friday evening to conjure up a calf whose flesh they roasted and ate as their Sabbath meal.

Even if the stern and scholarly Jewish elite preferred the sober precincts of the study house and the prayer house, the *Am Ha'aretz* relied on amulets and incantations to drive off the invisible demons whom they blamed for their ills and misfortunes. Like so many other countertradi-tions in Jewish history, magic and mysticism may have started out as a hidden and forbidden movement, but they insinuated themselves into the heart and soul of Judaism—"one of the most powerful forces," as his-torian Gershom Scholem puts it, "ever to affect the inner development of Judaism."[34]

The most distinctively Jewish expression of magic and mysticism was the "name magic" that had long been associated with the personal name of the God of Israel—the so-called Tetragrammaton, the four Hebrew letters that correspond to YHWH in English (*yud, hay, vav, hay*), or "Yahweh," as it is conventionally rendered in English. By pious tradition, the name of God is not to be spoken aloud at all, and a variety of codes and euphemisms are used to avoid writing it down outside the Torah itself. The most common practice is to use the Hebrew letter *yud*, written twice, in place of the Tetragrammaton, and as so written, the name is pronounced "Adonai," the Hebrew word for "Lord." Even today, devout Jews will write "G-d" instead of "God" in homage to the old taboo, and they refer to God as *HaShem* ("The Name"). But the taboo against speaking or writing the name of God was not merely a matter of piety— it was also intended to discourage its use by entrepreneurial Jewish magicians who were known as "Masters of the Name" (*Ba'a'eli Shem*) and who offered to cure illness or find lost objects by pronouncing the forbidden name, all on a fee-for-service basis "and not always on behalf of Jewish customers."[35]

Perhaps the most famous example of "name magic" in Jewish tradition, and an especially touching one, is the wholly legendary tale of a real-life rabbi, Rabbi Judah Loew of Prague, who seeks to create a *golem*—a medieval Jewish version of Frankenstein's monster—to protect the Jewish community against the predations of a Jew-hating priest and his bloodthirsty followers. Rabbi Loew fashions the figure of a man out of clay, he recites a series of magical incantations over the lifeless form, and then he places in its mouth a scrap of parchment on which are written the four Hebrew letters that spell the name of God. Suddenly, the figure of clay stirs, comes fully alive, and stands upright before his creator and master. "Know that you are made of earth," says the rabbi to the *golem*. "Your name is Joseph, and your mission is to protect the Jews."[36]

The very sobriety of rabbinical Judaism may have encouraged mystical speculation and magical experimentation by Jews whose curiosities and passions were not satisfied by poring over a page of Gemarah or mouthing the words of the *Shema*. The same powerful yearnings that have inspired mystics in all faiths, all ages, and all places were at work in the hearts and minds of Jews throughout the Diaspora. They yearned to transcend the tedium and occasional terror of daily life, to experience the exaltation of oneness with God, and, lacking the patience of Maimonides, they sought to hasten the coming of the Messiah. Running beneath the surface of Talmudic Judaism is a hidden but powerful current of magic and mysticism whose highest expression is the arcane and cryptic discipline known as Kabbalah.

Practical Magic

"Kabbalah" literally means "reception," in the sense of something received from ancient and esoteric sources. And the practitioners of Kabbalah embraced a set of mystical beliefs and practices that can be traced back to the oldest traditions of Judaism—and far beyond the bounds of Judaism. Like all mystics, they sought to transcend ordinary existence and discover the higher truths that cannot be expressed in ordinary words—sometimes by magic and sometimes by meditative practices such as self-hypnosis and yogalike discipline.

The first stirrings of what eventually emerged as Kabbalah reach all the way back to biblical antiquity, and some of its most arcane notions are first expressed in fragments of the Dead Sea Scrolls. Other elements of Kabbalah originated in the seventh century C.E. in Babylonia and Byzantium, where a few especially imaginative rabbis and sages expressed their own mystical musings in lushly metaphorical terms—the seven celestial palaces (*Hekhalot*) or the fiery chariot (*Merkaba*) that served as the abode of God. By the thirteenth century, the mystical traditions had been embraced by a few earnest seekers in Spain who were apparently less interested in codifying the *Halakhah* than in cracking the secrets of the universe. Around 1286, not long after Maimonides finished the *Mishneh Torah*, a Jewish mystic named Moses de Leon (c. 1240–1305) completed his own magnum opus, a million or so words of pure and potent mysticism called the Zohar ("Book of Splendor"). The Zohar was (and is) the fundamental text of Kabbalism.

Not until the expulsion of the Jews from Spain in 1492, however, did the study and practice of Kabbalah begin to spread throughout the Dias-

pora. And the timing was not coincidental—the characteristic Jewish response to crisis and catastrophe was a sharp and urgent longing for redemption by some act of divine intervention, often in the guise of the
Messiah, and the expulsion from Spain stoked these longings to a white-
hot glow. From the town of Safed in Palestine, where a few leading Kabbalists from Spain found a common refuge, the obscure teachings of the
Zohar and the mystical speculations of Kabbalism began to attract attention in Jewish communities around the world.

At first, both the rabbinical authorities and the Kabbalists themselves tried to protect the mystical traditions of Judaism from ordinary
Jews. According to one tradition, for example, mystical teachings were
supposed to be communicated by a master to an acolyte only "in a whis-
per," and another tradition held that a man was forbidden to open the
Zohar until he reached the age of forty.[37] Ironically, the invention of
printing with movable type and the spread of literacy made it impossible
to keep the genie in the bottle. Ultimately, the study and practice of
Kabbalah was so pervasive that it was no longer a set of esoteric teachings or a countertradition but, in fact, "a veritable mass religion."[38]

Many of the oldest and strangest traditions of Judaism were absorbed
by the Kabbalists and expressed in wholly new ways. "*Kavannah*," a term
ordinarily used to describe the mindfulness and pious intent of a Jew at
prayer, was given a new and highly charged meaning by the Kabbalistic
master Rabbi Isaac Luria (1534–1572). He used it to describe the mystical state of mind in which the hidden meanings of the liturgy would be
revealed and the very presence of God would be felt. And the Shekinah,
an intentionally hazy notion that is used in rabbinical Judaism to identify
the "feminine aspect" of God and his physical manifestation in smoke
and fire, is understood and described in Kabbalistic writings in a shock-
ingly explicit way: the Shekinah, as we have already noted, is depicted as
the female counterpart, companion, and consort of God.

Here is where Kabbalistic imagination and Kabbalistic practice burn
the hottest. Harking all the way back to the long-lost and long-forbidden
inscriptions that refer to "Yahweh and His Asherah," the Kabbalists
conceived of the Shekinah as a queen and a bride whose spouse is God
himself. And their focus on the Shekinah was not always or purely

metaphorical. When a pious Kabbalistic couple made love on a Sabbath evening—as *all* Jewish couples were ordered to do by Joseph Caro, a master Kabbalist as well as a codifier of Jewish law, in the *Shulhan Arukh*—they fancied that they were acting "in direct imitation of the union which takes place at that very time between the Supernal Couple."[39]

"I fulfil the commandment of copulation," a husband is instructed by Rabbi Isaac Luria to say to his wife, "for the unification of the Holy One, blessed be He, and the Shekhina."[40]

All of these excitations were (and are) downright embarrassing to the scholarly practitioners of rabbinical Judaism. Until the twentieth century, when Gershom Scholem insisted on approaching the Kabbalah as an authentic and worthy expression of Judaism, the whole subject of mysticism was treated with "contemptuous neglect." When Kabbalism was mentioned at all, it was openly condemned as a "theological danger" to Judaism or dismissed as an example of "primitive mythological thinking" among the *Am Ha'aretz*.[41] One influential nineteenth-century historian blamed the rise of Kabbalism on the oppression that medieval Jews were forced to endure—and he declared himself to be more troubled by the mystical yearnings of his fellow Jews than by the suffering that stirred those yearnings.

"More deplorable even than the persecutions, expulsions and massacres of the Jews was the effect which the systematic afflictions had upon their spirit," argues Heinrich Graetz. "The cabala . . . now began to intoxicate the head, to delude the sound sense and to lead the weak astray."[42]

But the spirit of Kabbalah eventually penetrated even the sober precincts of the synagogue: "[T]he rabbis could fight only a sort of delaying action," explains historian Salo Baron, and "[t]hey finally tried to take it under their own aegis and cleanse it."[43] In fact, faint traces of Kabbalism can be observed in sedate congregations all over the Jewish world today.

To achieve the proper *kavannah* during the recitation of the *Shema*, for example, an ardent Kabbalist at prayer would close his eyes, cover his face, and sway back and forth with an exaggerated movement of the upper torso. No matter how he articulated the rest of the liturgy—and a pious Jew at prayer sometimes sounds as if he is mumbling rather than speaking—he would abruptly slow down and speak the words of the *Shema* with accuracy and crispness, especially on the final "d" sound in the last word of the prayer *Echad* ("One"). Some Jews at prayer in the modern synagogue, especially in Orthodox and Conservative congregations, unknowingly imitate the medieval Kabbalists by adopting all of the same gestures and practices.

"What lies behind this behavior pattern," Raphael Patai reminds us, "is the conviction that this most sacred confession of faith must be recited with such an intense concentration that it must manifest itself in shaking the whole body and soul."[44]

Even more sublime—and far more provocative—is an old tradition that has come to be attached to the singing of a particular Sabbath hymn, *"Le'cha Dodi"* ("Come, My Beloved"). The hymn was composed by one of the Kabbalists of Safed in the sixteenth century and adopted by their master, Rabbi Isaac Luria, as part of a ritual that took place on the eve of every Sabbath. The rabbi and his fellow mystics would leave the stuffy confines of the prayer house, climb one of the slopes around Safed, and address the words of the hymn to the setting sun and the oncoming Sabbath. To the pious mystics, roused to a state of ecstasy and exultation, the Sabbath manifested before their eyes as the Shekinah, garbed as befits a queen and bride on her way to a wedding night in the company of her betrothed, King of the Universe. "Come, my Beloved, to greet the bride," they sang. "Let us welcome the Presence of the Sabbath."[45]

Nowadays, the same hymn is sung within the walls of the synagogue, but something of the same mystical meanings can be glimpsed just beneath the surface. By tradition, as the hymn reaches its climax, the congregation will turn and face the entrance to the sanctuary as if to welcome the invisible Queen and Bride. And, although many of the congregants may not even suspect it, that is exactly why the tradition calls on us to bow in the direction of the empty doorway while singing the final words of the hymn: *"Bo'ee kallah, bo'ee kallah"*—"Enter O bride! Enter, O Bride!" We, too, are invited to behold the spectral bride on her way to join her divine spouse under the wedding canopy and in the marriage bed—and, if we delve into the *Shulhan Arukh*, we are encouraged to go home after the service and do the same.

The Jewish Vizier

An exquisite silver wedding ring on display in a Jewish museum in the Marais, the old Jewish quarter of Paris, tells a poignant but profound tale about the experience of Jews in the medieval Diaspora. The ring is elegant and ornate, a work of art fashioned out of precious metal and adorned with a tiny but highly detailed little house that is meant to symbolize the happy home that the bride hopes to make with her husband. *Shalom ba'bayit*—"Peace in the house"—is one of the core values of Judaism. But, significantly, the ring never belonged to a single wealthy woman—it was commissioned and owned by the Jewish community, and it was made available to any Jewish bride, rich or poor, on the day of her wedding because another core value of Judaism holds that *every* bride deserves to be adorned as a queen.

Let us imagine a typical wedding day when the ring was slipped onto the finger of a young bride. She stands with her husband-to-be under the *chuppah*, the wedding canopy that also symbolizes the sanctity of the Jewish home, and she is surrounded by father and mother, friends and loved ones, as the rabbi pronounces the traditional seven marriage blessings: "Blessed art Thou, Lord our God, King of the universe," goes the seventh blessing, "who created joy and gladness, groom and bride, mirth and song, pleasure and delight, love, brotherhood, peace and companionship."[46] Then a glass of wine is sipped, the wineglass is broken, and the celebration begins with singing and dancing, feasting and merriment.

Outside the synagogue, however, is a world of degradation and danger, a place where Jews are forced to wear the high-peaked cap or the yellow star that is meant to brand them and humiliate them as "Christkillers," a place where Jews are forced to convert on pain of torture or death, a place where the blood of Jewish men, women, and children is spilled whenever the rage or guile or raw superstition of the king or the church or the mob erupts yet again against the Jewish scapegoats who live among them. When the wedding is over and the couple returns to an apartment somewhere in the Marais, they are reduced once again to the precarious existence that is the life of every Jew, rich or poor, throughout the Diaspora.

Yet the wedding *did* take place, and countless others like it. Jewish communities across the Diaspora, whether living under the Cross or the Crescent—and each one had its own special terrors—managed to carve out little islands of safety and serenity. Behind the walls of the medieval ghetto, not only in Paris but in Cologne and Damascus and a thousand other cities and towns, a jeweler was able to work at making an ornate ring and a Jewish bride and groom were able to celebrate their nuptials, all thanks to the generosity of the *k'lal*, the community of Jews in which they lived. What is most remarkable about the history of the Jews in the Diaspora, then, is the fact that a civilization as rich and diverse as the one we have been exploring was able to survive and even thrive despite the worst moments of horror and pain.

In fact, some of the most exalted and enduring expressions of Jewish civilization in the Diaspora can be understood as a specific response to the suffering that the Jewish people were forced to endure. The single most solemn prayer of the Jewish High Holidays, *Kol Nidre* ("All Vows"), for example, is a renunciation of oaths and vows that may have originated among Jews who were forcibly converted to Christianity and Islam. And, as we have noted, the so-called Golden Age of Spain, never wholly free of its own anti-Semitic outrages, produced a rich and remarkable literature in both Arabic and Hebrew, a literature that does not begin or end with its most famous example, the writings of Maimonides.

Among the first and surely the most heroic figures of the Golden Age, by way of example, is the poet whose verse is quoted at the beginning of this chapter, a man known by the Arabic name Ismail ibn Nagrel'a (993–c. 1056) or, as his fellow Jews dubbed him, Samuel Ha'Nagid— Samuel the Prince. Like Maimonides, he was born in Cordoba, fled the city to escape an invasion of Islamic fundamentalists from North Africa, and ended up in service to a Muslim potentate. Indeed, Samuel Ha'-Nagid rose to the ranks of both vizier and general under the Muslim ruler of Granada, and he may have been the only Jew in history to command an Arab army in battle. Significantly, he believed himself to be a descendant of King David, and he was a rare example of a "fighting Jew" who distinguished himself on the field of battle during the long Diaspora.

Samuel Ha'Nagid campaigned with his Muslim army for nearly fifteen years, and all the while he was forced to defend himself against conspiracies that were raised against him by jealous courtiers back home in Granada. And yet he still managed to distinguish himself as a scholar and a poet as well as a statesman and general, producing commentaries on both *Halakhah* and the Koran and composing some of the most sublime Hebrew poetry of the Golden Age or any age. The turmoil and tumult of a life lived in danger, a life lived on the run, seemed to inspire in Samuel Ha'Nagid not only the dash of a battlefield hero but the deepest musings of a philosopher. Indeed, his writing reveals him to be both worldly and world weary, and—again like Maimonides—strikingly modern in sensibility, a kind of protoexistentialist of the High Middle Ages.

"I have nothing in the world but the hour in which I am," muses the soldier-poet on the occasion of achieving his fiftieth year. "It pauses for a moment, and then, like a cloud, moves on."[47]

The Woman Who Cast a Spell on a Bullet

One of the richest flowerings of creativity in all of Jewish history can be seen as an outgrowth of two terrible tragedies that befell the Jews in the seventeenth century. The first tragedy can be traced to the dangerous and highly conflicted role that the Jews were compelled to play in the daily life of the non-Jews among whom they lived. Precisely because Jews all over the Diaspora were excluded by law from schools and universities, guilds and professions, ownership and tillage of land, they were forced to earn their living at enterprises that exposed them to distrust and even hatred—Jews tended to be loan brokers and pawnbrokers, rent collectors and tax collectors, peddlers and petty merchants, none of whom are beloved by the people with whom they do business. And even the occasional Jew who rose to the highest available rank—a financial agent for an aristocrat, for example, condescendingly called a "court Jew"—was doubly despised as a Jew and as a symbol of the autocrat whom he served.

The Jewish plight was especially acute in the Ukraine in the seventeenth century, then under Polish rule, where a Jew might find himself caught between the Polish lord (or *pan*) whom he served as an estate manager and the Ukrainian or Russian peasant (or *khlop*) from whom he was obliged to extract the ancient feudal dues of labor, produce, and taxes. The ill feeling was aggravated by the fact that the Polish aristocracy was Catholic, the Ukrainian peasantry was Orthodox, and the Jews were detested, openly or secretly, by both. To make matters even worse, a typical occupation for Jews was the operation of the local tavern, where a hard-pressed serf might nurse his grudges over vodka, putting his kopeks into the open palm of the Jewish tavern keeper for each glass.

"Thus the Ukrainian Jew found himself between hammer and anvil: between the pan and the khlop, between the Catholic and the Greek Orthodox, between the Pole and the Russian," writes historian Simon Dubnow. "Three classes, three religions, and three nationalities clashed on a soil which contained in its bowels terrible volcanic forces—and a catastrophe was bound to follow."[48]

These forces erupted in the spring of 1648 when a Cossack leader (or *hetman*) called Bogdan Khmielnitzki led a peasant uprising against the Polish overlords of the Ukraine and adjoining regions in Eastern Europe. The Khmielnitzki insurrection can be understood as a social revolution and a war of national liberation—the Russian and Ukrainian peasantry making war against the Polish aristocracy—but the Jews turned out to be the targets of rage and cruelty of a kind that is still capable of shocking us even after the genocidal anti-Semitism that is within our own memory. Indeed, the excesses of the Khmielnitzki massacres can be seen as an early augury of—and a rehearsal for—the Holocaust.

"The victims were flayed alive, split asunder, clubbed to death, roasted on coals, or scalded with boiling water—even infants at the breast were not spared," goes a contemporary account of the massacres. "Scrolls of the Law were taken out of the synagogues by the Cossacks, who danced on them while drinking whiskey. They opened the bowels of women, inserted live cats, and then sewed up the wounds."[49] And, crucially, the point of these outrages was not merely the brutalization of the

Jews, which was a commonplace of life in the Diaspora, but something much more ambitious: "They were destined to utter annihilation, and the slightest pity to them was looked upon as treason."[50]

The Khmielnitzki massacres produced a new generation of Jewish martyrs and a new chapter in a martyrology that dates all the way back to the Maccabees. One young Jewish woman, for example, caught the eye of a Cossack, who was so smitten by her beauty that he resolved to spare her life, offering her a choice between conversion and marriage or forcible rape. The woman managed to extract herself from the dilemma by a clever but dire ploy. She persuaded the credulous peasant that she knew how to cast a spell that could change the direction of a bullet, and she offered to demonstrate her magical powers by having him fire a round at her head.

"The Cossack discharged his gun, and the girl fell down, mortally wounded," the story goes, "happy in the knowledge she was saved from a worse fate."[51]

Perhaps more to the point, however, is a telling detail that can be discerned in the historical account. By long experience and deep instinct, the Jews fled from the Cossacks and the peasantry in the direction of the fortified towns and cities, where they hoped to put themselves under the protection of the Polish king and his army. And, as one Jewish chronicler reports, the refugees were welcomed and sheltered by a Polish count and general who "took care of them 'as a father of his children.' "[52]

Counts and generals, of course, were more worldly—and more calculating—than the people over whom they ruled. They knew how useful a grateful Jewish community could be, sometimes by providing a "Court Jew" who was willing and able to lend money to the government and sometimes by serving as tax collectors and tavern keepers who extracted money from the peasantry. And the sheltering of Jews by a Polish king is an incident with rich precedent in Jewish history, a concrete example of the Talmudic aphorism that had already served as a strategy for survival since the era of Yohanan Ben Zakkai: "Pray for the peace of the ruling power, since but for fear of it men would have swallowed each other alive."[53]

By the time the massacres finally ended, a full decade after they had begun, the Jewish communities of Poland, Russia, and Eastern Europe were left in a state of both physical and spiritual devastation and dislocation. The death toll may have included as many as half a million Jewish men, women, and children, a body count that beggars even the Crusades, and many of those who managed to survive the carnage ended up as refugees, prisoners of war, or slaves. The repercussions were felt throughout the Jewish world, thanks to the so-called Scroll of Darkness, a detailed report of the atrocities that was composed in Vilna and circulated among Jewish communities across the Diaspora.

Indeed, as it turned out, it was the spilling of Jewish blood in the Ukraine that set in motion a second tragedy that began in the Jewish community of far-off Smyrna. As early as the summer of 1648, the first Jewish captives were brought to Turkey by the Tatars who had allied themselves with the Cossacks, and they were now offered for ransom to their fellow Jews. One of the Turkish Jews who witnessed the heartbreaking spectacle was a man called Shabbatai Zevi (1626–1676). So moved was he by what he saw that he began to imagine himself as their savior. Over the years, his imaginings only increased in grandeur, and by 1666, when the Khmielnitzki massacres had ended and the Jewish world was left in ruins, Shabbatai Zevi was ready to declare himself to be the Messiah. And, in defiance of the old taboo, he did so by purporting to speak aloud the secret and forbidden name of God.

"The Day of Revenge Is in My Heart"

The yearning for a savior, of course, is one of the oldest traditions in classical Judaism, and we have already seen how Jewish aspirations were frustrated by men who turned out *not* to be the Messiah. Simon Bar Kokhba, first hailed as "Son of the Star" and then condemned as "Son of a Lie," is an early example, and Jewish history is burdened with many others. But Shabbatai Zevi stands out among all the other False Messiahs as the one who won and then broke the hearts of a whole generation of Jews, and—almost inadvertently—thereby changed the course of Jewish history in ways that he could not have imagined.

Not coincidentally, Shabbatai Zevi was a student of the Zohar, and

he must have been familiar with the earlier efforts of his fellow Kabbalists to hasten the coming of the Messiah through the most forbidden of
all rituals of magic and mysticism. But Shabbatai went further. He convinced himself—and, crucially, a man known to history as Nathan of
Gaza (c. 1644–1680)—that he *was* the Messiah. So it was that Nathan,
an Ashkenazic Jew, served as the self-appointed prophet for Shabbatai
Zevi, a Sephardic Jew and the self-appointed Messiah, and the two of
them succeeded in bringing thousands of true believers throughout the
Jewish world to acclaim Shabbatai Zevi as the long-promised and long-
delayed Savior.

Their fellow Jews, thoroughly shattered and dispirited by the experiences of the last two decades, were surely ready for a Messiah. "The
frenzy of the Jews of Smyrna knew no bounds," sniffs Heinrich Graetz.
"Women, girls and children fell into ecstasies, and acclaimed Shabbatai Zevi the true redeemer."[54] As far away as Poland, Jews abandoned
their work and their homes in the sure conviction that the Messiah
would appear momentarily to "carry them on a cloud to Jerusalem."
While they waited, they mortified and purified themselves by strict fasting and ardent prayer, by rolling in the snow and burying themselves up
to the neck in the earth, and by immersing themselves in river water
through holes cut in the winter ice. And, like the zealots they had become, they imposed these rigors on not only themselves but "even their
little ones."[55]

Meanwhile, Shabbatai Zevi set himself up in an opulent house outside Constantinople—the so-called Castle of Splendor—and thousands
of the faithful managed to make their way to what quickly surpassed the
Wailing Wall as a Jewish pilgrimage site. The more distinguished callers
included deputations from Jewish communities all over the Diaspora, including a few emissaries who were dispatched by their rabbis to test the
Messianic credentials of the Jew from Smyrna. To one such delegation,
Shabbatai Zevi handed a letter to be carried back to Poland: "The day of
revenge is in my heart, and the year of redemption hath arrived," he
vowed, mindful of all that the Jews of Poland had suffered. "Soon will I
avenge you and comfort you."[56]

But the Jews of Poland—and, indeed, Jews all over the world—were to suffer one more outrage. A master of the Kabbalah from Poland arrived at the Castle of Splendor and insisted on putting the self-crowned Messiah-king to three days of close cross-examination to test his claims. The interrogator came away with the conviction that Shabbatai Zevi was a fraud—and, in fact, he denounced the False Messiah to the Turkish authorities, who arrested Shabbatai, draped him in chains, and delivered him to the sultan, who offered Shabbatai Zevi the age-old choice of conversion or death. To the shock of true believers all over the Diaspora, Shabbatai Zevi readily renounced his claims to Messiahship and, as the saying went, "put on the turban."

The Dance of Prayer

The apostasy of Shabbatai Zevi was even more damaging to Judaism than the crucifixion of Jesus of Nazareth had been to the first Christians, or so argues Gershom Scholem: "The paradox of a traitorous Messiah," he insists, "is far greater than that of an executed Messiah."[57] And, yet, from the soil stained with the blood and ashes of the Khmielnitzki massacres, from the ghettos and *shtetls* where a whole generation of brokenhearted Jews tried to explain to themselves why Shabbatai Zevi now wore the turban of Islam instead of the crown of the Messiah-king, something fresh and forceful began to bud and flower. The successive blows of these two tragic episodes may have left the Jewish world battered and bruised, but they also left it in a state of readiness for a refreshing and redemptive expression of Judaism—the movement called Hasidism.

"A more wounded human animal has rarely lived on earth," writes Raphael Patai of the Jews of Eastern Europe in the eighteenth century. "This was the creature whose misery Hasidism tried to heal."[58]

The man who inspired the reflowering of Judaism was Isaac Ben Eliezer (c. 1700–1760). The intellectual aristocracy in rabbinical Judaism, then and now, saw him as one of the *Am Ha'aretz*, someone who showed little aptitude for the study of Torah and Talmud during his early years in the traditional Jewish schoolhouse known as a *cheder*—indeed, he grew up to be a lime-digger in the Carpathian Mountains. Still, he burned with curiosity about the mystical secrets of the Kabbalah, and he possessed the charismatic personality and spiritual gifts that characterized a *Baal Shem*, a "Master of the Name," one of those wonder workers of Kabbalistic tradition who were believed to know the secrets of name magic. To distinguish him from an ordinary magus-for-hire, however, he was called the *Baal Shem Tov*—the "good" *Baal Shem*—and he is still known and revered in Hasidic tradition by the acronymic title *Besht*.*

The *Besht* preferred the solitude and beauty of the countryside to the crowded and stuffy prayer house. He valued authentic piety above mere scholarship—*Hasid* means "pious one"—and he rejected the old hierarchy of values in rabbinical Judaism that measured the quality of a man's Jewishness in terms of how many lines of Gemarah he had committed to memory. He expressed himself in simple stories rather than Talmudic casuistries, and the telling of tales is one of the cherished traditions of Hasidism. Above all, the *Besht* taught his fellow Jews to turn to God in a spirit of gladness rather than despair, and he encouraged them to seek a state of ecstasy in prayer rather than numbly and mindlessly repeating the liturgy.

"When Israel came down from the mountains, it was to teach men to live with abounding joy, for joy in every living thing, he said, is the highest form of worship," writes the novelist and playwright Meyer Levin in his collection of Hasidic folktales. "Every act of living: breathing, eating, walking should be accomplished with fervour, joy, ecstasy, for every act spoke to God."[59]

Thus inspired and thus taught by the *Besht*, Hasidism can be seen as a reinvigorated Judaism—a "Dionysian" Judaism, as Raphael Patai puts it [60]—and one that roused the Jewish world out of a mournful stupor and a stale bookishness. The *Besht* restored the mystical and ecstatic elements that had spoken to the needs of the Jewish people and kept Judaism alive for so many centuries of heartache. Just as King David, the "sweet singer of Israel," "danced before the Lord with all his might" (2 Sam. 6:14), the *Besht* taught the Jews to express their piety and prayerfulness through song and dance.

---

*As if to play down the original function of a *Baal Shem* in Kabbalistic tradition, *Baal Shem Tov* is rendered as "Master of the Good Name" or "Master of the Holy Name" in some devout sources.

A typical Hasidic song (*niggun*), for example, consists of a spirited melody but no lyrics at all; it may consist of a single word repeated over and over again or, even more commonly, a series of syllables that mean nothing at all. "[T]he singer returns to a stammering infant language," explains musicologist Hanoch Avenary, "in order to express before God feelings too delicate or too intimate for a conventional verbal statement."[61] The Hasidic style of davening (praying) consists of pronounced and sometimes violent bowing and swaying that reminded one Jewish historian of the Shakers. At certain moments, a Hasid might break into "ecstatic acrobatics" so spirited that he resembles a whirling dervish.[62]

"The Rabbi commands us to rejoice," goes a Hasidic folk tune. "It's a mitzvah to forget the gloom."[63]

Precisely because of the ecstasies that it offered, Hasidism spread through the Jewish communities of Eastern Europe and Russia like a flame through tinder, answering the urgent spiritual need of a demoralized people and capturing the loyalties of perhaps half the Jewish population. Soon after the death of the *Baal Shem Tov*, however, Hasidism began to morph into something quite different from the pure and simple faith that the *Besht* modeled. "Tzaddikism" describes the self-contained religious communities that arose within Hasidism, each one centering on its own powerful *rebbe*, the Yiddish term for "rabbi," a charismatic figure who was regarded as a *tzaddik*, a wise and righteous person. At its most degraded moments, Hasidism included *rebbes* whose luxurious "courts" were sustained at the expense of their mostly poor but wholly devoted followers.

The rabbinical establishment responded to the latest countertradition in Judaism with unrestrained horror. The most zealous of the so-called Mitnagdim ("Opponents") was Rabbi Elijah (1720–1797), the Gaon of Vilna, a revered figure in the Jewish community of Lithuania. He denounced Hasidism for its "perversities," ordered a Hasidic "seducer" who dared to preach in Vilna to be imprisoned and scourged, decreed that Hasidic writings be publicly burned, and pronounced a *herem* (ban) against the Hasidim in general.[64] "As they recite their fake prayers, they scream and shout so that the walls shake," he complained. "This is only one of their thousand ugly ways."[65] Like the other schisms in Judaism—the "Holy Seed" and the *Am Ha'aretz* of biblical antiquity, the Hasidim and the Hellenizers of the Maccabean revolt, or the Sadducees and the Pharisees of the first century c.e.—the Jews of eighteenth-century Europe were divided between the followers of the *Besht* and the followers of the Gaon of Vilna, the Hasidim and the Mitnagdim. Now and then, the two opposing factions would go beyond exchanging insults and excommunicating each other and actually come to blows.

The irony here—and, by now, we should not be surprised to find one—is that the Hasidim and the Mitnagdim have far more in common with each other than with secular Jews or any of the more progressive religious movements in Judaism. Indeed, even in the eighteenth century, the two factions were already borrowing from each other—some of the Hasidic *rebbes* sought to combine ecstatic prayer and Kabbalistic mysticism with the sober study of Torah and Talmud, and the Gaon of Vilna himself was willing to soften the harder edges of rabbinical Judaism and make the study of Talmud more accessible. Still, given the Jewish genius for finding and fighting over differences among fellow Jews, neither should we be much surprised that two ultraobservant Judaisms could never find a way to live in peace with each other.

The ultimate irony is that Jewish history had already begun to change its course—slowly, subtly, but unmistakably—at the very moment when the Hasidim and the Mitnagdim of the eighteenth century were struggling with one another over the right way to be a Jew. A whole new Judaism was just beginning to emerge, and all of the old Judaisms would be left behind. And the latest reinvention of Judaism would change not only the destiny of the Jewish people but the fate of the whole world.

Abominable Heresies

> Receiving every day more information about the abom-
> inable heresies practiced and taught by him, they have
> decided that the said Espinoza be excommunicated and
> banished from the people of Israel.
> —ORDER OF EXCOMMUNICATION AGAINST BARUCH SPINOZA

● ● ●

> I believe in Spinoza's God.
>
> —ALBERT EINSTEIN

Across the threshold of a synagogue in the Jewish quarter of Amsterdam lay the prostrate figure of a man called Uriel da Costa
(c. 1585–1640). Twice excommunicated for rejecting the sanctity of the
Oral Torah and the authority of rabbinical Judaism, da Costa had twice
recanted and performed the penitence that the rabbis required of him—
he dressed in the clothes of a mourner, held up a black wax taper while
confessing his crimes to the congregation, submitted to a public flogging
with a leather whip, and finally lay in the doorway as each of his fellow
Jews stepped on him on the way out of the synagogue. Even then, however, da Costa was still tormented by his fellow Jews and by his own free-
thinking ways. At last, he took his fate in his own hand, and literally so,
by putting a bullet through his head.

Among the Jewish children who used to follow da Costa around town and shout taunts at him—"There goes a heretic! There goes an imposter!"[1]—may have been a boy whose name was Baruch d'Espinoza, but who is better known in the history of philosophy as Benedictus de Spinoza (1632–1677). He was only eight years old when da Costa finally died a suicide, but he was an alert and curious child, and he showed as much aptitude for the study of astronomy and physics as for Mishnah and Gemarah. Indeed, it was his own curiosity about the world outside the Talmud and the Torah that eventually alienated Spinoza, too, from the Jewish community. Da Costa's fate became Spinoza's when the elders of the Jewish community in Amsterdam condemned *his* "evil ways" and issued a *herem* ("ban") against the twenty-four-year-old freethinker on July 27, 1656.[2]

The scene of Spinoza's excommunication is a famous one, but it is not quite what it seems to be. Contrary to appearances, the Jewish community of Amsterdam was not a fossilized remnant of medieval obscurantism. In fact, compared to the *shtetls* and ghettos of Eastern Europe or the Levant at the very same moment in history—the Khmielnitzki massacres and the False Messiahship of Sabbatai Zevi were still in full eruption—the so-called Jewish Street of Amsterdam was a worldly, sophisticated, and cosmopolitan place where Jews were already emerging from the confines of the ghetto and beginning to play an active role in the secular life of the non-Jewish world.

Spinoza, however, was moving faster in that direction than most of his fellow Jews, and he provoked some of the old terrors that had haunted the Jews since biblical antiquity. The elders of the Jewish community in Amsterdam were still fearful of attracting the attention of the ruling powers of the non-Jewish world to the question of their own loyalty and fidelity. Amsterdam, after all, was a place of refuge for Spanish and Portuguese Jews whose families had converted to Catholicism under the threat of the Inquisition and then reconverted to Judaism—Uriel da Costa, for example, was one of these "new Jews"—and they knew exactly what it meant for a Jew to be seen as a heretic by the crown or the church. Only a year before the excommunication of Spinoza, a Jewish man was burned at the stake as a heretic in Cordoba, and even in Amsterdam, the Jewish community was charged by the laws of the Dutch republic to ensure that "atheists and godless men" were "properly isolated and punished without mercy."[3]

So the musings of a young man like Spinoza were seen as threatening even by otherwise open-minded and easygoing Jews. After all, he did not merely reject the authority of rabbinical Judaism and repudiate his communal obligations by shunning the synagogue, failing to pay his dues, and breaking the laws of the Sabbath. When Spinoza pointed out the flaws and contradictions in the Bible and expressed doubts about its divine authorship, when he questioned the existence of the soul and the afterlife, when he suggested that God and nature were one and the same thing, he was denying some of the fundamental articles of faith in both Judaism *and* Christianity.

Ironically, Spinoza—"this freest and boldest spirit of his generation," as Israeli historian Yirmiahu Yovel puts it—acted according to an old Jewish tradition, the tradition of innovation and invention that had always preserved the Jewish people. No matter how audacious and confrontational he may have been, he never formally renounced Judaism and never converted to Christianity. Today, Spinoza is hailed as the archetype of the modern Jew precisely because he dared to set himself free from the old pieties, and, in doing so, he stoked the fires of freethinking that continue to burn in Judaism.

That's why, far more than figures like Simon Bar Giora and Yohanan Ben Zakkai, the *Besht* or the Gaon of Vilna, it is Spinoza who anticipates the dilemma of the modern Jew who seeks to participate fully in the secular world. And that's why David Ben-Gurion (1886–1973), yet another Jewish freethinker who was also one of the founding fathers of modern Israel, carried on a rather whimsical campaign to revoke the *herem* that had been pronounced against Spinoza by the Jewish community of Amsterdam some three hundred years earlier.

"[W]ho in the Jewish world today might be authorized to accept Spinoza back into the Jewish fold? The Lubavitcher Rebbe? The Prime Minister of Israel? The President of Yeshiva University? The B'nai B'rith?"

asks Yovel, pointedly reminding us of how much Judaism has changed since then. "There is no longer a single normative Judaism today—a development of which Spinoza himself was one of the harbingers."[4]

The Gates of Berlin

At the age of fourteen, a young man called Moses Mendelssohn (1729–1786) boldly presented himself at the gates of Berlin, a city from which all but a few privileged Jews were excluded by law, and managed to talk his way past the watchman whose job it was to turn away people just like him. Once inside the Prussian capital, he placed himself under the tutelage of a rabbi and continued his studies of the Talmud and the Torah—but he soon found his way to the philosophical musings of Maimonides and from there to the *philosophes* whose writings were shedding the light of rationalism over Europe. Emboldened by his new knowledge, and encouraged by the new spirit of the Enlightenment, Mendelssohn entered and won an essay competition sponsored by the Prussian Academy of Science, thus besting another contestant whose name was Immanuel Kant and calling attention to himself as an accomplished intellectual in a place where intellect was valued and praised.

"A second Spinoza" is how the German critic and dramatist Gotthold Lessing (1729–1781) described young Mendelssohn, "lacking only his errors to be his equal."[5]

Mendelssohn won a medal and a prize of fifty ducats, and he was ultimately elevated by the emperor himself, Frederick the Great, to the status of a *Schutzjude*, one of the few Jews permitted to reside in the imperial capital at the sufferance of the crown. But he was not content with grudging dispensation of a kind that had always been available to the occasional "court Jew." Rather, he aspired to full and public participation in the cultural life of Germany. Not unlike Josephus, who distinguished himself as a man of letters in the loftiest circles of the Roman Empire, Mendelssohn managed to win admirers among the literary elite of Berlin.

"Mendelssohn became a citizen of the republic of letters," enthuses the historian Heinrich Graetz (1817–1891), one of the direct beneficiaries of Mendelssohn's pioneering efforts on behalf of German Jewry.

"Mendelssohn recovered for the Jews what they had lost in the course of the degradation of a thousand years of enslavement."[6]

Significantly, Mendelssohn remained a proud Jew even as he rose in the esteem of his non-Jewish friends and patrons, and he replied to provocative public challenge to convert to Christianity with an equally public affirmation of his Jewish faith: "I am so firmly and absolutely convinced of the essential elements of my religion that I bear witness before God," he declared in an open letter, "that I will cling to them as long as my soul does not assume a different nature." And yet, even as he affirmed his Jewishness and defended Judaism, Mendelssohn conceded that the ancient faith might be in need of reform, thus speaking aloud an explosive idea that would soon work a revolution in the Jewish world. "I could not deny," he allowed, "that I have noticed in my religion human admixtures and abuses which, unfortunately, dim its lustre and which creep into all religions in the course of time."[7]

To encourage his fellow Jews to join him in reforming Judaism, Mendelssohn—the son of a scribe whose profession was making copies of the Torah with a quill pen on scrolls of parchment—undertook to translate the Pentateuch from Hebrew into modern German, and he published an influential commentary on the Torah in the same language. The rabbinical establishment, which regarded biblical Hebrew as the only appropriate language for the sacred text, threatened a *herem* against anyone who dared to read Mendelssohn's elegant translation. And their concerns were later shown to be well-founded—the publication of the Bible in modern German was the symbol of a powerful new countertradition in Judaism.

"A Veritable Magic Circle"

The ideas that Mendelssohn advocated were the first stirrings of a movement in Judaism that came to be called the Haskalah ("Enlightenment"). Like the Enlightenment that was at work all over Western Europe, the Haskalah celebrated the worth and dignity of the human being. As translated into the Jewish experience, however, the Enlightenment created yet another schism among Jews, a division of the Jewish

world into the so-called Maskilim ("enlightened ones") and the practitioners of traditional Judaism. And yet the schism is really nothing new
in Jewish history—the same bitter conflict existed between the Hasidim
and the Hellenizers of biblical antiquity, and it exists today between the
ultraobservant Jews and the secular Jews who are their modern descendants.

Like the ancient Jews who adopted Greek manners, language, and
dress in an effort to "Hellenize" themselves, the Maskilim now shaved
their beards, mastered modern German, and attired themselves in the
fashions favored by the cosmopolitan elite of Berlin—indeed, "Berlin-
ism" is how some Jewish traditionalists in Poland and Russia described
the Haskalah. As if to symbolize the soaring social ambitions of the first
Maskilim, a wealthy and beautiful Jewish woman called Henriette Herz
(1764–1847) hosted a literary salon in her elegant home, the first of several Jewish women to do so in Berlin and Vienna. "It was she who formed
a veritable magic circle that attracted to it every person of distinction,
native and foreign, who was in Berlin," reports Graetz, who was himself
"a late product of the Haskalah."[8] "This salon proved particularly attractive to cultivated Christian youths because of the pretty Jewish girls and
women who moved about their beautiful hostess like satellites . . . and
took an active part in the interchange of thought that accompanied
these social gatherings."[9]

Perhaps the single most eloquent fact about the aspirations of Judaism under the influence of the Haskalah is that *both* the Reform movement and the movement called Modern Orthodoxy, which are nowadays
regarded as adversaries and opposites, were established at roughly the
same time and place, and for the same purpose. Each one originally represented an effort by German Jewry to find a way to be both good Jews
and good Germans at the same time—and to keep the Maskilim from
abandoning Judaism altogether. "A Jew at home," according to the poet
Judah Leib Gordon (1830–1892), a leading exponent of the Haskalah in
Vilna, "and a man in the street."[10]

Reform and Modern Orthodoxy came to very different conclusions
when considering how much of Jewish law and ritual they were willing
to preserve—Reform preserved relatively little, and Orthodoxy pre-

served a great deal more—but both movements shared the goal of remaking Judaism for the modern world. Thus, for example, Reform Jews and Modern Orthodox Jews were not required to wear a beard or earlocks, a skullcap, or the ritual fringes called *tsit-tsit*, all of which were unmistakable signs of one's Jewishness, and thus they were able to move more easily in secular circles in nineteenth-century Germany. And the same is true today—in 2000, Senator Joseph Lieberman, the first Jewish vice-presidential candidate of a major political party in American history, was advertised as an Orthodox Jew, but his version of Orthodoxy did not require him to bear any of the external markings of a traditional Jew.

A Prayer for the Tsar

The Haskalah, in fact, collided with some of the most fundamental teachings of Judaism. The cherished theological assumption of Judaism, as we have already seen, is that the Jews are *not* like everybody else. Rather, the Jews are the Chosen People, "a kingdom of priests, and a holy nation" (Exod. 19:6), and they have been called upon by God to separate themselves from the rest of the world. That is, after all, the essential function of the ritual of circumcision, the dietary laws, the sanctity of the Sabbath, and much else in Jewish ritual and practice. Thus, as viewed from the stance of traditional Judaism, the shiny new aspirations of the Maskilim were not different from the old apostasies and heresies that had been luring Jews out of Judaism ever since God set the gods and goddesses of Canaan in front of the faithless Israelites as "a trap unto you" (Judg. 2:3).

So great was the threat of enlightenment and emancipation to the Hasidic *rebbes* of Russia and Eastern Europe that, when Napoleon invaded Russia, Shneur Zalman (1745–1813), founder of the Hasidic movement now known as Chabad, rose in *shul* to offer a prayer for the Tsar of All Russia. By doing so, the Lubavitcher *rebbe*, as Zalman came to be known, suggested that a pious Jew ought to prefer autocracy and anti-Semitism over "Liberty, Equality and Fraternity," and he readily explained why. "Should Bonaparte win, the wealth of the Jews will be increased and their position will be raised [but] their hearts will be estranged from our Heavenly Father," said the *rebbe*. "Should our Czar Alexander win, the Jewish hearts will draw nearer to our Heavenly Father though the poverty of Israel may become greater and his position lower."[11]

But history, if not God, was on the side of the Maskilim, or so it seemed at the time. Some of the old barriers began to fall in Germany and elsewhere in Western and Central Europe: the universities began to accept Jewish students, the learned professions began to admit Jewish doctors and lawyers, and Jewish men "of the higher classes" were even granted the right to carry a sword![12] But none of these concessions were universal or wholehearted; the French Revolution led to the formal emancipation of the Jews in France and the countries that came under French domination, but the Jews of Russia and Eastern Europe still lived under near-medieval laws and traditions. Even where the Jews were emancipated, the new rights and privileges were often subject to quotas and conditions. No amount of pretty rhetoric could conceal the ugly sewer of anti-Semitism that still ran beneath the feet of the emancipated Jews.

"Not only must the Jews again be shut in a ghetto and placed under constant police surveillance, and wear a badge on their sleeves, but the second sons of the 'Jew Boys' must be castrated to prevent the increase of their population," wrote a visionary anti-Semitic propagandist in the opening years of the nineteenth century. And one of his fellow pamphleteers complained bitterly that it was only getting harder to pick out (and pick on) the Jews now that they had begun to dress and speak like ordinary Germans, going clean-shaven and shunning Yiddish in order to ease their way into non-Jewish circles: "He no longer has even a beard by which one could pull him, and he no longer speaks a gibberish you could mimic!"[13]

At the brightest moments, however, the Jews of Germany and Western Europe were capable of looking beyond the atavisms of anti-Semitism and convincing themselves that a new age had now begun in Jewish history. In a sense, they were right—the Haskalah released a reservoir of energy and enterprise that had been dammed up behind the ghetto walls and "the wall around the Torah." Three Jews in particular, all of them born in Germany or Austria in the nineteenth century, can be seen as living proof of the proposition that the Jewish people, once set free from the deadweight of old traditions, were capable of literally changing the world.

In fact, all three of them—Karl Marx, Sigmund Freud, and Albert Einstein—belong to world history as much as to Jewish history, and their work helped to create and shape the modern world even more directly and more distinctly than biblical Judaism helped to create and shape its sister religions of Christianity and Islam. And yet, if Marx, Freud, or Einstein had been born only a few years earlier—or if they had been born in some *shtetl* rather than at ground zero of the Haskalah—their genius might have been contained within the four walls of the study house and devoted to the fine points of Talmudic pilpul rather than world-shaking and history-making innovations in politics, medicine, and science.

"On the Jewish Question"

"Judaism was not a religion," goes a sour witticism of the poet Heinrich Heine (1797–1856), "but a misfortune." Born, raised, and educated as a Jew—his Hebrew first name was Hayyim—Heine frankly confessed that he converted to Christianity not out of conviction but to improve his prospects for earning a living in the German civil service: "If the law had permitted the stealing of spoons," he quipped, "I should not have been baptized."[14]

The same cold calculation prompted a German Jew named Herschel Marx to renounce his religion in 1817: he was an attorney, but the cycle of revolution and counterrevolution in Western Europe meant that he could never be sure when and where he would be permitted to practice law. So he stepped around the practical problem of his Jewishness by converting to Christianity and changing his name from Herschel to Heinrich. And he even repudiated the old Ashkenazic taboo against naming a child after a living relative by christening his infant son, born the year after his conversion, with both the thoroughly non-Jewish name of Karl and his own name. Thus did Karl Heinrich Marx (1818–1883) come into a world that was even more troubled when he left it than when he entered it.

Karl Marx was not raised as a Jew, of course, but he was not actually baptized until shortly before he started school, and he could not fail to see through the halfhearted Christianity of his mother and father. Both his paternal and maternal grandfathers were rabbis, and the Marx family had provided rabbis to the Jewish community in his hometown of Trier since the sixteenth century. Indeed, Marx's uncle was serving as the town rabbi when his father submitted to conversion, and he was related by blood to rabbis all over Europe—in Poland, Italy, Bohemia, and Alsace. So deeply imprinted was young Karl with the values of Judaism that the essay he wrote on graduation from the *Gymnasium* echoes one of the cherished aphorisms of Rabbi Hillel as recorded in the Talmud: "If I am only for myself, what am I?"[15]

"If [a man] works only for himself, he may perhaps become a famous man of learning, a great sage, an excellent poet, but he can never be a perfect, truly great man," writes the future author of *The Communist Manifesto* at the age of seventeen. "History calls those men the greatest who have ennobled themselves by working for the common good."[16]

Of course, Marx later declared his hatred for *all* religion, not excluding Judaism: "The destruction of religion, the phantom happiness of the people, is a necessary condition for their real happiness."[17] But he reserved a special kind of contempt for the Jewish people, whom he saw as the ultimate practitioners of the capitalist system whose overthrow and obliteration he advocated with the white-hot zeal of a true believer. "Money is Israel's jealous God, and they can have no other God," writes Marx in his notorious tract *On the Jewish Question*. "The social emancipation of the Jew is the emancipation of society from Judaism."[18] At perhaps his most squalid moment, in a private letter to Friedrich Engels, his comrade, collaborator, and fellow Jew, Marx notoriously referred to one of his ideological rivals within the socialist movement as "the Jewish nigger."[19]

So Marx can be seen as an especially ugly example of a countertradition that is one of the shameful secrets of Jewish history, the phenomenon of "Jewish self-hatred." Indeed, Marx has been called "the most famous and most influential of all Jewish self-haters."[20] Even on the subject of Jewish self-hatred, however, Jewish opinion is divided. From one point of view, Jewish self-hatred can be seen as an off-putting but inevitable side effect of emancipation. "Ironically, self-hatred is an artifact of liberation as the oppressed regard their own traditions as outmoded, archaic, shameful, crude, inept, disgraceful," writes Marx biographer Murray Wolfson. "They turn on themselves, and often embrace their oppressors by hoping to convince them that 'We are really the same as you.' "[21] From another point of view, however, Jewish self-hatred is the curse that befalls anyone who commits the sin of assimilation—and so, when the traditional and observant Jew looks on *any* "enlightened" Jew, then and now, what he sees is the self-hating Jew.

The life and work of Karl Marx suggest, however, that even a self-hating Jew is indelibly marked with his own Jewishness. The idealism that shimmers beneath the surface of revolutionary socialism—the utopian vision of a world of peace and justice—is the same idealism that can be found in writings of the Prophets, and that is why Marxism resonated so powerfully within the oppressed Jewish communities of Europe and Russia in the nineteenth century. Ironically, the writings of Marx, a self-hating Jew, convey a fresh expression of an ancient article of faith in Judaism—the redemption of humankind, not by a God-sent Messiah but by a proletarian revolution.

According to one of the witticisms of the poet Heine, conversion to Christianity was an "entrance ticket" to the culture of Europe. For countless thousands of Jews, however, the struggle for social justice under the banner of socialism performed the same function. The poor and powerless Jews of Poland and Bielorussia and the Ukraine—the *Ostjuden* ("Eastern Jews"), as they were rather disdainfully called by the wealthier and more assimilated Jews of Germany—had no interest in recreating the salons of Berlin in the *shtetls* and ghettos of Cracow or Kiev. They burned with a righteous wrath against the near-medieval tsarist autocracy that imposed on the Jewish people a degraded and degrading poverty and the constant threat of pogroms and persecution. For a Jew like Leon Trotsky (1879–1940), founder of the Red Army in Bolshevik

Russia, it was conversion to Marxism rather than Christianity that served as an "entrance ticket."

Trotsky and his Bolshevik comrades, of course, regarded Judaism with the same cold contempt that Marx had expressed, and the most radical of the Jewish socialists imagined that they were liberating their fellow Jews from Judaism by rooting out its oldest religious traditions. But a far greater number of Jews saw socialism as a way to remake themselves, and to remake Judaism, in the image of the biblical prophets who embraced the highest ideals of social justice. And one modern theologian, Jacob Neusner, is willing to credit the Jewish disciples of Marx, and specifically the Jewish labor movement known as the Bund,[22] with an exalted and distinctively Jewish moral achievement. "Jewish Socialism, that most secular movement, seems to me to have preserved the most profoundly religious theme of Jewish tradition," writes Rabbi Neusner, "the primacy of morality."[23]

Freud's Revenge

Sigmund Freud (1856–1939), not unlike Marx, regarded all of organized religion as a symptom of profound human dysfunction. And when the founder of psychoanalysis strayed into amateur biblical scholarship in *Moses and Monotheism*, he issued the startling and off-putting pronouncement that there were actually two men called Moses, neither of whom was Jewish, and both of whom were murdered by their Jewish followers! Freud himself suffered from a kind of Moses complex, and he recruited Carl Gustav Jung (1875–1961) to serve as his Joshua, pointedly choosing a Swiss Protestant in the hope of convincing the world that psychoanalysis was not a strictly Jewish enterprise: "This Swiss," Freud told his resentful Jewish disciples, "will save me and all of you as well."[24]

But Freud, quite unlike Marx, never embraced Christianity and, in fact, remained a self-identified and self-affirming Jew even if a highly assimilated one. "A Gentile would have said that Freud had few overt Jewish characteristics, a fondness for relating Jewish jokes and anecdotes being perhaps the most prominent one," recalls his official biographer,

Ernest Jones. "But he felt himself to be Jewish to the core, and it evidently meant a great deal to him."[25]

In fact, Freud struck his official biographer—a non-Jew—as assertively Jewish. "He had the common Jewish sensitiveness to the slightest hint of anti-Semitism, and he made very few friends who were not Jewish," reports Jones. "He objected strongly to the idea of their being unpopular or in any way inferior."[26] Freud himself declared that he had "never been able to see why I should feel ashamed of my descent," and affirmed that he found "the attraction of Jewry and Jews irresistible."[27] Although he conceded that he was bound to Judaism by "neither faith nor national pride," he acknowledged his own debt to some of the oldest traditions in Judaism, including the one that is preserved in the passage of the Torah where Moses is shown to admonish God to his face for his various shortcomings as a deity.

"It is to my Jewish nature alone that I owe two characteristics that had become indispensable to me in the difficult course of my life," Freud told a convention of the B'nai B'rith in 1926. "Because I was a Jew, I found myself free from many prejudices which restricted others in the use of their intellect; and, as a Jew, I was prepared to join the opposition and do without agreement with the 'compact majority.' "[28]

Freud was blunt and unsentimental about what it meant to be a Jew. When a Jewish colleague wondered out loud whether to raise his newborn son as a Christian, Freud delivered a sharp rebuke: "If you do not let your son grow up as a Jew, you will deprive him of those sources of energy which cannot be replaced by anything else," said Freud. Jewish "energy," as Freud used the term, was not some airy-fairy notion extracted from the philosophical musings of Maimonides or the arcane mysteries of Kabbalah; it was a hard-edged weapon that Freud regarded as essential to survival in a world benighted by anti-Semitism—literally a matter of life and death. "He will have to struggle as a Jew," said Freud, "and you ought to develop in him all the energy he will need for the struggle."[29]

Indeed, Freud once revealed an experience from his own childhood that allows us to see for ourselves how thin and brittle was the shell of civilization within which the Haskalah first flowered. At the age of twelve, Freud recalls, his father told him about an incident that could have happened anywhere in the Diaspora and must have been a commonplace of Jewish life in the nineteenth century, especially in Germany. As Jakob Freud walked down the street, a Gentile knocked his new fur cap into the mud and shouted at him, "Jew, get off the pavement!"

"And what did you do?" the outraged young Freud asked his father with all the fearlessness of an adolescent.

"I stepped into the gutter," his father admitted, "and picked up my cap."

Freud was shocked and heartbroken by his father's confession, and he later showed himself to be made of sterner stuff when it came to anti-Semitic bullies. His son, Martin, recalled a similar incident from his own childhood, but one with a much different outcome. Father and son were on a mountain-climbing holiday in a German village, but when they returned to their hotel after a day of hiking, they ran into a crowd of villagers who barred their way and shouted anti-Semitic slogans at them. "Swinging his walking-stick, Freud unhesitatingly charged into them," reports Jones, "with an expression on his face that made them give way before him."[30]

Something of the same toughness of spirit was in evidence in 1939, when Freud's family and followers were urging him to leave Vienna before it was too late and put himself beyond the reach of the Third Reich. He literally faced down the Nazi bureaucrats in Vienna who were empowered to decide whether this famous Jew would be set free or sent to a concentration camp, and it was the Nazis who flinched—Freud and his family were allowed to leave Vienna and reached a safe haven in London. And when the Nazis demanded a written acknowledgment that he had not been mistreated—something they intended to use for propaganda purposes—Freud, the master of the Jewish joke, offered them a single sardonic line: "I can heartily recommend the Gestapo to anyone."[31]

On the very eve of his flight from Vienna, Freud was inspired to draw on his Jewish heritage in his conversations with friends and family. He likened himself to the patriarch Jacob, "whom in his old age his children brought to Egypt," and he wryly invoked Ahasverus, the so-called Wandering Jew of Christian tradition: "It is time for Ahasverus to come to rest someplace." And when his colleagues declared their intention to follow him into exile and set up the new headquarters of the Psychoanalytic Society wherever he settled, Freud was reminded—and, in turn, pointedly reminded them—of Rabbi Yohanan Ben Zakkai and the academy that the Roman general Titus permitted him to establish at Yavneh. "We are going to do the same," said Freud. "We are, after all, used to persecution by our history, tradition and some of us by personal experience."[32]

"Subtle but Not Malicious"

A minor scandal erupted within the Jewish community of Berlin in 1920 when a young man named Albert Einstein (1879–1955) refused to pay the communal dues that were assessed against every Jewish citizen. "Much as I feel myself a Jew," protested Einstein, "I feel far removed from the traditional religious forms." And he sought to make it clear that he was acting on principle and not out of penury by offering to make a voluntary contribution to the Jewish welfare fund. When it was pointed out that German law required *all* citizens, Jews and non-Jews alike, to pay dues to the religious communities to which they belonged, Einstein was moved to an expression of outrage that seems almost infantile in light of things to come. "Nobody can be compelled to join a religious community," he declared. "Those times, thank God, are gone forever."[33]

Einstein eventually relented and agreed to pay his dues. Still later, as he witnessed the crimes against the Jewish people by Nazi Germany and its collaborators, his sense of solidarity with his fellow Jews grew ever stronger. He could not fail to see that Jewish identity was not a matter of choice—Einstein's writings were among the first books to be publicly burned (along with those of Marx and Freud, among many others) when the Nazis came to power in 1933. Toward the end of his life, when he was arguably the most famous Jew in the world, Einstein was invited to serve as president of Israel, although his advanced age and failing health prompted him to turn down the honor. "I have to be satisfied with playing the Elder Statesman and the Jewish Saint," he wrote in a private letter in 1952, "mainly the latter."[34]

Einstein, in fact, was already playing a highly visible role in the struggle for a Jewish homeland in Palestine at the very moment when he was still dickering over his dues back in Berlin. At the invitation of Chaim Weizmann (1874–1952), the leading figure in the Zionist movement and the future president of Israel, Einstein traveled to Palestine in 1922 to deliver a lecture at the site on Mount Scopus in Jerusalem where Hebrew University was to be built: "The lectern has waited for you for two thousand years," went the formal greeting that was extended to Einstein, who responded with a greeting of his own in Hebrew, "which," as he privately confessed, "I read with great difficulty."[35]

Einstein, as it turns out, was a visionary in matters of politics as well as physics. At a time when most of his fellow German Jews still aspired to be both good Jews and good Germans—the old ideal of the Haskalah—Einstein was willing to put himself in the service of Zionism, a movement based on the idea that a Jewish homeland was the only safe refuge for the Jewish people. As early as 1933, when the Nazis were only beginning to put their anti-Semitic theories into practice, he recognized in Nazism what the rest of the world—and, tragically, much of the Jewish world—would come to see only later: a "war of annihilation," as Einstein put it, "against my fellow Jews."[36] And, just as he enlisted in the struggle to build Zionism, Einstein joined the larger struggle to defeat Nazism: he helped to compose and signed a letter to President Franklin Delano Roosevelt alerting FDR in 1939 to the urgent need to perfect and build the atomic bomb and use it against Nazi Germany.

"I believe that it is my duty to bring to your attention," Einstein wrote to Roosevelt, "that extremely powerful bombs of a new type may be constructed."[37]

The Nazis famously dismissed the groundbreaking scientific theories of Einstein as "Jewish physics" even as they were trying to use the same theories to build an atomic bomb of their own, and some Jews were (and are) offended by the notion that the work of Marx, Freud, or Einstein owes something to their Jewishness. "In truth, there was nothing specifically 'Jewish' about Socialism or Capitalism or any economic philosophy," insists Abram Leon Sachar, "just as there was nothing specifically 'Jewish' about the mathematics of Einstein."[38] But Einstein can be seen as just as deeply and uniquely Jewish as Marx and Freud, even if each expressed Jewishness in a slightly different way. Marx, as we have seen, was a messianist; Freud loved to tell Jewish jokes; and Einstein, like so many of the rabbis and sages who came before him, was a working theologian.

Indeed, even if Einstein shunned any formal affiliation with religious Judaism, he was a man who spent a lot of time thinking and talking about God. His theological credo, however, owed less to the Torah than to Spinoza, whom he revered as "one of the deepest and purest souls our Jewish people has produced."[39] And yet, even if he acknowledged only Spinoza, a man who was excommunicated by his fellow Jews, Einstein also embraced something of Maimonides, a man whose books were burned at the behest of his fellow Jews precisely because of his own pious rationalism. In fact, Einstein echoes not only the ideas but even the formal phrasing of Maimonides' thirteen articles of faith ("I believe with perfect faith that God is not physical").[40]

"I believe in Spinoza's God who reveals himself in the orderly harmony of what exists, not in a God who concerns himself with the fates and actions of human beings," Einstein declared when asked in 1929 if he believed in God. "The idea of a personal God is an anthropological concept which I cannot take seriously."[41]

Of course, Einstein often used "God" as a kind of code word for purely scientific notions. One of his metaphorical expressions was so famous—"I cannot believe that God plays dice with the universe"[42]—that it finally drew an exasperated retort from a fellow physicist: "I wish Einstein would stop telling God what he can and cannot do." Einstein himself acknowledged that "[i]t is always misleading to use anthropomorphical concepts in dealing with things outside the human sphere."[43] Still, he was fired with the same spirit that inspired the Prophets, no less than the Jewish Socialists, to define the sacred in terms of social justice in the here and now: "I believe that we have to content ourselves with our imperfect knowledge and understanding and treat values and moral obligations as a purely human problem," declared Einstein, "the most important of all human problems."[44] And, as if to affirm his idealism even in the face of all the horror that the world had witnessed, his final word on the subject of God is the most redemptive of all. "God may be subtle," said Einstein, "but He is not malicious."[45]

"Death to Dreyfus! Death to the Jews!"

One of the cherished assumptions among the emancipated and enlightened Jews of Germany and Western Europe in the nineteenth century was that the so-called Jewish question—the question of anti-Semitism, both its causes and its effects—had been solved once and for all. The poor, benighted *Ostjuden* might continue to suffer in Poland and Russia and the Ukraine, where they were still persecuted and oppressed, but the Jews of Germany, France, and England were now full-fledged and fully empowered citizens of their homelands. "[I]n the civilized world," wrote Graetz in 1871, "the Jewish tribe has found at last not only justice and freedom but also . . . unlimited freedom to develop its talents."[46]

Or so they thought until they first heard the name of Dreyfus.

Captain Alfred Dreyfus (1859–1935) was a Jewish officer in the army of France, the very first place in Europe where the Jews had been fully and formally emancipated, and he served as the only Jew on the French general staff—a measure of the lofty heights to which a Jew might ascend in modern Europe. But in 1894 Dreyfus was falsely accused of espionage on behalf of Germany, and—after a secret court martial and a quick conviction based on forged evidence—he was shipped off to Devil's Island under a life sentence. Although Dreyfus would later be exonerated, the Dreyfus Affair, as it was known, came as a shock to the complacent Jews of France and the rest of Western Europe—here was a recrudescence of anti-Semitic rhetoric and anti-Semitic violence in the very heart of "the civilized world."

"Soldiers!" cried Dreyfus at the ceremony where he was publicly stripped of his badges and buttons, and his sword was broken. "An innocent man is dishonoured!"

"Death to Dreyfus!" cried the mob. "Death to the Jews!"[47]

One man who watched the spectacle with a kind of fascinated horror was a foreign correspondent from Vienna named Theodor Herzl (1860–1904). Like Dreyfus himself, Herzl was a highly assimilated Jew from a

German-Jewish background, and—like so many of his fellow Jews—he was shattered by the latest eruption of the oldest and ugliest currents of anti-Semitism. After all, if such a thing could happen in France, the place where the Emancipation began, it could happen anywhere in the world. Six months later, Herzl had completed and published the little book *Der Judenstat*—"The Jewish State"—which would serve as the manifesto of modern political Zionism.

Here is a crucial moment in yet another countertradition in Judaism. Until then, the very idea that the exile of the Jewish people might come to an end—the idea that they might return to their ancient homeland in the land of Israel—was regarded by pious Jews as a matter of theology, not politics. A fundamental credo in traditional Judaism held that the Jewish people would be restored to *Eretz Yisrael* only when God sent the Messiah to carry them back to Jerusalem, and not a moment sooner. A few aging Jews might make their way to Jerusalem in order to die and be buried in the Holy Land—and there to await the day of resurrection in their graves—but the rest of the Jewish people were expected to stay where they were and, "though he may tarry," wait patiently for the coming of the Messiah.

Everything the pious Jew knew about the history of the Jewish people confirmed the accuracy of these articles of faith. Bar Kokhba had tried to take back Jerusalem from the Romans—indeed, he had been hailed by Rabbi Akiva himself as the Messiah-King—but he turned out to be the "Son of a Lie" rather than the "Son of the Star," and the whole effort had ended in defeat and dispersion. So, too, had Shabbatai Zevi promised to lead the Jewish people back to *Eretz Yisrael*, and then betrayed everyone who had believed him by taking the turban. So it was that most Jews—and virtually all observant Jews—were fearful of any act or any word that might be seen as yet another audacious attempt at "forcing the end."

Herzl was not burdened by these pious traditions, and he was mostly ignorant of the first stirrings of political Zionism among the Jews of Russia and Eastern Europe. At a time when the earliest *chalutzim* ("pioneers") had already made their way from the Pale of Settlement in Russia to the Turkish province of Palestine—"We have come to the land to build it," goes a Zionist folksong, "and be rebuilt by it"[48]—Herzl was still idling in Vienna, a failed lawyer and an aspiring playwright with a rich wife and a wealth of literary pretensions. Nor did Herzl evince much compassion for his fellow Jews: "Thirty or forty ugly little Jews and Jewesses," he once wrote home about a "grande soiree" that he had attended in Berlin. "No consoling sight"[49] Only after witnessing the public humiliation of Dreyfus did Herzl belatedly discover his own Jewishness and fall under the thrall of Zionism.

Still, Herzl brought something to Zionism that the rough-and-ready *chalutzim* lacked—a gift for cultivating rich and powerful men. Herzl possessed such charm and charisma and sheer *chutzpah* that he was compared by his contemporaries to a biblical prophet and the Messiah himself, although others said he resembled "an insulted Arab sheikh," likened him to Shabbatai Zevi, and suggested that he see a psychiatrist.[50] Like Ezra and Nehemiah, who enjoyed the patronage of a Persian emperor, or Josephus and Yohanan Ben Zakkai, who sought and won the favor of a Roman general, Herzl managed to secure audiences with various potential allies and benefactors, everyone from the kaiser of Germany to the sultan of Turkey to the pope at the Vatican. To each one, he conceded the existence of what was generally called "the Jewish question"—a "misplaced piece of medievalism" that regarded Jews as an alien and undesirable element everywhere in the Diaspora—and he proposed to solve the Jewish question once and for all by the simple expedient of giving the Jews a land of their own.[51]

"The Jewish question still exists—it would be foolish to deny it," writes Herzl in *The Jewish State*. "I consider the Jewish question neither a social nor a religious one—it is a national question."[52]

Among the first of the potentates upon whom Herzl called was a titled German Jew, Baron Maurice von Hirsch (1831–1896). The Hirsch family had started out as "court Jews," rose to ever greater respectability as bankers and railroad builders, and grew so rich and influential that Maurice von Hirsch's grandfather Jacob had been raised to a baronage. Mindful of the "Jewish question," and willing to spend his own money to improve the lot of his fellow Jews, Baron von Hirsch had already donated vast sums of money to establish trade schools and agricultural colonies for Jews all over the Diaspora, and he had even underwritten a few such projects in Palestine. But Zionism was not just another object of philanthropy, Herzl told von Hirsch—the goal of Zionism was nothing less than the creation of a sovereign Jewish state with its own land, its own army, even its own flag.

"What is a flag? A stick with a rag at the end of it?" Herzl mused in an audacious letter to Baron von Hirsch. "No, for a flag, people live and die. It is the one thing people are willing to die for, if they are taught to do so. With a flag, people are led—perhaps all the way to the Promised Land."[53]

The prospect of leaving behind the salons of Berlin and Vienna and pioneering in the malarial swamps and barren deserts of Palestine did not much appeal to the beneficiaries of the Haskalah. But it sparked a flame among the *Ostjuden* that burned even hotter than the messianic fervor that had once focused on Shabbatai Zevi or the religious ecstasies of Hasidism. And, ironically, the idea of mass emigration was especially appealing to the very worst enemy of the Jewish people in the nineteenth-century Diaspora, the tsar of Russia, who wanted to rid himself of the millions of Jews who were crowded into the so-called Pale of Settlement that ran from Lithuania through Bielorussia to the Ukraine.

"One-third will emigrate," one high-ranking minister to the Russian tsar predicted, "one-third will convert, and one-third will die."

The prediction was accurate on two out of three points. Only a tiny number of the *Ostjuden* converted, but a great many of them managed to emigrate, and a great many more were murdered by Nazi Germany and its allies during the Holocaust. Among the Jewish refugees who left Europe in the late nineteenth and early twentieth centuries, one hundred thousand or so actually made it to Palestine, but nearly three million reached safe havens in Western Europe, South Africa, South America, and, above all, the United States. To the Jews who sailed past the Statue of Liberty into New York harbor, America was not the Promised Land, not "the land of milk and honey," but the *Goldineh Medinah*—the Golden Land.

"A New Judaism and a New Jew"

If there is a pilgrimage site in American Judaism, it is (or, at least, ought to be) Ellis Island, the place where literally millions of Jews first set foot on American soil. The scene is conjured up in the poem by Emma Lazarus (1849–1887) that is affixed to the base of the Statue of Liberty— "Give me your tired, your poor, your huddled masses yearning to breathe free"—and those huddled masses include the ancestors of the greatest number of modern American Jews. My heart still goes to my throat when I recall the sight of the marble steps that lead from the boat landing to the reception hall on Ellis Island; so many feet have trod those steps, the feet of my own grandparents among them, that we can still see and touch the place where the risers are worn away.[54]

"The manner in which the people of different nationalities greet each other after a separation of years is one of the interesting studies at the Island," reads a placard that I copied out on my first visit, the recollections of a matron who witnessed many of the reunions that took place at the so-called Kissing Post on Ellis Island. "The Jew of all countries kisses his wife and children as though he had all the kisses in the world and intended to use them all up quick."[55]

The first Jews to reach America were a shipload of twenty-three Sephardim whose ancestors had been expelled from the Iberian Peninsula in 1492 and who had found a temporary refuge in Brazil. When they sailed into the port of New Amsterdam aboard the *St. Catarina* in 1654, they were first denied permission to land by the Dutch governor, Peter Stuyvesant; but he was eventually forced to admit them by the headquarters of the Dutch East India Company, whose stockholders included some influential Dutch Jews. When Stuyvesant continued to afflict the new arrivals, an assertive young Jew named Asser Levy raised such a protest that he was eventually granted all the rights and privileges of a full-fledged Dutch burgher, including the right to bear arms and the right to own land. From the beginning, then, Jews in America showed themselves to be assertive, proud, and successful, a very different kind of Jew from those who were still confined and oppressed in the ghettos of the Diaspora.

Not until the nineteenth century, however, did Jewish immigration to America begin in earnest. Jews from Germany and Austria arrived by the thousands in the wake of the Napoleonic Wars and the successive revolutions and counterrevolutions that continued to rock the cities of Europe. By 1880, when new and vastly larger waves of Russian and Eastern European Jews were reaching the United States, the German Jews in America already constituted a kind of landed aristocracy within American Judaism. By the opening shot of World War I in 1914, a quarter-million Jews from Austria and Germany had been joined by more than two-and-a-half million Jews from Russia and Eastern Europe. Today, the Jewish population of greater New York is significantly larger than that in the combined population of Jerusalem, Tel Aviv, and Haifa.

The arrival of Jews in America, from one perspective, was something very old and very traditional. After all, as we have seen, the Diaspora was already 2,500 years old when those two dozen refugees from the Spanish Inquisition landed at what is today New York City. And the same outflow of Jewish refugees from Russia and Eastern Europe that reached a flood tide in the late nineteenth century carried Jews to London and Paris, to Johannesburg and Rio de Janeiro, to Havana and Toronto. But, in a profound sense, something wholly new began right here in the United States—America was, in fact, the Golden Land that it was advertised to be, and Jews have thrived here with a degree of freedom, security, opportunity, and prosperity that is unknown anywhere else in the long history of the Diaspora.

"Here in the New World the refugees from every corner of the Old [produced] a new Judaism and a new Jew," enthuses historian Abram Leon Sachar, "upon whom rests the chief responsibility for the future of the race."[56]

Of course, Sachar understates the case—and slightly misses the point—when he refers to "*a* new Judaism." When the first Jewish refugees from Russia and Eastern Europe stumbled off the boats at Ellis Island, at least two other "Judaisms" already existed in America—the descendants of the Jews from Germany and Austria who had arrived in the mid-nineteenth century and the descendants of the Sephardic Jews who had arrived even earlier. And, in fact, the latest refugees were not warmly welcomed by their fellow Jews; what inspired Emma Lazarus, a woman from an old New York family of Sephardic origin, to write her welcoming verses was the scandalous fact that some of the harshest attacks on the *shtetl* Jews from Eastern Europe—"The wretched refuse of your teeming shore," as she put it—were uttered by wealthy and highly assimilated Jews who now called themselves "Hebrews" and felt nothing in common with those they considered "wretched refuse" indeed.[57]

Some of the same frictions—and many new ones—are still at work. An American Jew of Russian origin might still refer to a fellow Jew of German origin as a "Yekka," a disparaging and even insulting term. "My mother declared to me that German Jews, even newly arrived ones, were arrogant and heartless," says a character in E. L. Doctorow's *World's Fair*. "We were descendants of Eastern Europeans, a more natural, more humane people, who knew what suffering was."[58] But nowadays the Jewish community is so rich and diverse that the distinctions between Russian Jews and German Jews seem trivial; the Ashkenazic Jews in all of their varieties have been joined by Jews from Israel, Persia, North Africa, Ethiopia, and all over the Diaspora. And that is only one way to distinguish among the many Judaisms in contemporary America.

The fact is that Judaism reached a critical mass in America and exploded into a thousand fragments. Today, for example, the largest number of religiously affiliated Jews in America belong to the Reform and Conservative movements, but the majority of American Jews are not affiliated with *any* religious movement. Some Jews pray three times a day, some Jews go to synagogue only on the High Holidays, and the greatest number of all never set foot in a *shul*. Indeed, a self-identified and self-affirming Jew in America today might be a "BuJew" who keeps kosher and practices Zen meditation; or a Yuppie with a mystical bent who studies a thoroughly up-to-date form of Kabbalah that promises to improve his sex life as well as his spiritual life; or a wholly secular Yiddishist who plays in a klezmer band and prefers the *mamaloshen* ("mother tongue") to the *loshen ha'kodesh* ("sacred tongue") of Hebrew. And that's exactly what one Jewish historian meant when he declared, "There are six million Jews in America, and six million Judaisms."[59]

The Melting Pot

The Jewish dramatist Israel Zangwill (1864–1926) summed up the most powerful element in the American Dream in the image of "The Melting Pot." A Jew who reached America was urged to stop being a "greenhorn" and start being an American—"*oysgrinen zikh,*" according to the Yiddish phrase. Typically, the newly arrived Jew gave up the prayer house and took up the sweatshop, and replaced the study of Talmud with the study of English.[60] But the Melting Pot has done as much to ensure "the disappearance of Judaism," according to one Orthodox rabbinical commentator, than any other annihilating force that the Jewish faith has encountered.[61] Today, if Reform Jews and ultraobservant Jews agree on anything—indeed, if there is a "Jewish question" in the United States—it is not the age-old problem of anti-Semitism but the dilemma of what Alan Dershowitz calls "the disappearing American Jew."

"The good news is that American Jews—as *individuals*—have never been more secure, more accepted, more affluent, and less victimized by discrimination or anti-Semitism," Dershowitz frets. "The bad news is that American Jews—as a *people*—have never been in greater danger of disappearing through assimilation, intermarriage, and low birthrates."[62]

No greater or crueler irony can be found in all of Jewish history. America was the place of refuge where millions of Jewish lives were preserved during the Holocaust—my grandfather managed to travel from Boibruisk, Russia, to New York City via Jerusalem, Cairo, and Gallipoli, and he died in bed at the age of seventy-eight in Los Angeles; but his mother and father, who remained behind, were shot to death by the Germans in an open pit. And yet, if we believe what the alarmists are saying, American Jews are doing to themselves what Antiochus the Madman and the Grand Inquisitor and Adolf Hitler tried but failed to do.

Of course, alarmism is an old Jewish tradition, too. The hand-wringers who are predicting the disappearance of the Jewish people in the twenty-first century sound a lot like the ones who have predicted the very same thing throughout the history of Judaism. The Hasidim of biblical antiquity condemned the Hellenizers, the Talmudic sages attacked the Kab-

balists, the Mitnagdim and the Hasidic *rebbes* excoriated each other—
and joined in decrying the Maskilim. And yet, against every dire prophecy, the Jewish people are still here, and Judaism is only richer and
stronger precisely because Jewish civilization was constantly reinvigorated by a steady infusion of new ideas about what it means to be Jewish.

To be sure, the "Judaisms" of the modern world are very different
from the "classical" Judaism that excommunicated Spinoza. The twentieth century added a whole new martyrology and a whole new saga of redemption, and contemporary Judaism is defined as much by these very
recent events as by anything else in the long history of the Jewish people.
"On three things does the world stand," goes a cherished Talmudic aphorism, "on justice, on truth, and on peace."[63] Today, if the Jewish world of
the twenty-first century rests on three things, they are the American Diaspora, the Holocaust, and the State of Israel.

EIGHT

After Auschwitz

After Auschwitz, to write a poem is barbaric.
—THEODOR ADORNO

Among all the works of fiction that have been written about the Holocaust, a whole library of horror and heartbreak, an essential one is *The Last of the Just* by André Schwarz-Bart, a novel that allows us to witness the ordeal of the Six Million through the experiences of a single Jewish man with a name and a face. And yet, significantly, the book opens with a scene set in the English town of York on March 11, 1185, when a sermonizing bishop roused his congregants to riot against the Jews who lived among them.

A few Jewish families barricaded themselves in an old watchtower on the edge of town. For seven days, a monk approached the walls under an upraised crucifix and offered the besieged Jews a choice between conversion and death. And for seven days, the offer was refused. On the seventh day, the rioters who surrounded the watchtower heard "a great sound of lamentation" and then an ominous silence—and when they finally broke into the watchtower, they found that the Jews of York, just like the Jews who had sought refuge from a Roman army at Masada, had taken their own lives rather than die at the hands of their enemies.

"This anecdote in itself offers nothing remarkable," writes Schwarz-

Bart. "In the eyes of Jews, the holocaust of the watchtower is only a minor episode in a history overstocked with martyrs."[1]

Here is the first of a thousand troubling questions that are raised by the Holocaust: How do the events of the "War Against the Jews," as historian Lucy Dawidowicz puts it, fit into the long and often dismal experience of the Jewish people? Was the Holocaust something new and unique, or was it merely another chapter in the Book of Martyrs that is one version of Jewish history? And, whether or not the Holocaust *is* something new and unique, what sense can we make of the stomach-turning and soul-shaking ordeal that our blood relations endured in the concentration camp at Birkenau or the killing pits at Babi Yar?

It's a question that still haunts the Jewish world. For Jews who, like Abraham or Moses or Job, are willing to address a bold question to God, the Holocaust presents itself as a troubling theological mystery: Where was God at Auschwitz? For some Jews, especially in Israel, the Holocaust is a hard lesson in history and politics: it represents a caution against passivity and powerlessness, and it inspires in them a toughness and even a ruthlessness that harks all the way back to the "fighting Jew" of distant biblical antiquity: "Never again!" For other Jews, especially in America, the Holocaust is not a matter of theology or history or politics—rather, it is a matter of Jewish identity, and it fundamentally defines their Jewishness in terms of victimhood, real or imagined. "To be a Jew in America, or anywhere, today is to carry with you the consciousness of limitless savagery," writes journalist and author Leonard Fein. "It is to carry that consciousness with you not as an abstraction, but as a reality; not, God help us all, only as a memory but also as possibility."[2]

The notion that American Jews are at risk of a second Holocaust is surely a matter of rhetorical excess if not an outright paranoid fantasy. And yet no thinking or feeling Jew can look at the grainy black-and-white photographs that have become icons of the Holocaust without coming to the shattering realization that, but for an accident of history, he or she might have been one of those naked corpses. The whole question of Who is a Jew?—a question answered in pious Jewish circles by reference to the fine points of Jewish law—is rendered moot by the dire truth that many men, women, and children who were not Jews at all under the rigorous standards of *Halakhah* were Jewish enough for Hitler. The point is made in the recollection of a highly assimilated Jewish-American G.I. whose unit liberated a labor camp, where he came upon the sight of a few surviving Jewish slaves, starved and broken by the brutality of their German captors.

"On that day," he recalls, "I became a Jew."

Some Jews lament that the Holocaust is so prominent in Jewish memory and Jewish identity. Should we not spend less time commemorating the Holocaust and more time celebrating the rich and redemptive moments in Jewish history? Are we not in danger of turning Judaism into a wholly new faith—"Holocaustism"? Yet the Holocaust is a fact of Jewish history that simply cannot be ignored, and many Jews regard it as a kind of sacred duty to wring some kind of meaning out of the suffering and death of six million men, women, and children who were murdered by Nazi Germany and its collaborators simply because they were Jewish.

"Thou Shalt Not Forget"

Tragically, the search for the meaning of the Holocaust has provoked as much bitterness and contention within the Jewish world as any counter-tradition that we have so far encountered. At one extreme, some Jewish fundamentalists insist on blaming the victims of the Holocaust for their own sufferings: "A weeding-out process" is how one ultraobservant Jew describes the Holocaust, "a punishment for the spiritually dilapidated state of the Jews." Some pious Jews cast God himself in the role of torturer and executioner of the Jewish people, and they cite chapter and verse from the Torah itself to justify their theological stance: "The Lord will send upon thee cursing, discomfiture, and rebuke until thou be destroyed," God is shown to warn the Chosen People, "because of the evil of thy doings, whereby thou hast forsaken Me" (Deut. 28:20).[3] Thus, to the most anguishing of all questions—Where was God at Auschwitz?—they offer a heartbreaking and blood-shaking answer.

"God was in the gas chambers," insists one modern Jewish zealot, "telling the Jews: 'This is what happens when you turn your back on me.' "[4]

At the other extreme are a few deeply alienated Jews who also use the Holocaust as a weapon for attacking their fellow Jews, but for a starkly secular motive. A recent and particularly ugly example is *The Holocaust Industry* by Norman G. Finkelstein, an odious little tract that dismisses the bulk of Holocaust scholarship as "nonsense, if not sheer fraud" and condemns the "sacralization of the Holocaust." When the smoke of the author's hellfire and brimstone finally clears, what is left is Finkelstein's insistence that the Holocaust is an "ideological weapon" deployed in defense of Israel and certain "political and class interests," presumably those of his fellow Jews in the United States.[5] "The Holocaust," fumes Finkelstein, "is effectively a 'mystery' religion."[6]

Of course, the Holocaust *is* regarded by some Jews as a mystery so profound and so impenetrable that, like the personal name of God, it is dangerous even to speak it aloud. After all, how can we express in mere words what so many of our fellow Jews experienced in flesh and blood? At a certain sublime moment in *The Last of the Just*, for example, the author pauses for a moment in his storytelling and addresses a cry of despair to the reader before abruptly resuming the narrative: "I am so weary that my pen can no longer write," he laments. " 'Man, strip off thy garments, cover thy head with ashes, run into the streets and dance in thy madness. . . .' "[7]

Other Jews regard it as a sacred duty to testify to the crimes that were committed against the Jewish people. "Remember what the Amalekites did to you on your way out of Egypt," goes a passage in the Torah. "Thou shalt not forget" (Deut. 25:17, 19).[8] By long tradition, the Amalekites, an ancient enemy of the Israelites, are symbolic of *all* oppressors of the Jewish people, including the most recent and most terrible oppressor of them all. Even a strictly secular Jewish historian like Simon Dubnow, a man for whom the study of history was an instrument of Jewish liberation, understood and embraced the commandment "Thou shalt not forget." Thus, the last words that he uttered when he was shot down in the streets of Riga during the Holocaust were *"Schreibt und farschreibt!"*— "Write and record!"[9]

After Auschwitz

One reason that the Holocaust is so perplexing, so unsettling, and so hard to leave alone is that the depths of its horror and terror are literally unfathomable. Today, more than a half-century after the defeat of Nazi Germany, startling new facts about the Holocaust continue to boil up from the killing pits. Only very recently, for example, was it revealed to the world that the IBM corporation actively collaborated with Nazi Germany during the Holocaust by providing the cutting-edge computer technology that made it possible to identify, locate, seize, and murder six million Jewish men, women, and children. Thus, even if we regard the Holocaust as unique only in the number of its victims and the efficiency with which they were murdered, we are still presented with new data that explain how Nazi Germany and its collaborators were able to turn mass murder into an industrial-scale operation.

"IBM Germany . . . supplied the indispensable technologic assistance Hitler's Third Reich needed to accomplish what had never been done before," reveals historian Edwin Black in a book first published only in 2001, "the automation of human destruction."[10]

Most treacherous of all, however, is the impulse to tinker with the brutal facts of the Holocaust. "After Auschwitz, to write a poem is barbaric," wrote Theodor Adorno (1903–1969), a German-Jewish social scientist and Holocaust survivor, and I understand him to mean that the Holocaust is an event of such towering evil and such unfathomable horror that it casts a moral shadow over every human enterprise. But his words can also be taken as a caution—whenever we try to make sense of the Holocaust in our own words and images, and especially if we dare to "fictionalize" the historical record, we put ourselves at risk of trivializing an event that simply beggars the human imagination.

Perhaps the single best example of the moral peril against which Adorno warns us can be seen in the motion picture that Steven Spielberg made out of Thomas Keneally's admirable book, *Schindler's List*. Keneally, to his credit, alerts his readers to what he calls the "strange virtue" of Oskar Schindler, a Nazi war profiteer who managed to save the lives of a thousand or so Jewish men and women who worked as slaves in his factories. "[I]t is a feature of his ambiguity," explains Keneally, "that he worked within or, at least, on the strength of a corrupt and savage scheme."[11] By contrast, Spielberg made the mistake, however well-intentioned, of tampering with history in order to make what he regarded as a better movie, and he thereby conjured up a phony version of the Holocaust that pointedly omits one of its emblematic horrors.

As a filmmaker, Spielberg loves to toy with his audience. When Indiana Jones, armed only with a whip, finds himself face to face with a sword-wielding villain in *Raiders of the Lost Ark*, for example, we expect to see a set-piece fight scene. Then, abruptly, Spielberg directs Jones to pull out a revolver and cut short the fight by shooting his adversary. The scene plays against our expectations, and it is played for laughs. Exactly the same kind of game-playing is at work in *Schindler's List*, where we are shown a group of terrified Jewish women as they are herded into the "showers" at Auschwitz. We already know that signs were posted outside the gas chambers at Auschwitz to trick the Jewish victims into compliance: UNDRESS HERE FOR DISINFECTANT BATHS. FOLD CLOTHES NEATLY. REMEMBER WHERE YOU LEAVE THEM. Now it is Spielberg who is playing the trick: we see a tight closeup of the showerheads, and what comes out is water, not gas. Thus did Spielberg make the only movie about Auschwitz that even a Holocaust-denier can love, a movie in which we never actually see a single scene of mass murder, a movie in which the "showers" at Auschwitz are actually showers!

Still, Spielberg is wholly faithful to at least one tradition of the Holocaust—the Jewish experience of the Holocaust is almost invariably shown as the experience of the victim, passive and powerless. "Schindler's Jews," as his beneficiaries were known—and the very phrase reduces them to the status of chattel—were lucky enough to find themselves in the hands of a rare and even freakish Nazi factory owner who was willing to act as their protector, but they were always and wholly dependent on his whim. To see the Holocaust through the eyes of Oskar Schindler is to see the Jews as victims whose survival was the result of an act of heroism by a "Righteous Gentile," the title that is bestowed on the rare man or woman who was willing to shelter or rescue a Jew from the Holocaust.

Precious few Jews were so fortunate and that's exactly why they died by the millions.

But there were other Jews who refused to wait patiently and passively for rescue—whether by God, the Allies, or a Righteous Gentile—and refused to die as victims. They represent yet another countertradition in Jewish history—they were "fighting Jews" whose memory reached all the way back to the Maccabees and the defenders of Masada. Although few in number, these Jews can be found throughout the history of the Holocaust, in every ghetto and every camp, from the very beginning to the very end. If we are to make sense of the Holocaust, if we are to honor the commandment that we find in the Torah—"Thou shalt not forget"— then we must remember the Jews who fought back.

"In the Name of Twelve Thousand Persecuted Jews"

On November 7, 1938, a young man showed up at a sporting goods shop in Paris and asked to buy a handgun—a .45 caliber, the kind he had heard mentioned in Hollywood movies. But the shopkeeper persuaded him to choose a 6.35mm revolver—the gun was small and easily concealed, and its hammer was specially designed to make it easier to remove from a pocket without snagging. The gun carried only five rounds, and he purchased only one box of ammunition; he knew what he meant to do with the gun, and five bullets would be more than enough.

His name was Herschel Grynszpan (1921–c. 1942), and he is among the most intriguing figures in the history of the Holocaust, if also one of the more obscure. He was only seventeen years old on the day he purchased the gun, a handsome young man, dark and brooding—he bore a striking resemblance to Sal Mineo. His parents were Polish Jews who had fled to Germany in the wake of World War I to escape the anti-Semitic violence that had flared up across Eastern Europe. (Like the followers of Khmielnitzki some three hundred years before, the latter-day Cossacks who took up arms against the Bolsheviks often singled out Jews as their victims.) But Germany was no longer a safe refuge once the Nazis rose to power in 1933, and the Grynszpans sought a way to send their son out of

Nazi Germany. First, they signed him up with a Zionist organization for emigration to Palestine, but Herschel was deemed too young and too frail for the journey. Finally, in 1936, they sent him to live with his uncle in Paris.

Once he was safe in Paris, however, the news from home literally haunted young Herschel. Starting on the day the Nazis had assumed power in Germany, they had begun to build and use the apparatus of the Holocaust, and every day brought reports of new outrages. Jews were stripped of German citizenship, excluded from the schools and the professions, and subjected to public humiliation and worse if they ventured out of their homes. To make them more readily identifiable, all Jews in Germany were ordered to adopt "Israel" or "Sarah" as their first names, and the letter "J" was stamped in red ink on their identity cards.

At last, in November 1938, as Herschel read in the Yiddish newspapers of Paris, the German government announced that Polish Jews would be expelled from Germany, and the Polish government announced that they would be refused admission to Poland. Herschel's parents, along with some twelve thousand other Jews, were stranded in the no-man's-land on the Polish-German border, cold, hungry, and ill, as winter approached. The only word from his family was a despairing postcard from his sister, Berta: "You have undoubtedly heard of our great misfortune."[12]

So young Herschel Grynszpan, frantic over of the fate of his family and his fellow Jews, decided to do something about it. As soon as he left the shop where he had purchased the revolver, he stopped briefly at one of his hangouts, the Café Tout Va Bien ("All Goes Well"), and loaded the gun in the privacy of the basement lavatory. Then he presented himself at the German embassy on the Rue de Lille. "I would like to see a person of some importance," Grynszpan announced. "I have an important document to deliver." He was escorted to the office of the third secretary of the embassy, Ernst vom Rath, who invited him to take a seat and asked to see the document he had offered to turn over.

"You are a dirty *Boche*," said Grynszpan as he drew his gun and fired all five shots at the German diplomat, "and here, in the name of twelve thousand persecuted Jews, is your document!"[13]

At that moment, Grynszpan saw himself as a champion of the Jewish people, a single courageous Jew who was ready to carry out an act of blood vengeance against Nazi Germany for its crimes against his family and his fellow Jews. And he believed, too, that the rest of the world could be made to care about the fate of the Jews who remained in the clutches of Nazi Germany. If only the world paid attention to what was happening on a remote stretch of the Polish-German border, Grynszpan had convinced himself, something could and would be done to save the twelve thousand Jews whose lives were at urgent risk and more than a half-million other Jews who were still awaiting their fate within Nazi Germany.

"I have to protest in such a way that the whole world hears my protest," Grynszpan had written on the back of a photograph that was found in his pocket when he was arrested, "and this I intend to do."

The Night of Broken Glass

Grynszpan did not fully appreciate the will, the guile, or the ruthlessness of the enemy against whom he had delivered one sharp and largely symbolic blow. Within hours after the death of vom Rath, a new catastrophe befell the very people whose lives Grynszpan was trying to save. The Nazi regime seized upon the assassination of the German diplomat in Paris as an excuse for the latest escalation in the war against the Jews, a carefully choreographed night of terror that came to be known as Kristallnacht—"Night of Broken Glass"—because of the vast amount of glass that was left on the streets of Germany after the windows of Jewish homes and shops were shattered. In retrospect, Kristallnacht can be seen as the very first overt act of violence in the crusade that had been in preparation since in 1933 and later come to be known as the Holocaust.

On the night of November 10, 1938, several hundred Jews were killed outright, some 30,000 Jewish men were seized and sent to concentration camps, nearly 200 synagogues were burned to the ground and 75 more were demolished, and more than 7,500 Jewish-owned stores and houses were destroyed. Although the Nazi authorities made some half-hearted efforts to give Kristallnacht the appearance of a spontaneous act of vengeance by the German people—Nazi storm troopers were cautioned to leave their uniforms at home and wear civilian clothing—the operation was, in fact, planned and executed with typical discipline and precision. "Only such measures are to be taken that will not endanger German lives or property," went the orders issued by the Gestapo and the SS. "The whole operation is to be over by 5:00 A.M." Even the graffiti to be painted on shopfronts and synagogues were specified in advance: REVENGE FOR THE MURDER OF VOM RATH was one approved text, and another was DEATH TO INTERNATIONAL JEWRY.[14]

So, in a sense, the first act of Jewish armed resistance against Nazism can be seen as a backfire, and that is mostly how Grynszpan is remembered, when he is remembered at all. But Grynszpan only provided the Nazis with an excuse for Kristallnacht—the extermination of the Jews had been their goal all along, and if he hadn't assassinated a German diplomat on that November morning in 1938, the Nazis would have found (or fabricated) another pretext or, even more likely, acted without one. Grynszpan can be credited with ultimate success in his stated goal of exposing the plight of the Jews and the brutality of Nazi Germany to the rest of the world.

"Humanity stands aghast and ashamed at the indecency and brutality that is permitted in Germany," proclaimed one American newspaper in an editorial about Kristallnacht, and another one added: "Reprisal against a whole people for the crime of an overwrought youth is a throwback to barbarity."[15]

Grynszpan himself disappeared into the maw of history. On the day of the assassination, he was seized by the embassy staff and turned over to the French police, and he was still in a French prison, awaiting trial on murder charges, when Germany invaded France in 1940. Ultimately, Grynszpan ended up in the Sachsenhausen concentration camp near Berlin, and he presumably died there—his name is not mentioned in Nazi records after 1942. Ironically, his parents and siblings managed to survive the Holocaust by fleeing to the Soviet Union, and his older brother, Marcus, took his own measure of revenge against the Nazis by serving as a combat soldier in the Red Army. Long after the war, as if to honor his role in the struggle against Nazism, a tribunal declared that

Herschel Grynszpan would be deemed to have perished on May 8, 1945—the day of victory over Nazi Germany.

The Fatal Ideal

Among the most telling entries in the short biography of Herschel Grynszpan is the simple fact that the only thing he knew about firearms was what he had seen in Westerns and gangster movies from Hollywood. Like most Jews in Europe between the two world wars—and, in fact, like most Jews in the Diaspora since the Bar Kokhba Revolt—nothing in Grynszpan's upbringing or education or experience of the world had prepared him to embrace the idea of armed self-defense. Quite to the contrary: the civilized ideal of the Haskalah, as we have seen, encouraged the Jews of Germany to be like everyone else, "a Jew at home and a man in the street," and if they had been trained in the use of arms at all, it was when they served, often with great heroism, in the kaiser's army during World War I.

Of course, the fatal ideal was deeply rooted in Jewish tradition. By and large, the Jews had staked their survival in the Diaspora on the same strategy: they placed themselves under the protection of the powers that be in the countries in which they lived, and they relied on the army and the police to protect them against the Jew-haters. We have already seen several examples of the same tradition: Yohanan Ben Zakkai prevailed upon a Roman general to extract him from besieged Jerusalem, for example, and the Jews who fled the Cossacks during the Khmielnitzki massacre put themselves under the protection of a Polish general. Indeed, as we have noted, the tradition is so old and so deeply embedded in classical Judaism that it is articulated even within the Oral Torah.

"Pray for the peace of the ruling power," cautioned one of the sages of antiquity, "since but for fear of it men would have swallowed each other alive."[16]

Here, of course, is exactly where the Jews who fell under the ruling power of Nazi Germany and its allies made a fatal mistake. By long and mostly reliable tradition, the Jews had always resorted to the ruling power to protect them against acts of anti-Semitism. Even now, they continued to believe that law and order was the best protection against the latest eruptions of violence against the Jews. The Nazis, in fact, played upon these very traditions throughout the Holocaust—and with tragic results.

One of the oldest and most celebrated institutions of the Diaspora, for example, was the *kehillah*, a Jewish communal organization that attended to the internal concerns of the Jewish community—aid to the poor, maintenance of the synagogue, burial of the dead—and, at the same time, acted as a liaison between the Jewish community and the ruling power for the purpose of enforcing civil law and collecting taxes. At some times and places in Jewish history—Poland in the Middle Ages, for example—the Jewish communal authority was so powerful that it virtually amounted to Jewish self-government. And even in more recent experience, the Jews were accustomed to complying with the authority of the Jewish community—Albert Einstein, as we have seen, may have protested against the communal dues he was called upon to pay, but he ultimately paid them.

Thus, when the Nazis began to carry out the mass murder of the Jewish people in earnest, they set up in each Jewish community that fell under their control their own version of the old *kehillah*, an institution that they called a Judenrat ("Jewish council"). The idea was old, familiar, and even comforting—the Jews believed they could rely on the elders of the community to deal with the ruling power on their behalf and perhaps even to protect them from its worst excesses. But the Judenrat was actually a cynical and deadly device used by the Nazis to enforce law and order within the ghetto and to supply the machinery of the Holocaust with Jewish bodies.

Indeed, Jews were literally requisitioned by the Germans, and it was the Judenrat that filled the orders: a specified number of Jews must present themselves at a specified location in the ghetto for what was advertised as labor conscription or "resettlement in the east," according to a standard Nazi euphemism. Against the evidence of their own eyes, against all the rumors of what was really happening to Jews "in the east," the members of the Judenrat summoned their fellow Jews to the transports in the vain hope that the greater number would be spared. And the greatest number of Jews, by a long and mostly honorable tradition in Jewish history, complied without protest with the demands of their elders and betters. "Jewry, which had been without any arms even before the war, was committing itself to a strategy of accommodation," explains Holocaust historian Raul Hilberg. "There were to be no 'provocations.' There was to be no semblance of revolt."[17]

The strategy was an utter failure, of course. No lives were saved, and "accommodation" with the Nazis only made it easier for them to murder Jewish men, women, and children by the millions. And, in fact, the members of the Judenrat have been condemned in some Jewish circles as cynical collaborators who worked only to save their own friends and relations from the gas chambers. But it is too simple to blame the unfortunate few who were called upon to serve on a Judenrat and make up the lists of Jews who were sent "to the east." If the Jews were betrayed during the Holocaust, they were betrayed by their own cherished tradition of going along and getting along with "the ruling power"—and, in the end, it was the ruling power that devoured them.

To Die with Honor

Not every Jew in Europe, however, was quite so ill-prepared to deal with the deadly threat that Nazi Germany posed to the Jewish people. A few clear-eyed and courageous Jewish men and women constituted what Holocaust historian Lucy S. Dawidowicz calls a "counter-community," an underground movement that armed itself and fought back against the Nazis and their allies at every opportunity. They are the heroes of the Holocaust, but they are too often overshadowed by the vastly greater number of victims.

Significantly, the resistance movement in the ghettos and camps consisted largely of young men and women who had embraced the Jewish countertraditions of socialism or Zionism or both. The Jewish labor movement known as the Bund was the single largest component of the "counter-community" of resisters, but it also included Jewish members of the Communist Party and a whole constellation of parties that were committed to both socialism *and* Zionism, all of them united by what Dawidowicz calls "a mystique of fraternity" that can be traced back to the new and updated versions of messianism as articulated by Karl Marx and Theodor Herzl.[18] "The secular messianic vision—'We have been naught, we shall be all'— continued to inspire its adherents, even in the bleakness of the ghetto," Dawidowicz explains, "with the radiant promise of the future."[19]

Jewish resistance was never merely a matter of rhetoric. From the earliest days of World War II, as the Jews were herded into ghettos in towns and cities all over Eastern Europe, the Jewish underground set up and operated public kitchens, infirmaries, even newspapers that were printed in secret and passed from hand to hand. Above all, they drew on their own tradition of what they called *zelbshuts*, a Yiddish term for armed self-defense. The Bund had organized a militia in the aftermath of the Kishinev pogrom of 1903 in an effort to defend their fellow Jews against state-sponsored acts of anti-Semitic violence, using clubs and brass knuckles as weapons and recruiting "tough Jews" to fight with them—horse thieves, wagon drivers, slaughterhouse workers.

The Zionists, too, trained themselves in the use of arms in anticipation of the day when they would finally "make aliyah" to Palestine and begin the work of building and defending the Jewish homeland. Indeed, the tradition of armed self-defense was shared by all factions in modern political Zionism, both the socialist parties that represented the majority of Jews in the Zionist movement and their bitter ideological rivals, the so-called Revisionists, who rejected socialism and embraced a rightist political agenda. By 1941, according to a message smuggled out of Warsaw, the very highest priority of the Jewish underground was "[t]o strengthen the power of resistance and endurance of the Jewish masses in the face of terrible persecutions without parallel in human history."[20]

Resistance meant more than force of arms. The underground newspapers campaigned against the Judenrat and the Jewish police who served them, all of whom were condemned as "traitors who will get their well-merited punishment."[21] Jewish workers who labored in the factories that had been set up inside the ghettos were urged to "work badly and slowly" and to carry out acts of sabotage. Now and then, a strike or a public demonstration would be mounted within the ghetto walls in protest against the starvation rations that were provided to the Jewish slave laborers.

Meanwhile, the underground fighters smuggled in a few old rifles and pistols and stockpiled a meager supply of explosives and gasoline that could be used to make hand grenades and Molotov cocktails. Still, until the very end, the fear of Nazi reprisals against the ghetto population—or, later in the war, the hope of liberation by the Red Army or the Allies—persuaded even the most radical elements of the underground to hold their fire. Only when it became clear that the ghettos were being "liquidated"—and that the real meaning of "resettlement" was death—did the Jewish resistance finally rise up in open battle with the Nazis and their collaborators.

"Don't let yourself be destroyed like sheep!" cried the headline of an underground newspaper published by the Bundists in the Warsaw Ghetto in 1942. "Better to die with honor than to be gassed in Treblinka!"[22]

At this very moment, the young Jewish resistance fighters of the Warsaw Ghetto affirmed a Jewish tradition that reached all the way back to the Maccabees and the defenders of Masada—sometimes a Jew might be without the power to decide *whether* to die but still possessed the power to decide *how* to die. The same heroism was displayed in ghettos across Europe where the Jewish resistance rose up against the Germans and their collaborators. Thus, for example, an anguished conversation between two young men in the Bialystok Ghetto in 1943 echoes the words that must have been spoken by the Zealots who made their last stand on Masada some two thousand years earlier. Only a tiny remnant of the Jewish population of Poland remained alive, one of the two men said to his cohort, and so what difference did it make when or how the last few of them died?

"The only question facing the Jews," replied the other one, "was how to choose to die: 'either like sheep for the slaughter or like men of honor.' "[23]

"Jews! Weapons! Jews! Weapons!"

By January 18, 1943, when the Germans decided to liquidate the Warsaw Ghetto and send the last fifty thousand Jews in Warsaw to the concentration camp at Treblinka, the ghetto fighters had replaced the Judenrat as the de facto leadership of the doomed Jewish community, and they were ready to fire the first shot in what the world would come to remember as the single most dramatic example of Jewish resistance in the history of the Holocaust—the Warsaw Ghetto uprising.

Gestapo informers and other Jewish collaborators had been quietly put out of action in a series of secret executions. A network of fortified attics and cellars, bunkers and hideouts, had been provisioned with food and water and linked together with secret passageways. To finance the purchase of arms on the "Aryan" side of the ghetto wall, money had been extracted from a few wealthy Jews who still remained in the ghetto, and the Judenrat had been persuaded to make a contribution of a million zlotys out of its treasury. A small arsenal was made ready for battle—rifles and pistols, ammunition, hand grenades, Molotov cocktails—all of them smuggled into the ghetto or fabricated by the ghetto fighters out of smuggled explosives. At last, they had gone to ground, quite literally, in anticipation of the battle to come.

At first, the Germans resorted to their customary tactics to persuade the last Jews in the Warsaw Ghetto to present themselves for "resettlement" as compliantly as the three hundred thousand Jews who had gone before them. The Germans promised extra food rations to those who voluntarily signed up for the transports; they declared an "amnesty" for Jews who had gone into hiding in defiance of earlier deportation orders; and they distributed reassuring postcards from friends and relations who had already been sent "to the east"—the last letters to be written, at the instruction of the concentration camp guards, before they were murdered. Those postcards, like the promise of showers at Auschwitz, were among the weapons of psychological warfare by which the Germans had so far managed to intimidate and manipulate their Jewish captives. But new voices—Jewish voices—were now heard in the ghetto.

"Jews, citizens of the Warsaw ghetto, be on the alert, do not believe a single word or act of the SS bandits," warned a pamphlet circulated by the resistance. "No Jew should go to the trains."[24]

So the Germans themselves were forced to go into the ghetto and take out the last remaining Jews by force—or, at least, to try. When the first SS troops entered the ghetto, they were met by gunfire from the hidden bunkers where the Jewish defenders were waiting. Some fifty Germans were killed or wounded before the rest withdrew in haste and shock, and the weapons they left behind in their retreat were added to the meager arsenal of the ghetto fighters. Suddenly confronted with the previously unimaginable phenomenon of Jews who fought back, the Germans were now the ones who were terror-stricken.

"Juden! Waffen!" one German soldier was heard to cry out in panic and disbelief, repeating the amazing words over and over again: "Jews! Weapons! Jews! Weapons!"[25]

When the Germans reentered the ghetto on April 19, 1943, they came in force. A battalion of Ukrainian and Lettish soldiers, serving in an auxiliary of the SS, surrounded and sealed off the ghetto, and some seven thousand German army troops and Polish police officers were held in reserve. Three artillery detachments from the Wehrmacht were positioned outside the ghetto walls, and two thousand shock troops of the SS marched into the ghetto behind a screen of heavy tanks. But the second attempt at crushing the Jewish resistance ended in a second defeat—with casualties numbering two hundred, the Germans were forced to withdraw under fire. That night, the first night of Passover, a seder was conducted in one of the bunkers to the accompaniment of gunshots and explosions.

On the following day, a new assault was mounted, but Jewish resistance was even fiercer. A single homemade mine, planted in the street and fired by remote control from an observation point, killed a hundred or so. Tanks were stopped and set afire with Molotov cocktails. So the German troops withdrew once again, and a veritable siege army—tanks, field guns, anti-aircraft batteries, and heavy machine guns—fired into the ghetto from a safe distance. Between barrages, the Germans set fire to buildings inside the ghetto to kill or burn out those who remained alive. And yet, when the smoke lifted, they saw that one of the Jewish defenders had affixed a banner to a rooftop: "We shall fight to the last."[26]

The ghetto fighters continued to resist, day after day, even as the Germans returned to the ruined ghetto with flamethrowers and police dogs to hunt out the bunkers where the last of the Jews were sheltering. The ghetto fighters, mostly socialist Zionists, were joined by fresh volun-

teers, including their bitter ideological adversaries in the Zionist movement, the right-wing Revisionists. "There was no shortage of volunteers," writes Dawidowicz, "only of arms."[27] Not until May, after weeks of
hard fighting, did the Germans finally reach the bunker located at Mila
18, where the Jewish resistance was headquartered. The Germans sealed
the openings and introduced gas into the bunker, a method of killing
Jews that they had perfected long ago.

A hundred ghetto fighters at Mila 18, like the Zealots at Masada, resolved to take their own lives rather than die at the hands of the Germans and their allies. Not even the destruction of the leadership,
however, put an end to the resistance. Isolated bands of ghetto fighters
continued to hold out until shortly before the Polish uprising more than
a year later. And the Warsaw Ghetto uprising did not end in utter defeat—some 75 Jewish men and women managed to slip out of the scattered bunkers, reach the sewers of Warsaw, and escape from the doomed
ghetto. And, significantly, they did not merely survive—rather, they
lived to fight again.

"We Do Not Select"

Any Jew who managed to escape from a ghetto or a concentration camp
was immediately confronted with a new but no less deadly dilemma. The
prospect of reaching a safe haven outside the vast stretches of German-
occupied Europe was remote. Even if a Jew avoided betrayal and detec-
tion on the long trek out of *Festung Europa* ("Fortress Europe"), the fact
is that Jews were not welcome as refugees in most countries of the world,
Allied or neutral. Great Britain had closed Palestine to legal Jewish immigration, and the United States immigration quota for Germany went
unfilled while German Jews clamored at the U.S. Embassy in Berlin for
the visas that meant the difference between life and death. Indeed, one
reason that more of the victims of the Holocaust did not break and run is
that, quite literally, they had nowhere in the world to go.

As a practical matter, then, only a few choices were available to the
Jew who succeeded in avoiding the killing pits or the concentration
camps. Some Jews went into hiding within occupied Europe, either

"passing" as non-Jews with forged identity papers or—like Anne Frank and her family—putting themselves under the protection of a Righteous Gentile who was willing to put his or her own life at risk by concealing a fugitive Jew. Some Jews reached the war-ravaged territory still controlled by the Red Army, where they might be given a chance to join the Soviet armed forces—a half-million Jews served in the Red Army, and some two hundred thousand were killed in combat—or, at least, to share the brutal war experience of the Soviet people. And a few Jews picked up the gun and carried on the fight against the Germans and their allies as partisans.

Even the Jew who was determined to fight as a partisan, however, faced a whole new peril. Here and there, Jews were permitted to join the resistance movements that were operating within German-occupied territory—in France, Italy, Yugoslavia, and the Netherlands. The French *Maquis* actually welcomed Jewish fighters on the assumption that their loyalty to the resistance was far beyond doubt. More often, however, and especially in Russia and Eastern Europe, the partisans were not much friendlier to Jews than the Germans and their collaborators. For that reason, although some two hundred partisan units operating on the Eastern Front were captained by Jews, many of them took Ukrainian or Russian names to conceal their Jewish identity from their own comrades in arms. Still, at some rare but stirring moments in the otherwise benighted history of the Holocaust, Jews gathered in partisan bands of their very own and made war on Germany.

The single most remarkable example of Jewish resistance outside the ghettos and the camps—and the one that represents a crucial countertradition in itself—is the so-called Bielski partisans, a little army of some twelve hundred Jewish men, women, and children who operated in the forests of Bielorussia, under German occupation until western Russia was finally liberated by the Red Army in 1944. Led by a remarkable man called Tuvia Bielski (1906–1987), a figure with all the courage and charisma of the biblical David in *his* days as a guerilla fighter, they modeled a spirit of resistance and rescue that is wholly unique in the history of the Holocaust.

In some ways, the Bielski partisans resembled other Jewish fighters who fought the Germans and their allies in the forests and marshes throughout the Eastern Front. The band consisted of Jews who had managed, against all odds, to escape from the ghettos where their fellow Jews were awaiting "resettlement." They set up camp only in the wildest and most remote places, far from German patrols and civilian eyes. They survived on the game and edible plants that they could find in the wilderness, and the provisions that they could carry away from isolated farms and villages, sometimes as an act of generosity and solidarity by a friendly civilian, perhaps more often as an "expropriation" at gunpoint. They were armed only with the guns and ammunition that they managed to smuggle out of the ghetto or seize from the Germans whom they attacked and killed in ambushes and hit-and-run raids.

But the Bielski partisans were unique in one crucial way—they welcomed *any* Jew and *every* Jew who succeeded in finding his or her way to their wilderness encampment in the forests of Bielorussia. "Would that there were thousands of Jews who could reach our camp," Tuvia told his comrades in arms, "we would take all of them in."[28]

Most partisan bands, out of simple and brutal necessity, accepted only those who were fit, healthy, and capable of fighting. The very survival of a partisan unit, according to the cruel calculus of guerilla warfare, depend on the ability of each member to hit the enemy and then run. For that reason, some partisans accepted only young men who showed up with weapons of their own. Everyone else was turned away— the elderly, the children, the frail, or even otherwise vigorous young men who did not possess a firearm. Some bands refused to accept women even if they were both armed and fit. And the Jews who were sent back after reaching the partisans were forced to survive as best they could on their own resources. Most of them, of course, did not survive at all.

Tuvia Bielski, however, embraced a very different principle—he placed the highest value on saving Jewish lives even if it placed his own life at risk. "I don't promise you anything—we may be killed while we try to live, but we will do all we can to save more lives," he would tell each new arrival. "This is our way—we don't select."[29]

The very word used by Bielski conjures up one of the characteristic horrors of the Holocaust—the so-called "selection," when the Jewish inmates of a concentration camp would pass in review before a clutch of

German officers who decided which ones would live and which ones would die. Some Jews were selected for the gas chambers, and some were spared in order to work as slaves, at least until the next selection. For Tuvia Bielski, however, the very principle of selection was morally impermissible. His more ruthless comrades protested against the ever-growing burden of the men, women, and children who had joined their ranks—a grandfather, for example, carrying a toddler on his shoulders, neither of them able to kill Germans—but Bielski insisted that it was their duty to welcome precisely those Jews who would be most at risk if they were turned away.

"Tuvia Bielski was filled with the pain of and the love for Jews," recalls Abraham Viner, a Bielski partisan. "He was grateful that he could save Jews. For him, it was a privilege."[30]

He was atypical in other ways, too. The Bielski family earned its living in prewar Poland by farming, not shopkeeping. Tuvia's schooling ended at the age of thirteen when he was sent to work in the fields. Later, he enlisted in the Polish army, and he came away from his military service with the skills of a sharpshooter. So Tuvia and his brothers were, quite literally, the modern equivalent of *Am Ha'aretz*, "people of the land," and they had acquired skills that were not valued much in Jewish tradition but turned out to be essential for survival when dealing with Nazi Germany.

"Father used to say that with fine people we have to be good and proper, but with bad people we have to be bad," recalled Zus Bielski, one of Tuvia's brothers and fellow partisans. "We would not let others push us around. We knew how to fight."[31]

Tuvia was a tough Jew, to be sure, but he was neither a thug nor a bumpkin. He read both the Polish and Yiddish newspapers, and he was alerted to the dangers of fascism when he came across an article by Albert Einstein, "Under the Shadow of Death." He briefly joined and soon withdrew from one of the Zionist parties—Tuvia was too headstrong and high-spirited to submit to the leadership of others—but his political instincts were so sure and his charismatic appeal so strong that others were drawn to him. In 1941, when the German armed forces invaded and conquered the corner of eastern Poland and western Russia where the

Bielski brothers lived, they managed to evade the *Einsatzgruppen*, who murdered Jews by marching them to open pits and shooting them; and they refused to join the rest of the Jews in the ghettos that were set up as holding pens for the industrial-scale abbatoirs at Auschwitz and Treblinka. Tuvia and his brothers, like Judah and the Maccabees, headed into the forests of Bielorussia, and there they stayed—and fought—until the day of liberation.

Bielski, like the biblical King David, was no plaster saint—rugged and handsome, he was the object of adoration among the women in his partisan band, and he was willing to welcome one or another of them into his tent by night. He wielded strict authority over the partisans who followed him into the forest; just as Jerusalem was renamed "the City of David," the encampment where Tuvia's band was headquartered was called "Bielsk." But, at the same time, he was precisely the kind of heroic figure that Herschel Grynszpan aspired to be, and he reminds us that Jewish survival during the Holocaust did not always depend on putting oneself under the protection of a Nazi war profiteer who treated his Jewish slaves well. At the very darkest moment of the Holocaust, Bielski kindled the very same light that had burned so brightly in Jewish history some two thousand years earlier.

"When he got on the horse with his leather coat and the automatic gun," recalls one of his comrades, "we called him '*Yehuda HaMaccabee*' "—Judah Maccabee.[32]

In the Belly of the Beast

The Jews who fought back, of course, represent only a tiny fraction of the Jewish population in Europe during the Holocaust. By far the greatest number of Jews—trapped, terrorized, abandoned, and betrayed—died in the killing pits and the concentration camps, a total of six million Jewish men, women, and children. Millions were herded at gunpoint to open trenches and ravines, stripped naked, and shot to death. Millions more were shipped in cattle cars to concentration camps, where most of them were stripped, shaved, and sent directly to the gas chambers and some were spared so that they could be worked, starved, and tortured to death.

And the German genius for torture and death was endlessly inventive—Jews were subjected to grotesque medical experiments, for example, and they were used to test various new methods of mass murder. And yet, even in the belly of the beast, the Jews fought back.

Some 667 attempted escapes from concentration camps are recorded in the history of the Holocaust, although only 76 of them were ultimately successful, and revolts took place at five of the death camps whose only purpose was the murder of Jews. At the Sobibor death camp, for example, a Red Army officer named Alexander Pechersky led 600 fellow Jews in an uprising on October 14, 1943, and as many as 400 of them managed to break out of the camp, leaving behind ten dead Germans and 38 casualties among the Ukrainians who served as camp guards. Two days later, orders were given to destroy the death camp where 600,000 Jews had so far been murdered.

At Treblinka, the death camp that was the destination for transports from the Warsaw Ghetto and other Jewish communities from Germany to Greece, three combat units armed themselves with weapons lifted from the camp armory and rose up on August 2, 1943, killing 20 Germans, setting the camp on fire, and leading as many as 200 Jews out of the death camp where 800,000 Jews were murdered.

The Jewish resistance penetrated even Auschwitz, the bloodstained icon of the Holocaust and the place where the greatest number of Jews were murdered. The Holocaust, as we have already noted, depended on a whole complex of systems and installations, all on an industrial scale—not only the tabulating equipment provided by IBM's German subsidiary, but also the gas chambers, the Zyklon B poison gas, and the crematoria where the vast number of Jewish corpses were burned to ash. And, precisely because mass murder was a German industry, the loss of any single component would slow down or stop the machinery of the Holocaust. So it was that the Jewish resistance chose the crematoria as the target of a crucial act of sabotage.

The heroine of the operation was a young woman whose name comes down to us as Rosa Robota—"Robota" is a Russian word for "worker," and it is surely the *nom de guerre* that she chose when she joined the Jewish underground. A member of the Zionist socialist youth movement

known as Hashomer Hatzair ("The Young Watchmen"), Rosa first joined
the resistance movement in the Ciechanow ghetto in Poland. Even after
she was caught in a roundup and sent to Auschwitz along with her family
in 1942—she survived the selection that took place upon arrival, and
she watched as her parents and siblings were marched off to the gas
chambers—Rosa found a way to carry on the fight.

Because she was still young and fit, Rosa was assigned to work as a
slave laborer in one of the factories that were scattered around the
Auschwitz-Birkenau complex. She worked in a clothing factory, and
other women from Ciechanow worked in a munitions factory operated
by Krupp, where they had access to high explosives in the form of small
disks that they called "buttons." Rosa was asked by the Jewish underground inside Auschwitz to recruit the women in the munitions factory
to smuggle out the explosives that were urgently needed for a planned
operation whose target was the crematoria.

Each day, twenty women managed to hide a few "buttons" in secret
pockets sewn into their camp uniforms and carry them back to the bar-
racks. Day by day, Rosa passed the explosives along to other members of
the resistance within Auschwitz, sometimes hiding them in a loaf of
bread or a food canister with a false bottom. Eventually, the supplies
reached the bomb makers, who used empty sardine tins as bomb casings
and packed them with "buttons" to create the explosive devices that
would be used to destroy the crematoria. On the day of the operation,
the bombs were hidden on the handcarts that were used to haul corpses
from the gas chambers to the crematoria, and the task of planting and
setting off the bombs fell to the so-called Sonderkommando, the doubly
cursed souls whose work assignment in Auschwitz was tending to the
dead bodies of their fellow Jews.

On October 7, 1944, Rosa witnessed the result of her courageous exploits: Crematorium III at Auschwitz-Birkenau was shattered and set
afire by the exploding bombs, and the Sonderkommando fell upon their
guards, killing four SS men and throwing one especially vicious officer
into the very crematorium where so many of their fellow Jews had been
sent up in smoke. Taking advantage of the panic that the explosion created among the Germans, they headed for the barbed-wire fence, cut

their way through, and led some six hundred Jews out of Auschwitz. But the moment of liberation lasted only briefly—the SS pursued the escaping Jews in force, and all of them were hunted down.

Rosa and three of her comrades—only their first names are recorded: Esther, Ella, and Regina—were taken to the notorious Block 11, where the torture cells were located, and they emerged only on the day they were led to the gallows for a hanging that all of the Jewish prisoners were compelled to witness. But, even as Rosa Robota mounted the gallows, she left her fellow Jews with a stirring example—her last scribbled message, smuggled out of her torture cell, was the traditional Hebrew greeting of Hashomer Hatzair, the words that we read in the Torah when Moses charges Joshua with command of the army that will fight its way into the Promised Land: *"Khazak v'amatz"*—"Be strong and courageous!" (Josh. 1:6).

"The Weight of Dying Jews"

More than one survivor of the Holocaust was so afflicted by his ordeal that he was ultimately driven to take his own life long after liberation. "Whoever was tortured, stays tortured," observed Jean Améry, an Austrian-Jewish philosopher and resistance fighter who survived the Holocaust by thirty-three years before finally dying a suicide.[33] As if to signify his own lifelong struggle to explain the Holocaust to himself, Primo Levi (1919–1987) recalls in *Survival in Auschwitz* how he once glimpsed what a fellow prisoner called Iss Clausner had scratched into the bottom of the tin bowl in which each prisoner received his daily ration of gruel. "Where others have carved their numbers, and Alberto and I our names, Clausner has written: '*Ne pas chercher à comprendre.*' "—"Do not try to understand."[34]

Still, something deep inside us—something that attests to our Jewishness as well as our humanity—forces us to look at the horrors of the Holocaust and try to make sense of them. The experience of the Holocaust is too intense, too tormenting, and too enduring to be reduced to a "crime against humanity" that is unique only in the size of the body count. We are compelled to imagine ourselves in the plight of those who suffered and died and ask ourselves the searing question: What would *I* have done? Would I have walked to the "showers" or would I have fought back? And, even if it cannot be answered, asking the question is the most authentically Jewish impulse of all, precisely because it draws on and honors the feeling of empathy that is one of the core values of Judaism.

The traditional observance of Passover, for example, is meant to place us, literally as well as symbolically, in the plight of the ancient Israelites who were "slaves unto Pharaoh in Egypt." Thus, for example, all of the traditional Passover foods served as the Passover meal known as a seder are what Rabbi Jacob Neusner calls "action-symbols"[35]—we dip a sprig of parsley into salt water to remind ourselves of the tears of the Israelites, for example, and we taste the dish of bitter herbs called *maror* to remind ourselves of the bitterness of their lives. And, at one sublime moment in the seder, we are called upon to project ourselves, body and soul, into a distant time and place—perhaps a wholly mythical time and place—and to speak in the first person about what happened there.

"This is done," we are instructed to tell our children, "because of what God did for *me* when *I* went free out of Egypt."[36]

Exactly the same empathetic impulse is at work when Jews ponder the Holocaust. The idea is expressed, for example, in a guidebook to Holocaust sites published by a Jewish organization: "We want only that the visitor standing at the gate of Dachau or the graves of Bergen Belsen recognize that he too was behind barbed wire; that his own children were led into the gas chamber."[37] And it is expressed, too, by Emil Fackenheim, a survivor of the Sachsenhausen concentration camp, when he muses on the cattle cars that were used by the Germans to carry countless Jews to the death camps during the Holocaust: "I confess I have imagined myself in one of those cars many times, and consider any Jew less than Jewish—any human less than human—who has not imagined himself in that position at least once."[38]

Indeed, the mental exercise of putting oneself in the mind and body of a Holocaust victim takes on a terrifying but illuminating momentum of its own. The novelist Herman Wouk, for example, insists on putting us through the experience of the Holocaust in a searing scene in *War and*

Remembrance. A character called Aaron Jastrow, ironically, a highly assimilated and even a "self-hating" Jew, ends up with his fellow Jews inside the gas chamber at Auschwitz. No water flows from the showerheads as in Spielberg's phony version of the Holocaust—Wouk allows us to smell, taste, and feel the poison gas that fills the darkened chamber, packed tight with Jewish men, women, and children. Suddenly, spontaneously, the words of the *Shema* return to Jastrow's lips: "Hear O Israel, the Lord our God, the Lord is One." But Wouk refuses to let us off by fading to black at this moment of pious martyrdom—he insists on subjecting us to every sensation that he has experienced in his own private act of empathy.

> Naked flesh presses on his face and all over him, stilling his contortions. He cannot move. He does not die of the gas. Very little enters his system. He goes almost at once, the life smothered out of him by the weight of dying Jews. Call it a blessing, for death by the gas can take a long time.[39]

Still, a moment of empathy with the Jews who rode in the cattle cars and died in the gas chambers, no matter how earnest and intense, is not enough to make sense of the Holocaust. Indeed, the exercise poses its own risks: when we sentimentalize and "sacralize" the Holocaust by focusing on its martyrs, when we elevate the Holocaust from the realm of history and politics into the pristine realm of theology, we strip away some of its most vital and urgent meanings. And we simply cannot begin to understand and appreciate the most powerful countertradition in all of Jewish history—the upwelling of will, courage, vision, strength, and heroism that created the modern state of Israel—unless we ponder some of the lessons that we learn when we turn our gaze from the martyrs and focus on the heroes of the Holocaust.

"A State for Which Jews Need No Visas"

The first of the many lessons that can be learned from the Holocaust is that the Jews of Europe were betrayed by their own tradition. Ever since a Persian emperor permitted the Jews to return from exile in Babylon and rebuild the Temple in Jerusalem—an act of largesse for which he is hailed in the Bible as "Messiah"—the Jewish people sought to place themselves under the protection of a ruler or a ruling power. By now, we have seen many examples: Yohanan Ben Zakkai was able to preserve rabbinical Judaism by making a deal with a Roman general during the destruction of Jerusalem; some Polish Jews were able to spare themselves from the Khmielnitzki massacres by seeking refuge with a Polish count and his army; and, as recently as 1917, Chaim Weizmann was able to persuade Great Britain to endorse the notion of a Jewish homeland in Palestine. Significantly, the so-called Balfour Declaration takes the form of a note from the British foreign minister to Lord Rothschild, the modern equivalent of the *shtadlan* or Court Jew who had long enjoyed access to the crowned heads of Europe: "His Majesty's Government view with favour the establishment in Palestine of a national home for the Jewish people."[40]

But the strategy was a complete and catastrophic failure when it came to a ruler like Adolf Hitler and a ruling power like Nazi Germany. The Germans were clever and cynical enough to take advantage of an old and honorable Jewish tradition by, for example, setting up the Judenrat to do their dirty work in the ghettos of Europe. They played on the old habits of the Jews by holding out the familiar prospect of official largesse—the Jews who climbed into the cattle cars were told that they were headed to a place that the German government had set aside as a refuge for the Jewish people. *"Arbeit Mach Frei"* was the slogan over the gates of Auschwitz: "Work sets you free." Until the very end, when the "showers" turned out to be gas chambers, the Germans tried to fill their brutalized and terrorized Jewish victims with the false hope that the brutality and terror would finally end if only they followed orders.

Indeed, the whole world was fooled by German artifice and euphemism. The International Red Cross was repeatedly invited to inspect the camp at Theresienstadt, a showplace where food was set out on the dining tables while the inspectors were making their rounds and then taken away again when they left. The ultimate destination for the inmates of Theresienstadt was one of the death camps; but not even the

Jews themselves, whose long history is full of carnage and outrage, were able to conjure up what awaited them at Auschwitz or Treblinka. Conditioned by two thousand years of going along and getting along, they were twice victimized, first by their own inability to imagine that the government of a civilized country might resolve to exterminate them and then by the deception and brutality practiced upon them by that government.

"The question is not why all the Jews did not fight," offers Elie Wiesel, "but how so many of them did."[41]

A second lesson of the Holocaust is that the Jewish people found no place of refuge anywhere in the world. Only a few months before Kristallnacht in 1938, for example, delegates from thirty-two nations gathered at a French resort in Evian to discuss under what circumstances they might be willing to rescue some of the Jews who were already trapped inside Nazi Germany—and Hitler saw for himself that the German Jews were no more welcome in the United States or Great Britain or France than they were in Germany itself. The gas chambers were already in full operation in 1943 when the question was raised again at the so-called Bermuda Conference, where the Allies responded to the desperate plea for rescue of the surviving Jewish men, women, and children of Nazi-occupied Europe with a shrug of indifference. When U.S. Secretary of State Cordell Hull proposed to British Foreign Secretary Anthony Eden that the Allies evacuate and shelter some sixty or seventy thousand Bulgarian Jews who were destined for the concentration camps, for example, the British diplomat was unmoved by their plight and unwilling to do anything to save them.

"If we do that, then the Jews of the world will be wanting us to make similar offers in Poland and Germany," Eden protested. "Hitler may take us up on any such offer, and there simply are not enough ships and means of transportation in the world to handle them."[42]

Nor were the Allies willing to use their military might to slow down or stop the Holocaust. The Allied armed forces fought fascism with great courage and determination, but Jews and non-Jews alike in the highest circles of government and command were fearful of characterizing the war as an effort to save Jewish lives. A mass meeting was held in New York's Madison Square Garden to call attention to the fate of the doomed Jews of Europe, and three hundred rabbis demonstrated on the steps of the Capitol, but President Franklin D. Roosevelt pointedly refused to meet with them because he was fearful of giving the impression that the war against Nazism was a "Jewish war."

Nor was the Allied high command willing to take *any* action, no matter how slight or surreptitious, to strike at the machinery of mass murder. The facts of the Holocaust were well known to the Allied war leaders—indeed, wartime aerial reconnaissance photographs of Auschwitz show the gas chambers, the crematoria, and the long lines of Jews at a "selection," and the deportation of some three hundred thousand Hungarian Jews to Auschwitz in 1944 was actually reported in the pages of *The New York Times*. But even when Chaim Weizmann himself begged the Allies to bomb the railroad lines to Auschwitz, the man who had once been able to secure the Balfour Declaration was told that it was not "technically feasible."[43]

A third lesson of the Holocaust is that the Jews were dangerously out of touch with their own ancient tradition of armed self-defense. For two thousand years, Jewish culture had emphasized piety and scholarship at the expense of physical and military training. The notion that athletics are somehow foreign to Judaism can be traced all the way back to the era of the Maccabees, when the Hellenizers scandalized their more pious fellow Jews by shedding their clothing to participate in Greek sporting competitions. The tradition of the "fighting Jew," which begins in the Torah itself, was finally renounced by rabbinical Judaism after the Bar Kokhba uprising, and the Jewish people forfeited a crucial element of its own authentic heritage.

"[O]ver hundreds of years," Hilberg proposes, "they had 'unlearned' the art of revolt."[44]

Although the counterhistory of the Jewish people records a few isolated instances of Jewish self-defense during the Middle Ages in such German cities as Cologne, Mainz, and Frankfurt, the spirit of resistance was largely replaced by the spirit of accommodation among the Jews of Europe. Indeed, by a strange and cruel irony, not a few victims of the Holocaust shared something in common with Adolf Hitler—they were all veterans of the German army who had won the Iron Cross in combat during World War I. When confronted by a Germany that now sought to murder all of the Jews within its grasp, only a few Jews found it within themselves to pick up a weapon and fight back. And, significantly, the Jews who joined the resistance were, by and large, the same Jews who embraced the newest and boldest Jewish countertraditions of socialism and Zionism.

The tantalizing question of what might have happened during the Holocaust if there had been more Jews like Herschel Grynszpan or Tuvia Bielski or Rosa Robota was raised by no less a villain than Joseph Goebbels, the zealous Nazi who served as minister of propaganda in the Third Reich. Even his contempt for the Jewish people quite cannot conceal his admiration for what they had managed to achieve during the Warsaw Ghetto uprising: "[T]he joke cannot last much longer," Goebbels confided to the pages of his journal, *"but it shows what the Jews are capable of when they have arms in their hands."*[45]

A fourth lesson of the Holocaust is implicit in everything else we have considered so far. The Jews of Europe were forced to rely on what turned out to be wholly unreliable and inadequate resources precisely because they had so few resources of their own: they were, yet again, "strangers in a strange land," as the Torah puts it so memorably (Exod. 2:22). The old "Jewish question," which Herzl had once dismissed as "a misplaced piece of medievalism," turned out to be an urgent concern of modern Judaism: when it was literally a matter of life and death for millions of Jewish men, women, and children, there was no Jewish state to shelter the victims of the Holocaust, and no Jewish army to protect or vindicate them.[46]

Whether out of xenophobia or isolationism or plain anti-Semitism, or a queasy blend of all three, not even the United States was willing to shelter the endangered Jews of Europe. The point is made with heartbreaking clarity in one of the defining moments of the Holocaust. When the S.S. *St. Louis*, a ship carrying a few hundred desperate refugees from Nazi Germany, arrived in America in 1939, it was refused permission to disembark any of its Jewish passengers at any port in the United States. Unlike the *St. Catarina*, which brought the first Jewish refugees to America in 1654, and unlike the thousands of ships that brought millions of

Jews to America in the nineteenth and early twentieth centuries, the *St. Louis* was turned away and sent back to Germany. The fact that America was unwilling to welcome even a few Jewish refugees was not lost on Germany. At the very moment when it mattered most of all—and to the shame of "the land of the free and the home of the brave"—the doomed Jews of the *St. Louis* had nowhere to go.

All of these lessons can be focused on a single compelling answer to the "Jewish question": the Jews must have a land of their own, a place where they will be assured of the dignity of full citizenship, including the right and the duty to defend themselves against their enemies. The tragic vulnerability of the Jewish people during the Holocaust only underscored what critic Leon Wieseltier defines as "a classical meaning of Zionism"— and, we should add, the ultimate lesson of the Holocaust—"[T]here must exist a state for which Jews need no visas."[47] Thus we come to the most recent and the most revolutionary countertradition in the long history of the Jewish people, a countertradition that challenged every cherished assumption of "classical" Judaism and redefined, fundamentally and forever, what it means to be a Jew.

NINE

Measured in Blood

It is by the amount of blood shed that you can evaluate
a revolution, and not by the beautiful ideas for which it
is shed.

—VLADIMIR JABOTINSKY

Within the confines of a neighborhood in Jerusalem called Mea Shearim, a community of self-ghettoized Jewish fundamentalists known as the Neturei Karta ("Guardians of the City") is making a last stand against the modern world. As in the ghettos of medieval Europe, a chain is drawn across the streets that lead into the Jewish quarter at sunset on Shabbat. Like other ultraobservant Jews around the world, the men wear the garb of eighteenth-century Poland—black caftans, white stockings, and the headgear that earns them the nickname of "black hats." So zealous are the Neturei Karta that some of them have been known to spit upon Jewish women who wander into their quaint old neighborhood in shorts or skirts, and they have ventured into the streets of Jerusalem to stone the occasional automobile whose driver dares to violate the Sabbath.

What the Neturei Karta regard as the greatest threat to Judaism, however, is not short skirts or Sabbath-breaking or any of the other sins of assimilation. In their eyes, the very worst enemy of the Jewish people is the State of Israel itself. Just as Arab militants insist on calling Israel "the Zionist entity," the Jewish militants of the Neturei Karta call it "the Zionist state." The most dedicated of them use scrip instead of Israeli currency and refuse to carry an identity card like other Israeli citizens. To these Jews, Israel represents not only the triumph of secularism over piety but something much worse—the sin of "forcing the end." And the homeland that Zionism created as a refuge for the Jewish people is what they call the "ultimate heresy."[1]

"Zionism is a complete denial [of] the Holy essence of the Jewish people," rails one of the faithful, condemning both the Jewish Enlightenment of the nineteenth century and the Zionist movement of our own times in a single furious tirade. "The former breached the wall of the citadel of the faith, and the latter, disguised in an imitation of Jewish garb, entered through the breaches in order to carry on the work of destroying the main structure."[2]

As strange as the Neturei Karta may seem—a nest of Jewish anti-Zionists in the very heart of Israel—they are a living reminder that, until the emergence of modern political Zionism in the late nineteenth century, the yearning for a return to *Eretz Yisrael* was strictly a matter of theology and true belief. In that sense, every pious Jew over the last two thousand years was a "Zionist" because he or she was taught to believe that the Jewish people, both the living and the dead, would be gathered and conveyed to land of Israel by the Messiah. Until the moment of redemption, however, a pious Jew was obliged to offer an earnest prayer to God, but he was forbidden to do anything more. "By the End of Days He will send our Messiah," goes one of the traditional morning blessings still recited by observant Jews, "to redeem those longing for His final salvation."[3]

Zionism worked nothing less than a revolution in Jewish history by boldly and even ruthlessly severing the linkage between Jewish messianic longings and Jewish national aspirations. The Zionists rejected the pious teachings of Maimonides, who counseled the Jewish people to wait patiently for the coming of the Messiah "though he may tarry," and they embraced the stirring and empowering notion that the Jewish people need not wait for the Messiah to carry them to Israel on a cloud—Jewish

men, women, and children would return to Israel whenever they summoned up the daring and determination to go there. "If you will it," goes
one of Theodor Herzl's most famous aphorisms, "it is no dream."[4]

To describe Zionism as a revolution is not merely a matter of rhetoric.
If we look back on the long history of the Jewish people as a series of
traditions and countertraditions, Zionism is the most radical countertradition of all. Indeed, the early Zionists rejected the brittle piety of
traditional Judaism just as emphatically as the pious Jews rejected the political derring-do of Zionism. "Zionism and Judaism are not merely different but in all likelihood contradictory," insists a character in a short story
by Hayim Hazaz (1897–1973). "Zionism starts where Judaism collapsed."[5]

The Zionist pioneers who came to Palestine in the late nineteenth
and early twentieth centuries aspired to answer the age-old "Jewish question" once and for all by giving the Jews a country of their own. Indeed,
they sought to remake the Jewish people in a wholly new image, and
when they sang of their determination to "rebuild the land and be rebuilt
by it," they meant it quite literally. "All other revolts, both past and future, were uprisings against a system," declared David Ben-Gurion in
1944. "Our revolution is directed not only against a system, but against
destiny."[6] Of all the many "Judaisms," then, Zionism stands out as the
one that has worked the single most dramatic change in what it means to
be a Jew.

Bialik's Children

Among the oldest and ugliest scourges of Jewish life in the Diaspora was
the so-called blood libel, the false and malicious accusation that Jewish
ritual requires the use of blood in the making of matzoh. Whenever a
blood libel was raised, it prompted the trial and execution of some un-
lucky Jew on charges of murder, or an incident of raw mob violence
against the Jewish community, or both. This particular medievalism
was still rearing its head in 1903, when a newspaper in the Ukraine published the accusation that a Christian child had been murdered to supply blood for the upcoming observance of Passover. Thus provoked, a
mob attacked the Jewish quarter of a Russian town called Kishinev at the

instigation of agents of the Interior Ministry while the tsarist troops and police watched from a safe distance and did nothing.

The latest outbreak of state-sponsored anti-Semitic violence was familiar enough, but the Kishinev pogrom provoked a new and challenging response within the Jewish communities of Russia—a sense of shame over Jewish passivity in the face of violence, and a sense of resolve that Jews ought to do something to protect themselves. The events at Kishinev inspired a young Jewish poet called Haim Bialik (1873–1934) to write a poem that has come to be known as "City of Slaughter"—and, remarkably, the poem itself contributed to a revolution in Judaism.

Bialik's poem was first published under the title "The Burden of Nemirov"—a reference to one of the sites of the Khmielnitzki massacres in the seventeenth century—in an effort to escape the strict censorship of the tsarist government. Still, Bialik's readers clearly understood the poem as a description of the more recent events in Kishinev, where some fifty Jews had been killed, five hundred more had been raped or beaten, and the Jewish quarter had been destroyed. And yet, significantly, Bialik did not direct his anger at the pogromists who had committed the outrages at Kishinev or the tsarist regime that had instigated them. Rather, Bialik was outraged at his fellow Jews, and his poem is full of contempt for the Jewish men who cowered in their hiding places and tried to save their own sorry lives while their mothers and sisters, wives and daughters, were raped by "seven uncircumcised ones."[7]

> *Beneath this matzah-trough and behind that cask,*
> *Lay husbands, bridegrooms, brothers, peeping from holes,*
> *While holy bodies quivered beneath asses' flesh . . .*
> *Lying down in their shame and seeing—neither stirring nor moving.*
> *Their eyes they did not gouge out nor did they go out of their mind—*
> *But, perhaps, a man even prayed in his heart for his life:*
> *"Master of the world, make a miracle—and let not evil come upon me."*[8]

The poem sizzles with disdain, not only for the cowardly Jewish men—"Concealed and cowering—the sons of the Maccabees!"[9]—but also for the oldest traditions of Judaism in which they have placed their faith. As soon as the gang rape is over and the rioters are gone, the men who proudly claim descent from the ancient priesthood, the *Kohanim*, hasten to the rabbi and demand to know: "Rabbi! My wife, what is she? Permitted or forbidden?"[10] Once the sacred law is consulted and the question of ritual purity is answered, the outrage itself will be forgotten.

> *The matter ends; and nothing more.*
> *And all is as it was before.*[11]

Among the Jewish readers of "City of Slaughter" were men who felt the sting of rebuke and resolved to do something about the latest indignities that had been visited upon the Jews. Among the Zionists and Bundists alike, as we have already seen, the first valiant efforts at Jewish armed self-defense began to appear in towns and villages all over Russia. Here and there, a few brave Jews undertook to stockpile a few weapons and learn how to use them. Then, at the first sight of the so-called Black Hundreds, an anti-Semitic militia organized and armed by the tsarist government, the Jewish fighters sallied forth to skirmish with the enemy. All was not to be "as it was before"; rather, the Jews would stand up and fight.

The tradition was carried from the *shtetls* and the ghettos all the way to the *kibbutzim*, the collective farms in Palestine where Jewish *chalutzim* were remaking themselves as tillers of the soil. Against the predations of their Arab neighbors, the *chalutzim* organized the first Jewish defense force in Palestine, at first called *Bar Giora*, after the Jewish freedom fighter of the first century C.E., and later called HaShomer ("The Watchman"). The members of the HaShomer, known as Shomrim ("Watchmen"), patrolled the Jewish settlements to warn away any attackers and, if necessary, to drive them off by force of arms. "In blood and fire Judah fell," went the slogan of HaShomer; "in blood and fire Judah shall rise again."[12]

The outbreak of World War I in 1914 inspired a new expression of the same fierce idea. Jews were serving in great numbers in the armies of all the European countries that went to war, but they served in the ranks as ordinary soldiers: "Jews fight everywhere," as Chaim Weizmann put it, "and are recognized nowhere."[13] Here the Zionists saw a critical opportunity: the British hoped to take Palestine away from the Turks, and so the Jews would show the rest of the world their love of Zion and their courage in battle by offering to join the British army in the battle to liberate Palestine. Crucially, they offered to serve in the British army and fight in the British cause, but they proposed to do so *as Jews.*

The man who championed the cause of a Jewish regiment in the British army was Vladimir (Ze'ev) Jabotinsky (1880–1940), a journalist, poet, and orator from the Ukraine. He showed up in Alexandria to lobby the British authorities in Egypt to set up a Jewish regiment, and as a result two specifically Jewish units of the British armed forces were created: the Zion Mule Corps, which served with distinction in the fighting at Gallipoli in 1915 and 1916, and later the Jewish Legion, which was first organized in 1917 and fought in the battle to liberate Jerusalem in 1918. Drawing volunteers from within Palestine and as far away as Russia, England, and the United States, the Jewish Legionnaires wore a uniform emblazoned with a Star of David—the symbol that would later mark the Jewish victims of the Holocaust was used, there and then, to identify the first Jewish army since Bar Kokhba.

Courage in battle was a point of honor among the Jewish soldiers, who sought to disabuse their skeptical British cohorts—and the rest of the world—of the notion that Jews could not fight. Thus, for example, the ranking Jewish officer in the Zion Mule Corps, a highly decorated veteran of the tsarist army named Joseph Trumpeldor (1880–1920), insisted on putting himself in the heat of the battle. Trumpeldor was a handsome young man who had lost an arm in battle while serving the tsar, and he cut a dashing figure that was not lost upon the British officers who fought with him at Gallipoli.

"Many of the Zionists whom I had thought somewhat lacking in courage showed themselves fearless when under heavy fire," wrote one British officer who witnessed the Zion Mule Corps in action, "while Captain Trumpeldor actually reveled in it, and the hotter it became the more he liked it, and would remark: 'Ah, it is now *plus gai!*' "[14]

Nothing in the history of Zionism better symbolizes the remaking of the modern Jew. Trumpeldor himself died in 1920 in the defense of a

Jewish settlement in the upper Galilee from an Arab attack. "Never mind," he told his comrades in arms, "it is good to die for our country."[15] From the ranks of the Zion Mule Corps and the Jewish Legion, however, came the first officers of the Haganah ("Defense"), a Jewish militia that was set up to defend the Jewish community in Palestine after World War I. Later, during World War II, new Jewish regiments were organized within the British army, and a few of the most courageous of the Jewish soldiers from Palestine volunteered to parachute behind the German lines to act as liaison with resistance fighters in occupied Europe. The most famous of them, but hardly the only one, was yet another Jewish poet, a beautiful young woman named Hannah Senesh (1921–1944), who left a legacy of stirring poetry and an example of heroism before she died at the hands of the Gestapo at the age of twenty-three.

> *Blessed is the heart with strength to stop its beating for honor's sake.*
> *Blessed is the match consumed in kindling flame.*[16]

Shortly before his death in 1940, looking back on the tradition of Jewish armed self-defense, Jabotinsky himself recalled the moment when he first read "City of Slaughter" and, like so many other Jews, was stirred to answer the bitter challenge in Bialik's poem. "The revival of Maccabean tendencies in the Ghetto really dates from that poem," wrote Jabotinsky. "The self-defense organizations which sprang up everywhere in Russia, the *Shomrim* movement in Palestine, even the Jewish Legion which fought for the Holy Land in 1918—they are all Bialik's children."[17] Although Jabotinsky did not live long enough to see it for himself, Bialik's children include the ghetto fighters of Warsaw, the Jewish resistance inside Auschwitz, the Bielski partisans, and the soldiers of the Israel Defense Forces who are the modern incarnation of the fighting Jew.

Practical Zionism

The heroism and dedication of Jewish soldiers in the field during World War I only strengthened the hand of the Jewish leaders in London, including Chaim Weizmann and Lord Rothschild, who were lobbying the British government to publicly affirm its commitment to a Jewish homeland in Palestine. Eager to secure Jewish support for the war effort, especially in the United States and Russia—and eager, too, to stake a British claim on the former provinces of the Ottoman Empire—Great Britain was persuaded that a nod in the direction of Zionism was strategically sound, if also slightly cynical in light of the promises that had already been made to the Arabs by T. E. Lawrence, "Lawrence of Arabia." "Apart from the merits of the question itself," confided one British diplomat to the British foreign minister, Lord Balfour, "our political interests seem to lie in encouraging the Zionists."[18]

Herzl had died in 1904, only forty-four years old, and leadership of the Zionist movement had settled on Chaim Weizmann; but here was the prize that Herzl had struggled to win—a promise from one of the great powers to sponsor a Jewish state in Palestine. Ironically, Herzl had been harshly criticized in some Zionist circles for what was called a "charter psychology," and he struck the younger and more radical Zionists as just another *shtadlan*—the term for one of the Jewish emissaries of the Middle Ages who bowed and scraped before a powerful potentate to win some grudging favor for his fellow Jews.[19] Weizmann, by contrast, represented the new spirit of "Practical Zionism," an empowering notion that the Jewish people must not wait on the kindness of strangers; rather, they must begin to build a homeland in Palestine with their own hands. Still, it was Weizmann who secured the charter that Herzl had always sought—the Balfour Declaration of 1917. "His Majesty's Government view with favour the establishment in Palestine of a national home for the Jewish people," wrote Lord Balfour, "and will use their best endeavours to facilitate the achievement of this object."[20]

The Balfour Declaration is really nothing more than a "declaration of sympathy" in the form of a one-page letter from Lord Balfour to Lord Rothschild. The crucial paragraph in which the British policy toward Palestine is briefly and obliquely summarized is only sixty-six words long, and the very sentence that seems to promise a Jewish homeland goes on to hedge the promise: "[N]othing shall be done which may prejudice the civil and religious rights of existing non-Jewish communities in Palestine."[21] Still, the Balfour Declaration can be seen as "the decisive diplomatic victory of the Jewish people in modern history," as Israeli diplomat and historian Abba Eban (b. 1915) puts it, and a crucial first step in what he rightly calls "the Israeli revolution."[22]

What is truly revolutionary, however, is not the Balfour Declaration itself but the remarkable enterprise of nation-building that Weizmann and his fellow Zionists managed to put into place in reliance on the guarded words and phrases that Balfour put on paper. Practical Zionism, as the phrase implies, was less interested in elaborate ideologies or grand schemes than in "creating facts on the land," according to a memorable and oft-quoted aphorism that was (and is) the credo of Zionism. Even before the British were formally granted a mandate to govern Palestine by the League of Nations in 1922, the Jewish community in Palestine—known as the *Yishuv* ("Settlement")—was already creating its own government-in-waiting in anticipation of the day when, sooner or later, the Jewish national state would come into existence.

Thus, for example, the executive branch of the World Zionist Organization, known as the Jewish Agency, served as a kind of Jewish shadow government in Palestine. The trade union federation known as *Histadrut* functioned as a welfare and public works agency. The security of the Jewish towns and settlements in Palestine was entrusted to the Haganah. All of these institutions amounted to what was proudly called "the state on the way." By May 14, 1948, when the British mandate finally came to an end—and Ben-Gurion, Weizmann, and the other founding fathers and mothers of modern Zionism promptly declared the independence of *Medinat Yisrael*, the State of Israel—Jewish self-government in Palestine had been a "fact on the land" for several decades.

The Jewish Cop and the Jewish Hooker

Like every other countertradition in Jewish history—the Hellenizers, the Kabbalists, the Hasidim, the Maskilim, and many others besides—the first Zionists discovered that their earliest and longest-enduring adversaries were to be found among their fellow Jews. Indeed, if Jewish fundamentalists, Jewish atheists, and Jewish assimilationists shared anything in common, it was a hatred of Zionism and a conviction that it represented a catastrophe for the Jewish people, although each faction came to the conclusion for very different reasons.

Observant Jews of all colorations—and not just the radical fringe—distanced themselves from Zionism in its early years. At one end of the religious spectrum within Judaism, fundamentalist Jews regarded Zionism as nothing less than a sin against the God of Israel: "We are in the Golus for our sins," goes the radical Jewish critique, pointedly using the Yiddish pronunciation of the word for "exile" in place of the Hebrew, "*Galut.*" "We must lovingly accept our sentence."[23] At the other end, Reform Jews in the early twentieth century distanced themselves from Zionism because they aspired to full citizenship in the lands of the Diaspora. "We denounce the whole question of a Jewish state as foreign to the spirit of the modern Jew of this land," declared one Reform rabbi in the United States in the 1920s, "who looks upon America as his Palestine."[24]

Jewish revolutionaries, too, who had embraced Marxism in place of Judaism and now aspired toward the new messianic ideal of international socialism, attacked Zionism as an imperialist enterprise. Leon Trotsky, for example, penned a pamphlet in 1904 in which he condemned Theodor Herzl as a "shameless adventurer" and dismissed the Zionist ideology as "hysterical sobbings."[25] Although the Soviet Union ultimately cast one of the crucial votes for Jewish statehood in the United Nations in 1947, Zionism was always one of the bogeymen of Soviet propaganda. In 1952, for example, a show trial was staged in Soviet-dominated Czechoslovakia, and fourteen Communist apparatchiks, eleven of them Jewish, were accused of espionage for Israel. Until the fall of the Soviet Union in 1989, generation after generation of Soviet Jews—known as "refuseniks"—were denied permission to emigrate to Israel.

Along with religious Jews and revolutionary Jews, many of the most highly assimilated Jews in the Diaspora, including those who wanted to be "a Jew at home and a man in the street"[26] and those who did not want to be Jews at all, condemned Zionism because they feared that the very idea of a Jewish state called their own patriotism into question in the eyes of their fellow citizens. As late as 1937, when the fate of the Jews in Germany was no longer in question, some Jews were still willing to criticize the effort to rescue their doomed brethren by arranging for their emigration to Palestine. "It is a gross slander on the German Jews whose love for the fatherland is proverbial," insisted one such Jewish writer, "to represent them as being ready to rush in panicky haste from it in a mass exodus at the first approach of misfortune."[27]

Of course, the high emotions cut in both directions: some of the Zionists were zealots, too, and they regarded any Jew who lingered in the Diaspora with suspicion and sometimes outright contempt. Weizmann himself, for example, railed against "that class of 'tame Jew' who doesn't want to be bothered with Zionism or national aspirations," and he borrowed from the vocabulary of the ultraobservant Jews in condemning both the "so-called assimilated cosmopolitan Jews" and the observant Jews for whom "Judaism had become 'a mere religious formula.' "[28] For the true believers in Zionism, the Jew who regards himself as "emancipated" from his Jewishness and remains in the Diaspora "becomes an inner cripple," as pioneering Zionist leader Max Nordau (1849–1923) put it. What's worse, he or she was committing the unpardonable sin of forgetting the lessons of history. "The whole of history has taught us that never have Jews been in a happier condition than they were in Spain," Nordau pointed out, "before . . . the Inquisition and the Expulsion of the fifteenth century."[29]

An even greater irony, however, is that Zionism preserved and even perfected some of the most cherished beliefs of its various enemies within the Jewish world. Thus, for example, Herzl consciously tapped into the same spiritual tradition in Judaism that had always focused the longings of the Jewish people on the coming of the Messiah—which is exactly why some of his critics compared him to Sabbatai Zevi. And Herzl himself conceded the merit of their concerns when he confided to the king of Italy that he avoiding riding a white horse or donkey while in Palestine lest he be accused of tacitly making a claim of his own Messiahship—the Messiah, according to ancient tradition, would ride a white ass. Even the Jews who embraced both Zionism and Marxism—and thus rejected the religious traditions of Judaism—acknowledged that a Jewish homeland must be built in Palestine and nowhere else in the world precisely because *Eretz Yisrael* had always been the object of longing among the Jewish masses. They might have been wholly secular Jews, but they were also practical Zionists.

Zionism also drew on the fiery idealism that begins in the Five Books of Moses and the writings of the Prophets, and thus links the oldest values of Judaism to the aspirations of revolutionary socialism. The single best example is also the single most resonant symbol of the Zionist ideal: the *kibbutz*, an experiment in strictly egalitarian communal living, reflects a conscious effort by the earliest Zionists to realize the socialist ideal in the here and now. Even as they were fighting for their lives against Arab terrorism in the 1920s and '30s, some Zionists embraced a faintly mystical doctrine known as *to'har haneshek* ("purity of arms"), which held that Jews ought to fight only when absolutely necessary, and, even then, they should fight in a way that minimizes the number of casualties. During the 1930s and the war years, the doctrine was expressed in the official policy of *havlaga* ("self-restraint" or "nonreaction"), a doctrine that called upon the Haganah to refrain from preemptive attacks on Arab terrorists and to act only and strictly in self-defense.

Finally, and above all, Zionism shared the aspiration of assimilated Jews in the Diaspora to transform the Jewish people from ghetto dwellers into a modern nation, enlightened and emancipated. That is what is meant by the Zionist aspiration to be "rebuilt" by the land of Israel. Jews must no longer be restricted to the hateful role of tavern keeper or tax collector or pawnbroker, nor must they aspire only to be doctors or lawyers or professors. Rather, Jews ought to be workers and farmers, soldiers and sailors, too. For that reason, some of the earliest and most idealistic Zionists refused to hire Arab labor—if a job of work needed to be done, no matter how arduous, it should be done by a Jew. Of course, the Zionists differed with Jewish assimilationists on one crucial point: the goal of "normalizing" Jewish life could be achieved only in a place where the Jews were citizens of their own sovereign state. According to a coarse if colorful witticism, the Zionist dream would be fulfilled "on the day when the first Jewish cop arrests the first Jewish hooker on a street-corner in Tel Aviv."

Thus did the early Zionists try to work out the contradiction that lies at the heart of Zionism. The most observant Jews condemned Zionism because they saw it as a betrayal of the sacred mission of the Jewish people. The Jews had been chosen by God as "My own treasure," "a kingdom of priests, and a holy nation" (Exod. 19:5, 6). As the Chosen People, they were expected to be "a light unto the nations" (Isa. 49:6), but they were expected to live separate and apart from the other nations—the Hebrew word is *goyim*. That is why the Jewish fundamentalists, then and now, regard the ultimate sin of Zionism as "the transformation of the Divine and Holy people into *merely* one of all the peoples of the earth."[30] And yet the most assimilated Jews, just like their distant biblical ancestors who clamored for a monarch in place of a theocracy, yearned only to be "like all other nations" (1 Sam. 8:5).

Zionism tried to answer both yearnings at once. The Zionist state would be uniquely and distinctively Jewish in its moral aspirations— what other country in the world, for example, embraced the lofty notion of "purity of arms"? And yet, at the same time, the Zionist state would afford the Jewish people an opportunity to be "like all other nations," a country with a flag and a passport, an army and a navy, and, yes, even cops and hookers. At the heart of the Zionist dream is a double bind that is best summed up in a Jewish witticism that reads like a Zen koan: "Jews are like everybody else," the saying goes, "only more so."

A Land Without a People

One of the cherished myths of early Zionism was the notion of Palestine as "a land without a people for a people without a land." As late as 1969, Golda Meir, then prime minister of Israel, was still insisting that "there are no such things as Palestinians."[31] And, in fact, myth and reality are sometimes hard to distinguish in the Zionist experience in Palestine. After all, when the first *chalutzim* arrived in the late nineteenth century, Palestine was underpopulated and underdeveloped, and they accomplished exactly what the Zionist saga claims for them, draining the malarial swamps, plowing and sowing the land, literally "making the desert bloom."

But the land was *not* empty. A significant Arab population was already in Palestine when the first waves of *chalutzim* began to arrive—a

fact that is obliquely noted in the Balfour Declaration itself—and the opportunities created by Zionist enterprise only attracted more Arabs from
the neighboring lands. Indeed, Palestine had passed in and out of Arab
sovereignty starting as early as the seventh century, and except for a couple of centuries of bloodthirsty rule by the Crusaders, Palestine remained
under Islamic sovereignty until the end of World War I. Not unlike the
Jews who lived under the Moors during the "Golden Age" of Spain, the
Jews who lived in Jerusalem during the Crusades fared far better under
Arab rulers than they had under the Crusader kings.

For one tantalizing moment in history, the prospect of peaceful coexistence between Jews and Arabs in Palestine seemed to be within
reach. Back in 1919, meeting in London under the approving eyes of
T. E. Lawrence, Chaim Weizmann and the Arab emir Faisal agreed in
principle on the division of Palestine into an Arab state and a Jewish
state. They vowed to "encourage and stimulate immigration of Jews into
Palestine on a large scale" while respecting the rights of "the Arab peasant and tenant farmers" and leaving the Islamic holy places in Jerusalem
under Muslim control.[32] The scene evokes the biblical saga of Jacob and
the Canaanite chieftain called Hamor, two patriarchs of rival tribes who
are shown to be willing to overlook their old grievances and share the
land between them: "I look forward, and my people with me look forward," Faisal assured Weizmann, echoing the very words spoken by Jacob
and Hamor, "to a future in which we will help you and you will help
us."[33] But, just as Jacob's efforts at peacemaking were frustrated by an act
of terrorism by his hotheaded sons, the noble words of Faisal were rendered meaningless by those of his fellow Arabs who were determined to
drive the Jews out of Palestine.

Even as Weizmann and Faisal were palavering in London, the Arabs
and the Jews were skirmishing with each other in Palestine. The Shomrim came into existence because Jewish settlements were being raided by
Arabs, if only for plunder or out of resentment over Jewish purchase of
Arab land from some absentee landlord in Beirut or Constantinople. As
the pace of Jewish immigration quickened and the scope of the Jewish
settlement increased, so did the pace and scope of Arab violence against
the *Yishuv*. And Arab violence took on the political and religious col-

orations that are so familiar to us today. Thus, for example, the Arab ri-oting that took so many Jewish lives in 1929 was sparked by an incident at the Temple Mount. A partition had been erected at the "Wailing Wall" to separate Jewish men and women at prayer, and Arab agitators characterized the pious gesture by a few observant Jews as the first step in an effort to take away the Temple Mount.

The terrorism and counterterrorism that afflict the Middle East today—the shooting and sniping, the bombing of buses and markets, the outbreaks of mob violence—were already facts of life from the earliest days of Zionist nation-building in Palestine. Hebron, for example, was the site of an old and well-established Jewish community until 1929, when Arab rioting drove out the last of the Jews. During World War II, Arab violence took on an ugly taint—the Grand Mufti of Jerusalem, an Arab leader from an old Palestinian family, put himself in service to the Third Reich, making propaganda broadcasts from Berlin and urging his German benefactors to put him at the head of an Islamic army to take back Palestine from the British and the Jews.

Ironically, despite all of the bitterness, the Jews and Arabs of Pales-tine have come to resemble each other in startling ways. Palestinian Arabs have been likened to "the Jews of the Arab world" precisely be-cause of their intellectual achievements and political aspirations, and the struggle of the Palestinian Arabs for statehood has been called "Arab Zionism." Thus, the Palestinian Authority can be seen as a "state on the way" in the West Bank and Gaza in much the same way the Jewish Agency once served as a shadow government in Palestine under the British mandate. And if Yasir Arafat was condemned as a terrorist before he became a head of government, so were Menahem Begin and Yitzhak Shamir, both of whom started out as terrorists and ended up as prime ministers of Israel.

"In Fire and Blood"

As if to affirm its authentic and essential Jewishness, the countertradi-tion of Zionism spawned its own set of countertraditions. Not every Zionist, for example, was committed to Palestine as the site of the Jewish homeland—the so-called territorialists advocated any number of alternative Zions, ranging from Argentina to Saskatchewan. Even the worst enemies of Zionism came up with their own twisted versions of a Jewish homeland. Nazi Germany, for example, toyed with the notion of settling some four million Jews on the island of Madagascar in the Indian Ocean before resolving to murder them instead. In 1928 the Soviet Union actually set up a Jewish "autonomous region" in a Siberian backwater called Birobidjan, although only 30,000 of the anticipated 300,000 Jews showed up there.

"If you ask them about Palestine, they laugh," one Soviet propagandist insisted in the 1930s. "The Palestine dream will long have receded into history when in Biro Bidzhan there will be motor cars, railways and steamers, huge factories belching forth smoke."[34]

Theodor Herzl himself, for example, briefly endorsed the so-called Uganda scheme, a proposal by the British government to establish a Jewish colony in British East Africa. Herzl embraced the Uganda scheme only as an emergency measure to rescue the endangered Jews of Russia in the wake of the Kishinev pogroms, but the Zionist Congress of 1904 voted him down with such passion that his leadership of the Zionist movement was called into question. Even the most secular Zionists understood the uniquely powerful appeal of Palestine as a Jewish homeland, and, significantly, the delegates from Kishinev itself were among the majority that voted against the Uganda plan.

"If I forget thee, O Jerusalem," Herzl declared at the closing session of the Zionist Congress, quoting a cherished line of biblical text and thereby conceding his own doctrinal error, "may my right hand lose its cunning."[35]

Ironically, an even more violent schism within Zionism was prompted by the seeming erosion of Herzl's grand vision of a Jewish homeland in all of Palestine. In 1922, after the League of Nations had formally confirmed the British mandate to rule Palestine, the British abruptly closed half of Palestine to Jewish settlement; roughly one-half of the territory of Palestine, everything to the east of the Jordan River, was lopped from the mandate and handed over to a new and autonomous Arab monarchy called Transjordan. At the same time, some Zionists saw the policies of accommodation and compromise that characterized the "Practical Zionism" of Chaim Weizmann as a betrayal of Zionism itself. The most visible and the most vocal of the critics was Vladimir Jabotinsky, who complained about the "meekness" and "weakness" of Weizmann in dealing with the British authorities in Palestine and resigned in protest from the Zionist leadership in 1923.[36]

The schism between Jabotinsky and Weizmann ultimately led to the creation of a countermovement within Zionism that called itself Revisionism and set itself in opposition to the Labor Zionists and their various allies on the left wing of Zionism. Under the leadership of Jabotinsky, the Revisionists called for Jewish settlement on *both* banks of the Jordan River. To accelerate the pace of Jewish settlement, they were willing to defy British limits on Jewish immigration. To defend the Jewish population, and to deter Arab violence, they called for the creation of a standing Jewish army—and they were willing to punish Arab violence by answering terror with terror. Indeed, the Revisionists were unwilling to make any deals with the Arabs. Jabotinsky conceded that both Arabs and Jews were able to state a claim to Palestine, but the Jewish claim was more compelling because of the dire threat to Jewish lives in Europe.

"It is like the claims of appetite," as Jabotinsky put it, "versus the claims of starvation."[37]

Clashes between the Revisionists and the Labor Zionists who made up the leadership of the Jewish Agency struck sparks on virtually every point of conflict. The Revisionists condemned the doctrine of "purity of arms" and the policy of "self-restraint," and demanded that vengeance be taken for acts of Arab terrorism. They rejected the socialist agenda of Labor Zionism and called for greater investment in private industry and agriculture. Meanwhile, the Labor Zionists attacked Jabotinsky as a dangerous demagogue with "the brilliance and great personal charm of the *Fuehrer*," and likened the Revisionist youth movement—Betar (*B'rit Trumpeldor*) or "Covenant of Trumpeldor"—to the "brownshirts" of Nazi Germany.[38] Now and then, the Jewish Agency and the Haganah went so far as to cooperate with the British authorities in tracking down and arresting the Jewish terrorists who carried out reprisals against both the Arabs and the British.

But the real flash point was a crisis that befell the Jewish world in 1939 when the British issued a "White Paper" on Palestine. At the very moment of greatest threat to the Jewish people, when the Jews of Europe were able to find no place of refuge anywhere in the world, Great Britain announced a series of drastic changes in its interpretation of the Balfour Declaration, all designed to placate the Arabs in Palestine. The purchase of land in Palestine by Jews would be flatly prohibited. Jewish immigration to Palestine would be limited to only seventy-five thousand over the next five years. Beyond the meager five-year quota, no more Jews would be admitted to Palestine without Arab consent. Thus, at precisely the moment in history when six million Jewish men, women, and children were being murdered in Europe, the gates of the Jewish homeland were closed against them.

"There is the abandonment of the Balfour Declaration," declared Winston Churchill on the floor of the House of Commons. "There is the end of the vision, of the hope, of the dream."[39]

"These Abominable Outrages"

The White Paper provoked anguish and outrage throughout the Zionist movement. All of the factions issued statements of protest, and the Jewish Agency cooperated with the Revisionists in stepping up the pace of "Aliyah B," an underground operation that smuggled Jews by the thousands into Palestine in defiance of the British immigration policies. But the Revisionists went further. Acting through their underground military organization, Irgun Zvai Leumi ("National Military Organization"), they took the battle against the White Paper to the streets, striking at British government facilities and British soldiers and police in uniform.

The Irgun, originally known as Haganah B, was a breakaway faction of the Haganah that had come to serve as the military arm of the Revisionists. Its slogan was the same as the one that had been embraced by the first Jewish militia in Palestine, HaShomer: "In blood and fire Judah fell, in blood and fire Judah shall rise again." Its symbol was a map of

Palestine—*all* of Palestine, both east and west of the Jordan River—
overprinted with an uplifted arm holding a rifle and the words *"Rakh
kakh,"* "Only thus." From its earliest days, the Irgun freed itself from the
official Jewish policy of "self-restraint" and carried out reprisals against
both Arab violence and British arrests, beatings, and even executions of
Irgunists.

To punish the Arabs for a fresh outbreak of rioting in 1936, for example, the Irgunists ambushed and killed Arabs and set off bombs in Arab
bus stations and marketplaces. One Irgunist, an eighteen-year-old named
Jacob Rass, disguised himself as an Arab villager, concealed a handmade
bomb under a pile of vegetables in a wheelbarrow, and tried to leave the
barrow behind in the crowded market street. But Rass was spotted by an
Arab woman, who began to cry out, *"Yahud! Yahud!"* ("Jew! Jew!"), and
he was set upon by the crowd and shot by British police while trying to
escape. Awaiting interrogation by the British, he unfastened his ban-
dages and allowed himself to bleed to death lest he be forced to give away
the names of his fellow Irgunists.[40]

The outbreak of World War II, only a few months after the issuance
of the White Paper, prompted the Revisionists and the Jewish Agency to
declare an armistice in the struggle against the British and their own
skirmishes with each other. "We should help the British in their war as if
there were no White Paper," declared Ben-Gurion, "and we should fight
the White Paper as if there were no war."[41] Once again, Jews clamored
for the opportunity to fight in Jewish units of the British army, and once
again the Star of David appeared on the uniform sleeves of the Jewish
Regiment. At the same time that thousands of Jews were serving as
British soldiers and sailors, however, thousands of other Jews were working to evade the British armed forces by smuggling Jewish refugees from
the Holocaust into Palestine.

Only the most radical elements of the Zionist movement continued
to strike at British targets even during the war. One such splinter group
of the Irgun, led by Avraham Stern (1907–1942), called itself Lohamei
Herut Yisrael ("Lehi" or "Israeli Freedom Fighters") but was known by
everyone else as the Stern Gang. Rejecting both Jabotinsky *and* Weizmann—and seeing Britain rather than Germany as the worst enemy of

the Jewish people—Stern actually sent emissaries to make contact with German agents in Syria during World War II. He was struck with the bold if ludicrous idea of inviting Germany to send tens of thousands of Jews to Palestine by ship, thus saving Jewish lives and disrupting British naval operations. We will never know what the Nazis would have made of Stern because all of his emissaries were arrested before they could deliver their messages. But the Stern group was much more effective when it came to terrorism against the British, and they succeeded in assassinating the British resident minister in Egypt, Lord Moyne, in 1944.

The Irgun honored its cease-fire until the day of victory over Germany in 1945. But when the British announced that the White Paper would remain in effect—and the homeless survivors of the Holocaust would be denied entry to Palestine—the underground war was resumed with an ever greater fury. On a single day in 1946, for example—a Sabbath day, when the British did not expect Jewish military operations—sixteen targets were struck at the same time. British bases were attacked with mortars and machine guns, British military vehicles were fired on, and a bomb was set off in an officers club in Jerusalem, causing some eighty casualties. And the emblematic act of insurrection came on July 22, 1946, when the Irgun managed to set off a powerful bomb in the landmark King David Hotel in Jerusalem where the British military and other colonial offices were headquartered.

The bombing of the King David Hotel prompted the Jewish Agency to issue a condemnation of "the dastardly crime perpetrated by the gang of desperados" and to call upon the Jewish community in Palestine to "rise up against these abominable outrages."[42] But, in a real sense, the Irgun was winning its underground war. The British were unwilling to hold on to Palestine at the price in blood that the Irgun was willing and able to inflict—GOVERN OR GET OUT! went one London newspaper headline—and the decision was made to hand the problem to the United Nations.[43] On November 29, 1947, the U.N. narrowly voted to relieve Great Britain of its mandate and to divide the land of Palestine into two sovereign states, one Jewish and the other Arab. And Great Britain set May 15, 1948, as the date when the Union Jack would be struck for the last time on the flagstaffs of Palestine.

Now the conflict within the Jewish community took on a new and ominous coloring. The "state on the way" would soon become a state in both fact and law, and the rivalries between the Labor Zionists and the Revisionists, the Haganah and the Irgun, raised the ugly prospect of a Jewish civil war. At the same time, the Arab bloc had rejected the partition of Palestine and announced its intention to kill the infant Jewish state at birth. Indeed, Arabs and Jews began to skirmish within Palestine even while the British were still there, and the armies of five Arab nations invaded within hours after the declaration of Jewish statehood in 1948. Not unlike the rival bands of Jewish freedom fighters who rose up against the Romans in the first century c.e., the splintered factions within the Jewish community were forced to fight a war against a powerful and determined enemy while, at the same time, keeping an eye on each other.

The moment of crisis—and a defining moment in the history of Israel—came on June 20, 1948, when the Irgun attempted to bring in a ship called the *Altalena* in defiance of a truce that had been formally accepted by the Arabs and the government of Israel. "Altalena" was a *nom de guerre* of Jabotinsky's, and the ship carried a cargo of arms and ammunition from France to supply the units of the Irgun that were fighting alongside the Haganah in the War of Liberation—five thousand Lee-Enfield rifles, five million rounds of ammunition, and two hundred fifty Bren submachine guns. On that day, the War of Liberation threatened to turn into a civil war, and the question of whether Israel would survive as a democracy—indeed, whether Israel would survive at all—was at stake.

Ben-Gurion, now prime minister of Israel, was willing to allow the *Altalena* to land so long as its precious cargo was turned over to the Haganah, which now constituted the official armed force of the State of Israel, but the Irgun insisted that 20 percent of the weapons be released to its own units. Thus, when the *Altalena* dropped anchor off the beach at a place called Kfar Vitkin, a detachment of soldiers awaited the ship, and a pair of corvettes steamed up to block an escape by sea. Orders were given to surrender the ship and its cargo, and when the orders were defied, the Jewish soldiers and sailors of the State of Israel opened fire on the Jewish soldiers of the Irgun. Under naval escort, the *Altalena* steamed to Tel Aviv, where it was run aground and a fresh round of firing broke out from the shore. By the end of the incident, sixteen Irgunists had been killed and forty more wounded, and the ship was destroyed along with most of its cargo.

"Blessed be the gun that destroyed her," declared Ben-Gurion, as if to invoke once again the doctrine of "purity of arms" even as they were used by Jews against their fellow Jews.[44]

At precisely this moment, however, the State of Israel was spared a civil war. The leader of the Irgun, Menachem Begin (1913–1992), stepped out of the shadows and declared his solidarity with the new Jewish state. "The Irgun Zvai Leumi is leaving the underground within the boundaries of the Hebrew independent state," Begin had previously declared. "In the State of Israel we shall be soldiers and builders. We shall respect its Government, for it is our Government."[45] Begin had directed the Irgun in some of its most radical acts of violence, including the bombing of the King David Hotel and the massacre of Arab civilians in the village of Deir Yassin, but now he chose the role of statesman rather than that of terrorist—the Irgun would be disbanded, its fighters would join the ranks of the armed forces of Israel, and, eventually, the former terrorist would serve as prime minister of Israel and share the 1978 Nobel Peace Prize with Egyptian premier Anwar el-Sadat (1918–1981) in recognition of those first critical steps toward the very first peace treaty between Israel and an Arab state.

"There are times when the choice is between blood and tears," writes Begin in his memoir, *The Revolt*. "Sometimes, as the 'Altalena' taught us, it is essential that tears should take the place of blood."[46]

The New Jew

The very first official act of the newly declared State of Israel in 1948 had been the abolition of the White Paper by which the British had excluded even the most desperate and endangered Jews from the shores of Palestine. Under the so-called Law of the Return, formally enacted in 1950, a place of refuge and the rights of citizenship in Israel are extended to any Jew in the world. Within the first five years of Israel's existence, its population doubled, and today the number of Jewish men, women, and children living proud and free in the State of Israel is nearly equal to the number who were murdered during the Holocaust.

Among the first Jews to be welcomed to Israel, of course, were the Holocaust survivors whom the British had so callously excluded. But equally urgent was the rescue of Jewish communities throughout the Arab world, where the Mizrahim had lived for centuries but now faced a new era of oppression precisely because they were a convenient target for the Arab nations that had been defeated in the War of Liberation. Thus, for example, "Operation Magic Carpet" evacuated the Jewish community that had existed in Yemen since the destruction of Jerusalem in 70 C.E., and "Operation Ali Baba" did the same for the Jews of Iraq. More than a half-million "Oriental" Jews were brought to Israel in the early years of statehood, leaving behind their homes, businesses, and other property, and some Israelis regard the settlement of these refugees as a fair exchange for the half-million or more Arabs who fled Israel during the War of Liberation.

The in-gathering of the Jewish people, surely the single most essential and successful mission of Zionism, focused all of the diversity in Jewish history and tradition on the little nation of Israel. The pioneers of the Zionist movement may have been mostly Ashkenazic Jews—and they continued to provide the political elite in Israel for several generations—but now Israel is a richly, even wildly multicultural society that included significant numbers of Sephardic and Eastern Jews and, more recently, a whole new generation of Russian Jews who were allowed to reach Israel only after the disintegration of the Soviet Union. Tellingly, more than a dozen parties are now represented in the legislature of Israel, the Knesset, and they represent every shade of opinion—and every shade of skin color—in the fractured and contentious political landscape of modern Israel, ranging from white-hot religious fundamentalists to die-hard Communists and every one of the sects and schisms in between.

At the same time, Israel has been forced to defend its very existence virtually without interruption. The so-called War of Liberation between the newly declared State of Israel and its Arab enemies ended in an armistice in 1949, but Israel was compelled to fight again and again, each time winning on the battlefield much greater territory than it had been willing to accept in exchange for statehood in 1948. Israel captured the Sinai Peninsula in the so-called Sinai Campaign of 1956, an ill-fated effort by Britain and France to punish Egypt for nationalizing the Suez Canal, but the United States pressured Israel to return the captured territory to Egypt. The historic victory in the Six-Day War of 1967 restored all of Jerusalem to Jewish sovereignty—something that the Zionists had been willing to sacrifice in 1948—along with the Golan Heights, the West Bank, Gaza, and the Sinai Peninsula. Israel succeeded in keeping the territories despite an effort by the Arab bloc to take them back in the Yom Kippur War of 1973, although the Sinai was once again restored to Egyptian rule when Begin and Sadat signed the historic peace treaty between Israel and Egypt in 1979. Even when Israel is not at war with the sovereign states of the Arab bloc, of course, the undeclared war of the Palestinian Arabs is always being fought with greater or lesser ferocity.

Under such pressures, the very nature of Zionism—already splintered into dozens of rival factions—has changed along with the human face of Israel. The utopian and even messianic ambitions of the founding generations have been mostly forgotten. Nowadays, for example, the *kibbutzim* cater to high-tech industry and the tourist trade, and ideologues who still spout the grandiose rhetoric of Zionist tradition are dismissed by a new generation of Israelis with a condescending turn of phrase: "Pretty souls." According to historian Jay Gonen, born and raised in Israel, " 'Stop talking Zionism' became a popular phrase for rejecting any eloquent but impractical idea."[47]

Instead, the core values of Zionism are expressed in the tough, pragmatic, unsentimental, "can-do" approach that Israelis bring to the governance and defense of the Jewish state—and these are values that can be seen as specifically Israeli rather than specifically Jewish. The point is made, for example, in a tale told about the origins of *sabra*, the Hebrew word used to describe a native-born Israeli. A *sabra* is a cactus fruit to which native Israelis are likened because, like the fruit itself, they are supposedly "tough and prickly on the outside, sweet on the inside."

But there is another and more revealing way to understand how the term came to be applied to Israelis. During the early years of nation-building in Palestine, native-born children often found themselves out-shined in the classroom by European-born Jews who had been raised in the more bookish traditions of the Diaspora. To put them in their place, a native-born child might challenge a newly arrived child to peel the spiky skin of a *sabra*, a task that required dexterity and experience rather than book learning. After a defeated rival dropped the *sabra* in frustration, nursing a wounded finger or two, the native-born Jewish child would show off his or her skill by deftly peeling the skin and sharing the delicious fruit inside.

The same qualities of pragmatism, skill, and resourcefulness came to be summed up in a distinctively Israeli phenomenon called *bitzuism*, a term that derives from the Hebrew word for "implementing" or "expediting."[48] As used by an earlier generation of Zionists, the word was tinged with disapproval and disparagement—*bitzuism* was "Zionism without ideology," an approach to problem-solving that is highly practical but stripped of moral content. "The bitzu'ist is the builder, the irrigator, the pilot, the gunrunner, the settler," explains critic Leon Wieseltier. "In the history of the Jewish state, the bitzu'ist is really a social type: crusty, resourceful, sardonic, effective, not much in need of thought, not much in need of sleep either." But, as Wieseltier insists on pointing out, *bitzuism* must be seen as among the most authentic and enduring expressions of Zionism, and one charged with "supreme moral seriousness."

"One of the characteristic features of bitzu'ism is a contempt for circumstances that extenuate," he explains. "Rescue first, worry later. Better the most bitter warfare within the Jewish state than ceremonies of commemoration for a lost Jewry."[49]

The Masada Complex

A fierce and profound sense of duty still suffuses the Jewish state. An article of faith among Israelis is that the lessons of history—not only the Holocaust but *all* of Jewish history—must not be forgotten. Thus, for example, a 1927 poem by Yitzhak Lamdan (1899–1954) provided Zionism with one of its credos: "Masada shall not fall again." Significantly, the ancient site where the Zealots committed mass suicide rather than surrender to a besieging Roman army in the first century c.e. has been elevated from a symbol of martyrdom to a symbol of survival, and it has served as a kind of national shrine where new generations of Jewish soldiers take a solemn oath to defend the State of Israel, a place where Jews do not need visas and where the tradition of the fighting Jew is honored and preserved.

Still, the memory of Masada is somehow less perplexing to Israelis than the memories of the Holocaust. Almost inevitably, Jewish children who are raised with the fighting Jew rather than the praying Jew as their exemplars—"Every boy is good with his gun" went the rousing anthem of the Palmach, the shock troops of the Haganah during the War of Liberation[50]—are deeply troubled by the question of why so few Jews fought back. During the 1950s, for example, some newly arrived Jewish refugees from Europe found themselves taunted by native-born or Eastern Jews with an especially cruel epithet, *sabon*—a word that means "soap" and refers not only to their pallid skin color but also to the notion that the Germans used the rendered fat of Jewish corpses to make soap. The same rebuke that Bialik once expressed toward the Jews of Kishinev is thus brought to bear against the six million Jews who died in the Holocaust, the great of majority of whom did *not* fight back.

Still, no less than Masada, the Holocaust is the focus of a new credo in Zionism: *Asur she'ha'sho'ah tahazor*—"It is forbidden for the Holocaust to return."[51] And the memory of the Holocaust charges every new threat to Israel with ominous possibilities. When the Arabs engage in rhetorical overkill by threatening to "drive the Jews into the sea," as they first did during the War of Liberation and still routinely do, they are poking an old wound.[52] Thus, the victory in the Six-Day War was seen by Israelis to "avert another Holocaust," and the heroism of the Jewish soldiers on the battlefield was not only a vindication but a kind of corrective to the experience of the Holocaust: "Right after the war," recalls historian Jay Gonen, "one could hear voices in Israel say: 'If only the six million could see us now!' "[53]

Indeed, the Holocaust and the founding of Israel are explicitly linked in Jewish consciousness. The Proclamation of Independence that was read out loud by David Ben-Gurion on May 14, 1948, invokes the memory of "the catastrophe which recently befell the Jewish people" as evidence of "the urgency of solving the problem of its homelessness by re-establishing in Eretz-Israel the Jewish state."[54] Significantly, the Zionist rhetoric is strictly and even pointedly secular: the new Jewish homeland is called *Medinat Yisrael* ("State of Israel") rather than *Eretz Yisrael* ("Land of Israel") because the biblical term is so freighted with religious and messianic baggage; and the Holocaust is called "the catastrophe" (*Shoah*) because the Hebrew word for "holocaust" (*Olah*) is used in the Bible to indicate a living creature that is slaughtered and burned whole as an offering to God. But it is equally significant that the most recent innovations in Judaism are the addition of two days of ritual observance to the Jewish calendar—*Yom HaShoah*, a day of remembrance for the Six Million, and *Yom Ha'Atz'ma'ut* ("Independence Day"), a day of celebration for the creation of the Jewish state.

All of these complex feelings feed into a psychological mechanism that has been called the Masada complex—a grim determination among Israelis not only to fight for their existence but, if necessary, to go down fighting. After all, what other option is available to a tiny sliver of a country that is wedged between the Arabs and the deep blue sea? And nowhere is the Masada complex expressed more forcefully, if also wordlessly, than in the simple fact that Israel was among the first countries in the world to acquire a nuclear capability. Without ever threatening to use nuclear weapons—indeed, without ever openly conceding that it *has* nuclear weapons—Israel has allowed the rest of the world to understand that it is both willing and able to bring down a nuclear holocaust on any enemy foolish enough to attack the Jewish state with weapons of mass destruction or ruthless enough to carry out the threat to "drive the Jews into the sea."

But the whole notion of a Masada complex can be overstated. To its credit, and contrary to its image in the Arab world, Israel has often embraced the old Zionist tradition of *havlaga*—self-restraint—and has been willing to accommodate its enemies in the interest of peace. Thus, as we have already noted, it was Menahem Begin, the Irgun commander who ordered the bombing of the King David Hotel, who shared a Nobel Peace Prize with Anwar el-Sadat. And it was Itzhak Rabin (1922–1995), the chief of staff of the Israel Defense Forces during the Six-Day War, who shared the same prize with Shimon Peres (b. 1923) and Yasir Arafat (b. 1929) for attempting to make peace between Israel and the Palestinian Arabs. Notably, both Sadat and Rabin paid for their efforts as peacemakers with their lives, each one the victim of an assassination by religious fundamentalists of his own faith.

Perhaps the most stirring example of *havlaga* is the heroism of the Israelis during the Gulf War in 1990–91, when the United States prevailed on Israel to endure a sustained missile attack by Iraq without launching a preemptive strike or retaliating after the missiles began to fall. The ordeal was rendered all the more horrific by the knowledge that the incoming missiles might be armed with poison gas or bacteriological weapons. So it was that the Israelis were compelled to put on gas masks and to retreat to "sealed rooms"—a nightmarish experience for a people whose blood relations had been gassed to death in the sealed rooms at Auschwitz and Treblinka.

Still, if there *is* a deeply felt spiritual and psychological impulse among Israelis that prompts them to pick up the gun—an impulse that is only mistakenly called a Masada complex—it is one of the oldest and most cherished traditions of Judaism: *"Kol Yisrael haverim"*—"All Israel are brethren."[55] "Israel" is used here in its classical sense as a term that encompasses the whole of the Jewish people and not merely the citizens of the State of Israel. Indeed, the indelible and enduring Jewishness of Israel is evidenced by the fact that Israel sees itself as the ultimate guarantor of Jewish security throughout the world. Thus, when Arab and German terrorists hijacked an Air France airliner to Uganda in 1976—and promptly carried out a "selection," keeping the Jewish passengers at gunpoint and setting the non-Jews free—it was Israel, rather than France or Germany, that executed the daring rescue of the Jewish men, women, and children at Entebbe without bothering with the formality of which country had issued their passports.

The Victory of Judaism

The ultimate victory of Zionism is expressed in yet another example of diversity in Jewish history and destiny. The fact is that Israelis do *not* share all of the values, experiences, and ideals of the Jews in the Diaspora. Indeed, the differences are so pronounced that a distinction can be drawn between "Israelism" and "Judaism," and some Israelis insist on distancing themselves from their brethren in the Diaspora by calling themselves "Hebrews" rather than "Jews." One faction of early Zionists, in fact, reached all the way back to the distant biblical origins of the land of Israel by styling themselves as "Canaanites"!

"Most sabras prefer the remote to the recent . . . Israel to the galut, the Bible to the Talmud, and nationality to religion," explains Jay Gonen. "Their historical view of their own heritage leads directly from an independent nation nearly 2,000 years ago to an independent nation now. The years that are skipped and rejected are considered abnormal, shameful, and boring, as well as more or less irrelevant to the present national identity."[56]

Indeed, a certain tension and even open confrontation sometimes divides Israel and the Jewish communities of the Diaspora. No longer can Israel count on the reflexive support of American Jewry, for example, and some Jews in the Diaspora are willing to condemn Israel for specific policies and actions. For example, when Ariel Sharon (b. 1928), campaigning against Ehud Barak in 2000 in the prime ministerial election, sparked a new intifada by making a highly public and intentionally provocative visit to the Temple Mount in Jerusalem, an American rabbi and a prominent Jewish leader published an Op Ed piece in which they publicly condemned the "fetishized adulation" with which the site is now regarded by both Arabs and Jews. After all, they pointed out, observant Jews are forbidden to set foot on the Temple Mount lest they inadvertently tread on the spot where the Holy of Holies once stood, and the Israeli government has always been willing to cede authority over the Temple Mount to Arab authorities who are responsible for the Muslim holy places that now stand there.

"Nor, for that matter, do American Jews do Israel any service," they boldly insisted, "by declaring, as a recent advertisement proclaimed, that 'Israel must not surrender Judaism's holiest site, the Temple Mount.' "[57]

Such pronouncements suggest that the relations between Israel and the Jews of the Diaspora have now come full circle. The pioneering Zionists, as we have seen, were regarded with caution and sometimes outright hostility by certain factions in American Jewry. After the Six-Day War in 1967, the survival of Israel inspired a closing of the ranks among the Jews in the Diaspora, and only rarely, if ever, would a prominent American Jew publicly criticize the State of Israel. Now, more recently, the Jews of the Diaspora feel empowered—some of them even feel obliged—to condemn Israel for specific actions or policies that strike them as "un-Jewish." Still, the lessons of recent history always assert themselves, and that is why most of the Jews who live in comfort and safety in the *Goldeneh Medinah* ultimately defer to the Jews who live under the threat of Arab violence in Israel.

"Every Jew in the world has the right to an opinion," explains Abraham Foxman, an official of the B'nai B'rith Anti-Defamation League, "but it is the Jews whose kids stand guard on the borders of Israel, whose kids might die on the Temple Mount, who have the right to make the decision."[58]

Indeed, if there is a single common value within the Jewish world today, a single shared belief that binds together *K'lal Yisrael*, it is the necessity for the secure existence of the State of Israel as the Jewish homeland it was always intended to be. That is an article of faith among the Jewish people, but it has less to do with theology than with the hard facts of history. With the exception of a radical fringe on the far edges—a few ultraobservant Jewish fundamentalists on one end and a few deeply alienated secular Jews on the other—the old enmity toward Zionism among assimilated Jews and religious Jews alike has largely disappeared. "My final word is: Judaism will either be Zionist or not be at all," declared the early Zionist leader Max Nordau—and history had proved him to be wholly correct.[59] Significantly, when Israeli general and politician Moshe Dayan recalled the day the Jewish state was declared in Jerusalem, he characterized it not as "the victory of Zionism" but as "the victory of Judaism."[60]

TEN

A Useful Past

Like a great tree, with its roots in heaven,
and its branches reaching down to the earth.

—JUDAH AL-HARIZI, *"The Sun"*

On the wall of my brother's apartment during his college years was a chart that depicted the rise and fall of peoples and civilizations across the sweep of history in various color-coded bands. Assyria and Babylon, the ancient conquerors of Israel, started as slivers of purple and blue, bulked up to imperial dimensions, then quickly thinned out and disappeared. But a tiny thread of red ran across the chart without interruption from the beginning of recorded history to our own era—the thread that represented the Jewish people.

The simple fact that the Jews have survived since distant biblical antiquity, of course, is one of the stirring truths of Jewish history. Over the centuries and millennia, our enemies tried to exterminate us and obliterate our faith and our culture—but we are still here. Even so, we put ourselves at risk of distorting and diminishing the saga of Judaism and the Jewish people if we celebrate only our survival. Although the Jews have always represented only an infinitesimal fraction of the world population, Jews have influenced and enriched what we call Western civilization in profound and enduring ways.

"Something to conjure with, what this small people has done!"

observed Marc Chagall, whose art offers one rich and resonant vision of the Jewish experience. "When it wished, it brought forth Christ and Christianity. When it wanted, it produced Marx and socialism."[1]

Exactly here, however, we bump into the problem that has perplexed us from the opening pages of this book. If, on one hand, we define Judaism so expansively that we are willing to credit it with the creation of both Christianity and Marxism—each of which, from its own point of view, regards Jews and Judaism as obsolete or worse—then we are at risk of reducing three thousand years of Jewish history to nothing more than a vague and vaporous idea. And yet, on the other hand, if we define Judaism so narrowly that we recognize as Jews only those who strictly observe the ritual law as it is preserved in classical rabbinical tradition, then we are in danger of overlooking some of the greatest achievements of Jewish civilization and, even more tragically, writing off all but a few of the Jews who are alive today.

The problem, of course, is fully as ancient as the Jewish people itself. The struggle to define what it means to be a Jew begins in the Bible, where the very first generation of Jewish fundamentalists were already scolding their brethren for their unseemly fascination with those ivory figures of naked goddesses called *teraphim*, and it is still going on today, as the latest generation of Jewish fundamentalists are still scolding the rest of their fellow Jews for aspiring to be "a Jew at home and a man or woman in the streets." So far, despite three thousand years of hot and sometimes bitter debate, the Jewish people have not yet agreed upon a single answer to the simple question: Who is a Jew? Indeed, the essential point of *The Woman Who Laughed at God* is that Jewishness can be defined only through its richness and diversity.

"The reward of being Jewish," wrote Holocaust historian Lucy S. Dawidowicz, "lies in defining oneself, not in being defined."[2]

What Judaism Isn't

Any definition of what Judaism *is* must begin with what Judaism *isn't*.

Judaism, for example, is not a race. According to pious tradition, the original twelve tribes of Israel all descended from a single common ancestor, but they were not a separate and distinct race in any sense. Indeed, the Bible itself reports that the Israelites were related by blood to various other peoples around the ancient Middle East, and biblical tradition proposes that the Arabs, too, descend from the very first patriarch, Abraham, although not from his wife, Sarah. And the Bible, as we have seen, is full of fruitful intermarriages, including not only Moses and his pagan wife, Zipporah, but the coupling of Judah and his daughter-in-law, an act of illicit love between an Israelite and a Canaanite that spawned the tribe of Judah and, therefore, the Jews.

Recently, some genetic researchers have proposed that Jewish men who are identified as *kohenim*—descendants of the high priest Aaron—do, in fact, have a higher incidence of certain genetic markers than the Jewish population in general. But the bloodlines of the Jewish people are so diluted by thousands of years of life in the Diaspora that it is meaningless to speak of a common genetic inheritance, much less a common race. Indeed, the evidence of three thousand years of intermarriage with non-Jews can be seen on the faces of the Jewish men and women who live in Israel today. Those who descend from German Jews may be fair and blond and blue-eyed, for example, and those who descend from Iraqi Jews are likely to be swarthy and black-haired and brown-eyed. And, unless each of their non-Jewish ancestors underwent the demanding ritual of conversion to Judaism, many of those couplings were in plain violation of the strict prohibition against intermarriage that is written into the Torah.

Judaism is not a nationality. To be sure, the creation of the State of Israel has given Jews an opportunity that they have not enjoyed since the defeat of Bar Kokhba—the opportunity to live as citizens of a Jewish state. Under the Law of the Return, any Jew in the world may claim and carry an Israeli passport. But millions of Jews have chosen to remain in the Diaspora, and they regard themselves as citizens of the various countries where they live now. Today, just as in antiquity, when parallel editions of the Talmud were being compiled in both Jerusalem and Babylon, Jewish communities are not merely surviving but flourishing in both Israel and the Diaspora.

Judaism cannot even be defined as a religion—or, at least, not as a religion with a single creed. The "Judaisms" of the modern world are even greater in number and variety than the sects and schisms that contended with each other in ancient Israel. Even within the broad categories of Hasidic, Orthodox, Conservative, Reform, and Reconstructionist Judaism, we will find a rich array of rituals, practices, and beliefs, some of them so contradictory that an Orthodox Jew will not sit down to a meal in the home of a Reform Jew. On the fringes of organized religion in Judaism are even more inventive expressions of Jewishness, ranging from the Jewish fundamentalists in Jerusalem who are even now fashioning priestly vestments and temple furnishings in urgent expectation of the coming of the Messiah and the building of the Third Temple, to the Jewish innovators in New York and Los Angeles who have organized their own gay and lesbian congregations precisely because the older traditions in Judaism regard homosexuality as a capital crime.

The easy way out of the dilemma is to define Judaism as a "culture" or a "civilization" and leave it at that. But the cultural diversity of the Jewish people is even richer than its religious diversity. The tapestry of Jewish civilization includes the Ashkenazic, Sephardic, Persian, and other "Eastern" Jews, each of whom represents a separate and distinct cluster of traditions with their own language, music, cuisine, attire, and folkways. Thus, for example, the language of Ashkenazic tradition is Yiddish, a blend of medieval German and biblical Hebrew, while the language of Sephardic tradition is Ladino, a blend of Spanish and Hebrew; but Persian Jews speak Farsi, "Eastern" Jews speak Arabic, and Jews from all three traditions in America and elsewhere in the world speak English. Then, too, the fulfillment of the Zionist dream has created a distinctively Israeli culture whose native tongue is a reinvented version of biblical Hebrew and whose national identity draws on all of these "Judaisms" but presents itself as a new, vigorous, and distinctive Judaism in itself.

The Untold History of the Jewish People

What do these many "Judaisms" actually have in common?

"There are three traits to this nation," King David is made to say in the Talmud. "They are compassionate, modest and charitable."[3]

King David says no such thing in the biblical account of his life, however, and rarely is he shown to embody any of these lofty qualities. Indeed, if rabbinical Judaism had embraced the example of David as he is actually depicted in the Bible—a ruthless and cunning warrior, a man of insatiable carnal appetite, a king with imperial ambition—the history of the Jewish people might have turned out much differently. Still, rabbinical Judaism itself was only one of many "Judaisms," and that is why it is hard, and perhaps impossible, to reduce Judaism to a simple credo or a catechism.

Of course, many efforts have been made to do so. Hillel, the kind and gentle rabbi of the first century B.C.E., refined a single nugget of moral truth out of the complexities of the Torah: "Do not unto others what is hateful unto you." The prophet Micah, however, was unable to pare the list down to fewer than three entries: "Only to do justly, and to love mercy, and to walk humbly with thy God" (Mic. 6:8). And Maimonides, the medieval metaphysician, bulked it up to thirteen articles of faith: "I believe with perfect faith that the Creator, Blessed is His Name, creates and guides all creatures," and so on.[4]

According to the most traditional Jews—who are often the most visible and vocal Jews—the *only* authentic Judaism is the one that embraces all of the beliefs and practices that were so compelling to the rabbis of antiquity and the Middle Ages. The point is made with ugly bluntness at the place that is regarded as the most sacred site in Judaism—the Western Wall in Jerusalem, the last remnant of the Temple that Herod built. When Reform or Conservative Jews approach the Western Wall to pray, especially if the minyan consists of women only or both men and women together, they are likely to be cursed and pelted with rocks, bottles, and dirty diapers by the *haredim*. At such moments, ironically enough, the fundamentalists in Judaism seem to have more in common with fundamentalists in Christianity and Islam than with most of their fellow Jews.

Indeed, if we embrace the strict definition that is offered by the most traditional and highly observant factions of Judaism, then 90 percent or more of the Jewish men, women, and children in the world today are not entitled to call themselves Jews at all—or, at least, they are not entitled to call themselves Torah Jews. But the same thing might have been said at several other crucial moments over the last three thousand years when

Judaism reached a turning point and what had been only a countertradition managed to weave itself into the tapestry of Jewish history and Jewish destiny. The untold history of the Jewish people, as we have now seen for ourselves, is the struggle of tradition and countertradition, a constant process of invention and reinvention that has kept Judaism and the Jewish people alive.

"Get Souled"

At the Chochmat HaLev ("Wisdom of the Heart") Jewish Meditation Center in Berkeley, California, Shabbat services include both davening (praying) and drumming, an innovation that may appeal to the spirited young Jews who come to *shul* with their own drums but one that is sternly prohibited by sacred Jewish law. "On the Sabbath, it is forbidden to make a musical sound, either with an instrument or with the limbs of the body," goes a provision of the *Shulhan Arukh*. "It is even forbidden to snap the fingers or to strike on a board to make a sound."[5] And yet, when the sounds of drumming fill the synagogue, the scene conjures up a moment that is described in perhaps the single oldest fragment of text in the Torah.

> Then Miriam the prophetess, Aaron's sister, took a timbrel in her hand; and all the women went out after her in dance with timbrels. And Miriam chanted for them:
>
> > *"Sing to Yahweh, for he has triumphed gloriously,*
> > *Horse and driver he has hurled into the sea."*
> > (Exod. 15:20–21)[6]

Indeed, the Bible plainly reveals—and even celebrates—the fact that singing and dancing, music and percussion, once accompanied the sacred rituals of ancient Israel: "David and the House of Israel danced before the Lord to the sound of all kinds of instruments, lyres, harps, timbrels, sistrums, and cymbals." King David himself, "the sweet singer of Israel," danced with such dervishlike ecstasy, "leaping and whirling before Yahweh," that his priestly tunic flew up and revealed the royal privates to the gathered crowd (2 Sam. 6:5, 16).[7]

Only after the destruction of the Temple in 70 c.e. did classical Judaism come to see the use of musical instruments as unseemly and inappropriate. According to rabbinical tradition, the ban on music is a gesture of mourning over the loss of the Temple—we must await the coming of the Messiah and the building of the Third Temple before we are entitled to follow David's spirited example. Another explanation, less pious but perhaps more telling, is that the rabbis of the Talmudic era sought to distinguish Jewish worship services from those of the renegade Jews who now called themselves Christians and continued to use choirs and musical instruments in their houses of worship. If the Christians accompanied their prayers with harps and timbrels, the rabbis decreed, then the Jews must pray *a capella.*

By the early nineteenth century, the Reform movement was willing to put aside the ancient tradition of bereavement, and Reform Jews began to install organs and choir lofts in their synagogues. From the Orthodox point of view, they were shamelessly aping the Christians, trying to make the synagogue into a church; but if we take a longer view, they were simply coming full circle and embracing the oldest traditions of Judaism. Today, the more progressive movements in Judaism fill their synagogues with the joyous sounds that were once heard in the Temple, and it is a new tradition in many congregations for the cantor—often accompanying himself or herself on the guitar—to sing the concluding prayer of the Saturday morning service, *Adon Olam,* to the tune of the latest pop song to go into heavy rotation on MTV. What better way, after all, to catch the attention and spark the interest of a new generation of Jews in their three-thousand-year-old faith?

Drums and guitars, however, are only one example of the spirit of innovation and invention at work in the Jewish world today. Every tradition and countertradition in the long history of Judaism, no matter how old or how obscure, is brought fully up to date. Metivta, "a center for contemplative Judaism," offers a lecture on "Rereading the Hasidic Masters." "Get souled!" exhorts the Manhattan Jewish Experience, "and unlock your spiritual potential with insights from the Kabbalah." The

Orthodox Union convenes a panel of rabbis and doctors to discuss "Halachic and Practical Considerations in Hospice and Terminal Care." The Israel Aliyah Center offers "Hi-Tech Employment Opportunities in Israel," and the Bureau of Jewish Education announces a summer program for teenagers at archaeological sites: "Teenagers Dig Israel." The Hasidic movement called Chabad, followers of the late Lubavitcher *rebbe*, announce their latest fund-raising telethon with a logo right out of Chagall and *Fiddler on the Roof*.[8]

An even more revolutionary expression of Judaism has emerged in Israel. Religious observance tends to be highly traditional—the progressive movements such as Reform and Conservative Judaism are only beginning to establish themselves in the Jewish homeland—but the fact is that the vast majority of Israelis are *not* observant, and they define their Jewishness in terms of national character and national culture rather than religious practice. And yet even the most secular Jew in Israel is called upon to affirm the most ancient Judaism of all—when Israeli men and women put on the uniform of a Jewish army and take an oath to defend the Jewish state atop the ancient fortress of Masada, they are reenacting a Jewish tradition that is far older than even the oldest expression of "classical" Judaism.

The rich flowering of Judaism in our own age is deeply unsettling to some Jews. Even if the most traditional Jews find themselves forced to concede the point that Judaism changes and grows, they insist that we must go through the proper channels. The slightest degree of innovation in ritual or practice must be based on "sound religious scholarship," justified and defended according to "halakhic rules of interpretation," and ratified by "authoritative, ordained scholars," according to Rabbi Haym Donin.[9] One who improvises on Jewish tradition on his or her own initiative and according to his or her own imagination, Rabbi Donin insists, goes beyond "the legitimate boundaries of Judaism." And what is at stake, goes the traditional argument, is nothing less than the survival of the Jewish people. "[Assimilation] begins when Jews discard the binding character of the halakha," he argues, "and it ends with the disappearance of Judaism."[10]

By the deepest irony of all, the debate between the traditionalists and the innovators in Judaism is something very ancient, something very familiar, something deeply and authentically Jewish. The traditionalists in the Jewish world have *always* feared and condemned the prospect of growth and change in Judaism. "He who studies Jewish history," wrote Simon Rawidowicz in an essay titled "The Ever-Dying People," "will readily discover that there was hardly a generation in the Diaspora that did not consider itself the final link in Israel's chain."[11] And yet Judaism has *always* survived by growing and changing. "Despite everything," insists Simon Dubnow, "the law of survival has never stopped working things out in its own way."[12]

The secret of Jewish survival, as I have argued in these pages, is to be found in the genius of the Jewish people for reinventing themselves. Starting in antiquity, continuing across three thousand years of Jewish history, and even in our own brave new world, each generation of Jews, each community of Jews, has succeeded in redefining itself, sometimes in subtle ways and sometimes in dramatic ones. "All Judaisms therefore testify to humanity's power of creative genius: making something out of nothing," explains theologian Jacob Neusner. "Each Judaism begins in its own time and place, then goes in search of a useful past. Orthodoxy no less than Reform takes up fresh positions and presents stunningly original and relevant innovations."[13] So it is that Judaism and the Jewish people are far more vigorous and vital than even their most zealous defenders are ready to admit.

Skeptics, Agnostics, and Atheists

Ironically, the countertraditions of Judaism may be more familiar today than some of the oldest articles of faith. Nowadays, for example, far more attention is paid to such famous latter-day Kabbalists as Madonna and Roseanne than to the rabbinical scholars and sages who continue to devote their lives to the study the Talmud and Torah. Only a few "Torah Jews" still pore over the ancient texts and observe the ancient rituals— and the rest of us, like our fellow Jews throughout history, are searching for other ways to understand and affirm what it really means to be a Jew.

How many Jews in the world today, I wonder, know that the thirteen articles of faith, as first articulated by Maimonides in the thirteenth century and still embraced in traditional Judaism, expects them to affirm "with perfect faith" that "there will be a resuscitation of the dead whenever the wish emanates from the Creator"?[14] Or that Jewish religious law, as codified in the *Shulhan Arukh* by Joseph Caro in the sixteenth century and still regarded as binding by traditional Jews, prohibits a husband from touching his menstruating wife even to nurse her during an illness?[15] And, among those Jews who *know* the oldest and strictest traditions of Judaism, how many of them affirm and practice them?

The fact is that fewer than half of the Jews in America are affiliated with *any* branch of Judaism, and only 10 percent of them embrace some form of Orthodoxy. The percentage of purely secular Jews in Israel is even higher, perhaps as much as 80 percent of the population. Among the vast majority of Jews in the world today, the old messianic traditions of Judaism have been wholly forgotten, and the old strictures that govern the separation of the sacred and the profane—women who are menstruating no less than food that is *trayf*—are a dead letter. For most Jews, if they pause to ponder such matters at all, it is with a worldliness that owes less to Maimonides than to Spinoza or, for that matter, Marx, Freud, and Einstein.

Even at the moment of greatest innovation, however, the worldly Jew still stands solidly on the bedrock of Jewish tradition. "[A] humble agnosticism often ranks higher than theological certainties," writes Emil Fackenheim about the rabbinical literature known as Midrash.[16] The Talmud, according to Leonard Fein, is the best evidence that "Judaism abides skeptics, agnostics, and atheists."[17] And it is the Torah, which Jewish fundamentalists regard as the revealed word of God, that gives us the moral example of Abraham, who argues with God, and Sarah, who laughs at God. If we read the Torah with open eyes, we can find a way to be fully and truly Jewish without being a true believer, and the argument can be made that the audacity—the sheer *chutzpah*—that Abraham and Sarah displayed in some of their encounters with God is one of the core values of Judaism. Significantly, the name by which the Jewish people and the Jewish state are now known—"Israel" (*Yisrael*)— is explained in the Torah as identifying "one who strives with God."[18]

The friction between free-thinking and true belief in Jewish theology is expressed in one of the folktales that are the glory of the Hasidic tradition. A young man presents himself to a *rebbe* in order to find out how to be a good Jew. But the student balks at the very first lesson—the Thirteen Principles of Faith of Maimonides, each of which begins with the formulaic phrase: "I believe with perfect faith . . ." Heartbroken, he confesses to the rabbi that he cannot recite the words in good conscience—there is *nothing* he believes "with perfect faith." But the rabbi is quick to reassure the earnest young man.

"It is not a statement," explains the rabbi. "It is a prayer: 'May I believe!' "[19]

A Tree with Its Roots in Heaven

At the heart of Judaism, then, is the freedom and perhaps even the duty to question oneself, to question one's teachers, to question God himself. All of the traditions and countertraditions in the Jewish experience can be seen as examples of the same impulse, and all of them have been woven into the rich and colorful tapestry that is Jewish history. By teasing apart these strands of tradition, by tracing them back to their points of origin in the Torah and beyond, as I have tried to do here, we come upon "a useful past" that is the ultimate source of Jewish identity.

The Maccabees, for example, dared to interpret the Torah to permit a Jewish soldier to fight on the Sabbath—and thus set into motion the vast enterprise of scriptural interpretation that is "classical" Judaism. The Hellenizers aspired to master the secular civilization of the Greeks—and thus inspired an open-mindedness among their fellow Jews that can be traced from Josephus to Spinoza to Marx, Freud, and Einstein. The Kabbalists and the Hasidim liberated themselves from the sober discipline of Talmudic scholarship—and thus set Judaism afire with powerful currents of mysticism and ecstasy. Rabbi Akiva saw in a guerilla fighter like Bar Kokhba the long-promised and long-awaited Messiah—and thus anticipated the day when Jewish men and women from the ghetto and the *shtetl* would reinvent themselves as modern Maccabees and take up arms to restore Jewish sovereignty in the ancient homeland.

At various moments in Jewish history, each of these "Judaisms"—

along with many others—was condemned as something alien and dangerous. Then, as now, some Jews fought their fellow Jews in order to extinguish what they regarded as a threat to the very existence of Judaism. And yet each of these contending "Judaisms" managed not only to survive but to thrive. The countertraditions that were once regarded as apostasy are today accepted by most Jews, if not all of them, as authentic and worthy expressions of one's Jewishness. That's exactly why the old Jewish joke "Two Jews, three opinions" is as crucial to understanding Judaism as the prayerful credo that we are taught to recite by our rabbis: "Hear O Israel, the Lord thy God, the Lord is One."

The point is made at a certain sublime moment in the service that takes place in the synagogue on every Shabbat morning. After the scrolls of the Torah have been read out loud to the congregation—the very same words that have been written by hand with a quill pen on sheets of parchment for at least two thousand years—we recite a traditional prayer that affirms its divine origins: "This is the Torah that Moses placed before the children of Israel," goes the ancient liturgy in a literal English translation, "from the mouth of God to the hand of Moses."[20] By invoking *Moshe Rabbeinu* (Moses, Our Teacher), we are reminded of one of the most cherished and enduring moments in Jewish tradition, a scene that appears often in the iconography of Judaism—Moses coming down from Sinai with a pair of tablets in his arms, each one bearing the commandments that have been written in stone, quite literally, with the finger of God.

And then a second verse is recited, echoing a few lines from the Book of Proverbs, and a very different image of the Torah is invoked.

> *It is a tree of life for those who grasp it,*
> *and all who uphold it are blessed.*
> *Its ways are pleasantness, and all its paths are peace.*[21]

Here, then, is a more accurate and more agreeable symbol for Judaism in all of its richness and diversity—Judaism is a "tree of life," not a tablet of stone. It is not hard, brittle, and unchanging; rather, it is fecund and fully alive, and it survives precisely because it grows and changes. While

Judaism may be a tree "with its roots in heaven," in the pious words of the medieval Jewish poet Judah Al-Harizi (c. 1170–1235),[22] it is a tree that grows right here on earth. And the abundance of its shoots and branches—the many "Judaisms" that make up the untold history of the Jewish people—is the best measure of our vitality and the best hope for our survival.

NOTES

ONE: *And Sarah Laughed*

1. All biblical quotations are from *The Holy Scriptures According to the Masoretic Text* (Philadelphia: Jewish Publication Society [JPS], 1961) unless otherwise indicated by an abbreviation or note that identifies another translation. A complete list of Bible translations and their abbreviations can be found on page 296.

2. Shmuel Ettinger, "Graetz, Heinrich," *Encyclopedia Judaica [EJ]*, 17 vols., corr. ed. (Jerusalem: Keter Publishing House, n.d.), vol. 7, 849.

3. Quoted in Yirmiahu Yovel, "Why Spinoza Was Excommunicated," *Commentary*, vol. 64, no. 5, July–December 1977 (November 1977), 46–52, 46.

4. Adapted from (Rabbi) Nosson Scherman, ed. and trans., *The Rabbinical Council of America Edition of the ArtScroll Siddur* (Brooklyn, N.Y.: Mesorah Publications, 1987), 179.

5. Quoted in Ari L. Goldman, *Being Jewish: The Spiritual and Cultural Practice of Judaism Today* (New York: Simon & Schuster, 2000), 27.

6. Adapted from JPS.

7. Adapted from JPS, New JPS, and AB.

8. Aaron Rothkoff, "Sarah," *EJ*, vol. 14, 868, citing, inter alia, BB 58a, Ex. 4. 1:1, BM87a, and Gen. R. 53:9.

9. Elaine A. Phillips, "Incredulity, Faith, and Textual Purposes: Post-Biblical Responses to the Laughter of Abraham and Sarah," in *The Function of Scripture in Early Jewish and Christian Tradition*, eds. Craig A. Evans and James A. Sanders (Sheffield, England: Sheffield Academic Press, 1998), 22–23.

Two: *The People of the Book*

1. Emil L. Fackenheim, *What Is Judaism? An Interpretation for the Present Age* (New York: Summit Books, 1987), 43.

2. Ibid., 59.

3. Adapted from JPS.

4. Heinrich Graetz, *Popular History of the Jews*, trans. A. B. Rhine, 6 vols. (New York: Hebrew Publishing Company, 1930; orig. pub. 1919), vol. 1, 13.

5. Quoted in Richard Elliott Friedman, *Who Wrote the Bible?* (New York: Summit Books, 1987), 19.

6. Quoted in ibid., 21.

7. Adapted from JPS.

8. Adapted from JPS.

9. Scholarly consensus attributes the Binding of Isaac, as Gen. 22:1–19 is known in Jewish tradition, to the source called the Elohist or E "with scarcely a dissenting voice," according to Ephraim Speiser, "and with only a few minor reservations." Speiser himself, however, suggested that the passage is a "fusion" of J and E. "The issue is thus not a closed one by any means." E. A. Speiser, trans., intro., and notes, *Genesis*, Anchor Bible (AB), vol. 1 (Garden City, N.Y.: Doubleday, 1987; orig. pub. 1962), 166.

10. Quoted in Ralph Klein, "Chronicles, Book of, 1–2," in *The Anchor Bible Dictionary (ABD)*, ed. David Noel Freedman, 6 vols. (Garden City, N.Y.: Doubleday, 1992), vol. 1, 997.

11. Adapted from JPS.

12. Harold Bloom and David Rosenberg, *The Book of J* (New York: Grove Weidenfeld, 1990), 273.

13. Jacob Neusner, *Torah Through the Ages: A Short History of Judaism* (Philadelphia: Trinity Press International, 1990), 2.

14. Donald Harman Akenson, *Surpassing Wonder: The Invention of the Bible and the Talmuds* (New York: Harcourt Brace, 1998), 28.

15. (Rabbi) Nosson Scherman, ed. and trans., *The Rabbinical Council of America Edition of the ArtScroll Siddur* (Brooklyn, N.Y.: Mesorah Publications, 1987), 399.

16. *Elim* is translated as "the mighty" in the JPS and as "the celestials" in the New JPS.

17. Adapted from NEB.

18. Adapted from JPS and NEB.

19. Hayim Halevy Donin, *To Be a Jew: A Guide to Jewish Observance in Contemporary Life* (New York: Basic Books, 1972), 243.

20. Nahum M. Sarna, *Understanding Genesis: The World of the Bible in the Light of History* (New York: Schocken Books, 1966), 3.

21. Sigmund Freud, *Moses and Monotheism* (New York: Vintage Books, 1967; orig. pub. 1939), 51.

22. Paul Johnson, *A History of the Jews* (New York: Harper & Row, 1987), 4.

23. Ibid.

24. Magnus Magnusson, *Archaeology of the Bible* (New York: Simon & Schuster, 1977), 42.

25. Quoted in Amy Dockser Marcus, *The View from Nebo: How Archaeology Is Rewriting the Bible and Reshaping the Middle East* (Boston: Little, Brown, 2000), 31.

26. Elias Auerbach, *Moses*, trans. and ed. Robert A. Barclay and Israel O. Lehman (Detroit: Wayne State University, 1975), 216. Yet Auerbach begs the question of whether or not Moses actually existed. "There can be no doubt whatever about the historicity of Moses' personality," he insists, "certainly no more than about the historicity of Buddha or Jesus."

27. Ibid., 179.

28. Israel Finkelstein and Neil Asher Silberman, *The Bible Unearthed: Archaeology's New Vision of Ancient Israel and the Origin of Its Sacred Texts* (New York: Free Press, 2001), 81–82.

29. Ibid., 118.

30. Quoted in Marcus, *The View from Nebo*, 2000, 91.

31. Ibid., 97.

32. Adapted from JPS. The boundaries of Israel are given in the Book of Genesis, where God is shown to promise the land of Israel to the descendants of Abraham. Scholarship suggests that the boundaries describe the empire of David at its greatest reach and were written into the Bible during or after his reign.

33. Magnusson, *Archaeology of the Bible*, 156.

34. Thomas L. Thompson, *The Mythic Past: Biblical Archaeology and the Myth of Israel* (New York: Basic Books, 1999), xv.

35. Ibid.

36. Finkelstein and Silberman, *Bible Unearthed*, 3.

37. Ibid., 2–3.

38. Ibid., 275, 276.

39. John M. Berridge, "Jehoiachin," *ABD*, vol. 3, 662–63.

40. A'hron Oppenheimer, "Am Ha-Arez," *EJ*, corr. ed., vol. 2, 836.

41. Adapted from New JPS.

42. Adapted from JPS and NEB.

43. Adapted from JPS and NEB.

44. Adapted from JPS.

45. Sarna, *Understanding Genesis*, 20.

THREE: *A Goddess of Israel*

1. Adapted from JPS and NEB.

2. Adapted from NEB.

3. Adapted from NEB.

4. Salo Wittmayer Baron, *A Social and Religious History of the Jews*, 2d ed.,

19 vols. (Philadelphia: Jewish Publication Society / New York: Columbia University Press, 1952–1983), vol. 1, 112.

5. Quoted in Ilana Pardes, *Countertraditions in the Bible: A Feminist Approach* (Cambridge, Mass.: Harvard University Press, 1992), 19.

6. Elizabeth Cady Stanton, *The Woman's Bible* (New York: Arno Press, 1972; orig. pub. 1898), 12, 36.

7. Ibid., 7.

8. Anne Michele Tapp, "An Ideology of Expendability," in *Anti-Covenant*, ed. Mieke Bal (Sheffield, England: Almond Press, 1989), 173.

9. Ibid., 171.

10. J. Cheryl Exum, *Fragmented Women: Feminist (Sub)versions of Biblical Narratives*, Journal for the Study of the Old Testament, suppl. ser. 163 (Sheffield, England: JSOT Press, 1993), 173, 174, 175.

11. Phyllis Trible, *God and the Rhetoric of Sexuality* (Philadelphia: Fortress Press, 1978), 202.

12. Ibid.

13. Adapted from JPS.

14. Leila Leah Bronner, "Valorized or Vilified? The Women of Judges in Midrashic Sources," in *A Feminist Companion to Judges*, vol. 4 of *The Feminist Companion to the Bible*, ed. Athalya Brenner (Sheffield, England: Sheffield Academic Press, 1993), 78.

15. Adrien Janis Bledstein, "Is Judges a Woman's Satire of Men Who Play God?" in ibid., 34.

16. David Penchansky, "Staying the Night," in *Reading Between Texts*, ed. Danna Nolan Fewell (Louisville: Westminster–John Knox Press, 1992), 84–85.

17. Ibid. Penchansky describes but dissociates himself from these speculations about a "feminist intelligentsia."

18. Harold Bloom and David Rosenberg, *The Book of J* (New York: Grove Weidenfeld, 1990), 26.

19. See Jonathan Kirsch, *The Harlot by the Side of the Road: Forbidden Tales of the Bible*, chap. 7, "The Woman Who Willed Herself into History."

20. Adapted from JPS.

21. Karen Armstrong, *Jerusalem* (New York: Alfred A. Knopf, 1996), 39–40.

22. Elias Auerbach, *Moses*, trans. and ed. Robert A. Barclay and Israel O. Lehman (Detroit: Wayne State University Press, 1975), 50.

23. See Kirsch, *The Harlot by the Side of the Road*, chap. 9, "The Bridegroom of Blood."

24. Adapted from JPS.

25. Adapted from JPS.

26. Pardes, *Countertraditions*, 89–92.

27. Sigmund Freud, *Moses and Monotheism* (New York: Vintage Books, 1967; orig. pub. 1939), 39, citing Eduard Meyer.

28. Murray Lee Newman, Jr., *The People of the Covenant* (New York: Abingdon Press, 1962), 26.

29. Martin Buber, *Moses: The Revelation and the Covenant* (New York: Harper & Row, 1958), 42.

30. Jan Assmann, *Moses the Egyptian* (Cambridge, Mass.: Harvard University Press, 1997), 4.

31. Ari Z. Zivotofsky, "The Leadership Qualities of Moses," *Judaism* (American Jewish Congress) 43 (3), 171 (Summer 1944): 259.

32. Adapted from JPS.

33. Louis Ginzberg, *The Legends of the Jews*, trans. Henrietta Szold, 7 vols. (Philadelphia: Jewish Publication Society, 1909–1938), vol. 3, 384–86, citing, inter alia, *Sanhedrin*.

34. Auerbach, *Moses*, 64–65.

35. Adapted from JPS and NEB.

36. Adapted from JPS and NEB.

37. P. Kyle McCarter, Jr., trans., intro., and comm., *I Samuel*, AB, vol. 8 (Garden City, N.Y.: Doubleday, 1980), 418.

38. Adapted from JPS and AB.

39. Buber, *Moses*, 7, n.1.

40. Adapted from JPS.

41. Peggy L. Day, "From the Child Is Born the Woman," in *Gender and Difference in Ancient Israel*, ed. Peggy L. Day (Minneapolis: Fortress Press, 1989), 69, n.14, citing the work of Gustav Bostrom.

42. Robert G. Boling, trans., intro., and comm., *Judges*, AB, vol. 6A (Garden City, N.Y.: Doubleday, 1975), 209. Boling himself finds the suggestion "doubtful."

43. Quoted in Raphael Patai, *The Hebrew Goddess*, 3d ed. (Detroit: Wayne State University Press, 1990; orig. pub. 1967), 53 (emphasis added).

44. Ibid., 36–38

45. Quoted in ibid., 94.

46. The familiar passage in the Book of Exodus where Aaron fashions a golden idol in the shape of a calf is believed by some scholars to be a relatively late invention that was written into the biblical text as a covert attack on King Jeroboam and the golden calves that decorated his sanctuaries at Bethel and Dan. A clue is found in the words that Aaron is made to speak: "These are your gods, O Israel" (Exod. 32:4). Aaron makes only one golden calf but refers to them in the plural; later, Jeroboam makes several golden calves and uses the very same phrase in addressing the Israelites (1 Kings 12:28).

47. Quoted in Patai, 84. Rashi refers to "a midrashic passage attributed to Rabbi Pinhas ben Yair, a 2nd-century C.E. Palestinian teacher who seems to have been an Essene" (83).

48. Ibid., 31–32.

49. Ginzberg, *Legends of the Jews*, vol. 3, 52, citing, inter alia, Mekilta Wa-Yassa' 5, 51b.

50. Ibid., 53, citing, inter alia, Tan. B. 4, 127–28, and Tan. B. 3, 74–75.

51. *The Alphabet of Ben Sira* is not to be confused with a work called *The Wisdom of Ben Sira*, also known as *Ecclesiasticus*, which is included in the Apocrypha in Christian tradition; the two works are apparently unrelated.

52. Joseph Dan, "Ben Sira, Alphabet of," *EJ*, corr. ed., vol. 4, 550.

53. Adapted from *The Alphabet of Ben Sira* as quoted in Aviva Cantor Zuckoff, "The Lilith Question," *Lilith* 5–8 (1976): 38, citing *The Alphabet*, 23a–b.

54. Quoted in Patai, *Goddess*, 224.

55. Quoted in ibid., 225.

56. Ibid., 32.

57. (Rabbi) Lynn Gottlieb, *She Who Dwells Within: A Feminist Vision of Renewed Judaism* (San Francisco: HarperCollins, 1995), 21.

58. Ibid., 22.

59. Patai, *Goddess*, 142, citing Tiqqune haZohar, Tiqqun 34, 77, Zohar 3, 296a, and Zohar 1, 12b.

60. Ibid., 145, citing Zohar 3, 69a.

61. Quoted in ibid., 114–15.

62. A. Cohen, *Everyman's Talmud* (New York: E. P. Dutton & Co., 1949) 98, 161, citing Keth. 65a and Ber. 61a.

63. (Rabbi) Solomon Ganzfried, *Code of Jewish Law (Kitzur Shulhan Arukh): A Compilation of Jewish Laws and Customs*, trans. Hyman E. Goldin, anno. rev. ed. (New York: Hebrew Publishing Co., 1963), 20.

64. Cohen, *Everyman's Talmud*, 160–61, citing Gen. R 45, 5, Kid. 49b, and Aboth 2, 8.

65. Rachel Adler, "The Virgin in the Brothel and Other Anomalies: Character and Context in the Legend of Beruriah," *Tikkun* 3/6 (1988): 31–32, citing Midrash Mishlei on Prov. 31:10.

66. Ibid., 29, citing Mishnah Horayot.

67. Ibid., 28–32, 103–8.

68. Patai, *Goddess*, 33.

69. Pardes, *Countertraditions*, 24.

70. "From the Editors," *Lilith* 1/1 (Fall 1976): 3.

71. Gottlieb, *She Who Dwells Within*, 20.

FOUR: *The Fighting Jew*

1. Robert Alter, *The David Story: A Translation with Commentary of 1 and 2 Samuel* (New York: W. W. Norton, 1999), 374.

2. Louis Ginzberg, *The Legends of the Jews*, trans. Henrietta Szold, 7 vols. (Philadelphia: Jewish Publication Society, 1909–1938), vol. 4, 101, 103, citing, inter alia, Sukkah 26b, Baba Batra 17a.

3. Rich Cohen, *Tough Jews: Fathers, Sons and Gangster Dreams* (New York: Simon & Schuster, 1998), 55.

4. Ibid., 20, 21.

5. Menachem Begin, *The Revolt* (New York: Nash Publishing, 1977; orig. pub. 1951), xxv.

6. Elimelech Epstein Halevy, "Alexander the Great," *EJ*, vol. 2, 578, citing Josephus and Yoma 69a.

7. Abram Leon Sachar, *A History of the Jews*, 5th ed. (New York: Alfred A. Knopf, 1967; orig. pub. 1930), 99.

8. Simon Dubnow, *A Short History of the Jewish People*, trans. D. Mowshowitch (London: M. L. Cailingold, 1936), 89.

9. Heinrich Graetz, *Popular History of the Jews*, trans. A. B. Rhine, 6 vols. (New York: Hebrew Publishing Company, 1930; orig. pub. 1919), vol. 1, 331.

10. Ibid., 336.

11. Ibid., 326.

12. Sachar, *History of the Jews*, 100.

13. Thomas L. Thompson, *The Mythic Past: Biblical Archaeology and the Myth of Israel* (New York: Basic Books, 1999), 199.

14. Flavius Josephus, *The Works of Josephus*, trans. William Whiston (Peabody, Mass.: Hendrickson Publishers, 1987), *Antiquities of the Jews*, 12.5.4, 324.

15. Adapted from JPS.

16. Emil L. Fackenheim, *What Is Judaism? An Interpretation for the Present Age* (New York: Summit Books, 1987), 67, 68.

17. Steven Weitzman, "Forced Circumcision and the Shifting Role of Gentiles in Hasmonean Ideology," *Harvard Theological Review* 92/1 (January 1999): 59.

18. Graetz, *Popular History*, vol. 1, 355.

19. S. Schwartz, quoted in Erich S. Gruen, *Heritage and Hellenism: The Reinvention of Jewish Tradition* (Berkeley: University of California Press, 1998), 5, n. 8. Gruen, however, disagrees with the premise that the Maccabean revolt ought to be seen as a "Kulturkampf."

20. Herman Wouk, *This Is My God* (New York: Doubleday, 1959), 99.

21. Ibid., 104.

22. Ben M. Edidin, *Jewish Holidays and Festivals* (New York: Hebrew Publishing Company, 1940), 102.

23. Ironically, the ancient sources who preserved the saga of the Maccabees have never been warmly embraced in Jewish tradition. All four of the Books of the Maccabees are excluded from the Jewish biblical canon, and they appear only in the Apocrypha and Pseudepigrapha as preserved in Christian tradition.

24. Gruen, *Heritage and Hellenism*, xiv, xv.

25. Paul Johnson, *A History of the Jews* (New York: Harper & Row, 1987), 108.

26. Solomon Grayzel, *A History of the Jews* (Philadelphia: Jewish Publication Society of America, 1947), 81.

27. Ibid., 89.

28. Josephus, *The Jewish War*, rev. ed., trans. G. A. Williamson (New York: Dorset Press, 1981), 2: 223, 144.

29. Richard A. Horsley, "Josephus and the Bandits," *Journal of Jewish Studies* (Oxford) 10/1 (1979): 37, quoting Josephus.

30. Quoted in Grayzel, *History of the Jews*, 90.

31. Quoted in L. I. Levine, "Herod the Great," *ABD*, 3, 67, citing b. B. Bat. 4a.

32. Quoted in Cecil Roth, *A Short History of the Jewish People* (London: East and West Library, 1959), 92.

33. Ibid., 93.

34. Josephus, *The Jewish War*, I. 660, 117.

35. A. H. M. Jones, Travers Herford, and Eduard Meyer, quoted in Shimon Applebaum, "The Zealots: The Case for Revaluation," *The Journal of Roman Studies* 41 (1971): 156–70, n. 4.

36. Roth, *Short History*, 52.

37. Ibid., 54; Klausner, quoted in Applebaum, "The Zealots," 156–70, 156.

FIVE: *Twenty-four Judaisms*

1. Yohanan Ben Zakkai and other early sages are known in the Talmud by the title "Rabban," a Hebrew word that literally means "teacher" and is a more exalted version of the term "rabbi." For that reason, rabbinical Judaism is sometimes called "Rabbanite" Judaism, especially in older and more traditional sources.

2. Cecil Roth, "The Zealots—A Jewish Religious Sect," *Judaism* 8/1 (Winter 1959): 40.

3. Adapted from (Rabbi) Nosson Scherman, ed. and trans., *The Rabbinical Council of America Edition of the ArtScroll Siddur* (Brooklyn, N.Y.: Mesorah Publications, 1987), 445.

4. Quoted in Jacob Neusner, *A Life of Rabban Yohanan Ben Zakkai, ca. 1–80 C.E.* (Leiden: E. J. Brill, 1962), 142. Yohanan Ben Zakkai is quoting Hos. 6:6.

5. Quoted in Jacob Neusner, ed. and trans., *The Talmud of the Land of Israel: A Preliminary Translation and Exposition* (Chicago: University of Chicago Press, 1984), vol. 31, *Sanhedrin and Makkot*, 360.

6. Cecil Roth, "Simon Bar Giora, Ancient Jewish Hero: A Historical Reinterpretation," *Commentary* 39 (Jan.–June 1960): 56.

7. Flavius Josephus, *The Works of Josephus*, trans. William Whiston (Peabody, Mass.: Hendrickson Publishers, 1987), 737, *The Jewish War* 6: 210.

8. Adapted from JPS.

9. Zvi Kaplan, "Hanina Segan Ha-Kohanim," *EJ*, vol. 7, 1266–67, citing Avot 3:2.

10. Adapted from NEB.

11. Adapted from NEB.

12. Josephus, *Works*, 743, *Jewish Antiquities*, 6:310.

13. Ibid., 793, *Against Apion*, 2:320.

14. Mireille Hadas-Lebel, *Flavius Josephus: Eyewitness to Rome's First Century Conquest of Judea*, trans. Richard Miller (New York: Macmillan Publishing Company, 1993), 238.

15. Donald Harman Akenson, *Surpassing Wonder: The Invention of the Bible and the Talmuds* (New York: Harcourt Brace & Company, 1998), 363–64.

16. Karen Armstrong, *Jerusalem: One City, Three Faiths* (New York: Alfred A. Knopf, 1996), 153.

17. Yigal Yadin, *Bar-Kokhba: The Rediscovery of the Legendary Hero of the Second Jewish Revolt against Rome* (New York: Random House, 1971), 22.

18. Adapted from Neusner, *Rabban Yohanan Ben Zakkai*, 141, citing, inter alia, TP Taanit 4.7.

19. Cecil Roth, *A Short History of the Jewish People* (London: East and West Library, 1959), 114.

20. Quoted in David Hendin, *Guide to Biblical Coins*, 3d ed. (New York: Amphora, 1996), 184.

21. Yadin, *Bar-Kokhba*, p. 27.

Six: *In the Ruined Citadel*

1. Salo Wittmayer Baron, *A Social and Religious History of the Jews*, 2d ed., 19 vols. (Philadelphia: Jewish Publication Society/New York: Columbia University Press, 1952–1983), vol. 2, 313, quoting Rabbi Abbahu.

2. Banesh Hoffmann, *Albert Einstein: Creator and Rebel* (New York: New American Library, 1972), 152.

3. Sander L. Gilman, "Introduction: The Frontier as a Model for Jewish History," in Sander L. Gilman and Milton Shain, *Jewries at the Frontier: Accommodation, Identity Conflict* (Urbana and Chicago: University of Illinois Press, 1999), 1.

4. Ibid.

5. Quoted in Baron, *History of the Jews*, vol. 2, 189.

6. Adin Steinsaltz, *The Essential Talmud*, trans. Chaya Galai (New York: Basic Books, 1976), 3.

7. Quoted in Geza Vermes, *Scripture and Tradition in Judaism* (Leiden: E. J. Brill, 1961), 2–3.

8. Quoted in Isaac Bashevis Singer, *Love and Exile: A Memoir* (Garden City, N.Y., Doubleday & Co., 1984), 65.

9. Steinsaltz, *Essential Talmud*, 26.

10. Ibid., 25–26.

11. Quoted in ibid., 6.

12. Nathan Schur, *History of the Karaites* (Frankfurt am Main: Verlag Peter Lang, 1992), 142.

13. Don Seeman, "Ethnographers, Rabbis and Jewish Epistemology: The Case of the Ethiopian Jews," *Tradition: Journal of Orthodox Jewish Thought*, 25/4 (Summer 1991): 13–29, 17.

14. Steven Kaplan, " 'Falasha' Religion: Ancient Judaism or Evolving Ethiopian Tradition?" *Jewish Quarterly Review* 59/1 (July 1988): 49–67, 51, n. 8.

15. Seeman, "Ethiopian Jews," 20, quoting Chief Rabbi Herzog.

16. Quoted in Matthew D. Slater, "The Jews of Cochin," *Judaism* 24/96 (Fall 1975): 486.

17. Ibid., 494.

18. Zhou Xun, "Jews in Chinese Culture: Representations and Realities," in *Jewries at the Frontier: Accommodation, Identity Conflict*, eds. Sander L. Gilman and Milton Shain (Urbana and Chicago: University of Illinois Press, 1999), 226.

19. Arthur Koestler, *The Thirteenth Tribe* (New York: Random House, 1976), 16.

20. Raphael Patai, *Tents of Jacob: The Diaspora Yesterday and Today* (Englewood Cliffs, N.J.: Prentice-Hall, 1971), 18.

21. Israel Shahak, *Jewish Fundamentalism in Israel* (London: Pluto Press, 1999), xiv.

22. (Rabbi) Alfred J. Kolatch, *The Jewish Home Advisor* (Middle Village, N.Y.: Jonathan David Publishers, 1990), 233.

23. (Rabbi) Nosson Scherman, ed. and trans., *The Rabbinical Council of America Edition of the ArtScroll Siddur* (Brooklyn, N.Y.: Mesorah Publications, 1987), 475, 992. (The Mourner's Kaddish is actually composed in Aramaic, a sister language of biblical Hebrew and the vernacular language of ancient Israel after the fifth century B.C.E.)

24. Quoted in Paul Johnson, *A History of the Jews* (New York: Harper & Row, 1987), 186.

25. Adapted from Scherman, *ArtScroll Siddur*, 179.

26. Quoted in Francine Klagsbrun, *Voices of Wisdom* (Middle Village, N.Y.: Jonathan David Publishers, 1980), 442.

27. Quoted in Meyer Waxman, *A History of Jewish Literature* (New York: Bloch Publishing Company, 1930), 3 vols., vol. 1, 297, 302.

28. Quoted in Haim Hillel Ben-Sasson, "Maimonidean Controversy," *EJ*, vol. 11, 749.

29. Johnson, *History of the Jews*, 118, 192.

30. Quoted in R. J. Zwi Weblowsky, "Caro, Joseph Ben Ephraim," *EJ*, vol. 5, 197.

31. Louis Isaac Rabinowitz, "Maimonides, Moses," *EJ*, vol. 11, 762, quoting Avodat Kokhavim 11:16.

32. Martin Buber, *Moses* (New York: Harper & Row, 1958), 7, n. 1.

33. Joseph Dan, "Magic," *EJ*, vol. 11, 707, quoting Sot. 48a.

34. Quoted in Raphael Patai, *The Jewish Mind* (New York: Charles Scribner's Sons, 1977), 150.

35. Gershom Scholem, *Kabbalah* (New York: Dorset Press, 1987), 30–31.

36. Poul Borchsenius, *Behind the Wall: The Story of the Ghetto*, trans. Reginald Spink (London: George Allen & Unwin, 1964), 14.

37. Scholem, *Kabbalah*, 14.

38. Raphael Patai, *The Hebrew Goddess*, 3d ed. (Detroit: Wayne State University Press, 1990, orig. pub. 1967), 114.

39. Patai, *Goddess*, 14.

40. Quoted in ibid., 275.

41. Ibid., 157, 163, quoting Gershom Scholem and Isaiah Tishby.

42. Heinrich Graetz, *Popular History of the Jews*, trans. A. B. Rhine, 6 vols. (New York: Hebrew Publishing Company, 1930; orig. pub. 1919), vol. 3, 391.

43. Baron, *History of the Jews*, vol. 2, 17.

44. Patai, *Goddess*, 166.

45. Adapted from Scherman, *ArtScroll Siddur*, 316–19.

46. (Rabbi) Hayim Halevy Donin, *To Pray as a Jew: A Guide to the Prayer Book and the Synagogue Service* (New York: Basic Books, 1980), 316.

47. Quoted in T. Carmi, ed. and trans., *The Penguin Book of Hebrew Verse* (New York: Penguin Books, 1981), 285.

48. Simon M. Dubnow, *History of the Jews in Russia and Poland: From the Earliest Times Until the Present Day*, trans. I. Friedlaender, 3 vols. (Philadelphia: Jewish Publication Society, 1916), vol. 1, 142.

49. Quoted in ibid., 145–46.

50. Ibid., 146.

51. Ibid., 147.

52. Quoted in ibid., 149.

53. Zvi Kaplan, "Hanina Segan Ha-Kohanim," *EJ*, vol. 7, 1266–67, citing Avot 3:2.

54. Graetz, *Popular History*, vol. 5, 163.

55. Dubnow, *History of the Jews*, vol. 1, 205.

56. Quoted in ibid., 206.

57. Quoted in H. H. Ben-Sasson, ed., *A History of the Jewish People* (Cambridge, Mass.: Harvard University Press, 1976), 706.

58. Patai, *Jewish Mind*, 191.

59. Meyer Levin, *Classic Hassidic Tales* (New York: Dorset Press, 1959), iv.

60. Patai, *Jewish Mind*, 180.

61. Hanoch Avenary, "Music," *EJ*, vol. 12, 638.

62. Patai, *Jewish Mind*, 197.

63. Quoted in ibid., 219.

64. Graetz, *Popular History*, vol. 5, 347.

65. Quoted in Patai, *Jewish Mind*, 197.

SEVEN: *Abominable Heresies*

1. Uriel da Costa, "My Double Life," in *Memoirs of My People: Through a Thousand Years*, ed. Leo W. Schwartz (Philadelphia: Jewish Publication Society, 1945), 87.

2. Quoted in Yirmiahu Yovel, "Why Spinoza Was Excommunicated," *Commentary* 64/5 (November 1977): 46.

3. Quoted in ibid., 49.

4. Ibid., 52.

5. Quoted in Abram Leon Sachar, *A History of the Jews*, 5th ed. (New York: Alfred A. Knopf, 1967; orig. pub. 1930), 268.

6. Heinrich Graetz, *Popular History of the Jews*, trans. A. B. Rhine, 6 vols. (New York: Hebrew Publishing Company, 1930; orig. pub. 1919), vol. 5, 301–2.

7. Quoted in ibid., 309.

8. Raphael Patai, *The Jewish Mind* (New York: Charles Scribner's Sons, 1977), 467.

9. Graetz, *Popular History*, vol. 5, 361.

10. Quoted in Howard M. Sachar, *A History of Israel* (New York: Alfred A. Knopf, 1979), 8.

11. Quoted in Alan M. Dershowitz, *The Vanishing American Jew: In Search of Jewish Identity for the Next Century* (Boston: Little, Brown, 1997), 30.

12. Graetz, *Popular History*, vol. 5, 329.

13. Ibid., 402, 404.

14. Quoted in A. Sachar, *History of the Jews*, 289; and in Emil L. Fackenheim, *What Is Judaism? An Interpretation for the Present Age* (New York: Summit Books, 1987), 61 ("entrance ticket").

15. Quoted in Francine Klagsbrun, *Voices of Wisdom* (Middle Village, N.Y.: Jonathan David Publishers, 1980), 5.

16. Quoted in Murray Wolfson, *Marx: Economist, Philosopher, Jew* (London: Macmillan, 1982), 14.

17. Quoted in A. Sachar, *History of the Jews*, 384.

18. Quoted in H. H. Ben-Sasson, ed., *A History of the Jewish People* (Cambridge, Mass: Harvard University Press, 1976), 806.

19. Quoted in Patai, *Jewish Mind*, 470.

20. Ibid.

21. Wolfson, *Marx*, 12.

22. The full and formal name of the Bund is *Algemeyner Yiddisher Arbeterbund in Lite, Poilen un Russland* ("General Jewish Workers' Union in Lithuania, Poland and Russia").

23. Jacob Neusner, *The Way of Torah: Introduction to Judaism* (Belmont, Calif.: Dickenson Publishing Co., 1970), 64, 73.

24. Quoted in Helen Walker Puner, *Freud: His Life and His Mind* (New York: Charter Books, 1978; orig. pub. 1947), 134.

25. Ernest Jones, *The Life and Work of Sigmund Freud*, abr. and ed. Lionel Trilling and Steven Marcus (New York: Basic Books, 1961), 18–19.

26. Ibid.

27. Quoted in Patai, *Jewish Mind*, 379.

28. Ibid.

29. Quoted in Puner, *Freud*, 153.

30. Jones, *Life and Work of Freud*, 244.

31. Quoted in ibid., 518.

32. Ibid., 514–15.

33. Banesh Hoffmann, *Albert Einstein: Creator and Rebel* (New York: New American Library, 1972), 144.

34. Quoted in ibid., 244–45.

35. Ibid., 150–51.

36. Ibid., 237.

37. Ibid., 206.

38. A. Sachar, *History of the Jews*, 297.

39. Quoted in Hoffman, *Albert Einstein*, 95.

40. Adapted from (Rabbi) Nosson Scherman, ed. and trans., *The Rabbinical Council of America Edition of the ArtScroll Siddur* (Brooklyn, N.Y.: Mesorah Publications, 1987), 179.

41. Hoffman, *Albert Einstein*, 94–95.

42. Quoted in (and adapted from) Lincoln Barnett, *The Universe and Dr. Einstein*, rev. ed. (New York: Bantam Books, 1968), 36.

43. Quoted in Hoffman, *Albert Einstein*, 195.

44. Ibid., 94–95.

45. Quoted in Mendel Sachs, *Einstein Versus Bohr* (LaSalle, Ill.: Open Court, 1988), 3.

46. Quoted in Paul Johnson, *A History of the Jews* (New York: Harper & Row, 1987), 380.

47. Quoted in ibid.

48. Quoted in Leonard Fein, *Where Are We? The Inner Life of America's Jews* (New York: Harper & Row, 1988), 6.

49. Quoted in Johnson, *A History*, 390–91.

50. Quoted in ibid., 391.

51. Quoted in (and adapted from) Walter Laqueur, *A History of Zionism* (New York: Holt, Rinehart and Winston, 1972), 86.

52. Ibid., 86.

53. Ibid., 89.

54. "Liberty, Statue of," *Encyclopedia Britannica Online* (EBO).

55. Maud Mosher, "Ellis Island As the Matron Sees It," 1910, posted at "The Kissing Post" on Ellis Island.

56. A. Sachar, *History of the Jews*, 308.

57. "Liberty, Statue of," EBO.

58. E. L. Doctorow, *World's Fair* (New York: Fawcett Crest, 1985), 188.

59. Quoted in Ari L. Goldman, *Being Jewish: The Spiritual and Cultural Practice of Judaism Today* (New York: Simon & Schuster, 2000), 27.

60. Irving Howe, *World of Our Fathers* (New York: Harcourt Brace Jovanovich, 1976), 121.

61. Hayim Halevy Donin, *To Be a Jew: A Guide to Jewish Observance in Contemporary Life* (New York: Basic Books, 1972), 32.

62. Dershowitz, *Vanishing American Jew*, 1.

63. Quoted in Jacob Neusner, *Torah Through the Ages: A Short History of Judaism* (Philadelphia: Trinity Press International, 1990), 22, citing, Mishnah-Tractate Abot 1:1–18.

E I G H T: *After Auschwitz*

1. André Schwarz-Bart, *The Last of the Just*, trans. Stephen Becker (New York: Atheneum, 1961), 4.

2. Leonard Fein, *Where Are We? The Inner Life of America's Jews* (New York: Harper & Row, 1988), 60.

3. Adapted from JPS.

4. Quoted in Joshua Hammer, *Chosen by God: A Brother's Journey* (New York: Hyperion, 2000), 57.

5. Norman G. Finkelstein, *The Holocaust Industry: Reflections on the Exploitation of Jewish Suffering* (London and New York: Verso, 2000), 1, 7, 45, 55, quoting Peter Novick ("sacralization of the Holocaust").

6. Ibid., 45.

7. Schwarz-Bart, *Last of the Just*, 370.

8. Adapted from NEP and JPS.

9. Adapted from Koppel S. Pinson, ed., *Dubnow: Nationalism and History* (Philadelphia: Jewish Publication Society of America, 1958), 39.

10. Edwin Black, *IBM and the Holocaust: The Strategic Alliance Between Nazi Germany and America's Most Powerful Corporation* (New York: Crown Publishers, 2001), 8.

11. Thomas Keneally, *Schindler's List* (New York: Simon & Schuster, 1982), 14.

12. Quoted in Anthony Read and David Fisher, *Kristallnacht: The Unleashing of the Holocaust* (New York: Peter Bedrick Books, 1989), 39.

13. Quoted in ibid., 6–7.

14. Quoted in ibid., 63, 64, 78.

15. Ibid., 151.

16. Zvi Kaplan, "Hanina Segan Ha-Kohanim," *EJ*, corr. ed., vol. 7, 1266–67, citing Avot 3:2.

17. Raul Hilberg, *Perpetrators, Victims, Bystanders: The Jewish Catastrophe, 1933–1945* (New York: HarperCollins, 1992), 177–78.

18. Lucy S. Dawidowicz, *The War Against the Jews, 1933–1945* (New York: Holt, Rinehart and Winston, 1975), 264.

19. Ibid.

20. Quoted in ibid., 266.

21. Ibid., 273.

22. Ibid., 310.

23. Ibid., 312.

24. Ibid., 333.

25. Quoted in Yuri Suhl, ed. and trans., *They Fought Back: The Story of Jewish Resistance in Nazi Europe* (New York: Schocken Books, 1967), 98.

26. Quoted in Dawidowicz, *War Against the Jews*, 338.

27. Ibid., 334.

28. Quoted in Nehama Tec, *Defiance: The Bielski Partisans* (Oxford and New York: Oxford University Press, 1993), 45.

29. Quoted in (and adapted from) Tec, *Defiance*, 3.

30. Ibid., 47.

31. Ibid., 8.

32. Ibid., 4.

33. Jean Améry, *At the Mind's Limit* (Bloomington: Indiana University Press, 1980), 34.

34. Primo Levi, *Survival in Auschwitz* (New York: Collier Books, 1993; orig. pub. 1958), 103.

35. Jacob Neusner, *The Way of Torah: Introduction to Judaism* (Belmont, Calif.: Dickenson Publishing Company, 1970), 25.

36. Adapted from Rachel Anne Rabinowicz, *Passover Haggadah: The Feast of Freedom*, 2d ed. (The Rabbinical Assembly, 1982), 39.

37. Quoted in Neusner, *The Way of Torah*, 84.

38. Emil L. Fackenheim, *What Is Judaism? An Interpretation for the Present Age* (New York: Summit Books, 1987), 36.

39. Herman Wouk, *War and Remembrance* (Boston: Little, Brown, 1985), 1307.

40. Quoted in Abba Eban, *My People: The Story of the Jews* (New York: Behrman House and Random House, 1968), 357.

41. Quoted in Suhl, *They Fought Back*, 4.

42. Quoted in Deborah E. Lipstadt, *Beyond Belief: The American Press and the Coming of the Holocaust, 1933–1945* (New York: Free Press, 1986), 208.

43. Quoted in Suhl, *They Fought Back*, 2.

44. Paraphrased in Jay Y. Gonen, *A Psychohistory of Zionism* (New York: New American Library, 1975), 153.

45. Quoted in Suhl, *They Fought Back*, 6 (emphasis added).

46. Quoted in (and adapted from) Walter Laqueur, *A History of Zionism* (New York: Holt, Rinehart and Winston, 1972), 86.

47. Leon Wieseltier, *The New Republic*, 192/6 (February 11, 1985): 22.

NINE: *Measured in Blood*

1. I. Domb, *The Transformation: The Case of the Neturei Karta* (Brooklyn and Jerusalem: Hachomo, 1989), vii, 133.

2. Ibid., 7.

3. (Rabbi) Nosson Scherman, ed. and trans., *The Rabbinical Council of America Edition of the ArtScroll Siddur* (Brooklyn, N.Y.: Mesorah Publications, 1987), 15.

4. Jay Y. Gonen, *A Psychohistory of Zionism* (New York: New American Library, 1975), 31.

5. Paraphrased in ibid., 21.

6. Quoted in David Biale, *Power and Powerlessness in Jewish History* (New York: Schocken Books, 1986), 4.

7. Steven L. Jacobs, *Shirot Bialik: A New and Annotated Translation of Chaim Nachman Bialik's Epic Poems* (Columbus, Ohio: Alpha Publishing Company, 1987), 134.

8. Ibid., 134, 136.

9. Hayyim Nahman Bialik, *Selected Poems of Hayyim Nahman Bialik,* ed. and intro. Israel Efros, rev. ed. (New York: Bloch Publishing Company, 1965; orig. pub. 1948), 119.

10. Jacobs, *Shirot Bialik,* 136.

11. Bialik, *Selected Poems,* 119.

12. Quoted in Gonen, *Psychohistory,* 276.

13. Quoted in Martin Gilbert, *Exile and Return: The Struggle for a Jewish Homeland* (Philadelphia and New York: J. P. Lippincott and Company, 1978), 80.

14. Quoted in (and adapted from) ibid., 85–86.

15. Quoted in Yehuda Slutsky, "Trumpeldor, Joseph," *EJ,* vol. 15, 1412–13.

16. Quoted in Peter Hay, *Ordinary Heroes: Chana Szenes and the Dream of Zion* (New York: G. P. Putnam's Sons, 1986), 171.

17. Quoted in Jacobs, *Shirot Bialik,* 124.

18. Quoted in Gilbert, *Exile and Return,* 101.

19. Gonen, *Psychohistory,* 44.

20. Quoted in Abba Eban, *My People: The Story of the Jews* (New York: Behrman House and Random House, 1968), 357.

21. Ibid.

22. Eban, *My People,* 359.

23. Walter Laqueur, *A History of Zionism* (New York: Holt, Rinehart and Winston, 1972), 408, quoting I. Domb.

24. Quoted in ibid., 394.

25. Quoted in Gonen, *Psychohistory,* 264.

26. Howard M. Sachar, *A History of Israel* (New York: Alfred A. Knopf, 1979), 8, quoting Judah Leib Gordon.

27. William Zukerman, quoted in Laqueur, *History of Zionism,* 429.

28. Quoted in Gilbert, *Exile and Return,* 100, 101.

29. Quoted in ibid., 56.

30. Domb, *The Transformation,* 118.

31. Paraphrased in Gonen, *Psychohistory,* 191.

32. Quoted in Gilbert, *Exile and Return,* 116.

33. Ibid., *Exile and Return,* 118.

34. Quoted in Laqueur, *History of Zionism*, 427.

35. Quoted in Gilbert, *Exile and Return*, 60.

36. Quoted in Laqueur, *History of Zionism*, 344, 349.

37. Quoted in ibid., 370.

38. Marie Syrkin, "Essence of Revisionism," in *Jewish Frontier Association, Inc.*, *Jewish Frontier Anthology, 1934–44* (New York: Jewish Frontier Association, 1945), 68, 69.

39. Quoted in Gilbert, *Exile and Return*, 230.

40. Samuel Katz, *Days of Fire* (Garden City, N.Y.: Doubleday, 1968), 32.

41. Quoted in Gonen, *Psychohistory*, 93.

42. *The Times* (London), "39 Killed in Jerusalem Headquarters," July 23, 1946, p. 4.

43. Quoted in Katz, *Days of Fire*, 125.

44. Quoted in ibid., 248.

45. Ibid., 229.

46. Menachem Begin, *The Revolt* (New York: Nash Publishing, 1977; orig. pub. 1951), 176.

47. Gonen, *Psychohistory*, 118.

48. Ibid., 96.

49. Leon Wieseltier, "Brothers and Keepers," *The New Republic*, 192/6 (February 11, 1985): 22,23.

50. Quoted in Samuel G. Freedman, *Jew vs. Jew: The Struggle for the Soul of American Jewry* (New York: Simon & Schuster, 2000), 46.

51. Quoted in Gonen, *Psychohistory*, 154.

52. Quoted in Raphael Patai, *The Arab Mind* (New York: Charles Scribner's Sons, 1976), 51.

53. Gonen, *Psychohistory*, 167.

54. Quoted in Eban, *My People*, 455.

55. Gonen, *Psychohistory*, 37.

56. Ibid., 115.

57. David N. Myers and (Rabbi) Chaim Seidler-Feller, "Jews Shouldn't Adulate Temple Mount," *Los Angeles Times*, January 21, 2001, page M5.

58. Quoted in Mary Curtius, "Diaspora Jews Add Voice to Jerusalem Debate," *Los Angeles Times*, January 25, 2001, page A4.

59. Quoted in Simon Dubnow, *Nationalism and History: Essays on Old and New Judaism*, ed. Koppel S. Pinson (Philadelphia: Jewish Publication Society of America, 1958), 169.

60. Quoted in Gilbert, 306.

TEN: *A Useful Past*

1. Quoted in Lucy S. Dawidowicz, *What Is the Use of Jewish History?*, ed. and intro. Neal Kozodoy (New York: Schocken Books, 1992), xii.

2. Ibid., xix.

3. Quoted in Raphael Patai, *The Jewish Mind* (New York: Charles Scribner's Sons, 1977), 8.

4. Adapted from "The Thirteen Principles of Faith" in (Rabbi) Nosson Scherman, ed. and trans., *The Rabbinical Council of America Edition of the ArtScroll Siddur* (Brooklyn, N.Y.: Mesorah Publications, 1987), 179.

5. (Rabbi) Solomon Ganzfried, *Code of Jewish Law (Kitzur Shulhan Arukh): A Compilation of Jewish Laws and Customs*, anno. rev. ed., trans. Hyman E. Goldin (New York: Hebrew Publishing Company, 1963), vol. 2, 103.

6. Adapted from New JPS.

7. Adapted from New JPS.

8. Quoted from various advertisements and announcements appearing in *The Jewish Journal of Greater Los Angeles*, 15: 43, December 22, 2000, and *The Jewish Week* (New York), December 22, 2000.

9. Hayim Halevy Donin, *To Be a Jew: A Guide to Jewish Observance in Contemporary Life* (New York: Basic Books, 1972), 32.

10. Ibid.

11. Quoted in Samuel G. Freedman, *Jew vs. Jew: The Struggle for the Soul of American Jewry* (New York: Simon & Schuster, 2000), 26.

12. Simon Dubnow, *Nationalism and History: Essays on Old and New Judaism*, ed. Koppel S. Pinson (Philadelphia: Jewish Publication Society of America, 1958), 40.

13. Jacob Neusner, *Torah Through the Ages: A Short History of Judaism* (Philadelphia: Trinity Press International, 1990), 17.

14. Quoted in Scherman, 180–181.

15. Ganzfried, vol. 4, 23–24.

16. (Rabbi) Emil L. Fackenheim, *What Is Judaism? An Interpretation for the Present Age* (New York: Summit Books, 1987), 15, 73.

17. Leonard Fein, *Where Are We? The Inner Life of America's Jews* (New York: Harper & Row, 1988), 31–32, citing Bab. Met. 59B.

18. "Your name shall no longer be Jacob but Israel," says Yahweh to Jacob after he wrestles with a mysterious figure who may be God himself, "for you have striven with beings divine and human, and have prevailed" (Gen. 32:29) (New JPS).

19. Quoted in Fackenheim, *What Is Judaism?*, 22.

20. Adapted from Scherman, 445.

21. (Rabbi) Jules Harlow, ed. and trans., *Siddur Sim Shalom: A Prayerbook for Shabbat, Festivals and Weekdays* (New York: The Rabbinical Assembly and The United Synagogue of America, 1985), 427. The quoted portion of the liturgy is adapted from Prov. 3:17 and 3:18.

22. Judah Al-Harizi, "The Sun," in *The Penguin Book of Hebrew Verse*, ed. and trans. T. Carmi (New York: Penguin Books, 1981), 389.

BIBLIOGRAPHY

Reference Works

Browning, W. R. F., ed. *A Dictionary of the Bible*. Oxford and New York: Oxford University Press, 1996.

Comey, Arie, and Naomi Tsur, *NTC's Hebrew and English Dictionary*. Chicago: NTC Publishing Group, 2000.

Doniach, N. S., and Kahane, A. eds. *The Oxford Hebrew-English Dictionary*. Oxford: Oxford University Press, 1996.

Encyclopedia Judaica. Corrected ed. 17 vols. Jerusalem: Keter Publishing House Jerusalem, n.d.

Freedman, David Noel, ed. *The Anchor Bible Dictionary*. 6 vols. Garden City, N.Y.: Doubleday, 1992.

Roth, Cecil, ed. *The Concise Jewish Encyclopedia*. New York: New American Library, 1980.

Wigoder, Geoffrey, ed. *The New Standard Jewish Encyclopedia*. New York: Facts on File, 1992.

Bibles

AUTHOR'S NOTE: When quoting from biblical sources, I use the phrase "adapted from" in the Notes to indicate, that I have omitted or rearranged portions of the text or combined text from more than one translation of the Bible. Throughout, I have taken the liberty of making minor changes in punctuation and capitalization, or omitting words and phrases that do not alter the meaning of the quoted passage, without indicating those changes in the text.

New JPS   *Tanakh The Holy Scriptures: The New JPS Translation According to the Traditional Hebrew Text.* Philadelphia: Jewish Publication Society, 1985.

JPS   *The Holy Scriptures According to the Masoretic Text.* Philadelphia: Jewish Publication Society.

AB   Boling, Robert G., trans., intro., and commentary. Judges. Anchor Bible, vol. 6A.
McCarter, P. Kyle, Jr., trans., intro., and commentary. I Samuel. Anchor Bible, vol. 8.
McCarter, P. Kyle, Jr., trans., intro., and commentary. II Samuel. Anchor Bible, vol. 9.
Speiser, E. A., trans., intro., and notes. Genesis. Anchor Bible, vol. 1. (orig. pub. 1962).

Books

Akenson, Donald Harman. *Surpassing Wonder: The Invention of the Bible and the Talmuds.* New York: Harcourt, Brace & Company, 1998.
———. *Saint Saul: A Skeleton Key to the Historical Jesus.* Montreal and Kingston: McGill-Queen's University Press, 2000.
Albright, William Foxwell. *From the Stone Age to Christianity: Monotheism and the Historical Process.* 2d ed. Baltimore: Johns Hopkins Press, 1957.
Alter, Robert. *The David Story: A Translation with Commentary of 1 and 2 Samuel.* New York: W. W. Norton, 1999.
Améry, Jean. *At the Mind's Limit.* Bloomington: Indiana University Press, 1980.
Armstrong, Karen. *Jerusalem: One City, Three Faiths.* New York: Alfred A. Knopf, 1996.
———. *The Battle for God.* New York: Alfred A. Knopf, 2000.
Assmann, Jan. *Moses the Egyptian.* Cambridge, Mass.: Harvard University Press, 1997.
Auerbach, Elias. *Moses.* Trans. and ed. Robert A. Barclay and Israel O. Lehman. Detroit: Wayne State University Press, 1975.
Bal, Mieke. *Lethal Love: Feminist Literary Readings of Biblical Love Stories.* Bloomington: Indiana University Press, 1987.
———. *Death & Dissymmetry: The Politics of Coherence in the Book of Judges.* Chicago: University of Chicago Press, 1988.
———. ed. *Anti-Covenant.* Sheffield, England: Almond Press, 1989.
Barnett, Lincoln. *The Universe and Dr. Einstein.* Rev. ed. New York: Bantam Books, 1968 (orig. pub. 1948).
Baron, Salo Wittmayer. *A Social and Religious History of the Jews.* 2d ed. 19 vols. Philadelphia: Jewish Publication Society New York: Columbia University Press, 1952–1983.
Begin, Menachem. *The Revolt.* Rev. ed. New York: Nash Publishing, 1977 (orig. pub. 1951).

Beilenson, Edna. *Simple Jewish Cookery.* Mount Vernon, N.Y.: Peter Pauper Press, 1962.

Ben-Sasson, H. H., ed. *A History of the Jewish People.* Cambridge, Mass.: Harvard University Press, 1976.

Biale, David. *Power and Powerlessness in Jewish History.* New York: Schocken Books, 1986.

Bialik, Hayyim Nahman. *Selected Poems of Hayyim Nahman Bialik.* Ed. and intro. by Israel Efros. New York: Bloch Publishing Company, 1965 (orig. pub. 1948).

Black, Edwin. *IBM and the Holocaust: The Strategic Alliance Between Nazi Germany and America's Most Powerful Corporation.* New York: Crown Publishers, 2001.

Bloom, Harold, and Rosenberg, David. *The Book of J.* New York: Grove Weidenfeld, 1990.

Borchsenius, Poul. *Behind the Wall: The Story of the Ghetto.* Trans. Reginald Spink. London: George Allen & Unwin Ltd., 1964.

Brenner, Athalya, ed. *A Feminist Companion to Judges.* Vol. 4 of *The Feminist Companion to the Bible.* Sheffield, England: Sheffield Academic Press, 1993.

Buber, Martin. *Moses: The Revelation and the Covenant.* New York: Harper & Row, 1958.

Carmi, T., ed. and trans. *The Penguin Book of Hebrew Verse.* New York: Penguin Books, 1981.

Chatwin, Bruce. *The Songlines.* New York: Viking, 1987.

Cohen, A. *Everyman's Talmud.* New York: E. P. Dutton, 1949.

Cohen, Mark R. *Under Crescent & Cross: The Jews in the Middle Ages.* Princeton: Princeton University Press, 1994.

Cohen, Rich. *Tough Jews: Fathers, Sons and Gangster Dreams.* New York: Simon & Schuster, 1998.

Cohn-Sherbok, Dan, and Cohn-Sherbok, Lavinia. *Jewish & Christian Mysticism: An Introduction.* New York: Continuum, 1994.

Comay, Joan. *The Diaspora Story: The Epic of the Jewish People Among the Nations.* Jerusalem: Steimatzky's Agency Ltd., 1981.

Crown, Alan D., Pummer, Reinhard, and Tal, Abraham, eds. *A Companion to Samaritan Studies.* Tubingen, Germany: J. C. B. Mohr, 1993.

Dawidowicz, Lucy S. *The War Against the Jews, 1933–1945.* New York: Holt, Rinehart and Winston, 1975.

———. *What Is the Use of Jewish History?* Ed. and intro by Neal Kozodoy. New York: Schocken Books, 1992.

Day, Peggy L., ed. *Gender and Difference in Ancient Israel.* Minneapolis.: Fortress Press, 1989.

Dershowitz, Alan M. *The Vanishing American Jew: In Search of Jewish Identity for the Next Century.* Boston: Little, Brown, 1997.

Doctorow, E. L. *World's Fair.* New York: Fawcett Crest, 1985.

Domb, I. *The Transformation: The Case of the Neturei Karta*. Brooklyn and Jerusalem: Hachomo, 1989.

Donin, Hayim Halevy (Rabbi). *To Be a Jew: A Guide to Jewish Observance in Contemporary Life*. New York: Basic Books, 1972.

———. *To Pray as a Jew: A Guide to the Prayer Book and the Synagogue Service*. New York: Basic Books, 1980.

Dorf, Elliot N., and Rosett, Arthur. *A Living Tree: The Roots and Growth of Jewish Law*. Albany: State University of New York Press, 1988.

Dubnow, Simon. *History of the Jews in Russia and Poland: From the Earliest Times until the Present Day*. Trans. I. Friedlaender. 3 vols. Philadelphia: Jewish Publication Society of America, 1916.

———. *A Short History of the Jewish People*. Trans. D. Mowshowitch. London: M. L. Cailingold, 1936.

———. *Nationalism and History: Essays on Old and New Judaism*. Ed. Koppel S. Pinson. Philadelphia: Jewish Publication Society of America, 1958.

Eban, Abba. *My People: The Story of the Jews*. New York: Behrman House and Random House, 1968.

Edidin, Ben M. *Jewish Holidays and Festivals*. New York: Hebrew Publishing Company, 1940.

Exum, J. Cheryl. *Fragmented Women: Feminist (Sub)versions of Biblical Narratives*. Journal for the Study of the Old Testament, Supplement Series 163. Sheffield, England: JSOT Press, 1993.

Fackenheim, Emil L. *What Is Judaism? An Interpretation for the Present Age*. New York: Summit Books, 1987.

Fein, Leonard. *Where Are We? The Inner Life of America's Jews*. New York: Harper & Row, 1988.

Fewell, Danna Nolan, ed. *Reading between Texts*. Louisville: Westminster–John Knox Press, 1992.

Finkelstein, Israel, and Silberman, Neil Asher. *The Bible Unearthed: Archaeology's New Vision of Ancient Israel and the Origin of Its Sacred Texts*. New York: Free Press, 2001.

Finkelstein, Norman G. *The Holocaust Industry: Reflections on the Exploitation of Jewish Suffering*. London and New York: Verso, 2000.

Freedman, Samuel G. *Jew vs. Jew: The Struggle for the Soul of American Jewry*. New York: Simon & Schuster, 2000.

Freud, Sigmund. *Moses and Monotheism*. New York: Vintage Books, 1967 (orig. pub. 1939).

Freund, Roman. *Karaites and Dejudaization: A Historical Review of an Endogenous and Exogenous Paradigm*. Stockholm: Almqvist & Wiksell International, 1991.

Galnoor, Itzhak. *The Partition of Palestine: Decision Crossroads in the Zionist Movement*. Albany: State University of New York Press, 1995.

Ganzfried, Solomon (Rabbi). *Code of Jewish Law (Kitzur Shulhan Arukh): A*

Compilation of Jewish Laws and Customs. Trans. Hyman E. Goldin. Anno. rev. ed. New York: Hebrew Publishing Company, 1963.

Gibbon, Edward. *The Decline and Fall of the Roman Empire.* Abridgment by D. M. Low. New York: Harcourt Brace, 1960.

Gilbert, Martin. *Atlas of Jewish History.* Rev. ed. Dorset Press, 1976.

———. *Exile and Return: The Struggle for a Jewish Homeland.* Philadelphia and New York: J. B. Lippincott and Company, 1978.

Gilman, Sander L., and Shain, Milton, eds. *Jewries at the Frontier: Accommodation, Identity Conflict.* Urbana and Chicago: University of Illinois Press, 1999.

Ginzberg, Louis. *The Legends of the Jews.* Trans. Henrietta Szold. 7 vols. Philadelphia: Jewish Publication Society of America, 1909–1938.

———. *Students, Scholars and Saints.* New York: Meridian Books, 1958.

———. *On Jewish Law and Lore.* New York: Atheneum, 1981.

Gitlitz, David M. *Secrecy and Deceit: The Religion of the Crypto-Jews.* Philadelphia and Jerusalem: Jewish Publication Society, 1996.

Goldhagen, Daniel Jonah. *Hitler's Willing Executioners: Ordinary Germans and the Holocaust.* New York: Vintage Books, 1997.

Goldin, Judah, ed. *The Living Talmud: The Wisdom of the Fathers and Its Classical Commentaries.* New York: The Heritage Press, 1960.

Goldman, Ari L. *Being Jewish: The Spiritual and Cultural Practice of Judaism Today.* New York: Simon & Schuster, 2000.

Goldman, Robert N. *Einstein's God: Albert Einstein's Quest as Scientist and as a Jew to Replace a Forsaken God.* Northvale, N.J.: Jason Aronson, 1997.

Gonen, Jay Y. *A Psychohistory of Zionism.* New York: New American Library, 1975.

Gottlieb, Lynn. *She Who Dwells Within: A Feminist Vision of Renewed Judaism.* San Francisco: HarperCollins, 1995.

Graetz, H. *Popular History of the Jews.* Trans. Rabbi A. B. Rhine. 6 vols. New York: Hebrew Publishing Company, 1930 (orig. pub. 1919).

Grayzel, Solomon. *A History of the Jews.* Philadelphia: Jewish Publication Society of America, 1947.

Greenberg, Sidney (Rabbi), and Levine, Jonathan D. (Rabbi), eds. *The New Mahzor for Rosh Hashanah and Yom Kippur.* Enhanced ed. Bridgeport, Conn.: The Prayer Book Press, 1998.

Gruen, Erich S. *Heritage and Hellenism: The Reinvention of Jewish Tradition.* Berkeley: University of California Press, 1998.

Hadas-Lebel, Mireille. *Flavius Josephus: Eyewitness to Rome's First-Century Conquest of Judea.* Trans. Richard Miller. New York: Macmillan, 1993.

Halevi, Ilan. *A History of the Jews: Ancient and Modern.* Trans. A. M. Berrett. London and New Jersey: Zed Books, Ltd., 1987.

Hammer, Joshua. *Chosen by God: A Brother's Journey.* New York: Hyperion, 2000.

Harlow, Jules (Rabbi), ed. and trans. *Siddur Sim Shalom: A Prayerbook for Shab-*

bat, Festivals and Weekdays. New York: The Rabbinical Assembly and The United Synagogue of America, 1985.

Harris, Stephen L. *Understanding the Bible: A Reader's Introduction.* 2d ed. Palo Alto, Calif., and London: Mayfield Publishing Company, 1985.

Hartman, David. *Israelis and the Jewish Tradition: An Ancient People Debating Its Future.* New Haven & London: Yale University Press, 2000.

Hay, Peter. *Ordinary Heroes: Chana Szenes and the Dream of Zion.* New York: G. P. Putnam's Sons, 1986.

Heilman, Samuel. *Defenders of the Faith: Inside Ultra-Orthodox Jewry.* New York: Schocken Books, 1992.

Heller, Joseph. *God Knows.* New York: Alfred A. Knopf, 1984.

Hendin, David. *Guide to Biblical Coins.* 3d ed. New York: Amphora, 1996.

Hilberg, Raul. *Perpetrators, Victims, Bystanders: The Jewish Catastrophe, 1933–1945.* New York: HarperCollins, 1992.

Hindus, Milton, ed. *The World of Maurice Samuel: Selected Writings.* Philadelphia: Jewish Publication Society of America, 1977.

Hoffmann, Banesh. *Albert Einstein: Creator and Rebel.* New York: New American Library, 1972.

Howe, Irving. *World of Our Fathers.* New York: Harcourt Brace Jovanovich, 1976.

Jacobs, Steven L. *Shirot Bialik: A New and Annotated Translation of Chaim Nachman Bialik's Epic Poems.* Columbus, Ohio: Alpha Publishing Company, 1987.

Jewish Frontier Association, Inc. *Jewish Frontier Anthology, 1934–44.* New York: Jewish Frontier Association, 1945.

Johnson, Paul. *A History of the Jews.* New York: Harper & Row, 1987.

Jones, Ernest. *The Life and Work of Sigmund Freud.* Abr. and ed. Lionel Trilling and Steven Marcus. New York: Basic Books, 1961.

Josephus, Flavius. *The Jewish War.* Trans. G. A. Williamson. Rev. ed. New York: Dorset Press, 1981.

———. *The Works of Josephus.* Trans. William Whiston. Peabody, Mass. Hendrickson Publishers, 1987.

Kamentz, Rodger. *The Jew in the Lotus.* San Francisco: HarperSanFrancisco, 1994.

Katz, Samuel. *Days of Fire.* Garden City, N.Y.: Doubleday, 1968.

Keneally, Thomas. *Schindler's List.* New York: Simon & Schuster, 1982.

Klagsbrun, Francine. *Voices of Wisdom.* Middle Village, N.Y.: Jonathan David Publishers, 1980.

Koestler, Arthur. *The Thirteenth Tribe.* New York: Random House, 1976.

Kolatch, Alfred J. *The Jewish Book of Why.* Middle Village, N.Y.: Jonathan David Publishers, 1981.

———. *The Jewish Home Advisor.* Middle Village, N.Y.: Jonathan David Publishers, 1990.

Laqueur, Walter. *A History of Zionism.* New York: Holt, Rinehart and Winston, 1972.

Levi, Primo. *Survival in Auschwitz*. New York: Collier Books, 1993 (orig. pub. 1958).

Levin, Meyer. *Classic Hassidic Tales*. New York: Dorset Press, 1959.

Lipstadt, Deborah E. *Beyond Belief: The American Press and the Coming of the Holocaust, 1933–1945*. New York: Free Press, 1986.

Magnusson, Magnus. *Archaeology of the Bible*. New York: Simon & Schuster, 1977.

Marcus, Amy Dockser. *The View from Nebo: How Archaeology Is Rewriting the Bible and Reshaping the Middle East*. Boston: Little, Brown, 2000.

Mazar, Amihai. *Archaeology of the Land of the Bible, 10,000–586* B.C.E. New York: Doubleday, 1992.

Meyer, Michael A. *The Origins of the Modern Jew: Jewish Identity and European Culture in Germany, 1749–1824*. Detroit: Wayne State University, 1967.

Milman, Henry Hart. *The History of the Jews*. 2 vols. London: J. M. Dent & Sons / New York: E. P. Dutton, 1909 (reprinted 1913; orig. pub. 1863).

Modrzejewski, Joseph M. *The Jews of Egypt: From Ramses II to Emperor Hadrian*. Trans. Robert Cornman. Philadelphia: The Jewish Publication Society, 1995.

Nadell, Pamela S. *Women Who Would Be Rabbis: A History of Women's Ordination, 1880–1985*. Boston: Beacon Press, 1998.

Nathan, Joan. *The Jewish Holiday Kitchen*. New York: Schocken Books, 1988.

Neusner, Jacob. *A Life of Rabban Yohanan Ben Zakkai, Ca. 1–80* C.E. Leiden: E. J. Brill, 1962.

———. *The Way of Torah: Introduction to Judaism*. Belmont, Calif.: Dickenson Publishing Company, 1970.

———. *Foundations of Judaism*. Philadelphia: Fortress Press, 1989.

———. *Torah through the Ages: A Short History of Judaism*. Philadelphia: Trinity Press International, 1990.

———, ed. and trans. *The Talmud of the Land of Israel: A Preliminary Translation and Exposition*. Chicago: University of Chicago Press, 1984. Vol. 31, *Sanhedrin and Makkot*.

Newman, Murray Lee, Jr. *The People of the Covenant*. New York: Abingdon Press, 1962.

Owings, Alison. *Frauen: German Women Recall the Third Reich*. New Brunswick, N.J.: Rutgers University Press, 1993.

Pardes, Ilana. *Countertraditions in the Bible: A Feminist Approach*. Cambridge, Mass.: Harvard University Press, 1992.

Patai, Raphael. *Tents of Jacob: The Diaspora Yesterday and Today*. Englewood Cliffs, N.Y.: Prentice-Hall, 1971.

———. *The Arab Mind*. New York: Charles Scribner's Sons, 1976.

———. *The Jewish Mind*. New York: Charles Scribner's Sons, 1977.

———. *The Hebrew Goddess*. 3d ed. Detroit: Wayne State University Press, 1990 (orig. pub. 1967).

Phillips, Elaine A. "Incredulity, Faith and Textual Purposes." In *The Function of Scripture in Early Jewish and Christian Tradition*, eds. Craig A. Evans and James A. Sander. Sheffield, England: Sheffield Academic Press, 1998.

Puner, Helen Walker. *Freud: His Life and His Mind*. New York: Charter Books, 1978 (orig. pub. 1947).

Rabinowicz, Rachel Anne. *Passover Haggadah: The Feast of Freedom*. 2d ed. The Rabbinical Assembly, 1982.

Rajak, Tessa. *Josephus: The Historian and His Society*. Philadelphia: Fortress Press, 1983.

Read, Anthony, and Fisher, David. *Kristallnacht: The Unleashing of the Holocaust*. New York: Peter Bedrick Books, 1989.

Roth, Cecil. *A History of the Marranos*. New York: Meridian Books & Philadelphia: Jewish Publication Society of America, 1959 (orig. pub. 1932).

———. *Short History of the Jewish People*. London: East and West Library, 1959.

Rubin, Israel. *Satmar: An Island in the City*. Chicago: Quadrangle Books, 1972.

Sachar, Abram León. *A History of the Jews*. 5th ed. New York: Alfred A. Knopf, 1967 (orig. pub. 1930).

Sachar, Howard M. *A History of Israel*. New York: Alfred A. Knopf, 1979.

Sachs, Mendel. *Einstein Versus Bohr*. LaSalle, Ill.: Open Court, 1988.

Sarna, Nahum M. *Understanding Genesis: The World of the Bible in the Light of History*. New York: Schocken Books, 1966.

Schäfer, Peter. *Judeophobia: Attitudes toward Jews in the Ancient World*. Cambridge, Mass.: Harvard University Press, 1997.

———. *Toward the Millennium: Messianic Expectations from the Bible to Waco*. Leiden: Brill, 1998.

Scherman, Nosson (Rabbi), ed. and trans. *The Rabbinical Council of America Edition of the ArtScroll Siddur*. Brooklyn, N.Y.: Mesorah Publications, 1987.

Schneider, Susan Weidman. *Jewish and Female: A Guide and Sourcebook for Today's Jewish Woman*. New York: Simon & Schuster, 1985.

Scholem, Gershom. *Kabbalah*. New York: Dorset Press, 1987.

Schur, Nathan. *History of the Karaites*. Frankfurt am Main: Verlag Peter Lang, 1992.

Schwartz, Leo W., ed. *Memoirs of My People: Through a Thousand Years*. Philadelphia: The Jewish Publication Society of America, 1945.

Schwarz-Bart, André. *The Last of the Just*. Trans. Stephen Becker. New York: Atheneum, 1961.

Shahak, Israel. *Jewish Fundamentalism in Israel*. London: Pluto Press, 1999.

Singer, Isaac Bashevis. *Love and Exile: A Memoir*. Garden City, N.Y.: Doubleday, 1984.

Stanton, Elizabeth Cady. *The Woman's Bible*. New York: Arno Press, 1972 (orig. pub. New York: European Publishing Company, 1898).

Steinsaltz, Adin. *The Essential Talmud*. Trans. Chaya Galai. New York: Basic Books, 1976.

———. (Rabbi). *The Talmud: The Steinsaltz Edition, a Reference Guide*. Trans. and ed. Israel V. Berman (Rabbi). New York: Random House, 1989.

Suhl, Yuri, ed. and trans. *They Fought Back: The Story of Jewish Resistance in Nazi Europe*. New York: Schocken Books, 1967.

Tec, Nehama. *Defiance: The Bielski Partisans*. Oxford and New York: Oxford University Press, 1993.

Thompson, Thomas L. *The Mythic Past: Biblical Archaeology and the Myth of Israel*. New York: Basic Books, 1999.

Trible, Phyllis. *God and the Rhetoric of Sexuality*. Philadelphia: Fortress Press, 1978.

Van Den Haag, Ernest. *The Jewish Mystique*. New York: Stein and Day, 1969.

Vaux, Roland de. *The Early History of Israel*. Trans. David Smith. Philadelphia: The Westminister Press, 1978 (orig. pub. 1971, 1973).

Vermes, Geza. *Scripture and Tradition in Judaism*. Leiden: E. J. Brill, 1961.

Waxman, Meyer. *A History of Jewish Literature*. 3 vols. New York: Bloch Publishing Company, 1930.

Wolfson, Murray. *Marx: Economist, Philosopher, Jew*. London: Macmillan, 1982.

Wouk, Herman. *This Is My God*. New York: Doubleday, 1959.

———. *War and Remembrance*. Boston: Little, Brown, 1985.

Yadin, Yigael. *Bar-Kokhba*. New York: Random House, 1971.

Journals and Periodicals

Adler, Rachel. "The Virgin in the Brothel and Other Anomalies: Character and Context in the Legend of Beruriah." *Tikkun* 3/6 (1988), 28–32, 103–105.

"Against the Tide: An Interview with Maverick Scholar Cyrus Gordon." *Biblical Archaeology Review* 26/6 (November/December 2000): 52–63, 71.

Applebaum, Shimon. "The Zealots: The Case for Revaluation." *Journal of Roman Studies* 61 (1971): 156–70.

Blum, Raymond Blum. "Letters: Joseph Lieberman." *Jewish Journal*, vol. 15, No. 26, August 25, 2000, p. 4.

Brandon, S. G. F. "The Zealots: The Jewish Resistance Against Rome." *History Today* 15/9 (September 1965): 632–42.

Curtius, Mary. "Diaspora Jews Add Voice to Jerusalem Debate." *Los Angeles Times*, January 25, 2001, page A4.

Emerton, J. A. "New Light on Israelite Religion: The Implications of the Inscriptions from Kuntillet Ajrud." *Zeitschrift für Die Alttestamentliche Wissenschaft* 94/1 (1982): 2–20.

———. " 'Yahweh and His Asherah': The Goddess or Her Symbol?" *Vetus Testamentum* 49/3 (July 1999): 315–37.

Fax, Julie Gruenbaum "T. K." *Jewish Journal of Greater Los Angeles* 14/51 (February 11, 2000): 10–11.

Fischer, Dov (Rabbi). "The Price of Freedom." *Jewish Journal* 15/49 (February 2, 2001): 54.

Franck, Isaac. "Spinoza's Onslaught on Judaism." *Judaism*, Vol. 28, No. 2, Issue 110, Spring 1979, pps. 177–201.

"From the Editors." *Lilith* 1 1 (Fall 1976): 3.

Horsley, Richard A. "Ancient Jewish Banditry and the Revolt Against Rome, A.D. 66–70." *Catholic Bible Quarterly* 43/3 (July 1931): 409–32.

————. "Josephus and the Bandits." *Journal of Jewish Studies* (Oxford) 10/1 (1979): 37–63.

————. "The Sicarii: Ancient Jewish 'Terrorists.' " *Journal of Religion* 59/4 (October 1979): 435–39.

————. "The Zealots: Their Origin, Relationships and Importance in the Jewish Revolt." *Novum Testamentu* 28, Fasc. 2 (April 1986): 159–92.

Jews for Truth Now. "An Important Message from Ehud Barak," advertisement. *Jewish Journal* 15/47 (January 19, 2001): 24.

Kaplan, Steven. " 'Falasha' Religion: Ancient Judaism or Evolving Ethiopian Tradition?" *Jewish Quarterly Review* 79/1 (July 1988): 49–67.

Katz, Nathan. "The Judaisms of Kaifeng and Cochin: Parallel and Divergent Styles of Religious Acculturation." *Numen* 42/2 (May 1995): 118–40.

Lemaire, Andre. "Who or What Was Yahweh's Asherah?" *Biblical Archaeology Review* 10/6 (November–December 1984): 42–51.

Lichtenstein, Aharon. "The Israeli Chief Rabbinate: A Current Halakhic Perspective." *Tradition* 26/4 (1992): 26–38.

Lobdell, William. "Doubting the Scouts." *Los Angeles Times*, January 20, 2001, p. B2.

Margalit, B. "The Meaning and Significance of Asherah." *Vetus Testamentum* 40/3 (July 1990): 264–97.

Masliyah, Sadok. "The Bene Israel and the Baghdadis: Two Indian Jewish Communities in Conflict." *Judaism* 43/171 (Summer 1994): 279–93.

Myers, David N., and Seidler-Feller, Chaim (Rabbi). "Jews Shouldn't Adulate Temple Mount." *Los Angeles Times*, January 21, 2001, p. M5.

Nagorski, Andrew, et al. "The Last Days of Auschwitz." *Newsweek*, January 16, 1995, 46–56.

Neusner, Jacob. "Religious Authority in Judaism: Modern and Classical Modes." *Interpretation* 39/1 (January 1985): 373–87.

————. "The Next Battle." *Jewish Journal* 15/42 (December 15, 2000): 62.

Polon, Moshe. "Torah Not an Evolving Document." *Jewish Journal of Greater Los Angeles* 15/19 (July 7–13, 2000): 9.

Ramras-Rauch, Gila. "Fathers and Daughters: Two Biblical Narratives." In "Mappings of the Biblical Terrain: The Bible as Text," eds. Vincent L. Tollers and John Maier. *Bucknell Review* 33/2 (1990): 158–67.

Rappaport, U. "John of Gischala: From Galilee to Jerusalem." *Journal of Jewish Studies* 33/1–2 (Spring–Autumn 1982): 479–93.

Roth, Cecil. "The Zealots—A Jewish Religious Sect." *Judaism* 8/1 (Winter 1959): 33–40.

————. "Simon Bar Giora, Ancient Jewish Hero: A Historical Reinterpretation." *Commentary* 29 (Jan.–June 1960): 52–58.

Schulweis, Harold M. (Rabbi). "Other Voices: Creating Pariahs in the Jewish Community." *Jewish Journal of Greater Los Angeles* 15/2 (March 10–16, 2000): 54.

Seeman, Don. "Ethnographers, Rabbis and Jewish Epistemology: The Case of the Ethiopian Jews." *Tradition: Journal of Orthodox Jewish Thought* 25/4 (Summer 1991): 13–29.

Shanks, Hershel. "Idol Pleasures." *Biblical Archaeology Review* 26/5 (September–October 2000): 22–25.

Shkop, Esther M. "And Sarah Laughed . . ." *Tradition* 31/3 (Spring 1997): 42–51.

Slater, Matthew D. "The Jews of Cochin." *Judaism* 24/96 (Fall 1975): 482–94.

Smith, Morton. "Zealots and Sicarii, Their Origins and Relation." *Harvard Theological Review* 64/1 (January 1971): 1–19.

Soskis, Benjamin. "Washington Diarist: Walking the Walk." *New Republic*, 223 9–10 (August 28 and September 4, 2000): 50.

Stillman, Yedida K., and Stillman, Norman A., eds. *From Iberia to Diaspora: Studies in Sephardic History and Culture.* Boston: Brill, 1999.

Swed, Mark. "Fanfare for an Uncommon Man." *Los Angeles Times*, January 20, 2001, pp. F2, F20.

"39 Killed in Jerusalem Headquarters." *Times of London.* July 23, 1946, p. 4.

Weinberg, Judy. "Lilith Sources." *Lilith* 1/1 (Fall 1976): 9, 38.

Weitzman, Steven. "Forced Circumcision and the Shifting Role of Gentiles in Hasmonean Ideology." *Harvard Theological Review* 92/1 (January 1999): 37–59.

Wiener, Julie. "Condemning the Vote." *Jewish Journal of Greater Los Angeles*, 15/1 (April 7, 2000): 25.

Wieseltier, Leon. "Brothers and Keepers." *New Republic* 192/6 (February 11, 1985): 21–23.

Wilkinson, Tracy. "Pope's Presence Awes Survivors of the Holocaust." *Los Angeles Times*, March 24, 2000, p. A10.

————. "Fiery Israeli Rabbi Faces Criminal Probe." *Los Angeles Times*, March 28, 2000, pp. A1, A4.

————. "Politician's Jailing Deepens Divide in Israel." *Los Angeles Times*, September 4, 2000, pp. A1, A8.

————. "Pragmatist or Hawk? New Premier Not Tipping His Hand." *Los Angeles Times*, March 8, 2001, p. A6.

Yovel, Yirmiahu. "Why Spinoza Was Excommunicated." *Commentary* 64/5 (July–December 1977) (November 1977), pp. 46–52.

Zeitlin, S. "Critical Notes: Zealots and Sicarii." *Journal of Biblical Lierature* 81, Part 4 (December 1962): 396–98.

Zivotofsky, Ari Z. "The Leadership Qualities of Moses." *Judaism* (American Jewish Congress) 43(3), 171 (Summer 1994): 258–69.

Zuckoff, Aviva Cantor. "The Lilith Question." *Lilith* 1/1 (Fall 1976): 5–10, 38.

On-Line Sources

Andrews, Edmund L. "The Business World: I. G. Farben: A Lingering Relic of the Nazi Years." *The New York Times* on the Web, May 2, 1999.

Encyclopedia *Britannica Online* (various articles).

Gustav Niebuhr. "US Jewish Leader Enters Fray Over Religious Control in Israel." New York Times News Service (National Desk), April 17, 1997.

www.kabbalah.com (Web site of The Kabbalah Centre).

Other Sources

Michael H. Gavshon, producer. "Whose Country Is It?" *60 Minutes*, August 20, 2000. CBS News (Burrelle's Information Services), vol. 32, no. 50, 13–18.

"Heaven on Earth/The One Hour Workout" (Advertisement). *Jewish Journal* 15/49 (February 2, 2001): 12.

INDEX